READING, SOCIETY AND POLITICS IN EARLY MODERN ENGLAND

Reading, Society and Politics in Early Modern England ranges over private and public reading, and over a variety of religious, social and scientific communities to locate acts of reading in specific historical moments from the sixteenth to the eighteenth centuries. It also charts the changes in reading habits that reflect broader social and political shifts during the period. A team of expert contributors cover topics including the processes of book production and distribution, audiences and markets, the material text, the relation of print to performance, and the politics of acts of reception. In addition, the volume emphasizes the independence of early modern readers and their role in making meaning in an age in which increased literacy equalled social enfranchisement and interpretation was power. Meaning was not simply an authorial act but the work of many hands and processes, from editing, printing and proofing, to reproducing, distributing and finally reading.

KEVIN SHARPE is Professor of Renaissance Studies at the University of Warwick and a Fellow of the Royal Historical Society and the English Association. He has authored or edited eleven books, including *Remapping Early Modern England: The Culture of Seventeenth-Century Politics* (2000), *Reading Revolutions: The Politics of Reading in Early Modern England* (2000) and *Criticism and Compliment* (1987).

STEVEN N. ZWICKER is Elkin Professor of Humanities at Washington University in St Louis. He has written widely on seventeenth-century literature and politics, and together with Kevin Sharpe has edited *Refiguring Revolutions: Aesthetics and Politics from the English Revolution to the Romantic Revolution* (1998) and *Politics of Discourse: The Literature and History of Seventeenth-Century England* (1987). His own monographs include *Politics and Language in Dryden's Poetry: The Arts of Disguise* (1984) and *Lines of Authority: Politics and English Literary Culture, 1649–1689* (1993).

READING, SOCIETY AND POLITICS IN EARLY MODERN ENGLAND

EDITED BY

KEVIN SHARPE

AND

STEVEN N. ZWICKER

CAMBRIDGE
UNIVERSITY PRESS

PUBLISHED BY THE PRESS SYNDICATE OF THE UNIVERSITY OF CAMBRIDGE
The Pitt Building, Trumpington Street, Cambridge CB2 1RP, United Kingdom

CAMBRIDGE UNIVERSITY PRESS
The Edinburgh Building, Cambridge, CB2 2RU, UK
40 West 20th Street, New York, NY 10011–4211, USA
477 Williamstown Road, Port Melbourne, VIC 3207, Australia
Ruiz de Alarcón 13, 28014 Madrid, Spain
Dock House, The Waterfront, Cape Town 8001, South Africa

http://www.cambridge.org

First published 2003

Printed in the United Kingdom at the University Press, Cambridge

Typeface Adobe Garamond 11/12.5 pt.   *System* LaTeX 2$_\varepsilon$ [TB]

A catalogue record for this book is available from the British Library

ISBN 0 521 82434 6 hardback

Contents

Illustrations

Contributors

HEIDI BRAYMAN HACKEL   Oregon State University

ADRIAN JOHNS   University of Chicago

DAVID SCOTT KASTAN   Columbia University

SETH LERER   Stanford University

JOSEPH LOEWENSTEIN   Washington University, St Louis

KIRSTIE M. McCLURE   University of California, Los Angeles

JOAD RAYMOND   University of East Anglia

MICHAEL SCHOENFELDT   University of Michigan

KEVIN SHARPE   University of Warwick

RICHARD WENDORF   Director of the Athenaeum Library, Boston

STEVEN N. ZWICKER   Washington University, St Louis

Acknowledgements

The idea for this volume had its origins in a conference held at the Huntington Library, San Marino, California. We would like to express our warm thanks to Professor Roy Ritchie and the staff of the Huntington for providing an opportunity to discuss this relatively new subject in a stimulating and critical environment. We should also like to thank Josie Dixon, who from the outset encouraged us to consider both a conference and a volume of essays and who contributed helpful suggestions about the range of topics. Some of the essays in this collection originated in papers for the conference and these have been revised for the collection; other essays were commissioned for the volume. We would like to thank all the contributors for their ready willingness to debate and to revise in the light of the editors' and readers' comments.

After the departure of Josie Dixon from Cambridge University Press, Linda Bree has worked with us in preparing the volume for publication and we thank her and the Press readers for their helpful suggestions, which have undoubtedly improved the shape of the whole.

More personally we would like to thank Malcolm and Jane Van Biervliet for the warm hospitality that facilitated the writing of the introduction together in a delightful environment in Oxford and Judy for all her sustenance and good company over a glass.

KEVIN SHARPE
STEVEN N. ZWICKER

Introduction: discovering the Renaissance reader

Kevin Sharpe and Steven N. Zwicker

Learning to read is one of our earliest rites of passage. Reading is the first test in a system of public pedagogy; acquiring its skills is our entrance into the world of letters. Reading makes possible at once public and private identity. Because learning to read is fundamental and reading is ubiquitous, it scarcely occurs to us that reading has a history, that its forms and practices have a past, that it is neither universal nor natural but socially specific and culturally constructed. Yet for all our insistence on the natural and the universal character of reading, we also recognize its difficulties and artificialities. Debates in educational psychology, the growing public awareness of dyslexia and the crisis over adult illiteracy serve to remind us that reading is neither natural nor ubiquitous, that geography, race and class are among the determinants that enable and delimit literacy.

To appreciate, in our own time, that reading is a variable product of circumstance impels us to address its history, to tell its stories of long continuity, of specific moments and of change. And our own moment is particularly opportune to return reading to its histories.[1] In a broad public way, talk of the end of the book, the dominance of the electronic image and the pervasiveness of the sound bite not only suggest the fragility of literary culture but also underscore the historicity of reading. Within the academy disciplinary developments have similarly opened a series of inquiries into the nature of the text and the meaning of reading.

Most famously, or perhaps infamously, deconstruction has claimed the death of the author. Without the author, the deconstructed text has no fixed meaning; words themselves act as unstable signifiers, purveyors of multiple meanings. In the critic's world of the endlessly multivalent text, any determination, any fixing of meaning is the property and prerogative of the reader.[2] With text (rather than book) in hand, the reader becomes the authoritative determiner, indeed the author, of meaning. For whatever mischief postmodern criticism has made, deconstruction, by permanently discrediting simply positivist notions of meaning, intention and authorship, has foregrounded the reader as a central subject of study.[3]

No less importantly, changes in historiography have, albeit unintentionally, opened possibilities for a history of reading. Where literary theory has decentred the author, the new history has deconstructed the traditional narrative of dynasty and ministry. In the new social history, in microhistories, case studies and alternative histories, authority itself has been seen to be not centred and fixed but dispersed and uncertain, contingent and contestable. Though these histories have not taken reading as their subject of enquiry, the implication of their address to fragmented authority and multiple narratives is the reader as subject and citizen.

Less publicly, and even more surprisingly, developments in that most traditional form of literary scholarship, bibliography, have refigured texts, authors and readers. Where the old bibliography aimed at a perfect text, reflecting in every accidental and recovering in every archaeology of syntax and typography the imprint and immanence of the author, new bibliographical traditions have wholly discredited the authorial imprint, the authentic material text.[4] Research in printing practices, design and format, punctuation and typography has disclosed the distance between authorial intention and the material text and revealed both the wilful transgressions and the slippages that transformed authorial utterance into a myriad of textual variants.[5] Textual variance demonstrates that meaning is a confluence of activities, a narrative of multiple collaborations and transformations performed by authors, publishers, licensers, printers, typesetters, proofreaders, booksellers – and readers. Modern bibliography invites study of the text not as the single act of a transcendent author but as a set of events within the social histories of production and consumption.[6]

Deconstruction, social history and the new bibliography have, along their various paths, led us to the reader. They have theorized the position of the reader; they have suggested the social dimensions of reading; they have sketched the material culture of the book. What they have not achieved, or even attempted, is a history of reading or a historicizing of readers. The beginnings of that enterprise have been most in evidence among those scholars often referred to as historians of the book. Here, studies of *bibliothèques bleues*, of an Elizabethan facilitator annotating classical texts, of the construction of heterodoxy by a Friulian miller and of the new sensibility of a Romantic reader have pointed up the rich possibilities of particular histories.[7] Such cases have questioned earlier assumptions that the history of reading might be simply written as a chronology from script to print, from intensive to extensive reading, from the authority of state control to the freedom of individual readers. The prospect of a more nuanced narrative of reading will surely depend upon many more such case studies. As practised, however, the case study has its limitations.[8] For all their revelation of the social dimensions of readers and their texts, the case histories of Menocchio, Harvey and Ranson remain attached to a stable notion of the text and assume the transparency of language. In part this attachment to stability and transparency goes to the core of the historian's own reading practices and to a historic resistance to theorizing.[9] Where the historian typically reads the document for its content, theorists and critics have located signification in forms and grammars, in metaphors and figures, in elisions and repressions.

Such a reading of our own contemporary practices suggests a way forward: a true collaboration between case study and theory, between materiality and aesthetics, between social history and exegesis. It is such an interdisciplinary conversation that this volume of essays seeks to open and extend. Interdisciplinarity is, of course, not a new mode of conversation: we are quite familiar with the politics of literature, with the aesthetics of revolution, with the ideologies of modernism. But such interdisciplinary praxis has in the past been delimited, constrained by the notion that meanings and events are principally the story of authorial acts. A new history of reading will turn our attention to all those performances of texts from the very moments of their conception and constitution. That history only begins to be written with the act of authorship. Every reconstitution of the text – its journey to the publisher, the copy prepared for the printer, the compositor's work with text and the processes of printing, distribution, acquisition and binding are all crucial moments in the lives of texts, in the continuous configurations and refigurations of meaning. In such a history all these performances complicate any simple or stable notion of authorship. We also need to recognize that all these acts and moments of production are acts and moments of interpretation, too – in the most literal sense, acts of reading.

Rather than the simple story of constitution and reception, our new history of reading stresses continuous transactions between producers and consumers, negotiations among a myriad of authors, texts and readers. Our address in this volume is therefore to all the ways and all the moments in which those negotiations shaped texts, fashioned modes of reading and even positioned authors. What we want to stress is the power and centrality of the reader in all the commerce of the book.

HUMANISM, PROTESTANTISM AND PRINT

Textual negotiations, of course, predate the age of print and no doubt will outrun it. Martial's epigrams are everywhere marked by awareness of the troubling exchanges between authors and readers, and of the potential independence of script. The electronic text would seem to dissolve authorial identity and textual stability into a myriad of transactions and rescriptions, an ever-opening set of permutations. It is the age of print, however, that not only multiplies and intensifies all the complex negotiations between texts and readers but also releases a new self-consciousness about textual strategies and relations. One facet of that self-consciousness was surely humanism. As Joseph Loewenstein demonstrates so fully for the case of Ben Jonson,[10] humanism was centrally concerned with the recovery of texts, with translation, emendation, reproduction and appropriation in all of its forms. No less, humanist pedagogy was preoccupied with the constitution of the ideal reader. While the ideology of humanism sought the textual production of the Christian commonwealth and virtuous subject, the practices of humanism, its curriculum of exegesis and rhetoric, opened the book to alternative interpretation. As well as directing and policing readers, that is, humanism educated and enabled readers to perform their own readings, and to construct their own, often dissenting, values and polities.[11]

There is no more obvious manifestation of that capacity for dissent than Protestant reformation. The reformers, of course, no less than Catholic expositors or humanist pedagogues, sought to exercise control over the meaning of Scripture; it was the purpose of a preaching ministry to expound and to gloss the word in every parish. Yet the Protestant emphasis on individual conscience and personal scripturalism, on each godly man's reading and wrestling with Scripture, ultimately democratized the word. For Protestantism throughout Europe drove the great project of vernacular Bibles. An English Bible in every parish and nearly every household literally placed Scripture within everyone's reach. For the literate and learned the Bible became not only an authority but a text to be edited, emended, retranslated, glossed, interrogated and, *in fine*, deconstructed. Beyond the intellectual elites the synchronism of Protestantism and print drove and made possible expanding literacy, what we might even call the beginnings of a reading nation.[12]

We have long understood the ways in which the synchrony of print, Protestantism and humanism constituted a textual revolution, a radical transformation in the authorship and production of, and in the marketplace for, books.[13] What we have not addressed is their collaboration in the creation of the modern reader. The modern reader, we would argue, emerged from the new availability of texts and techniques, the marketing not only of books but of hermeneutic strategies. Protestant humanism preached the need and fostered the skills for a new criticism – the capacity to hear and to read, to compare and conflate, to discern and apply meaning. It is these skills and these readers that this volume seeks to return to their central place in the narratives of early modern spirituality, politics and culture.

Those narratives begin, of course, with the book itself. For historians and critics the early modern book has often appeared more a simple object than a complex subject for study. But what we are learning from the new bibliography and from the history of the book is all the complexities of the book's composition, construction and production and the relation of those complexities to the creation of meaning. The early modern book conveyed meaning even before its pages were opened. The size and format at once determined and responded to audience and traced the hierarchies of class and authority. The stately folio was destined for the gentleman's library, the pamphlet and broadsheet for wide distribution.[14] But format was also imprinted with genre; the epic could best be imagined in folio sheets, the scatological woodcut on the ephemeral quarto. Though the playbook always appeared as a cheap quarto, it is hardly surprising that the aspiring laureate, Ben Jonson, determined to publish his works as a folio. The folio probably secured permanence as well as authority. Whereas most early modern books were sold unbound, the expensive folio was likely to be bound and hence preserved for posterity.[15] In the gentleman's library a hierarchy of texts was structured not only by binding itself, by all the qualities and character of binding and by the owner's decisions as to what texts to bind together. In addition, the binding stamp, often the armorial insignia of family and descent, not only marked the reader's ownership and authority but rendered the book an emblem of lineage and pedigree. The psychology of such materiality should not pass without comment: the book bound with family arms performed, we might say was enclosed within, a nexus of aristocratic codes and values which shaped its meaning. How different was the experience of reading the unbound penny pamphlet, seldom a prized object, more likely promiscuously distributed in alehouses, hung on bushes or hawked on street corners.[16]

Size, format and binding, then, begin the work of signification before the book has even been opened. The book once opened may seem to us more obviously, more transparently the script of meaning; but before the early modern reader confronted what we regard as the book, an elaborate set of paratexts unfolded in various ways to engage the reader and to shape the reading experience. The presence and style of a frontispiece portrait, an image frequently of the author, not only underscored writerly authority but vividly conveyed that authority to the reader.[17] Similarly the architecture of the title page framed the authority of and entrance to the text, at times literally with column, arch and cartouche. The bold superiors of the title itself, often the Latin epigraph or scriptural verse, the licence, indeed place of publication, name of publisher and printer all functioned to locate and legitimize the text, to place the reader within a geography of textual, economic and political power. The cynosure of power and authority in early modern England was patronage. And patronage was immediately announced in the dedicatory epistle. Here, while humility and supplication were, more or less conventionally, expressed, the author simultaneously wrote the approval, taste and authority of the aristocratic patron into the text, as a public marker of intimacy with social privilege. In the case of Spenser's *Shepheardes Calendar*, it is the name of the patron, Sir Philip Sidney, rather than the author that appears on the title page.[18] In a similar fashion, literary authority might be appropriated and conveyed by commendatory epistle or verse. While a verse or two from a friend or intimate might commend and domesticate the author and book, sometimes a panoply of eulogies and commendations formed a virtual academy of association and mapped a community of literary and political validation.[19]

Other kinds of paratextual apparatus were less inflected with patronage and power but participated no less in constituting meaning. When they were deployed, tables of contents, indices, abstracts and epitomes worked to endow the text with substance and *gravitas*, and of course structured a journey through the book, an organization of its meaning.[20] Indices also suggested the uses of the book and marked the passages that might, perhaps should, be extracted and commonplaced. All the paratextual matter of the early modern book was part of its design, in every sense of that word.

The early modern page, from the inception of print to what Richard Wendorf describes as the artfulness of Augustan typography, was a site of complex designs. Most obviously in either its promiscuous or calculated mingling of typefaces and styles – gothic or roman, italic or bold, literals of various sizes – the early modern page orchestrated and modulated the word. Gothic type was for a long time associated with tradition and authority; until the Restoration all proclamations were published in black letter; even now we speak of red-letter days, which once graphically distinguished important calendrical celebrations. But white space could signify as much as black or red. In early modern England, space, like leisure, was a mark of privilege. When paper was the most expensive element of any book, the wide margin and generous ruling announced the conspicuous consumption of both publisher and purchaser. By contrast, the crowded and irregular teeth of the radical pamphlet, where lines teemed to the edge of the page, suggest not only thrift but the urgency of salvation and revolution.[21]

Nor should we forget the margins of the early modern page. For here space was designated for a series of relations with and commentaries on the page. Printed marginal annotations might privilege the citation of author-ities, translations, glosses and polemical debates. In some cases – in print polemic, for example – marginalia threaten to invade and overwhelm the page, from the side or below. Nor was the margin, whatever the desires of authority, a space preserved for the privileges of print. The long-standing traditions of manuscript adversaria and the habit of commonplacing invited the reader into and instructed the reader in active engagement with the text.[22] Sometimes this was simply the correction of typograph-ical error – though, as Seth Lerer shows us, there was even a 'poetics' of errata.[23] Often correction swelled into the dispute and contest of argument. Frequently readers marked their texts with simple or complex signs of re-turn: underscoring, cross-hatching in the margin, pointing fists, flowers, astrological figures.[24] All witness the busy, at times turbulent, activity of the early modern reader. When as modern readers we open the early modern book, we are often confronted with the teeming business of the page, with the traces of multiple hands and dissonant voices.

While many of these features and traces are continuous facets of the early modern book, they both have a history and still need to be historicized. Such gestures as preface and dedication have a continuous life through the history of the book. But not least because such practices were implicated in all the social arrangements and transformations of the age, they were in-flected by long-term cultural shifts as well as by particular crises, in ways that have yet to be studied. We can surely hear in the dedications of Restoration histories and plays the memories of civil strife and social dislocation some-times distanced and tempered by new tones of irony and scepticism. Other features of the book – from black-letter print to erratic punctuation – decline, while the advertisement and the subscription list announce a thorough commercialization of the book.[25] Changes in the material book both trace and inscribe historical change in the culture and commerce of print.

Scholars have long recognized and theorized the relations, in the late seventeenth century, between the new commercialization of print and the emergence of a public sphere.[26] The growth of the gazette, the development of a periodical press and the proliferation of news in coffee house, theatre and spa are surely central to the historical narrative of Augustan England.[27] What recent work is beginning to indicate is that the confluence of print and publicity both requires deeper historicizing and a different chronology. Elizabethan religious polemics and providential narratives, early Stuart ballads and squibs and the deluge of Civil War pamphlets all press the claim for a public sphere of print and news a century before its Habermasian moment.[28] What they also demonstrate is a new, vibrant, often unruly commodity culture of print and a commercialization of author, book and reader.

But in the traditional story of the commercialization of print, somewhat surprisingly, it is the reader who has been neglected. Historians have of course debated and disputed the nature and extent of literacy,[29] but no study has placed readers at the centre of a history of the publication, distribution and commercialization of print, nor recognized the commanding presence of the reader as consumer. The new history of consumption has yet to recognize the position of the reader not just as economic consumer but as a driver for change in taste, fashion and value.

Our discussion of the early modern reader is, of course, a simplification. Any consideration of the market naturally leads to notions of targeted markets, market sectors and market share, not least because such language, for all its anachronistic qualities, quite properly describes both the conditions and perceptions of the early modern book trade. Authors, publishers and printers, that is, responded with increasing sophistication to the changing circumstances and constituencies of reading. Most obviously, across the period as a whole increasing literacy beyond the metropolis among women and the lower orders opened new markets for different forms of print. Changing tastes and fashions in turn formed new markets for new or newly constituted genres of writing – romance, travel narrative, lyric miscellany and, importantly, as Adrian Johns demonstrates, the emergent forms of learned periodical and scientific paper.[30] The drive of events, too – the Thirty Years' War, Civil War and Exclusion, colonialization and Popish Plot – excited new curiosities and literary forms such as newsbooks, state trials and poems on affairs of state. What the early modern book trade recognized was the diversity of communities of reading. The concept of reading communities – 'interpretive communities' – is well known to us from literary theory. Stanley Fish has interestingly theorized the shared conditions, ideologies and strategies of reading collectives.[31] Though he himself has not pursued its historical dimension, the model of interpretive communities draws attention to the specific historical circumstances and contingencies, as well as the geographies, of reading communities.

As soon as we glance back to early modern England, the historical force of interpretive communities is immediately obvious. At the most basic level Catholic and Protestant readers defined themselves through distinctive forms of the book and modes of reading. Though the different theologies of confession and election are fundamental to religious history, they are also crucial psychologies and soteriologies of reading in an age when the word was the key to salvation. Similarly, class has long helped to define forms and modes of literacy; we speak frequently of the gentleman scholar or the middle-class reader. Here, too, as well as economic boundaries, class inflected a range of reading sensibilities and psychologies: the salon constitutes a different interpretive community as well as social environment for reading from the dissenting academy.[32] And in an age of revolution, political difference powerfully defined reading parties. In their divisions of court and country, Royalist and Roundhead, Whig and Tory, contemporaries discerned and delineated not only political alliance but generic proprieties and interpretive sensibilities. The obvious communities of Catholic and Protestant, Royalist or Roundhead, only begin to open what we might call a historical psychology of the book. How differently a Quaker sister interiorized the word from a Presbyterian minister, let alone a recusant or latitudinarian. And how differently a Whig grandee and his circle imbibed political invective from the members of the Green Ribbon Club or Jacobite mob.[33] And religion, class and politics in all their complexities and combinations do not exhaust the sites of reading and communities of readers. Throughout this period, the household, godly or profane, the family, humble or aristocratic, the classroom at the petty school or university were elemental sites of reading. What these sites recall is the multiplicity of reading communities to which an individual at any time might belong, and the shifting affiliations and associations formed and reformed by the book. The theory of interpretive communities awaits not only historical specificity but a more nuanced, a more finely graded sense of the shifting and contending force of these communities in forming reading habits and hermeneutic principles.

Hermeneutic principles and reading communities were encoded by and within genres. Literary scholars have traditionally written the histories of literature almost exclusively as narratives of genre: the emergence of the city comedy, the eclipse of Cavalier lyric, the rise of the novel. Nor is this inappropriate for a humanist culture that described literary transmission as a generic process and that determined literary value by generic hierarchy from the lofty epic to the lowly comedy, from forensic to epideictic rhetoric.[34] Historians do not often deploy the lexicon of genre, yet there can be no doubt that forms and genres, and not just annal, chronicle and history but scaffold confession, statute and state trial, have always been the conveyers of cultural meaning. The discussion of genre, however, has been curiously confined to the creation and content of books: we are perfectly aware of the way writers deploy the verse epistle, epic diction and the familiar rising and falling structures of tragedy. What has not been charted is the complex interplay between the generic coding of texts and communities of consumers and individual readers. We appreciate the ways in which genre assumes shared interpretive habits, indeed readerly complicity – the romance in all of its transmutations anticipates and inscribes gender, class and sensibility;[35] but we should not assume a neat and straightforward move from textual genre to readerly experience. Whatever the hopes of authors and publishers, and however idealized the 'implied reader' of traditional literary criticism, early modern readers followed generic prescription neither homogeneously nor slavishly.[36] Not every reader came to his or her text with a full command of the complex codes of classical or modern genres and rhetorics. Irony and play, on the other hand, were the prerogatives as much of sophisticated readers as of authors. The history of translation, parody and adaptation, not least of Shakespeare himself, speaks to the force of readerly play and desire.[37] Frequent authorial appeals to the sceptical or resistant reader, finally, betray and point us to the importance of readerly contest of generic mark and freight. Any full history of the material book, of the marketplace and of the interpretive community in early modern England must address genre theory and history as the site of subtle and shifting negotiations between readers and authors.

PRINT, PRIVACY AND PERSONALITY

The social arrangements of genre, the marketplace of print and the many interpretive communities we have identified constitute the public arenas and conditions of early modern reading. But our modern sense of reading as private, personal and isolate certainly had early modern precedence and defenders. It is to these more personal and intimate sites and circumstances of reading that we now turn.

For all the emphasis on the preaching ministry – on godly household and the invisible community of the elect – at the core of Protestant doctrine, the priesthood of all believers, we find the individual Christian struggling alone with faith and the word. Where Catholic doctrine and ecclesiology

emphasized the hierarchy of saints and intercessors and the communal rituals of liturgy and mass, at the heart of the Protestant service the sermon,
albeit expounded, was ultimately addressed to the conscience of each individual believer. Official attempts to exclude women and apprentices from
the reading of vernacular Scripture also evidence that within the patriarchal
household Bible reading was a personal impulse as well as familial ritual.
The reformed experience centred on the individual conscience, the heart
of each believer; the journey to faith was a continuous process of interiorizing the word. And that interiorization often involves strenuous acts of
writing and reading. Historians of religion identify the sermon notebook,
the spiritual diary and the private prayer as the manifestations and sites of
Protestant, indeed Puritan, spirituality.[38] What we would emphasize is that
such writings were simultaneously acts of reading: of reading the word and
God's providences – of reading also the conscience and the self.[39] Protestant
self-identity, we might say, was formed through a progression of readings
and rereadings of the texts of Scripture, sermon and self.

Such stress on individual readers and personal reading carried important
hermeneutic implications. The obligation of the godly reader and exegete
was ever to unfold the personal meaning of Scripture, to apply the sacred
texts to the self. The logic, indeed the historical outcome, of such a self-
centred hermeneutic, as the enemies of Protestantism had warned, was an
assertion of each believer as determinant of meaning. Throughout our period the official teachings of editors, scholars and exegetes were contested
by the claims of the unlearned and enthusiastic. And ultimately the Baptist,
the Fifth-Monarchist, the Quaker and the Ranter proclaimed the interpretive authority of the spirit. The claim of the spirit in early modern England
emerges from a particular and individual experience of the text and by the
end of our period results in a validation of the individual as hermeneut.[40]

Protestantism may have been the main engine of individual exegesis,
but – paradoxically – other social arrangements and mechanisms opened
space and freedom for individual interpretation. Though humanist editions
and education reified textual and interpretive authority, the techniques and
skills fundamental to the humanist curriculum equipped each reader to
be editor and exegete.[41] While the schoolroom and lecture hall were the
locales of critical dialogue and learned community, we should not lose
sight of the individual humanist scholar in his study poring over his texts –
translating, conflating, emending, interrogating – silently and privately.
Montaigne's description of his study as solarium is a perfect exemplar of
study as privacy.[42] Such aspects of the humanist programme helped to forge
ideas of individuality and a culture of self-fashioning.[43]

Whatever the tensions between the sacred and the secular, between Protestantism and classical humanism, both programmes urged self-development and self-improvement in the broadest sense. We have glanced at the Puritan diary as self-analysis. But the popular providential narrative was also a script for self as well as for society; in its most famous and canonical expression, Bunyan's *The Pilgrim's Progress*, the providential script becomes a text for self-discovery and even for self-realization.[44] While Bunyan exemplifies a strain of early modern Protestant spirituality, his allegory also gestures to new, more secular figurations of the self and to a new hermeneutic of everyday experience. By the end of the seventeenth century, self-improvement was a common idiom of social discourse, not just the terrain of the godly and the radical. It was manifest in the preoccupation with the reformation of manners, institutionalized in the penitentiary, with its new conviction of incarceration as reformation, and aestheticized in the novel, that herald of self-dramatization and self-psychology.[45]

In early modern England, then, the self was discovered in all the acts of writing and reading. And, as the novel so fully displays, not only discovered but endlessly refashioned. Though the novel clearly emerges from the Protestant fascination with the self in daily experience and in all its particularity, it fashions new modes of reading texts – and of imagining the self. The novel, we know, both depends upon and forms new relations with the text; it effects what we may, in a long historical arc, see as a transformation from reading as exegesis to reading as sensibility. Over the course of the eighteenth century, we might argue, it was reading as sensibility that extended from the page to the world.[46] Men and women of feeling were first and foremost modelled by new ways of reading.[47] And in the Romantic sensibility, the very landscape, newly spiritualized and interiorized, was read as lyric and drama.[48] The Romantic reader, alone in nature with a slender volume of lyrics, not only experienced the self, but interiorized and interpreted the world through, and as, text.

The novel and sensibility direct us to questions of female readership and gendered modes of feeling and affect. At the beginning of our period, of course, literacy was almost exclusively a male prerogative. Women, except in the most progressive and aristocratic households, were seldom taught to read; as importantly, the sites of reading, and not just the university and schoolroom but more generally the study and library, were male terrains.[49] Although we tell, throughout this period, the story of growing literacy, that story remains too largely a narrative of expanding male readership, of the literacy of urban, mercantile classes, the apprentice and the parish constable. Indeed, whatever the enlightened views of an Erasmus, Vives or Ascham on female literacy, much courtesy literature prescribing silence as well as obedience and chastity, proscribed the female from the reading community.[50] And even those aristocratic women whose privilege and determination overrode the cultural proscription of reading appear to have internalized a notion of active reading as male prerogative. Few women, even of the upper orders, were significant collectors of books, fewer yet actively engaged with their texts through marginal commentary and contest.[51] In the slow evolution of female literacy, it is again Protestantism that is the important opening chapter. For whatever the early proscriptions against female reading of the Bible, Protestant preaching urged the fundamental importance of the word for both male and female spirituality and salvation. And in more radical Protestant circles female reading of Scripture opened into preaching, prophesying and a sisterhood of believers – that is, a community of female readers.[52] Historians of gender and literacy alike have yet fully to tell the story of the way the radical spiritual foundations of female literacy drove a broader culture and ultimately a validation of women as readers and writers. From such Civil War exegetes and prophets as Eleanor Douglas and Mary Cary we come to the full participation of Aphra Behn in Restoration literary culture, to forms of the novel that not only embrace but privilege female reading.[53] Any full telling of progress from patriarchy to female emancipation must, more than has been recognized, be a narrative of literacy and all the complex relations between the practices and experiences of reading.

The relation of gender to reading returns us to the question of genre. At the beginning of our period female reading was not only restricted by education and literacy but delimited by genre. Despite the success of the *Arcadia* among an aristocratic coterie, the romance, until its full novelization in the eighteenth century (and even then), remained a suspect mode; for most literate women the experience of the book was confined to spiritual genres and to household manuals, to books of housewifery, herbals, and cookery books. Even at this period gender is constituted through genres of reading.[54] Where the sixteenth-century gentleman with his books of heraldry, falconry and horsemanship was constituted for the *vita activa*, women's reading ever re-inscribed them within domestic circumstances and spaces. In disrupting the fixities of genre, civil war and revolution begin to deconstruct the stabilities and rigidities of the relations between genre and gender. The prophesying female is only the most obvious instance of the transgression of gender and genre; Lucy Hutchinson, for example, translated and interpreted Lucretius and we might even say read as well as wrote her husband's life.[55] The revolutionary disruptions of gender and genre are everywhere manifest in Restoration culture and society. From females on the stage to the pornographic squib avidly read by courtly women as well as by rakes, from Aphra Behn reading and reconstituting theatre to Mary Astell interpreting and refuting John Locke, every genre was opened by and to women as writers and hermeneuts.[56] By the beginning of the eighteenth century, the gendered system of genre was surely disrupted, if not, as some contemporaries feared, destroyed.[57]

Contemporary talk of the destruction of genre was a conservative, indeed a simplistic, response. For the ways in which genre helped to construct and define gender were at no point in our period straightforward. Even in the patriarchal world of Tudor England, the unruly woman was no doubt the audience for, as well as the subject of, popular ballad and comic drama.[58] Among the aristocratic coterie, women such as Lady Anne Clifford certainly consumed books across a wide variety of genres, often the preserve of males, and significantly deployed reading as an entrance into the male activities of litigation, property management and self-assertion.[59] The complications of gender and genre are not effected merely through the female transgression of male textual preserves. The promiscuous mixing of genres – the tragicomedy or mock heroic, for example – announce not just class miscegenation but generic slippage, the instability of gender and affect.

And not just the mixed genres themselves. It was the reading of tales of Moll Cutpurse and her progeny of female adventuresses which blurred the gendered implications of the heroic.[60] Texts such as *The Rape of the Lock* further cast in doubt the exact gendered constitution of heroic sensibility. The novel, with its appetite for and celebration of the mixing of forms, offered all the possibilities for a rescripting and rereading of all the significations of gender. Nothing more than the novel upset the traditional literary domains of the masculine and feminine. As contemporaries recognized, and in some cases lamented, the man of feeling was created through novel reading – both through reading the novel and through new literary sensibilities. And by the mid-eighteenth century the castigation of the feminized male, his boudoir stacked with novels, directly evidences the reconstitution of gender through reading.[61]

Talk of the feminized male may have expressed new concerns about the corporeality of reading, but, as Michael Schoenfeldt argues, it was by no means the first articulation of the physicality of reading, the intimacy of the body and the book.[62] The language of humanist classicism described the very processes of reading and understanding as physiologies of imbibing and ingesting.[63] The book itself as a repository of other readings and learning was frequently referred to as a digest. The active work of reading was figured as mastication and absorption; the consumption of the text was understood as digestatory in every real sense. In Protestantism, too, Scripture was the spiritual food of the godly, the heart the tablet inscribed by God, the conscience a text to be examined, the last judgement a reading of the book of life. Such language is too often treated as mere metaphor. In early modern England the book was implicated in and with the body in every way.[64] Reading, after all, was often literally physical labour: books were difficult of access, often read standing in the college library, heard in a chilly parish church, or strained over under flickering candles. From the very earliest stages reading was also associated with physical pain. Every memoir of school and college life recalls harsh beatings that marked the journey to literacy. Moreover, the active reading encouraged by spiritual and secular masters involved a veritable array of accoutrements – pen, knife, inkpot, sand, paper, candle – which involved the body laboriously and endlessly in the acts of reading and abstracting.[65] Such equipment situated the body in the study, at the desk, in postures of intensity and labour. Or at least this was the case for men. Women readers, by contrast, retired with the book to the intimacy of the closet. As Heidi Brayman Hackel points out, they deployed little of the paraphernalia of active reading, more the furniture and furnishings of the virginal and sewing box.[66] But no less than for men, the postures of female reading, as we shall see, implicated the body in the book. In the conditions of the early modern world, it is hardly surprising that reading was understood as a physiology, as the work of eye and hand.[67]

The processes of reading, then, were gendered – eroticized and sexualized. The active masculine reader with pen in hand mastered the text no less than his household; Renaissance portraiture displayed the acts of male writing and reading as dynastic, dominant, even priapic. The early modern woman as sexual object was figured and described as a book to be opened.[68] Female reading was frequently eroticized and implicated in the sexual body. The book held to the breast, in the lap, or concealed under the petticoats fetishized both the text and the reader. Male suspicion, even anxiety, variously imagined female reading as a source of ungovernable pleasure, by the eighteenth century even as self-pleasuring. As Alberto Manguel reminds us, we are not the first age to understand the erotic charge of taking a book to bed.[69]

REPRESENTING READERS

For the modern sensibility the body is the last preserve of the personal and the private. Any reading of the discourses of early modernism reveals rather the body as political site and public domain. Not least because it was so fully implicated in and with the body, the Renaissance book takes on rich symbolic, even totemic, import. In any signifying system in which the body was the primary analogue for ideology and politics, all representations of the body, in its physiological, intellectual and spiritual performances, carried public freight. What we would emphasize is that, in this period, it is often the book that activates, publicizes and blazons the spiritual, intellectual and social body. Given the centrality and the symbolic conjuncture of body and book, then, it is hardly surprising that the act of reading was so ubiquitously staged, depicted and represented.

Perhaps far more than for any other period in English history, the book was central to Renaissance portraiture. Everywhere in the representation of aristocratic men and women, the book disclosed and publicized degree, privilege, knowledge – authority. In a Protestant culture which foregrounds the word, the book interestingly and quite literally becomes the focus of visual attention. To begin with, representations of the saints (in particular St Jerome, translator of Scripture) were commonly figured with the book as the central element of the spiritual life and the act of reading as the demonstration of faith.[70] Interestingly, contemporary portraiture and paintings of the spiritual life tended to focus on reading as female piety; given the ubiquity of the word and low levels of female literacy, it is puzzling that these images were so selectively gendered. One is tempted to ask whether such representations were intended as a didactic programme, or how they performed to reconstitute female spirituality and religiosity.[71] Certainly, though there are few depictions of men at prayer with books in hand, the book is ubiquitous in the portrait of the humanist intellect. Everywhere in the portraiture of the icons of humanism – Erasmus, or More – the book is the centrepiece of the scholarly and intellectual life.[72] Not just books but all the equipment of active reading are scattered across the table, shelf and floor, announcing the colloquy of text and reader, the physical engagement of script and intellect.[73]

In the broadest sense, the humanist program was more than scholastic. In Renaissance England it constituted a curriculum that emphasized learning as service to the commonweal and the role of courtier and gentleman as public servant rather than warrior. We are familiar with this legacy in the literature of courtesy and conduct, in manuals for diplomats and justices.[74] Less familiar and less well understood are the portraits of Tudor and Stuart crown ministers and aristocrats which were at once the expressions and instruments of humanist ideology. How rare is the early modern portrait of the aristocrat as warrior knight; how ubiquitous is the image of the gentleman with book in hand. In these portraits the book stands as emblem of newly constituted ideals of aristocracy – learning, civility, service as social and political authority.[75] The courtier-aristocrat now announces his power not just with hand on sword hilt but with finger thrust into book. In such portraits we have a charismatic depiction of reading as authority.[76] Again, what is enigmatic is the demise of this genre – the disappearance, by the early eighteenth century, of reading and the book as important motifs of the aristocratic portrait. What we may discern here is not merely further evidence of the decline of humanism but the representation of new aristocratic values. The Augustan portrait, figuring the gentleman not at his desk but at leisure on his lands, represents a new culture of ease and elegance. From the canvases of Reynolds and Gainsborough, where scarcely a book is seen, we may begin to trace the anti-intellectualism of modern British aristocracy.

The painting is only the most graphic representation of the early modern reader; the early modern theatre stages reading at some of its most dramatic and climactic moments. In *Hamlet* meditation is epitomized by the actor with book in hand, the stage prop here a synecdoche of the intellectual life. Prospero's books were the very source of his magical powers; Caliban's education into language the foundation of his civilization into society. And the fatal plots of Renaissance tragedy repeatedly turn on acts of misunderstanding that are acts of misreading, literally and figuratively. It is scarcely surprising that acts of misreading and misapprehension are crucial to the plays of kings and aristocrats; but increasingly in this period the new genre of city comedy mocks and pillories illiteracy as social shame.[77] For all their celebration of the newly literate middle orders, we should not forget that such comedies were performed daily before audiences of the largely illiterate commonalty. Such mockery may evidence a growing acceptance of the centrality of literacy and the association of illiteracy with social exclusion. But the drama reminds us that in a broader sense, in a number of important circumstances, the illiterate participate in the consumption and interpretation of texts.[78] The sermon and proclamation took for granted an audience of consumers as auditors rather than readers. But it was the theatre that both assumed and constructed a dialogue between the performance and the audience, the script and the 'reader'. The very architecture of the early modern theatre foregrounds the illiterate auditor, since the poorest sort stood in the pit in closest proximity to, and in heckling distance from, the stage. There are some indications that audience participation was a not unwelcome part of performance, even that audience reading and reaction scripted the published text of the play. In such a sense, the trial screening may not be a modern invention.[79]

While for us the first folio is the emblem of theatre and print, in early modern England the ubiquity of the cheap quarto evidences a vibrant exchange between play-going and literacy. The commercial success of the playbook, hawked in the street as well as bundled in the gentleman's library, witnesses a broad cultural investment in the drama as representation of social experience. Indeed, if the playhouse was an agent of literacy in early modern England, literacy in its turn surely secured the survival of theatre in years of censorship and prohibition. The theatre may have been closed by parliamentary ordinance in 1642, but, as David Kastan demonstrates, the repeated publishing and republishing of Elizabethan and Stuart play texts not only guaranteed the survival of the theatre but was the very foundation of its repertoire and restoration.[80] At every point this survival was premised upon a marketplace – that is, a readership. With plays, as with so many other cultural texts and practices, it was readers who, during the 1640s and 1650s, secured and preserved the memory and so much of the legacy of pre-Civil-War England. By their collecting and circulating, copying and communicating, rediscovering and re-interpreting, readers, in ways that have yet fully to be explored, enabled and shaped an apparently seamless restoration of old cultural forms.

All cultural forms, we have learned, are political. Throughout our period the histories of authorship and print publication were, and are now perceived to be, narratives of politics. From the role of the book in disseminating Protestantism, through the force of the pamphlet in forging revolutionary consciousness, to the creation of political parties in and by print, the politics of authorship and publication have been well appreciated. What until recently has not even been constituted as a subject is reading as political experience and performance.

READING AS POLITICS

Politics is still too narrowly conceived as the exclusive business of pulpit, parliament and party. As recent work has begun to demonstrate, the reader alone in the study or closet with his – or her – books both imbibed politics and formed a political consciousness not only, or perhaps even primarily, from what we would categorize as political texts. Ways of reading, hermeneutic strategies, were, and of course remain, political performances. Famously, Elizabeth I read herself into, and political challenge in, the text of Shakespeare's *Richard II*.[81] In confinement Charles I read and marked his Shakespeare as a text of self and personal circumstance – a political performance recognized and castigated by Milton as regal weakness and corruption.[82] At the popular level, as social historians have begun to explore, the reading of ballads, squibs and news created a popular political consciousness, both loyalist and oppositional.[83] In early modern England men and women, we might say, read themselves into citizens.

The most familiar story of texts and politics in early modern England centres on licensing, regulation and censorship. In part because these subjects were bound up with guilds, clerical appointments and courtly offices, the history of censorship has long been told, and not unreasonably, as an institutional history. It has also been told primarily as a history of production, the mutilation of authors, the destruction of presses and the burning of books.[84] In early modern England – in many modern regimes, for that matter – the wrath of authority was inflicted upon the body of the writer and the book. But what our contemporary experience demonstrates, even within the most totalitarian regimes, is the limited power and inefficacy of censorship. The instruments, offices and penalties of censorship have limited effect on the mind of the author, still less on the imagination of the reader. Indeed, in societies heavily regulated by censorship there inevitably arise techniques and psychologies of reading created by the very instruments they undermine.[85] The indexing and banning of books is surely intended to police readers as much as writers, but, as we know, the forbidden bestseller is a recurring phenomenon from revolutionary pamphlet to pornographic novel.[86]

We have only just begun to understand that the reach of censorship in early modern England extended to interpretation as well as production. The calling in of books, the selective licensing of translations and the prohibition, by proclamation, of women and servants from the reading of vernacular Bibles were all obvious attempts by authority to censor acts of reading as much as writing. The penalties for failing to report or for reading and sharing illicit texts were scarcely less severe than those for writing or publishing and vending heterodox books. But early modern England lacked the resources of the modern state to reach into the corners of the realm for forbidden books and communities of dissenting readers.[87] And no less than in our modern experience, it would appear that such efforts as were made to police reading fostered rather than defeated reading against the state. Examples abound, in Star Chamber cases, treason trials and quarter sessions, of the pamphlet, satire or ballad which gained notoriety, frisson, to say nothing of commercial success, from a reputation for transgression. Ironically, in early modern England, as today, the practices and culture of censorship produced modes of reading and sensibilities of suspicion and resistance that fashioned the reading of all texts. Sir William Drake, like Menocchio, after all, formulated radical religious and political convictions from texts freely available and in many cases unquestionably orthodox.[88] How ironic that, in the end, the censoring state is the forge of the independent reader.

The collapse of censorship on the eve of civil war released a full flood of unlicensed text and independent thought. These radical pamphleteers, Levellers and Diggers, Fifth-Monarchists and Ranters, who turned the world upside down, have drawn generations of scholars interested in tracing and constituting a radical tradition.[89] More interestingly, critics and historians have of late turned from the writing of pamphlet literature to the marketplace, from analysis of authors and ideas to mechanisms and distribution.[90] Address to consumption and the market has opened new perspectives on the most basic questions of the nature and reach of radical ideas – perspectives that still await a full exploration of the interplay of the commercial and ideological. Such perspectives, as we have begun to discern, ultimately direct us to the reader. Some of the most interesting post-revisionist work on early modern England has focused not only on the materials of news information and its networks of association but on the social psychologies and political imaginings of communities of readers. Joad Raymond provides rich evidence of how the consumption of news in the various interpretive communities of assizes and alehouses, in their various contexts of courtesy book or ballad, created a multiplicity of readerly experiences and strategies.[91] As today, when we are fully aware of the way the same news item is spun and plays so differently across various media and social geographies, in early modern England the meaning of news was ultimately fixed by the reader. That is to say, the history of political ideology must fully incorporate the shifting receptions of texts as much as the purposes of authors and distributors.

Because it is moments of crisis that thrust values and ideologies into expression and contest, we must expect political crises also to be moments of hermeneutic crisis. In charting any history of reading in England the Civil War must be appreciated as climacteric – not least because contemporaries so understood it themselves. Seventeenth-century commentators, whether rightly or wrongly, explained the very origins of civil conflict in modes of education, methods of interpretation, ways of reading. Hobbes was the most famous but not the only social observer to identify the origins of turmoil with the circumstances and freedoms of reading.[92] The charge and countercharge of pamphlet warfare, after all, repeatedly turned upon accusations of misunderstanding and misreading. However accurate the contemporary belief that revolution was born of reading and misreading, there can be no doubt that the consequence of civil war was a revolution in the practices and psychologies of reading. Milton insisted that the success of the Good Old Cause, the fortune of the revolution, wholly depended upon right reading.[93] For him, only the education and construction of a nation of revolutionary readers would demystify, deconstruct and ultimately destroy the texts, images and idols of false authority.

'The Civil War' is a convenient shorthand for a series of political crises, of dislocations and transformations, in the constitution and reconstitution of the state. It must then be studied as not one but a series of hermeneutic crises. The term 'revolutionary reader' cannot do full justice to all the inflections and stances of reading across warring aristocrats, common soldiers and turbulent sects. Military victory and defeat forced the constant rereading of the texts of providence and Scripture; retirement and exile forged new Royalist communities of reading.[94] Most radically, the claim of the spirit led the Ranters to reject any interpretive authority, indeed to anticipate a postmodern textuality.[95] Full historicization of reading and revolution also demands a refined chronology, a close address to specific historical shifts and moments. We must imagine what it meant to read Scripture in a family with brother pitted against brother, what it was like to read statute and proclamation in the shadow of regicide. We must ask how commonwealth and republic returned the most conservative of readers to their classical texts, how the Protectorial court refashioned the reading of courtesy books, how the hopes and disappointments of millennium and Fifth Monarchy refigured the texts and meanings of prophecy.[96] Perhaps our critical perplexity over the ambiguities of Marvell's 'Horatian Ode' richly reveals how meaning can only be figured and fixed in all the variegations of persons and moments.[97]

One of the great consequences of civil war and interregnum was the unsettling of all textual stability and interpretive authority.[98] And the force of the Restoration was not simply the settling of political divide but the effort to heal hermeneutic fracture. The re-establishment of monarchy and church was more than a reconstitution of social authority: it was a reassertion of interpretive authority, a claim to sovereign signification. Official publications – editions, histories, treason trials – were themselves rereadings as well as rescriptings of the revolutionary past.[99] But in many other ways Restoration settlement endeavoured to police and reformulate the conditions and experiences of reading – past and present. Censorship was only the most obvious move. The erasures and elisions that everywhere mark Restoration literary and political culture were intended to delimit and direct the imaginations of readers.[100] And for some years after 1660, memories of past collaborations, guilt over regicide and anxiety about renewed conflict defined the conditions in which the past was read and present values were formed. Even that icon of modernity, Locke's *Two Treatises of Government*, was, as Kirstie McClure discloses, forged from ancient fable and amidst the turmoil of revolution.[101] As long as the Civil War remained so powerfully present, there was no reading outside its shadow.

Memory, however, was by no means a stable text. Whatever the efforts of authority to appropriate history and memory in the service of social harmony and political stability, former Parliamentarians and ex-Royalists naturally read all the texts of settlement as quite different promptings and admonitions. However urgent the desire for coherence and concord, it soon became apparent to contemporaries that hermeneutic division was a permanent legacy of political life. And not simply the divisions between Roundheads and Cavaliers. The defeat of a comprehensive religious settlement signalled, and ironically underwrote, a multiplicity of dissenting voices – a myriad of scriptural exegeses and appropriations.[102] The Popish Plot was not only scripted out of such religious divisions and unresolved political tensions, but was in large part textually manufactured – fabricated through narratives, depositions and readings.[103] And the Glorious Revolution was peacefully effected by the transmutation of violent conflicts into hermeneutic contests.[104]

We have learned how the acceptance of difference was gradually accommodated, indeed socialized, into a new political culture that embraced partisanship, and that ultimately institutionalized difference in party. What we need to address is the relation of these political changes to the history of reading. In the altered social and political circumstances of party, partisanship itself becomes the fundamental condition and indeed mode of reading. Where, for all their differences, early Stuart exegetes read to reveal one truth to which all might subscribe, Restoration hermeneutics accepted and even began to valorize interpretive distinction and difference. The recruitment of poets to party programmes assumes not only authorship as political practice but reading communities defined by political affiliation and party allegiance.

While difference may have been accommodated, violent division remained a powerful cultural fear. Party, as we have shown, endeavoured not only to socialize but to civilize division into coffee house, club, pleasurable social congress.[105] In its broadest cultural reach, this civilizing process is written as the history of politeness.[106] Reading, though it has not been studied as such, is very much part of that history. Politeness located practices of reading in the gentleman's academy, the ladies' salon, the society for the reformation of manners, the pump room at the spa. To mute coarseness and vituperation, it established an etiquette of civilized exchange – the wry observation, the ironic barb, the elegant put-down. Politeness, that is, ameliorated the violence of exchange and tempered the most aggressive modes of reading. It may be no coincidence that the age of politeness sees the departure of the irate reader from the margins, and more generally a decline of all readerly inscription and annotation.[107] Might we suggest that the shift from a world of endless reformations and revolutions to the relative peace of Hanoverian Britain owed something to the transformation of the active, purposeful, contesting humanist reader into the more leisured and passive reader, at pleasure with his or her books?

Reading for pleasure may seem to bring us straight and straightforwardly to the present. But neither the contours of the present nor the trajectories of the past are so simple. Neither 1642 nor 1688 signalled the end of revolutions driven by reading. Though at first glance the Romantic reader seems the embodiment of the isolate, the passive, the languid reader, utterly removed from reading as social action, the revolutions of the late eighteenth century, both political and aesthetic, were premised on revolutionary readers. The literary underground of *ancien régime* France evidences oppositional communities and the subversive capacities of readers.[108] In Wordsworth's England ways of reading nature and the book generated radical aesthetic and political sensibilities – ecological, republican, democratic.[109] The Romantic reader, of Rousseau, for example, read the book as the script of the self. In the Romantic hermeneutic, the reading of the most intimate of texts and experiences becomes perforce political performance. The Romantic reader, as Blake intuited, reconstituted the radical spirituality and social exegesis of godly enthusiasm.[110]

And who can doubt the politics of our own readings? Perusing any local bookshop, we immediately encounter the self-help manuals which not only evoke earlier humanist reading for action and self-improvement, but evidence a politics of selfhood and self-assertion. On the next shelf, feminist, black or gay literature assumes that political identity and community is constituted by reading. We are what we read.

READING POSSIBILITIES

And not only what, but how. The briefest review of our twentieth-century critical practices demonstrates that ways of reading determine our literary and historical praxis. The interpretive practices of twentieth-century literary criticism themselves constitute a history of reading. From biography and *belles lettres*, through the close formalism of New Critical hermeneutics, to the radical destabilization of deconstruction, it is first and foremost ways of reading that have figured and refigured the text and the canon. While the shifting hermeneutics of contemporary historiography have been less publicized and interrogated, shifts in the objects and fashions of historical enquiry are, no less than in literary criticism, changes in reading practices. The micro-history, the thick description and the long *durée* of the *annaliste* are fundamentally modes of interpreting – of reading – the past. The shifting strategies of literary criticism and historical interpretation are, of course, ideological narratives. It was the traumas of fascism and the Second World War that impelled the insistent universalism and transhistorical aestheticism of the New Criticism; equally, alternative politics discredited the 'master narrative' and fuelled a new social history. Whether we foreground them or not, the ways in which we read constitute our practices as critics and historians. Our purpose has been to foreground them, to bring into central focus the critical and historical hermeneutics of early modern reading. But this recentring has clear implications for our present and future as well as our past. It is to these implications we turn: to the ways in which reading might fashion us as scholars, students and citizens.

Traditional literary scholarship, for all its moves and turns, has taken, as the almost exclusive subject of its study, the text as object and production – authors and their histories, books and their formal properties. Only now are we beginning to understand the ways in which the reader is implicated in all stages of creation and production. In a marketplace of print, authors and, of course, to a greater extent publishers perforce imagined the consumer as a condition of creation and production. The absolute distinction of author and reader may be a convenient shorthand, but it is simplistic if not false. Of greater and broader import, address to the reader transforms the text from a site of sovereign authorial intention and meaning to a series of performances that ever complicate the very notions of authorship and meaning. Critical scholarship that embraces the reader as central actor newly opens and extends the text, not only to the moment of its creation and production but in all the interpretive communities and exegetical circumstances of its unfolding history. Such a perspective demystifies any residual, Romantic attachment to the author as isolate creative genius or to the aesthetic as timeless and universal; it makes all criticism historicized criticism. We have yet fully to understand and to practise the critical implications both of the sociology of the text and of the historicity of all its consumptions and receptions.[III]

This practice must begin with the material text itself. To ask the most basic question of who was capable of buying and reading a book is to return the text to the economic uncertainties and social dynamics of the market. The material text, we see, is permeable, open to all the exigencies of production within, and dislocations of, a market society. Opening books to their histories necessitates fundamentally revised principles and practices of editing. The new bibliography, concerned with form, design and typography as social indices has historicized editorial practice in new ways; what attention to the history of reception suggests is the editing of the readerly rather than the writerly text. Whereas the classic edition valorized, indeed reified, the text as embodiment of the single author, the new edition understands all texts as sites of multiple hands and voices.[112] What the future edition might valuably identify is all the traces of its textual multiplicity, its history of contingency and instability.

Textual instability is neither a term nor a concept familiar or welcome to historians. Historical method has been premised on the stable text as vehicle of authorial intention and coherent meaning. Even now most historians remain fixed in notions of textual stability largely because the destabilized text threatens and disrupts historical epistemology and practice. In their interpretive community, postmodern theory is feared as nihilism, as the end of history. But the readerly text, we would argue, invites rich historical contemplation. It gestures not to the univocal master narrative but to all the multiple actors and performative exigencies of texts, to the precise moments in which meanings are historically formulated. A proper account of the past, we suggest, should not merely tolerate the unstable text and its readers but license them to rewrite history.

In the classroom, the readerly text rewrites the script and transforms the experience of literary and historical study. All the material characters of the text as constituents of meaning quickly expose the limitations, indeed occlusions, of modern student editions. In a pedagogy centred on reading, the various and variant materialities of texts become central to our teaching and study. Where customarily the library and classroom constitute quite different sites of learning, in a reader-centred pedagogy, the library – that repository of the history of the book – becomes the classroom. Nor is the materiality of the text the limit of a pedagogy that newly stimulates the imagination. In releasing the text from single to multiple authorship, from fixity to multivalence, training in the history even of reading licenses the student as authority. As well as learning from master and exegete, the student-reader joins a community of readers, contributes to a history of reading; in appreciating and tracing all the negotiations that construct meaning, such a student begins to reconstruct the classroom, too, as a place of authorial and readerly exchange.

In the classroom, the history of reading is also and necessarily an interdisciplinary education. The history of reading studies the text in social history and as social history. It interrogates and explicates the text as spiritual and economic experience, rather than primarily as form and structure. In such a classroom, study of the text, even the most stringent formalist criticism, is practised also as historical sociology and anthropology.[113] In the history class, focus on reading directs the student of the past to all of its texts, to poem and play as much as to proclamation. It also insists on the rhetoricity, the 'readerliness' of all texts, and all the moments of interpretation, as historical actions and events. To return sermon or proclamation to their sites and successive moments of audition and reception is to disclose different imaginings of historical agency and authority – of history itself.

Habits of reading are not confined by the classroom; they are in the broadest sense public practices. If learning to read is the rite of entry into the social, reading as critical exegesis and engagement is traditionally held to be the qualification for citizenship. The health of democracy depends as much upon forms of literacy and modes of reading as on institutions and constitutions. Congress and Commons assume criticism and contest; the election requires discernment and discrimination; the free press is premised on the independent reader. Modes of reading in the present as in the past are barometers of the political temperature of the state. In our own time, not surprisingly, disquiet over the health and viability of democracy is analysed as a crisis of literacy. As the spin doctor and news manager endeavour to delimit damage, control meaning and direct perception, we correspondingly lament the apathy of the electorate, the passivity of the public, the 'dumbing down' of culture. Central to this analysis are both the decay of literacy and the decline of reading. All of us, it seems, opt lazily for the sound bite over the editorial; the young, we are told, discard books for images; attention deficit disorder is the diagnosed malady of our age.

A history of reading, however, suggests a less hysterical and more historical diagnosis. In the long *durée* of literacy we have heard articulated anxieties about the assault of print upon manuscript, the threat of digest to folio learning, the dangers of female and working-class literacy. Because they are so implicated in the public sphere, the technologies of writing, publishing and reading have always generated anxieties. But of course they have also structured what we have called progress. Today, progress, material, personal and public, is inseparable from the new technologies of communication, no less than from new ways of managing text and learning to read. For all the laments about the decline of literacy, we inhabit a culture more sophisticated than any we have seen in reading the image: decoding, enhancing, deploying, appropriating. The Internet, it is said, is the ultimate democracy. The radical optimist even talks of a new world order generated by the openness of the text and the freedom of the reader. The student of reading might prefer to temper prophecy with history.

NOTES

1. See R. Darnton, 'First Steps toward a History of Reading', *Australian Journal of French Studies*, 23 (1986), pp. 5–30; and A. Manguel, *A History of Reading* (London, 1996).
2. For classic texts in the history of reader response criticism, see W. Iser, *The Implied Reader* (Baltimore, 1974) and *The Act of Reading: A Theory of Aesthetic Response* (Baltimore, 1978); H. R. Jauss, *Toward an Aesthetic of Reception*, trans. T. Bahti (Minneapolis, 1982); and S. Fish, *Is There a Text in This Class? The Authority of Interpretive Communities* (Cambridge, Mass., 1980).
3. See, for example, R. Chartier, ed., *Histoire de la lecture: Un Bilan de recherches* (Paris, 1995), and his *Practique de la lecture* (Paris, 1995); E. Hannebut-Benz, *Die Kunst des Lesens: Lesenmobel und Leserverhalten von Mittelalter bis zur Gegenwalt* (Frankfurt, 1985); M. B. Parkes, *Scribes, Scripts and Readers: Studies in the Communication, Presentation and Dissemination of Medieval Texts* (London, 1991); J. Raven, H. Small and N. Tadmor, eds., *The Practice and Representation of Reading in England* (Cambridge, 1996); K. Flint, *The Woman Reader, 1837–1914* (Oxford, 1993); and J. Pearson, *Women's Reading in Britain 1750–1835: A Dangerous Recreation* (Cambridge, 1999).
4. On the new bibliography and the idea of authorial imprint, see P. Kamuf, *Signature Pieces: On the Institution of Authorship* (Cornell, 1988); S. Stewart, *Crimes of Writing: Problems in the Containment of Representation* (Oxford, 1991); R. Chartier, 'Figures of the Author', in Chartier, *The Order of Books* (Stanford, 1992); J. Maston, *Textual Intercourse: Collaboration, Authorship, and Sexualities in Renaissance Drama* (Cambridge, 1996); and J. Loewenstein, *Authorial Impression: The Production of Intellectual Property in Early Modern England* (forthcoming).
5. See D. F. McKenzie, 'Printers of the Mind: Some Notes on Bibliographical Theories and Printing-House Practices', *Studies in Bibliography*, 22 (1969), pp. 1–75; E. B. Tribble, *Margins and Marginality: The Printed Page in Early Modern England* (Charlottesville, Va., and London, 1993); L. E. Maguire, *Shakespearean Suspect Texts: The 'Bad' Quartos and Their Contexts* (Cambridge, 1996); and J. Loewenstein, 'Authentic Reproductions: The Material Origins of the New Bibliography', in L. E. Maguire and T. L. Berger, eds., *Textual Formations and Reformations* (Newark, Del., 1998).

6. See W. Speed Hill, ed., *New Ways of Looking at Old Texts* (Binghamton, N.Y., 1993); S. Orgel, 'What Is an Editor?', *Shakespeare Studies*, 24 (1996), pp. 23–9; and L. S. Marcus, *Unediting the Renaissance: Shakespeare, Marlowe, Milton* (London, 1996); and for a valuable survey of recent work see A. Johns, *The Nature of the Book: Print and Knowledge in the Making* (Chicago, 1998).

7. R. Chartier, *Lectures et lecteurs dans la France d'Ancien Régime* (Paris, 1987); Chartier, *The Cultural Uses of Print in Early Modern France* (Paris, 1987); L. Jardine and A. Grafton, ' "Studied for Action": How Gabriel Harvey Read His Livy', *Past and Present*, 129 (1990), pp. 30–78; W. H. Sherman, *John Dee: The Politics of Reading and Writing in the English Renaissance* (Amherst, Mass., 1995); C. Ginzburg, *The Cheese and the Worms: The Cosmos of a Sixteenth-Century Miller* (London, 1980); and R. Darnton, 'Readers Respond to Rousseau: The Fabrication of Romantic Sensitivity', in Darnton, *The Great Cat Massacre and Other Episodes in French Cultural History* (Harmondsworth, 1985), pp. 209–49.

8. Compare our remarks in K. Sharpe and S. N. Zwicker, eds., *Refiguring Revolutions: Aesthetics and Politics from the English Revolution to the Romantic Revolution* (Berkeley and London, 1998), introduction, especially pp. 20–1.

9. See, for example, E. P. Thompson, *The Poverty of Theory and Other Essays* (London, 1978); R. J. Evans, *In Defence of History* (London, 1997); and K. Sharpe, *Reading Revolutions: The Politics of Reading in Early Modern England* (New Haven and London, 2000), chapter 1.

10. See chapter 9 below.

11. Erasmus's *De Copia* is essentially a manual on reading practices. For humanism and reading, see T. Cave, *The Cornucopian Text: Problems of Writing in the French Renaissance* (Oxford, 1979); A. Grafton, *Commerce with the Classics: Ancient Books and Renaissance Readers* (Ann Arbor, Mich., 1997); M. Todd, *Christian Humanism and the Puritan Social Order* (Cambridge, 1987); and A. Grafton, 'The Humanist as Reader', in G. Cavallo and R. Chartier, eds., *A History of Reading in the West*, trans. L. G. Cochrane (Oxford, 1999), chapter 7. For emphasis on the resisting reader, see M. de Certeau, 'The Reader as Poacher', in de Certeau, *The Practice of Everyday Life* (Berkeley, 1984); Ginzburg, *The Cheese and the Worms*; and Sharpe, *Reading Revolutions*.

12. See J.-F. Gilmont, 'Protestant Reformations and Reading', in Cavallo and Chartier, eds., *A History of Reading*, chapter 8; Gilmont, ed., *La Réforme et le livre: L'Europe de l'imprimé* (Paris, 1990); R. Scribner, *For the Sake of Simple Folk: Propaganda for the German Reformation* (Cambridge, 1981); and D. Cressy, *Literacy and the Social Order: Reading and Writing in Tudor and Stuart England* (Cambridge, 1980).

13. See E. Eisenstein, *The Printing Press as an Agent of Change: Communication and Cultural Transformation in Early Modern Europe* (Cambridge, 1979).

14. For Congreve's proud progress from quarto to folio, see D. F. McKenzie, 'Typography and Meaning: The Case of William Congreve', in G. Barber and B. Fabian, eds., *Buch und Buchhandel in Europa im achtzehnten Jahrhundert: The Book and the Book Trade in Eighteenth-Century Europe* (Hamburg, 1981),

pp. 81–125; and chapter 2 below. See also M. Spufford, *Small Books and Pleasant Histories: Popular Fiction and Its Readership in Seventeenth-Century England* (Cambridge, 1981).

15. Moreover, folios were usually bound separately, cheap quartos more often together. We need to pay more attention to the different reading experiences fostered by binding practices.

16. See T. Watt, *Cheap Print and Popular Piety, 1550–1640* (Cambridge, 1991); and Spufford, *Small Books*.

17. See M. Corbett and R. W. Lightbown, *The Comely Frontispiece: The Emblematic Title-Page in England, 1550–1660* (London, 1979).

18. See A. F. Marotti, *Manuscript, Print, and the English Renaissance Lyric* (Ithaca and London, 1995), p. 310.

19. See, for example, Humphrey Moseley's folio edition of Beaumont and Fletcher's *Comedies and Tragedies* (London, 1647) with its thirty-seven commendatory poems, or his folio of William Cartwright's *Comedies, Tragi-Comedies, and Other Poems* (London, 1651) with its sixty-one leaves of commendatory verse.

20. One of the classic examples of paratext structuring text is the Geneva Bible with its dedication to Queen Elizabeth, its arguments, running heads, printed marginalia, illustrations, maps and tables, all of which serve not only to gloss meaning but also to prevent readers from glossing on their own. For typography and the presentation of play texts, see H.-J. Martin, *The History and Power of Writing*, trans. L. G. Cochrane (Chicago, 1994), pp. 319–30.

21. For typography and meaning, see N. Barker, 'Typography and the Meaning of Words: The Revolution in the Layout of Books in the Eighteenth Century', in Barber and Fabian, eds., *Buch und Buchhandel*. See also T. Corns, 'The Early Modern Search Engine: Indices, Title Pages, Marginalia and Contents', in N. Rhodes and J. Sawday, eds., *The Renaissance Computer: Knowledge Technology in the First Age of Print* (London, 2000), pp. 95–105; M. Elsky, *Authorising Words: Speech, Writing and Print in the English Renaissance* (Ithaca, 1989); S. Morison, *Politics and Script* (Oxford, 1972); and D. Olson, *The World on Paper: The Conceptual and Cognitive Implications of Writing and Reading* (Cambridge, 1994).

22. For manuscript adverseria and humanist scholarship, see the classic essay by Lisa Jardine and Anthony Grafton, 'Studied for Action'. For illustrations of the Renaissance systems of interlinear gloss and marginal commentary, see R. E. Stoddard, *Marks in Books, Illustrated and Explained* (Cambridge, Mass., 1985); and B. M. Rosenthal, *The Rosenthal Collection of Printed Books with Manuscript Annotations: A Catalogue of 242 Editions mostly before 1600 Annotated by Contemporary or Near-Contemporary Readers* (New Haven, 1997). One of the most complete catalogues of printed books with manuscript marginalia is R. C. Alston, ed., *Books with Manuscript: A Short Title Catalogue of Books with Manuscript Notes in the British Library* (London, 1994). See also Tribble, *Margins and Marginality*; and A. Grafton, *The Footnote: A Curious History* (London, 1997).

23. See chapter 1 below.
24. See W. E. Slights, 'The Edifying Margins of Renaissance English Books', *Renaissance Quarterly*, 42 (1989), pp. 682–716; R. C. Evans, *Habits of Mind: Evidence and Effects of Ben Jonson's Reading* (Lewisburg, Pa., 1995); S. N. Zwicker, 'Reading the Margins: Politics and the Habits of Appropriation', in Sharpe and Zwicker, eds., *Refiguring Revolutions*, pp. 101–15.
25. Sarah Clapp long ago addressed the history of book subscription in 'The Beginnings of Subscription Publication in the Seventeenth Century', *Modern Philology*, 29 (1931–2), pp. 199–224, and in 'Subscription Publishers prior to Jacob Tonson', *Library*, 13 (1932), pp. 158–83; more recent work has been done on Dryden, Pope and early eighteenth-century subscription publication; see, for example, M. Hodgart, 'The Subscription List for Pope's Iliad', in R. B. White Jr, ed., *The Dress of Words* (Lawrence, Kans., 1978), pp. 25–34; P. Rogers, 'Pope and His Subscribers', *Publishing History*, 3 (1978), pp. 7–36; and J. Barnard, 'Dryden, Tonson and Virgil', in P. Hammond and D. Hopkins, eds., *John Dryden: Tercentenary Essays* (Oxford, 2000). For book advertisement, see M. Seidel, 'Narrative News', *Eighteenth-Century Fiction*, 10/2 (1988), pp. 125–50; M. Harris, 'Timely Notices: The Uses of Advertising and Its Relationship to News during the Late Seventeenth Century', in J. Raymond, ed., *News, Newspapers, and Society in Early Modern Britain* (London, 1999), pp. 141–56; and C. Ferdinand, 'Constructing the Frames of Desire: How Newspapers Sold Books in the Seventeenth and Eighteenth Centuries', in Raymond, ed., *News, Newspapers, and Society*, pp. 157–75.
26. See J. Habermas, *The Structural Transformation of the Public Sphere* (Cambridge, 1989). See also J. Raymond, 'The Newspaper, Public Opinion, and the Public Sphere in the Seventeenth Century', in Raymond, ed., *News, Newspapers, and Society*, pp. 109–40; A. Halasz, *The Marketplace of Print: Pamphlets and the Public Sphere in Early Modern England* (Cambridge, 1997); and D. Zaret, 'Religion, Science, and Printing in the Public Spheres of Seventeenth-Century England', in C. Calhoun, ed., *Habermas and the Public Sphere* (Cambridge, Mass., 1992), pp. 212–35.
27. See T. Harris, 'The Parties and the People: The Press, the Crowd, and Politics "Out-of-Doors" in Restoration England', in L. K. J. Glassey, ed., *The Reigns of Charles II and James VII and II* (London, 1997), pp. 125–51; M. Harris, *London Newspapers in the Age of Walpole* (Cranbury, N.J., 1987); R. M. Wiles, *Freshest Advices: Early Provincial Newspapers in England* (Columbus, Ohio, 1987); and P. Rogers, *Grub Street: Studies in a Subculture* (London, 1972); see also *The Character of a Coffee-House with the Symptoms of a Town Wit* (London, 1673).
28. See R. Cust, 'News and Politics in Early Seventeenth-Century England', *Past and Present*, 112 (1986), pp. 60–90; A. Bellany, 'The Poisoning of Legitimacy: Court Scandal, News, Culture and Politics in England' (Ph. D. dissertation, Princeton University, 1995); D. Freist, *Governed by Opinion: Politics, Religion and the Dynamics of Communication in Stuart London, 1637–1645* (London,

1997); and J. Raymond, *The Invention of the Newspaper: English Newsbooks, 1641–1649* (Oxford, 1996).

29. David Cressy's classic study *Literacy and the Social Order* has been revised by K. Thomas, 'The Meaning of Literacy in Early Modern England', in G. Baumann, ed., *The Written Word: Literacy in Transition* (Oxford, 1986), pp. 97–131; M. Spufford, 'First Steps in Literacy: The Reading and Writing Experience of the Humblest Seventeenth-Century Spiritual Autobiographers', *Social History*, 4 (1979), pp. 407–35; and Watt, *Cheap Print and Popular Piety*.

30. See chapter 8 below.

31. Fish, *Is There a Text in This Class?*

32. Though this not to deny the important and increasing category of 'crossover texts', such as ballads and satires, which were collected by gentlemen and scholars as well as circulating among the populace.

33. See R. J. Allen, *The Clubs of Augustan London* (Cambridge, Mass., 1933); and J. R. Jones, 'The Green Ribbon Club', *Durham University Journal*, 49 (1956), pp. 17–20; on the partisan marking of Restoration texts, see Zwicker, 'Reading the Margins'.

34. See R. Colie, *The Resources of Kind: Genre Theory in the Renaissance* (Berkeley, 1973); and B. K. Lewalski, ed., *Renaissance Genres: Essays on Theory, History, and Interpretation* (Cambridge, Mass., 1986).

35. For gender, genre and early modern reading, see E. Hoby, 'The Politics of Gender', in T. Corns, ed., *The Cambridge Companion to English Poetry: Donne to Marvell* (Cambridge, 1993), pp. 31–51; W. Wall, *The Imprint of Gender: Authorship and Publication in the English Renaissance* (Ithaca, 1993).

36. Wolfgang Iser's *The Implied Reader* assumes too great a compliance by actual readers who, as authorial prefaces and epistles to readers manifest, were often resistant to reading with the grain.

37. For Shakespearean adaptation, see C. Spencer, ed., *Five Restoration Adaptations of Shakespeare* (Urban, Ill., 1965); M. Dobson, *The Making of the National Poet: Shakespeare, Adaptation and Authorship, 1660–1769* (Oxford, 1992); R. Strier, 'Impossible Radicalism and Impossible Value: Nahum Tate's *King Lear*', in Strier, *Resistant Structures: Particularity, Radicalism, and Renaissance Texts* (Berkeley and Los Angeles, 1995); and M. Walsh, *Shakespeare, Milton, and Eighteenth-Century Editing* (Cambridge, 1997).

38. See P. Seaver, *Wallington's World: A Puritan Artisan in Seventeenth-Century London* (London, 1985); and E. Boucier, *Les Journaux privés en Angleterre de 1600 à 1660* (Paris, 1976).

39. For reading providence, see A. Walsham, *Providence in Early Modern England* (Oxford, 1999).

40. See C. Hill, *The World Turned Upside Down* (Harmondsworth, 1972); and N. Smith, *Perfection Proclaimed: Language and Literature in English Radical Religion* (Oxford, 1989).

41. For an excellent essay on humanist education, see Q. Skinner, *Reason and Rhetoric in the Philosophy of Hobbes* (Cambridge, 1996), part 1.

42. Montaigne writes of his library as withdrawn 'from all intercourse, filial, conjugal and civic', where he can 'be by himself': M. de Montaigne, *The Complete Essays*, ed. M. Screech (Harmondsworth, 1987), pp. 459, 933.

43. Stephen Greenblatt's classic study *Renaissance Self-Fashioning: From More to Shakespeare* (Chicago, 1980) was not specifically addressed to reading practices. The relationship of the self to habits of reading is a subject that awaits exploration, though see M. T. Crane, *Framing Authority: Sayings, Self and Society in Sixteenth-Century England* (Princeton, 1993).

44. See Walsham, *Providence*; and P. Lake, *The AntiChrist's Lewd Hat: Protestants, Papists and Players in Post-Reformation England* (New Haven and London, 2001). We are grateful to Peter Lake for kindly allowing us to read this book in advance of publication. For Bunyan, see U. M. Kaufmann, *Pilgrim's Progress and the Tradition of Puritan Meditation* (New Haven, 1966).

45. See M. Foucault, *Discipline and Punish* (Harmondsworth, 1979); J. Bender, *Imagining the Penitentiary: Fiction and the Architecture of Mind in Eighteenth-Century England* (Chicago, 1987); M. McKeon, *The Origins of the English Novel, 1600–1740* (Baltimore, 1987); and G. Rousseau, ed., *The Languages of Psyche: Mind and Body in Enlightenment Thought* (Berkeley and Los Angeles, 1990).

46. For the emergence of sensibility, see G. J. Barker-Benfield, *The Culture of Sensibility: Sex and Society in Eighteenth-Century Britain* (Chicago, 1992); L. Klein, *Shaftesbury and the Culture of Politeness: Moral Discourse and Cultural Politics in Early Eighteenth-Century England* (Cambridge, 1994); and J. Ellison, *Cato's Tears and the Making of Anglo-American Emotion* (Chicago, 1999).

47. See H. Guest, ' "These Neuter Somethings": Gender Difference and Commercial Culture in Mid-Eighteenth-Century England', in Sharpe and Zwicker, eds., *Refiguring Revolutions*, pp. 173–97; and J. Campbell, *Natural Masques: Gender and Identity in Fielding's Plays and Novels* (Stanford, 1995).

48. See R. Paulson, *Literary Landscape: Turner and Constable* (New Haven, 1982); and Paulson, *Breaking and Remaking: Aesthetic Practice in England, 1700–1820* (New Brunswick, 1989).

49. Inventories of women's books often list them as in the bedroom; see N. Wheale, *Writing and Society: Literacy, Print and Politics in Britain, 1590–1660* (London, 1999), p. 106. We note that the study long remained, and indeed remains, a masculine domain.

50. See S. W. Hull, *Chaste, Silent, and Obedient: English Books for Women, 1475–1640* (San Marino, Calif., 1988); and H. B. Hackel, 'Impressions from a Scribbling Age: Recovering the Reading Practices of Renaissance England' (Ph.D. dissertation, Columbia University, 1995), chapter 4.

51. See Hackel, 'Impressions', chapter 4; and B. K. Lewalski, *Writing Women in Jacobean England* (Cambridge, Mass., 1993). The statement that Lady Clifford did not mark her books needs to be revised in the light of Stephen Orgel's acquisition of annotated books from her library. We are grateful to Stephen Orgel for this information.

52. See L. Pollock, *With Faith and Physic: The Life of a Tudor Gentlewoman, Lady Grace Mildmay, 1552–1620* (London, 1993); P. Crawford, *Women and Religion in England, 1500–1720* (London, 1993); P. Mack, *Visionary Women: Ecstatic Prophecy in Seventeenth-Century England* (Berkeley, 1992); and H. Hinds, *God's Englishwomen: Seventeenth-Century Radical Sectarian Writing and Feminist Criticism* (Manchester, 1996).

53. See E. S. Cope, *Handmaid of the Holy Spirit: Dame Eleanor Davies, Never soe Mad a Ladie* (Ann Arbor, Mich., 1992); and J. Todd, *The Secret Life of Aphra Behn* (London, 1996). For female readership in Restoration and eighteenth-century England, see T. Keymer, *Richardson's Clarissa and the Eighteenth-Century Reader* (Cambridge, 1992); P. McDowell, *The Women of Grubstreet: Press, Politics, and Gender in the London Literary Marketplace, 1678–1730* (Oxford, 1998); Pearson, *Women's Reading in Britain*; E. Gardiner, *Regulating Readers: Gender and Literary Criticism in the Eighteenth-Century Novel* (Newark, Del., 1999); and V. Jones, ed., *Women and Literature in Britain 1700–1800* (Cambridge, 2000).

54. At the most obvious level men were often depicted with big folio books on a desk, women more often with octavos in hand.

55. For Hutchinson, see L. Hutchinson, *Memoirs of the Life of Colonel Hutchinson* ed. J. Sutherland (Oxford, 1973); and *Lucy Hutchinson's Translation of Lucretius*, ed. H. De Quehen (Ann Arbor, Mich., 1996). For Margaret Cavendish, see K. Jones, *A Glorious Fame: The Life of Margaret Cavendish, Duchess of Newcastle, 1623–1673* (London, 1988); and A. Battigelli, *Margaret Cavendish and the Exiles of the Mind* (Lexington, Ky., 1998).

56. See W. Cherniak, *Sexual Freedom in Restoration Literature* (Cambridge, 1996); for Astell, see R. Perry, *The Celebrated Mary Astell: An Early English Feminist* (Chicago, 1986); and *Astell: Political Writings*, ed. P. Springborg (Cambridge, 1996). For Astell as critic of Locke, see P. Springborg, 'Mary Astell and John Locke', in S. N. Zwicker, ed., *The Cambridge Companion to English Literature, 1650–1740* (Cambridge, 1998), pp. 276–306. See also R. Weil, *Political Passions: Gender, the Family and Political Argument in England 1680–1714* (Manchester, 1999); and J. Todd, ed., *Aphra Behn Studies* (Cambridge, 1996).

57. The impact of the 'ladies' faction' on the theatre of the 1690s and the move towards sentimental comedy has been studied by R. Hume, 'The Change in Comedy: Cynical versus Exemplary Comedy on the London Stage, 1678–1693', *Theatre*, 1 (1983), pp. 101–18; for the feminization of the Quixote tradition, see C. Croft, 'Reworking Male Models: Aphra Behn's "Fair Vow-Breaker", Eliza Heywood's "Fantomina", and Charlotte Lenox's "Female Quixote"', *Modern Language Review*, 86 (1991), pp. 821–38.

58. See N. Davis, 'Women on Top', in Davis, *Society and Culture in Early Modern France* (London, 1975), chapter 5.

59. See Lewalski, *Writing Women*, chapter 5; G. Parry, 'The Great Picture of Lady Anne Clifford', in D. Howarth, ed., *Art and Patronage in the Caroline Courts* (Cambridge, 1993), pp. 202–19; and *The Diaries of Lady Anne Clifford*, ed. D. G. H. Clifford (Stroud, 1992).

60. Defoe's *Moll Flanders* and *Roxana* are the most obvious examples, but there is a rich *pícara* tradition that develops out of the work of Aphra Behn and Charlotte Lenox in eighteenth-century fiction; see M. P. Martin, ' "High and Noble Adventures": Reading the Novel in the Female Quixote', *Novel*, 31 (1997), pp. 45–62.

61. See J. Mullan, 'The Language of Sentiment: Hume, Smith, and Henry Mackenzie', in A. Hook, ed., *The History of Scottish Literature* (Aberdeen, 1987), pp. 273–89; C. Gallagher, 'Nobody's Story: Gender, Property, and the Rise of the Novel', *Modern Language Quarterly*, 53 (1992), pp. 263–77; and E. Cook, *Epistolary Bodies: Gender and Genre in the Eighteenth-Century Republic of Letters* (Stanford, 1996).

62. See chapter 7 below.

63. The metaphor of digestion was often taken from Seneca. See Sharpe, *Reading Revolutions*, p.182, for Sir William Drake's understanding of it.

64. For a stimulating study of the interrelations between the body and text, see J. Sawday, *The Body Emblazoned: Dissection and the Human Body in Renaissance Culture* (London, 1995).

65. For the connection between writing, labour and authority, see J. Goldberg, *Writing Matter: From the Hands of the English Renaissance* (Stanford, 1990).

66. See chapter 3 below. Dora Thornton observes that Renaissance women are most often shown with devotional books in their bedchambers, though there are occasional exceptions; see Thornton, *The Scholar in His Study: Ownership and Experience in Renaissance Italy* (New Haven, 1997), pp. 90–4.

67. See Johns, *The Nature of the Book*, chapter 6, and chapter 8 below.

68. Even in the court masque we find a vulgar reference to the 'two leaved book'; see *Coelum Britannicum*, lines 203–4, in S. Orgel and R. Strong, *Inigo Jones: The Theatre of the Stuart Court* (2 vols., London and Berkeley, 1973), vol. 2, p. 572.

69. Manguel, *A History of Reading*, p. 154.

70. See E. F. Rice, *Saint Jerome in the Renaissance* (Baltimore, 1985); other saints depicted with books include St Thomas Aquinas, St Filippo Neri, St Augustine and St Francis of Assisi.

71. See Crawford, *Women and Religion*. The reign of Elizabeth may well have had wider effects on attitudes towards female literacy, not least because the queen was represented, and presented herself, as a figure of learning who translated the classics and devotional works and wrote prayers. See *Elizabeth I: Collected Works*, ed. L. S. Marcus, J. Mueller and M. B. Rose (Chicago, 2000).

72. The most famous of these are the portraits of Desiderius Erasmus, Thomas More and Peter Gilles by Hans Holbein and Quentin Metsys; for these portraits and the rhetoric and iconography of Renaissance humanism, see L. Jardine, *Erasmus, Man of Letters: The Construction of Charisma in Print* (Princeton, 1993), pp. 27–55; for the famous Albrecht Dürer engraving of Erasmus, see E. Panofsky, *The Life and Art of Albrecht Dürer* (Princeton, 1955).

73. Images of active reading, including Agostino Ramelli's often reprinted design for a book-wheel and the beautifully detailed *Saint Jerome in His Study* by Antonello da Messina, can be consulted in Thornton, *The Scholar in His Study*.

74. See A. Bryson, *From Courtesy to Civility: Changing Codes of Conduct in Early Modern England* (Oxford, 1998).

75. See F. Heal and C. Holmes, *The Gentry in England and Wales 1500–1700* (Basingstoke, 1994).

76. See, for example, Van Dyck's portrait of Strafford with his secretary Sir Philip Mainwaring, in C. Brown and H. Vlieghe, *Van Dyck, 1599–1641* ([London], 1999), p. 332, plate 102.

77. For a discussion of the role of Envy in Marlowe's *Faustus* as a comment on the new importance of literacy, see Wheale, *Writing and Society*, pp. 1–5. See also Shakespeare's illiterate servant in *Romeo and Juliet* (1.2.38ff.), or his handling of literacy and illiteracy in Jack Cade's confrontation with the Clerk of Chatham in *2 Henry 6* (4.2.100ff); and E. R. Sanders, *Gender and Literacy on Stage in Early Modern England* (Cambridge, 1998).

78. Here the concepts of functional and partial literacy may be more helpful than the absolute divisions between literate and illiterate. See Thomas, 'The Meaning of Literacy'.

79. See Marcus, *Unediting the Renaissance*.

80. See chapter 5 below, and S. Wiseman, *Drama and Politics in the English Civil War* (Cambridge, 1998).

81. See D. Woolf, *The Idea of History in Early Stuart England* (Toronto, 1990), p. 31.

82. The copy of Charles I's annotated Shakespeare is in the Royal Library at Windsor; see Milton, *Eikonoklastes*, in *The Works of John Milton*, vol. 5, ed. W. H. Haller (New York, 1932), p. 84.

83. See A. Fox, 'Ballads, Libels and Popular Ridicule in Jacobean England', *Past and Present*, 145 (1994), pp. 47–83; T. Cogswell, 'Underground Verse and the Transformation of Early Stuart Political Culture', in S. D. Amussen and M. Kishlansky, eds., *Political Culture and Cultural Politics in Early Modern England* (Manchester, 1995), pp. 277–300; and Bellany, 'The Poisoning of Legitimacy'.

84. For the traditional emphasis on draconian censorship, see C. Hill, 'Censorship and English Literature', in Hill, *Collected Essays*, vol. 1: *Writing and Revolution in Seventeenth-Century England* (Brighton, 1995), pp. 32–71. See also the very different picture painted by C. Clegg in *Press Censorship in Elizabethan England* (Cambridge, 1997).

85. For this argument, see A. Patterson, *Censorship and Interpretation* (Madison, 1984).

86. See, for example, R. Darnton, *The Forbidden Bestsellers of Pre–Revolutionary France* (New York and London, 1995). The infamous trial and subsequent runaway success of Lawrence's *Lady Chatterley's Lover* provides an excellent modern example.

87. See A. B. Worden, 'Literature and Political Censorship in Early Modern England', in A. C. Duke and C. A. Tamse, eds., *Too Mighty to Be Free: Censorship and the Press in Britain and the Netherlands* (Zutphen, 1987), pp. 45–62; and S. Lambert, 'The Printers and the Government', in R. Myers and M. Harris, *Aspects of Printing from 1600* (Oxford, 1987), pp. 1–29.

88. See Sharpe, *Reading Revolutions*; and Ginzburg, *The Cheese and the Worms*.

89. Most famously Hill in *The World Turned Upside Down*.

90. See Raymond, *The Invention of the Newspaper*; chapter 6 below; and Johns, *The Nature of the Book*, chapters 2 and 3. See also Halasz, *The Marketplace of Print*.

91. See chapter 6 below; cf. F. Levy, 'The Decorum of News', in Raymond, ed., *News, Newspapers, and Society*, pp. 12–38; and *The Diary of John Rous, Incumbent of Stanton Downham*, ed. M. A. E. Green, Camden Society, 66 (1856).

92. Hobbes, Aubrey and Burnet all attributed the Civil War to the reading of texts of classical republicanism. See Sharpe, *Reading Revolutions*, p. 316.

93. See S. Achinstein, *Milton and the Revolutionary Reader* (Princeton, 1994).

94. See A. B. Worden, 'Providence and Politics in Cromwellian England', *Past and Present*, 109 (1985), pp. 55–99. On Royalist reading, see L. Potter, *Secret Rites and Secret Writing: Royalist Literature 1641–1660* (Cambridge, 1989); T. Corns, *Uncloistered Virtue: English Political Literature, 1640–1660* (Oxford, 1992), chapters 4 and 7; and J. Loxley, *Royalism and Poetry in the English Civil Wars* (Basingstoke, 1997).

95. See Smith, *Perfection Proclaimed*.

96. See D. Norbrook, *Writing the English Republic: Poetry, Rhetoric and Politics 1627–1660* (Cambridge, 1999); and chapter 4 below.

97. See, for example, the very different historical readings of A. B. Worden, 'Andrew Marvell, Oliver Cromwell and the Horation Ode', in K. Sharpe and S. N. Zwicker, eds., *Politics of Discourse: The Literature and History of Seventeenth-Century England* (Berkeley, 1987), pp. 147–80; D. Norbrook, 'Marvell's "Horation Ode" and the Politics of Genre', in T. Healy and J. Sawday, eds., *Literature and the English Civil War* (Cambridge, 1990), pp. 147–69; D. Hirst and S. N. Zwicker, 'Marvell and the Toils of Patriarchy', *English Literary History*, 66 (1999), pp. 626–54; and Norbrook, *Writing the English Republic*, chapter 6.

98. See S. N. Zwicker, *Lines of Authority: Politics and English Literary Culture, 1649–1689* (Ithaca, 1993).

99. After 1660, David Lloyd planned for an official history of civil war to be deposited in each parish. See D. Lloyd, *Eikon Basilike, or The True Portraiture of . . . Charles II* (1660), epistle dedicatory.

100. Most famously, the Act of Indemnity and Oblivion forbad the utterance of 'any reproach or term of distinction'; see J. P. Kenyon, *The Stuart Constitution, 1603–1688: Documents and Commentary* (Cambridge, 1966), p. 366.

101. See chapter 11 below.

102. For the Restoration church, see J. Spurr, *The Restoration Church of England* (New Haven and London, 1991); and J. Champion, *The Pillars of Priestcraft Shaken: The Church of England and Its Enemies, 1660–1730* (Cambridge, 1992).

103. See J. P. Kenyon, *The Popish Plot* (Harmondsworth, 1972); and R. Weil, ' "If I Did Say So, I Lyed": Elizabeth Cellier and the Construction of Legitimacy in the Popish Plot Crisis', in Amussen and Kishlansky, eds., *Political Culture*, pp. 189–212.

104. See, for example, the debates, in the Convention Parliament, over the meaning of the words 'abdication' and 'vacancy'; these can be followed in W. Cobbett, *Parliamentary History of England* (36 vols., London, 1806–20), vol. 5, pp. 31–110; see also T. P. Slaughter, ' "Abdicate" and "Contract" in the Glorious Revolution', *Historical Journal*, 24 (1981), pp. 323–37.

105. See also S. Pincus, ' "Coffee Politicians Does Create": Coffeehouses and Restoration Political Culture', *Journal of Modern History*, 67 (1995), pp. 807–34.

106. See, for example, Klein, *Shaftesbury and the Culture of Politeness*; and N. Phillipson, ed., *Politics, Politeness and Patriotism* (Washington, D.C., 1993).

107. See chapter 10 below, and S. N. Zwicker, *Producing Passions: Habits of Reading and the Creation of Early Modern Literary Culture* (forthcoming).

108. See R. Darnton, *The Literary Underground of the Old Regime* (Cambridge, Mass., 1982); and Darnton, *Forbidden Bestsellers*.

109. See D. Simpson, *Wordsworth's Historical Imagination: The Poetry of Displacement* (New York, 1987); G. Izenberg, *Impossible Individuality: Romanticism, Revolution, and the Origins of Modern Selfhood, 1787–1802* (Princeton, 1992); and Izenberg, 'The Politics of Song in Wordsworth's *Lyrical Ballads*', in Sharpe and Zwicker, eds., *Refiguring Revolutions*, pp. 116–37.

110. See J. Mee, *Dangerous Enthusiasm: William Blake and the Culture of Radicalism in the 1790s* (Oxford, 1992); for Blake's reconstitution of Milton, see the work of J. Wittreich, especially his *Angel of the Apocalypse: Blake's Idea of Milton* (Madison, Wisc., 1975).

111. See D. F. McKenzie, *Bibliography and the Sociology of Texts* (Oxford, 1985).

112. See, for example, the new edition of Chaucer under way at Cambridge University Press, published in paper and in a CD-ROM format, which features manuscript transcriptions, manuscript glosses, print editions, and digitized images of manuscripts, all available, through hypertext, for simultaneous consultation; see also J. Loewenstein, 'Legal Proofs and Corrected Readings: "Press-Agency" and the New Bibliography', in D. L. Miller, ed., *The Production of English Renaissance Culture* (Ithaca, 1991).

113. For an excellent example of a combination of formal analysis, anthropological approaches and close historicizing, see M. Schoenfeldt, *Prayer and Power: George Herbert and Renaissance Courtship* (Chicago, 1991).

PART I

The material text

CHAPTER ONE

Errata: print, politics and poetry in early modern England

Seth Lerer

Agnosco, fateor...

           Guillaume Budé, letter to Erasmus, 1 May 1516 (epistle 403)

I do not think that I have ever published anything that did not have an error in it. Typos have crept in and escaped proofreading. Mis-citations and mistranslations have refused correction. Facts and judgements have, at times, seemed almost wilfully in opposition to empirical evidence or received opinion. It is the duty of our readers, so it seems, to catch such errors. Referees for publishers and book reviewers for journals often begin well and well-meaningly enough. But praise soon shatters into pedantry, and reports and reviews will often end with catalogues of broken lines and phrases: errata uncaught by editor or author, blots on the reputation of the scholar's knowledge or his critical acumen.

I'm not alone. All creatures of the academic life subject themselves to such reviewing, and most practise it themselves. To have been savaged and to savage, whether veiled behind the scrim of the anonymous report or displayed in the full acknowledgement of the printed by-line, is the mark of my business: the rite of passage and the passing of one's rights. It is as if I've led an erroneous life, as if what should be totted up on the pages of the book of judgement – or, more prosaically, in annual decanal salary reviews – are not achievements but mistakes. We live, in the academy, by blunder.

What are the sources of this life, the origins of such a business?[1] I seek both cultural-historical and autotherapeutic answers to this question, and my working claim is that the origins of error – as an ideology, a practice, a defining mode of scholarly identity – lie in that nexus of the editorial, the academic and the political that shaped the textual adventures of the late fifteenth and early sixteenth centuries. My initial focus lies in the errata sheet, that marker not just of mistake but of authorial or editorial control, which emerges out of the early print shops and which stands, I argue, as the defining moment of both humanist erudition and early modern subjectivity.

The errata sheet is the place where the past is publicly brought into line with the present, where errors not just of typography but of usage, dialect, even of dogma, may be confessed and corrected. To explore its early history is to explore the loci of authority and action that make academic life both a performance and a defence. The form of the errata sheet – together with the rhetoric of humanist textual criticism, publishers' self-advertisements and the early Renaissance lyric – reveals the making of the text as (to appropriate Jonathan Crewe's phrasing) one of the 'trials of authorship', or, to put it in the words of Beth Pittenger, part of the 'noise' that fills 'a historically specific moment in which performative speech and theatrical handwriting meet a nascent technology and try to effect a translation into print conventions that have a different, although not completely separate, relation to writing'.[2]

What interests me are not so much the individuated errors of the early printers or even the techniques of collation, comparison and critical decision that went into the production of editions as the rhetoric of error and editorship and the stories told through prefaces, errata sheets and correspondence about the making (or mismaking) of books. The humanist account of error is invariably temporal: it locates the production of the book in a specific historical moment, charts its progress across time, and then invites the reader to locate it (and the reader's own act of reading) on a temporally defined continuum. The story of correction and the artifact of the errata sheet historicize the book, much as the humanist practice of philology historicized the text. For, by acknowledging the historical difference between text and reader, the humanist critic not only recognized linguistic change or corruption of copies, but also the fact that the completed work was not an autonomous object but a counter in the historical story of its making and reception. The early book is always a work in progress and in process, a text intruded upon for emendation, a text that invites the correction of the reader. There is nothing like an errata sheet to prompt the reader to seek out yet more errata – that is, nothing like the admission of *some* errors to provoke us to believe that the work is just *full* of errors. Moreover, the need to narrativize the story of such errors – to offer up a personal history of detection and correction – makes the true subject of the early humanist book not so much its content but the complex relationships among textual and political fealty that write the history of its own production.[3]

The errata sheet stands not as a static marker of uncaught mistakes but as a place holder in the ongoing narratives of book making and book reading themselves. Like many of the paratexts of early print – the prefaces, notes, correspondence and occasional handwritten comments in the margins of the book – errata sheets record the temporality of reading. They illustrate the ways in which the early printed book was used by the first ones to see it, and such sheets were often guides to reading itself. Several early books survive with handwritten corrections drawn from those sheets: illustrations of rereading, in which owner's pen corrected printer's faults.[4] More broadly, however, study of the errata sheet and of the rhetoric of error also helps us understand the ways in which the disciplines of editorial review, legal judgement, political control and religious devotional shared an idiom and imagery. In an age when the practice of confession came under close scrutiny, errata sheets and their accompanying paratexts became the places where the urge to confess could still find a voice, and where the seeking of forgiveness found its listener not among the booths of the church but in the stalls of the bookseller.

The rhetoric of early modern Europe (and, more specifically for my present purposes, of early modern England) is the rhetoric of error, whether it be in the form of the confession of the typo or the heresy.[5] In positing a history of that rhetoric, I offer here three interlocking areas of inquiry. First, I pursue the origins of the errata sheet itself in early European book making. Central to my inquiry is the awareness that these early sheets recorded errors typographical and substantive, if not doctrinal, and that in what I believe to be the earliest appropriation of this device in the English book – in the printed volumes of Sir Thomas More – the correction of error becomes both a method and a theme of intellectual self-presentation. More, and later Sir Thomas Elyot, use errata to tell stories of political correction, and in an extended reading of the corrections to Elyot's *Dictionary* (1538) I trace out the allegories of self-abnegation told through the emending of the typo. From this matrix of early sixteenth-century political and typographical alignment, I turn to the poetry of Wyatt, illustrating the way the instability of the handwritten text is often framed in terms directly borrowed from print, rather than manuscript, technologies. The 'quaking pen', in Wyatt's Chaucerian idiom, leads to reflections on the insecurities of 'proof,' while Wyatt's prose tracts seeking to defend himself against the accusations of heresy in the wake of Cromwell's death define political fealty in terms of editorial method. Together with Erasmus's reflections on the practices of textual criticism, and the work of More and Elyot that I examine in detail, these works of Wyatt open up a set of intellectual associations between forensic judgement and editorship. Wyatt posits a poetics of error for the early modern period – a poetics that has still-resonating implications for the history of scholarship itself, and in particular for modern confrontations with the texts of Wyatt and his age. But in the end this essay is itself a

confrontation with my own erroneous scholarship. And if it seeks to correct
claims I have made elsewhere, it implies (by argument and by example) that
the inheritance of humanist scholarship is not the unadulterated search for
truth but the all-too-often adulterated collations of the errant self.

I

From the start, errata sheets recorded more than typos. The earliest account
we have of one comes from the atelier of Sweynheim and Pannarz.[6] Library
catalogues record, for their edition of Lactantius published on October 29
1465, two concluding pages of the volume titled 'Lactantii Firmiani errata
quibus ipse deceptus est per fratrem Antonium Randesem theologicum
collecta et exarata sunt' ('The errata of Lactantius Firmianus, which he
himself did not catch, have been gathered and written down by brother
Antonio Randesi, theologian').[7] Other kinds of errors fill the sheets of
early Italian printers. Francesco Bonaccorsi published an edition of the
Laude of Jacopone da Todi in September 1490 that included not just
a list of typographical mistakes but also those of dialect and historical
idiom – in the words of Brian Richardson, an index that 'had a threefold
function as a glossary, an errata, and a kind of apparatus criticus'.[8] Early
editions of the works of Boccaccio, Sannazaro, Dante and other Italian
authors often contained, in addition to 'errori de la stampa', those of dialect and usage,[9] while classical texts used the errata sheet as the occasion
to review, re-edit and reprimand earlier editions or defective manuscripts.
A Horace *Opera* printed by Antonio Miscomini in Florence in 1482 has
on its last two pages the *errori* to be found in the edition. Here, what is
important is that this is not some tipped-in extra sheet but an integral part
of the foliation of the book. The errors noted are not printers' mistakes but
substantive emendations to the text. Errata sheets become the place where
textual criticism is done – not in the body of the poetry itself or in the
commentary.[10]

Similarly, in the *Miscellanea* of Poliziano (1489), also published by Miscomini, the final pages of 'Emendationes' offer up not only corrections to
the printed text but also new readings based, apparently, on fresh consultation with the manuscripts of Poliziano's sources. Comments, for example,
on the Greek text of Callimachus betray Poliziano's concern (voiced in his
letters, and in the later remarks to his readers at the close of this volume)
with the proper accents in the Greek. His final, general remarks bear noting,
too, as statements of the larger relationships of will and intention in the
making of the book and the establishing of author–audience association.

If any accents in the Greek words should be missing or wrongly written, let the well educated restore or emend them according to their judgement. But if, reader, you find in addition to these errors anything which escaped our hasty eyes, you will emend those too according to your judgement. Nor will you, whoever you are, consider ours that which is not quite right. Rather, you will ascribe all errors either to the printers or to the editors ['curatoribus']. For if you believe me to be responsible for any error herein, then I will believe you have nothing in your heart.[11]

Here, under the heading 'Emendationes', are emended not just textual but personal relationships. The author offers up avowals of diligence and good faith, and an invitation – or a threat – to readers for continued emendation 'pro iudicio'.

By the beginning of the sixteenth century, errata sheets had become commonplace in European books. They are the stuff of scholarship in Latin volumes – Aldus Manutius's famous printing of the *Hypnerotomachia Poliphili* (1499), for example, has a full page of errata – and the markers of interpretation in vernacular ones. Paolo Trovato has detailed the ways in which errata sheets were used in Italian-language books to correct differences in dialect, or even to emend the text. They appear under titles such as 'Errata corrige', 'Errori de la stampa', 'Errori notabili fatti nel stampare', and the like. They stood, as Trovato illustrates, as invitations for the reader to correct the text. 'Errori de la stampa' guided the corrections 'con la penna'. Any other corrections could be made, in the language of one mid-sixteenth-century Italian book, 'a la discretion de lettore', the equivalent of Poliziano's invitation, three-quarters of a century earlier, for readers to emend 'pro iudicio'.[12]

In England, the errata sheet becomes the stage for claiming authorial fidelity not only to text and type but to ruler and doctrine. There is evidence that, by the early 1520s, English printers were alert to the possibilities of typographical error. Of course, such sensitivities had been voiced half a century earlier by William Caxton, who had claimed that he himself had 'dylygently ouerseen' (i.e. proofread) the text of the revised, new edition of the *Canterbury Tales* of 1484 and who had similarly invoked John Skelton as overseer of the *Eneydos* of 1490.[13] Yet from Caxton's shop, and from that of his successor Wynkyn de Worde, there does not appear to be anything approaching the errata sheets or lists of emendations or corrections that were coming to be commonplace in continental printers. Only with the next generation is something like this European attention to error voiced. John Constable's *Epigrammata*, printed by Berthelet in 1520, has a letter from the printer mentioning the possibility of errors being introduced.[14]

By 1523, proofreading had become so central a part of the English print shop, that the printer Richard Pynson felt the need to define its task in an indenture between himself and John Palsgrave.[15]

Perhaps the earliest sustained engagement with errata in the English book, however, lies with Thomas More and the printing of a range of doctrinal texts he published in the 1520s and 1530s.[16] The *Responsio ad Lutherum* (*STC*[17] 18089), printed by Pynson in 1523, has an errata sheet appended to the second issue of the work.[18] The *Supplication of Souls* of 1529 (*STC* 18092, 18093), printed by Rastell, had in both of its editions errata sheets added to it.[19] And the 1533 *Apology* (*STC* 18078), also printed by Rastell, offers an errata sheet, followed by another four pages of errata for the second part of the *Confutation*, printed with it.[20] These texts have been explored in detail, most recently by the editors of the Yale edition of More's works, and there is some consensus that the role of More himself in their proofreading is debatable. The errata often list simple typographical errors. On occasion, there are substantive corrections made for sense or grammar. But what is significant, especially in the case of the *Supplication*, is the fact that the second editions of these works leave uncorrected 'dozens of... misprints' from the first editions. Are we dealing with the author reading proof or, in the case of the second text of the 1529 printing of the *Supplication*, what the Yale editors call 'a careless compositor [who] hastily proofread to produce the brief and inadequate list of errata'?[21]

In the case of the *Dialogue Concerning Heresies*, however, it is clear that More himself was very much involved in reading proof and offering corrections to his work. In the editions of 1529 (*STC* 18084) and 1531 (*STC* 18085) there are substantive changes made in the errata sheets, titled in both editions 'The fawtys escaped in the pryntynge'. Space does not permit an extensive engagement with the myriad alterations More made to his texts (indeed, the discussion of the textual condition of this work takes up nearly forty pages in the Yale edition).[22] But what should be pointed out, especially, is that More used the 'fawtys' pages to correct what he perceived to be doctrinal error in his text. For example, the phrase 'nothing faut worthy / only to enface that' is corrected in the errata sheet to 'nothing blame worthy / only to deface & enfame that'. The phrase 'pleasure and ellys' becomes 'plesure / where wha[n] and wherfore god shal worke his myracles / and ellys'.[23] The Yale editors also point out that More made substantive corrections between the 1529 and the 1531 edition; and, furthermore, when corrections to both editions needed to be made More had cancel slips inserted in the texts.[24] What is also significant is that the 1531 edition occasionally perpetuates some of the errors, typographical and doctrinal, of the 1529 edition — errors which were noted in the errata sheet to the 1529

edition. As the Yale editors put it, 'The fact that the text of the 1531 perpetuates mistakes in passages like these which deal with important matters of
doctrine raises the possibility that More did not proofread the entire second
edition as carefully as he did the first, in which the errors were emended
on the errata sheet.'[25]

These corrections do more than nuance an argument. They draw attention to the authority of More's authorship itself, the need for the writer to
'oversee' the publication of his work. But the main motive for this scrupulous proofreading was the theological purpose of the *Dialogue*. Calibrated
as a refutation of Protestant doctrine in the late 1520s, the *Dialogue* takes as
its very theme the problem of error. In its central character, the Messenger,
'More creates a composite picture of the layman who is tempted to break
from the ancient oral traditions of the church and accept the Protestant
idea that all doctrine and practices of the church must be based on the
written word of the Bible'.[26] Protestant texts, he argues, are 'maliciously'
printed books, and his own text – submitted, as he states, to 'the iudgement
of other vertuouse & connynge men' before publication – seeks to avoid
the problem of the wanton or corrupt book of Protestant belief. One of the
central images of the *Dialogue* is the issue of 'ocular proof'. Bad words blind
the eyes, and the poor benighted Messenger of the book takes what he has
heard rather than what he has read. In an argument against 'sola scriptura'
in Protestant doctrine (that is, the notion that the reading of Scripture alone
is enough to establish doctrine), More makes a claim for the importance of
getting words right. But the larger point is that More's Messenger is not so
much a reader as a listener. Much of what he knows comes from what he has
heard, and More defines this rough and unverifiable knowledge as 'hearsay'.
What you hear is not always what is right. 'For here may a man se that
mysse vnderstandynge maketh mysse reportynge.'[27] Thus, More advocates
'ocular proof', a conception of understanding keyed to vision and, as such,
correct reading. 'Hearsay', then, embraces all the misinformation conveyed
through the ear: rumour, false preaching, merry tales, popular belief and
jokes. It is, in short, the mark of 'heresy'. In the words of John Fisher, whose
sermon of 1526 against Martin Luther has been seen as doctrinal kin to
More's *Dialogue*, 'Heresy . . . is . . . the blyndyng of our sight.'[28]

The point of all this doctrinaire fine-tuning, it seems to me, is that
More represents himself in the actual publication of his book as his own
overseer and his own corrector. Self-correction in the print shop mimes self-
correction in the court or church. It represents the public acknowledgement
of error. Rhetorically, such an acknowledgement can only reinforce the
power of a work such as More's *Dialogue*, itself concerned with problems
of misrepresentation. Corrections of the press become a way of rectifying

the relationship of word and deed, of sign and substance. It has long been noted that More often puns on the two terms of his argument, 'heresy' and 'hearsay', and what I would suggest is that this wordplay works out, in a thematic way, the very notion of the printer's error that it is the purpose of the 'overseeing' to correct.[29] For if the logic of the *Dialogue* is ocular proof and careful reading, what better way to self-enact that logic than to offer up the author as his own best proofreader. And if the fear is that hearsay will lead to heresy, then what greater fear is there than that these two words might all to easily be shifted in the errors of the print shop. Correction is both moral and typographical.

Such multiple attentions to errata also govern the *Confutation of Tyndale*, published in 1532. In the preface to the first part of the volume, More returns to the imagery of sight and blindness in the discussion of heresy. He hopes, throughout the course of his refutation, 'to make euery chyld perceyue hys [i.e. Tyndale's] wyly folyse and false craftes . . . wherwyth he fayne wolde & weneth to blynde in such wyse the world'.[30] And then he states, reflecting on the great labour such correction requires:

I thynke that no man dowteth but that this worke both hath ben and wyll be some payne and labour to me / and of trouth so I fynde it. But as helpe me god I fynde all my laboure in the wrytynge not halfe so greuouse and pyanefull to me, as the tedyouse redynge of theyr blasphemouse heresyes / that wolde god after all my labour done, so that the remembraunce of theyr pestylent errours were araced out of englysshe mennes hertes, and theyr abomynable bookes burned vppe.

More then remarks that 'deuelysshe heresyes' are so strong in his time, that the heretical books are being read privately by people who believe them. But, he goes on,

it were nede as me semeth that dyuerse wyse & well lerned me sholde set thyr pennys to the boke / whych though they shall not satysfye them that wyll nedes be nought, yet shall they do good to such as fall to these folke of ouersyghte, wenyng y^t theyr new wayes were well.

I take this passage to imply that More imagines better readers coming to these heretical books and setting their pens to them, that is correcting them personally, and that even though such corrections shall not satisfy those readers who believe the heresies, that act may be a good one for those 'folke' (i.e. the good readers) who exercise their 'ouersyghte' in correcting or emending the books.[31]

This is the language of press correction applied to doctrinal debate. It takes words such as 'arace' and 'ouersee' and applies them to the discussion of the dissemination of heretical volumes. It also refers to a common

practice among early sixteenth-century readers themselves: the act of personally setting the pen to the book to correct its errors. In the two copies
of the *Confutation* I have seen in the Cambridge University Library, individual readers have corrected the text in pen according to the printed
errata sheet at the end of the first part of the volume.[32] But only one of
these two volumes actually has the errata sheet still in it (H.3.42). In the
other volume (Selden 3.135) only a stub of paper remains where the errata
sheet has obviously been cut out. Clearly what has happened is that in
one copy the reader has flipped back and forth in order to make the corrections, while in the other the reader has cut out the errata sheet, made
the corrections from it (probably keeping it at hand) and then discarded it
(the errata having been corrected and the sheet being no longer necessary).
Such personal corrections are perfectly in keeping with recorded practice.
Indeed, Pynson's own instructions in the second issue of the *Responsio ad
Lutherum* of 1523 (in an explanatory note at the end of the volume) ask the
reader to 'correct the errata which happened during the printing'.[33] And, as
Percy Simpson has noted in great detail, throughout the sixteenth and well
into the seventeeth century printers asked their readers to 'correcte those
faultes' which have been itemized in the errata sheets.[34]

Self-correction, then, becomes the impulse for the author and the reader.
Even in this preliminary survey of More's publications we can see how
the announcement and correction of errata links the act of typographical
overseeing with the larger imagery of sight and proof developed in doctrinal
contexts. More takes the idioms of the print shop and applies them to
the ideologies of argument. But, more pointedly, More may well be the
first English author to develop the errata sheet in England. Keyed to his
theological and political concerns, developed, perhaps, out of his knowledge
of continental humanist publishers' practices, and co-ordinated in the work
of two printers, Pynson and Rastell, deeply and self-consciously concerned
with their own place in various relationships of author, reader, court and
commerce (far more than Caxton or de Worde), the errata sheet emerges
from the English book of the 1520s as the venue for the staging of the
politics of reading and the reading of politics.

II

Such acts of self-correction are also acts of public fealty, and perhaps the
most elaborate, and most telling, of such public acts of overseeing are the
'Corrections' that appear at the beginning of Thomas Elyot's *Dictionary*
of 1538.[35] In the preface to the volume, Elyot notes that when the work

was already at the printers he became worried that he had neglected some aspects of its definitions. Henry VIII heard of Elyot's anxieties, and placed before him the resources of the royal library. Elyot stopped the presses and revised the entries after M – those before M having already been printed. He then had to revise the first half of the alphabet, and he did so by noting the corrections in the first part of the volume, but also by publishing a list of 'Additions' at the volume's end. Here is his version of the story:

But whyles it was in printyng, and uneth the half deale performed, your hyghnes being informed therof, by the reportes of gentyll maister Antony Denny, for his wysedome and diligence worthily callyd by your highnesse into your priuie Chamber, and of Wyllyam Tildisley, keper of your gracis Lybrarie, and after mooste specially by the recommendation of the most honourable lorde Crumwell, lorde priuie seale, fauourer of honestie, and next to your highnesse chiefe patron of vertue and cunnyng, conceyued of my labours a good expectation, and declaryng your moste noble and beneuolent nature, in *fauouryng* them that wyll be well occupied, your hyghnesse in the presence of dyuers your noble men, *commendynge* myne enterprise, *affirmed*, that if I wolde ernestely trauayle therin, your highnes, as well with your excellent *counsaile*, as with suche bokes as your grace had, and I lacked, wold therin ayde me: with the which wordes, I confesse, I receiued a newe spirite, as me semed; wherby I founde forthwith an augmentation of myn understandynge, in so moche, as I iuged all that, whiche I had writen, not worthy to come in your gracis presence, with out an addition. wherfore incontinent I caused the printer to cesse, and beginninge at the letter M, where I lefte, I passed forth to the last letter with a more diligent study. And that done, I eftesones returned to the fyrst letter, and with a semblable diligence performed the remenant. (sig. A2v–A3r, emphasis added)

The story of the *Dictionary* is a story of intrusions and informancy: a story of royal power worked through minion service and Cromwellian intrigue. For Henry, the manipulations of the printed word extended through the 1530s in an arc of parliamentary acts and statutes. Writing, reading and iconic presentation were the marks of fealty or treason. 'Writyng ymprintinge [and] cypheringe' could all be seditious acts. The forging of the 'kinges signe manuell signet and prevye seale' were treasonable, for which the punishment was death. And the control of the king's signs, and the inspections of his subjects' texts, found itself relocated in the Privy Chamber.[36]

Stephen Merriam Foley has argued that the publication of Elyot's *Dictionary*, and a passage such as this one in particular, reifies these relationships between the royal body and the public word. 'The king's body "literally" stands between the two incomplete alphabets of the work... [T]he king's intervention in the alphabetical order of the Dictionary demonstrates how the mechanical letters of the printing press and the human letters of the new learning could be reinscribed as the vehicles of a broadly nationalist and absolutist ideology.'[37] But a close reading of this passage shows us that it is not so much the king's body as that of his surrogates which interrupt the progress of the *Dictionary* and provoke the correction of Elyot and his book.

First among such surrogates is Anthony Denny. Throughout the 1530s, Denny had risen in the king's bodily service. From the position of Gentleman of the Chamber, he worked his way up through diligence, intrigue and patronage to that of Chief Gentleman of the Privy Chamber (installed by Cromwell in this position in the shake up after the Boleyn affairs), and he ended his royal service by being appointed, in October 1546, as Henry's last Groom of the Stool.[38] The roles that Denny played would have embraced the range of diplomatic and political intrigue, bodily service and even bawdry that had been filled by such predecessors as William Compton and Henry Norris. From wiping the royal bottom to securing mistresses for the king, the Gentlemen of the Chamber and the Stool were closest to the personality of power: in the words of David Starkey, 'the mere word of a Gentleman of the Privy Chamber was sufficient evidence in itself for the king's will, without any other form of authentication whatever'. Indeed, Starkey goes on, the Gentleman bore not just word and will but something of 'the indefinable charisma of monarchy' itself.[39] Denny himself clearly bore something of this charismatic flair, so much so that John Leland wrote that 'the whole court bore testimony to his "gratia flagrans" ' – what we might translate as his blazing repute with the king.[40]

What role, then, does Denny play in Elyot's story, and how does his placement introduce the string of intercessors and interrogators for the king? The *Dictionary* is the subject of inquiry, the object of intelligence gathering that filled the Henrician court in the late 1530s and that has been amply chronicled by G. R. Elton in his tellingly titled *Policy and Police*. The word is out, as it were, and Denny comes first as the chief spy of court and Privy Chamber. From Denny and the Chamber, we move to Tildesy and the library, and finally to Cromwell – here identified specifically as 'lorde priuie seale'. It is as if Elyot himself is walking through the anterooms and private apartments of power, as if he has been granted a succession of audiences, each one of which leads him closer and closer to the body of the king. Cromwell appears here as the 'fauourer of honestie, and next to your highnesse chiefe patron of vertue and cunnyng'. Virtue and cunning are, indeed, the two poles of Henrician courtly life here, and the language Elyot uses is the language not so much of the scholar or the printer as of the subject: 'fauouryng', 'commendynge', 'affirmed', 'counsaile'. Elyot is himself on trial of a sort here, called before the king and his creatures to render account. The king's words of permission and encouragement do more than stimulate the mind; they provoke a confession: 'with the which wordes, I confesse, I receiued a newe spirite, as me semed; wherby I founde forthwith an augmentation of myn understandynge.' This is the language of conversion, the accounting of a tale of turning from error to rectitude, from wandering to fealty found anew.

So just what was it that Sir Thomas Elyot felt the need to correct? Here is his account:

And for as moche as by haste made in printyng, some letters may happen to lacke, some to be sette in wronge places, or the ortography nat to be truely obserued, I therfore haue put all those fautes in a table folowing this preface: whereby they may be easily corrected: and that done, I truste in god no manne shall fynde cause to reiect this boke. (sig. A3v)

Certainly there are typos: haplographies, dittographies and transposed letters. But occasionally there are mistakes of a different sort. Take, for example, 'Qui', where Elyot has felt the need to correct the translation of a Latin phrase offered in definition:

reade after the latine wherefore was Epicurous more happy that he lyued in his owne countray, than Metrodorus whiche lyued at Athenes.

To read such a correction is to feel the need to go back to the source, to re-examine the supposedly erroneous text itself. Now, look at the actual entry for 'Qui', defined as 'the whyche. Alsoo sometyme it sygnifyeth howe.' What follows is a string of classical quotations illustrating not just grammatical but social and political correctness. The extracts tell a story of identity and power, of discovery and shame (I quote his English translations of the Latin excerpts):

> Doo what ye canne, howe or by whatte meanes thou mayste haue hyr.
> Howe arte thou callyd?
> . . .
> From whens is this suspycion happened vnto the?
> I pray god that a vengeaunce lyghte on hym.

And then we get to a remarkable self-reference:

For he spendethe his laboure in wrytynge of Prologues, not bycause he wyll telle the argumente, but for as moche as he wolde make answere to the yuell reportes of the olde envyouse Poete.

And finally, the quotation that Elyot corrects (and the last one in the entry):

Wherefore was Eypcure moore happye, that he *dydde dye* in his countrye, than Metrodours *that he dyed* at Athenes [emphasis added].

In this correction lies, perhaps, an allegory of an Elyotic scholarly devotion, a miniature story that recaps the longer story of the preface. Happy is the man who lives in his own country, who needs not Athens – more tempting for the scholar – but who serves a king whose generosity extends to opening an Athens of the mind before him in the library. Elyot changes 'die' to 'live', grants himself a reprieve after the intercessions of a king and his counselors. To read the entry 'Qui', now, is to see a story of the making of the man and the book: a story about which, and how, from whence, would to God, because, wherefore. It is the single word that sums up the stories of the preface, an entry that, corrected in the 'Corrections', invites the reader to understand the making of a lexicographical subject in a world of royal words and will.

Embedded in errata is the story of correction itself: correction not merely typographical or even theological but human and political. The Finis of the *Dictionary* closes with another appeal to correction, now hearkening back to the old manuscript appeals for readerly correction. But now the corrections of these readers, their 'honest labours', are described as 'being benefyciall vnto this theyr countrey'. This is the dictionary of English, the king's dictionary, the first text that, as Foley argues, 'helped to establish the schoolroom as a new cultural field for instituting royal absolutism'.[41] The story that this volume tells is, in the end, the story of a man publicly happy 'in his owne countray', and it is fitting, then, that at its close it should direct such nationalized ease to readers who, in finding fault, are offering not treason to a work published by Elyot, the servant, or Berthelett, *regius impressor*, but beneficence. The correction, as Elyot announced there, is 'an exquisite tryall', whether performed by author or by reader, one that affirms a shared participation in the trials of public service.

This image of the corrector on trial leads to a reconception of errata sheets, and indeed of all pages of editorial avowal, as legal transcripts: as account books in the judgements of political and scholarly loyalty. (I recall in passing that the structure of More's *Dialogue* itself became a trial, with the author 'defending the office of the priesthood and the divine right of the ecclesiastical courts to try heresy'.)[42] The text becomes a piece of evidence entered into the court of judgement. Erasmus recognized this judicial framework to the editorial condition in the letter to Thomas Ruthall of 7 March 1515, published as the preface to his edition of Seneca's *Lucubrationes* (Froben, August 1515). The product of his English sojourn, and addressed to one of the most powerful men in early Henrician England, the edition of Seneca begins with this epistolary meditation on the similarities between textual criticism and war. The letter begins, in fact, with an account of the Battle of Flodden Field (9 September 1513), and moves through, by analogy, the 'infinite army of corruptions' that Erasmus finds he must retake from the 'enemy' in making his edition. 'I had my pen for a sword,' he states, and goes on:

Nor had I any outside help in all these difficulties, except two ancient manuscripts, one of which was provided from his own library by the chief patron of my researches, that incomparable glory of our generation, William, archbishop of Canterbury [William Warham], and the other was sent to my assistance by King's College, Cambridge; but these were imperfect and even more full of error ['mendosum'] than the current copies, so that less confidence could be placed in one's auxiliary troops than in the enemy. One thing however helped me: they did not agree in error ['non consentiebant errata'], as is bound to happen in printed texts set up from the same printer's copy ['exemplari']; and thus, just as it sometimes happens that an experienced and attentive judge pieces together what really took place from the statements of many witnesses, none of whom is telling the truth, so I conjectured the true reading on the basis of their differing mistakes ['rem colligat, ita nos e diuersis mendis veram coniecimus lectionem'].[43]

Space does not permit a thorough unpacking of this remarkable letter. But it may suffice to say here that Erasmus's invocation of the trial judge, together with the military framing of his story, make editing an act shot through with the political and the forensic. At stake in his extended simile is a conception not just of the editorial but of the judicial: a recognition that no witness truly tells the truth, an appeal not to the authorities of history or text but to the judgement of conjecture.

III

If Erasmus deploys the language of the court to make a point about what we might now call, with David Greetham, 'textual forensics', then it is left to Thomas Wyatt to invoke the language of the editor in a plea for his own defence against accusations of treason.[44] Soon after Cromwell's fall in 1540, Wyatt's name appeared in papers once suppressed but now examined by the king's authorities.[45] In documents from 1538 they found complaints made by Dr Edmund Bonner and Dr Simon Heynes about Wyatt's potentially treasonous associations and remarks. With Cromwell dead, Wyatt could count on no one, at least at first, to counter the charges made by Bonner, in particular, that he had slandered Henry VIII. Though it was generally believed that Wyatt's arrest (on 17 January 1541) was a result of his loss of Cromwell as protector and his sympathy for Lutheran opinions, one of the central accusations was that he had said 'that he feared the King should be cast out of a cart's arse and that, by God's blood, if he were so, he were well served, and would he were so'. Wyatt wrote two prose texts in 1541 explaining his remarks and justifying his activities during his ambassadorial service in the late 1530s: 'A Declaration... of his Innocence' and 'Wyatt's Defence To the Iudges after the Indictement and the evidence'.[46] In these documents he goes to great lengths to affirm his habitual use of proverbs and to argue that Bonner, knowing of this habit, added one that Wyatt did not utter, in order to lend credence to a slanderous story about Wyatt himself. At the heart of his self-defence is concern with proper speaking, writing and receiving – a concern with language at the syllabic level. The altering of a single syllable, Wyatt argues, 'ether with penne or worde', can change the entire meaning of an utterance, an argument he marshals to claim that his statement was heard and transcribed inaccurately. Wyatt's 'Declaration' and 'Defence' are about many things – the nature of proverbial language, the problems of identity and impersonation – but, taken together, they also constitute a manifesto of editorial principles. Their comments on the modes of writing and reading bear directly on the circulation of Wyatt's own verse. Poem, book and letter are all forms of discourse equally subject to the slippage of the pen, the intrusions of the interceptor, or the mistakes of the proof.

Wyatt begins his 'Declaration' with a claim of innocence. His central task is to recall, years later, 'suche thynges as have passed me ... by worde, wrytinge, communinge, or receauing'.[47] This 'Declaration' is not so much an appeal to innocence as a remembrance of letters – an accounting of all the documents passed through his office while at the emperor's court. Letters upon letters stack themselves in Wyatt's prose.[48] '[L]ettres or wrytnges,' he tries to recall, 'came to my handys or thorow my handes vnopened' (p. 180). He never, he protests, knowingly communicated with a traitor. Those documents he could not verify were, as he put it, 'ether so secretly handlede or yett not in couerture' that he could not see them (p. 181). Some letters, he avers, never reached him, in particular the letters of Mason addressed to Wyatt and the earl of Essex (p. 183). And he goes on to define the province of 'an Imbassadoure' as secrecy itself, and to note that 'a prince were as good sende nakede lettres and to receaue naked lettres as to be at charge for Recidencers' (p. 184).

The 'Declaration' concludes, following Wyatt's signature, 'This withowte correctinge, sendinge, or ouerseinge' (p. 184), and in the 'Defence' that follows it Wyatt develops the activities of correcting, sending and overseeing into an essay on the nature of reading and writing itself. Reflection on the practice of diplomacy leads to a meditation on intention and expression:

Intelligens concludethe a familiarite or conferringe of devyses to gyther, which
may be by worde, message or wrytinge, which the lawe forbiddythe to be had with
anye the kinges traytours or rebels, payne of the lyke. Reherse the lawe, declare, my
lordes, I beseke you, the meaninge thereof. Am I a traytor by cawse I spake with the
kinges traytor? No, not for that, for I may byd him 'avaunte, traytor' or 'defye hym,
traytor.' No man will tayke this for treasone; but where he is holpen, counceled,
advertysed by my worde, there lyethe the treason, there lyethe the treason. In
wrytinge yt is lyke. In message yt is lyke; for I may sende hym bothe lettre and
message of chalinge or defyaunce. (p. 190)

Just because a man speaks with a traitor it does not mean he is a traitor.
Identity lies in intention, in the adherence to codes of conduct or the rules
of law. In writing, as in speech, the individual's identity should not be confused with that of the addressee. Such statements resonate profoundly with
Wyatt's own poetic practice. The gist of his epistolary satires, to Poyntz and
Bryan, lies precisely in these tensions between writer and addressee. It establishes a form of 'intelligens' between the two. Its understanding demands
a rehearsal of the laws of literary discourse, an inquiry into 'meaninge'
made through verse. But the verse epistle also sets up the conventions of
reported speech *as* conventions. It makes quotation the defining mode of
writer and addressee – indeed, it makes each poem operate entirely, as it
were, within quotation marks. The fiction of the letter, now, is the fiction
of the voice. The colloquy between friends is an act of 'intelligens' based
on 'familiarite'. The problem, therefore, lies along the line between the poetic and the historical. When is a quotation not a quotation? In the satire
addressed to Bryan, for example, the poem's speaker goes to great lengths
to distance himself from the pandering courtier, while at the same time
brilliantly ventriloquizing his position in the other's voice. 'Am I a traytor
by cawse I spake with the kinges traytor? . . . In wrytinge yt is lyke.' Am I a
panderer because I spoke with, wrote to, *wrote as*, the king's panderer?

How can one defend oneself against words quoted, reported and transcribed? This is the heart of Bonner's accusation and Wyatt's defence. 'And
what say my accusares in thes wordes? Do theie swere I spake them trayter-
ously or maliciously? . . . Rede ther depositions, theie say not so. *Confer*
ther depositions, yf theie agre worde for worde' (p. 197, emphasis added).
The accusations against Wyatt become texts; the texts become subject to
conferral – that is, comparison. Such documents are treated here as if they
were the objects of an editor: compared, collated and reviewed for accuracy.
Wyatt goes on:

Yf theie myseagre in wordis and not in substance, let vs here the woordes theie
varie in. For in some lyttell thynge may apere the truthe which I dare saye you seke

for your consciens sake. And besydys that, *yt is a smale thynge in alteringe of one syllable ether with penne or worde that may mayk in the conceavinge of the truthe myche matter or error.* For in thys thynge 'I fere', or 'I truste', semethe but one smale syllable chaynged, and yet it makethe a great dyfferaunce, and may be of an herer wronge conceaved and worse reported, and yet worste of all altered by an examyner. Agayne 'fall owte' 'caste owte', or 'lefte owte' makethe the dyfferaunce, yea and the settinge of the wordes one in an others place may mayke greate dyffer-aunce, tho the wordes were all one – as 'a myll horse' and 'a horse myll'. I besyche you therfore examen the matter vnder this sorte. *Confere* theire severall sayinges togyther, *confer* th'examynations vpone the same matter and I dare warrante ye shall fynde mysreportynge and mysvnderstandinge. (p. 197, emphasis added)

In the specific context of the defence, Wyatt argues that his words have been mistaken. His deployment of the proverb 'I am lefte owte of the cartes ars' (p. 198) has been taken out of context, misheard, misreported and mistranscribed into the environment of royal offence. Instead of saying what he has been accused of saying ('ye shall see the kinge our maister cast out at the carts tail'), what Wyatt claims he said was closer to 'I fere for all these menes fayer promyses the kinge shalbe lefte owte of the cartes ars.' He recalls that he may have very well said something like that, and may well have invoked this proverbial sentiment on occasion. 'But that I vsed it with Bonar or Haynes I neuer remembre; and yf I euer dyd I am sure neuer as thei couche the tale' (p. 198).

But in the larger world of Wyatt's discourse his appeal to memory and intention takes on the flavour of a theory of textual criticism. Comparison of manuscripts – signalled by the Latin verb 'conferre' and its past particip-ial form 'collatus' – was the hallmark of the early humanist philological method.[49] Erasmus frequently deploys the term in his accounts of editing and self-correction; but for my present purposes we can turn to a more local and contemporary analogue, Brian Tuke's preface to Thynne's 1532 edition of Chaucer:

as bokes of dyuers imprintes came unto my handes / I easely and without grete study / might and haue deprehended in them many errours / falsyties / and deprauacions / whiche euydently appered by the contrarietees and alteracions founde by *collacion* of the one with the other / wherby I was moued and styred to make dilygent sertch / where I might fynde or recouer any trewe copies or exemplaries of the sayd bookes. (sig. A2v, emphasis added)[50]

The collation of manuscripts helps what Tuke calls 'the restauracion' of Chaucer's works in their authorized form, and this process, he avers, is not just a literary but a political 'dewtie' growing out of his 'very honesty and loue to my countrey' (sig. A3r). Tuke's preface is a statement of national fealty, an appeal to King Henry VIII as patron to exercise his 'discrecyon and iugement' and accept the volume as it has been printed.[51] If Wyatt's 'Defence' reads as a statement of editorial principles, then Tuke's preface may stand as something of a defence of its own: a plea before a judging king for the authentic value of an author's works and, in turn, for a recognition of the editor's own searching out of falsity and error through the collation of texts.

As in the making of an edition, the slightest slip can change the meaning of a line: 'the settyng of the wordes one in an others place may mayke greate dyfferaunce'. 'I fere' or 'I truste', Wyatt offers, differ only in 'one smale syllable'. But what a syllable it is. Certainly, such a case is not a random call. Fear and trust are the two poles of Wyatt's poetic emotion. I have elsewhere adduced a whole range of Wyatt's uses of these terms, in the ballads, sonnets and songs, where these two words scope out the literary and emotional anxieties of someone who, as he puts it in the poem printed as the first of the Wyatt poems by Tottel, seeks the 'trust' of his beloved, yet also queries,

> What may I do when my maister feareth,
> But, in the felde, with him to lyve and dye?
> (4)[52]

Fear and trust play into the Petrarchan oxymora of love; in one poem, he distils the Italian lexicon of pain – sighing, hope and desire – into a unique concatenation of his own:

> An endles wynd doeth tere the sayll a pace
> Of forced sightes and *trusty ferefulnes*.
> (27.7–8, emphasis added)

And in one of the ballads preserved in the Blage manuscript Wyatt expounds not just on the nature of his trust but on the very problems of transcription and substitution that are the subject of his 'Defence'. Concluding the ballad, whose refrain line has been 'Patiens, parforce, content thy self with wrong', he offers:

> I Burne and boyle withoute redres;
> I syegh, I wepe, and all in vayne.
> Now Hotte, now Cold, whoo can expresse
> The thowsaund parte of my great payne?
> But yf I myght her faver Atteigne,
> Then wold I trust to chaunge this song,
> With pety for paciens, and consciens for wrong.
> (121.15–21)

Wyatt performs an act of critical self-revision. He suggests changing words for words, locates the change in 'trust', and posits a revisionary poetics that makes the language of the song always subject to rewriting, depending on the circumstances of performance.

'My word nor I shall not be variable' (11.13). In spite of this protest, Wyatt's words were variable. The very nature of the writing and transmitting of his poetry lies in the variations of the scribe, in the self-cancellations and revisions of the poet, and in the manipulations of the printer. It is, of course, a commonplace of Wyatt criticism to remark on the unstable quality of his verse line, on the idiosyncrasies of his spelling and on the variations generated by competing manuscript and print editions. The practice of textual criticism runs up against the intractable wall of Wyatt's own texts. As Jonathan Crewe recognizes, modern editions of Wyatt's poetry (as of much early sixteenth-century verse) are in themselves modernizations: recastings of his words and lines. 'In quite a fundamental sense,' Crewe notes, 'to print Wyatt modernized is to censor his work.'[53]

Let us examine an example of such censoring. The Penguin paperback edition of the poems of Sir Thomas Wyatt, edited by R. A. Rebholz, has, since its first publication over twenty years ago, become a standard text.[54] It is the form in which most students, and most teachers, will encounter Wyatt, and its prefatory explanations of the vexed problem of Wyatt's metres, the status of his work in manuscript, and the complex evidence – and scholarly debates – about the range of Wyatt's canon distil vast amounts of intricate material for modern readers. This is, admittedly, a modern-spelling edition. Rebholz has brought orthography and punctuation into line with current practices, he argues, because 'I became convinced that the sacrifices were eminently worthwhile because they make the poems genuinely available to modern readers when texts preserving old accidentals are frequently unintelligible' (pp. 14–15). He acknowledges that, on occasion, modernization may ruin a rhyme or metrical pattern and that added punctuation may fix syntax that, in Wyatt's time, would have been fluid enough to 'create ambivalent meanings' (p. 14).

I have discussed in detail elsewhere some of the textual problems raised by this edition, especially in the long poem to John Poyntz, where Rebholz's choice of base text and his selective recording of variants suppresses the controlling verbal relationship of this poem to its deep Chaucerian subtext (especially Chaucer's ballad 'Truth', itself a widely read text of the early Tudor period).[55] Here, I develop and correct an earlier engagement with this edition concerning one ballad that thematizes the problem of error and, in particular, locates that theme in the emergent print practices I

have discussed above. 'I see the change' (Rebholz 215) is a refrain ballad
appearing only in the Devonshire Manuscript of Tudor verse. Here is the
poem in the conservative, old-spelling edition of Kenneth Muir and Patricia
Thompson:

> I se the change ffrom that that was
> And how thy ffayth hath tayn his fflyt
> But I with pacyense let yt pase
> And with my pene thys do I wryt
> To show the playn by prowff off syght,
>   I se the change.
>
> I se the change off weryd mynd
> And sleper hold hath quet my hyer;
> Lo! how by prowff in the I ffynd
> A bowrnyng ffayth in changyng ffyer.
> Ffarwell my part, prowff ys no lyer!
>   I se the change.
>
> I se the change off chance in loue;
> Delyt no lenger may abyd;
> What shold I sek ffurther to proue?
> No, no, my trust, ffor I haue tryd
> The ffoloyng of a ffallse gyd:
>   I se the change.
>
> I se the change, as in thys case,
> Has mayd me ffre ffrom myn avoo,
> Ffor now another has my plase,
> And or I wist, I wot ner how,
> Yt hapnet thys as ye here now:
>   I se the change.
>
> I se the change, seche ys my chance
> To sarue in dowt and hope in vayn;
> But sens my surty so doth glanse,
> Repentens now shal quyt thy payn,
> Neuer to trust the lyke agayn:
>   I se the change.   (195)

Aside from certain orthographical conventions – the double 'f's, the early
sixteenth-century spellings, the consistent use of 'se' for 'see' – the most
important piece of verbal trickery in this text is the spelling of both the
definite article and the second person pronoun as 'the'. Wyatt's poems are
continually preoccupied with his own linguistic instability, and with the
inability of the poetic hand to transcribe the intentions of the heart. Even

when the author's own text is presented as a proof, he recognizes that it may never suffice. The logic of the poem hinges on the instability of 'the'. Who is to say that, in the refrain lines (6, 12, 18, 24, 30), the speaker of the poem sees 'the' change or sees 'thee' change? Similarly, in the first line of each successive stanza the ambiguity is only barely resolved as the reader completes its respective sentence. Line 19: I see 'the' change, or I see 'thee' change; line 25, I see 'the' change, or see 'thee' change. Following each refrain line, these first lines create an unresolvable conundrum. Indeed, they reify the very problem of the text posed by the poetry itself: the act of proofreading. Proof is no liar, or, more pointedly, the proof of sight that shows the writing of the pen plainly. What should, the poem's speaker asks, I seek further to prove? And yet, proofs always lie. For Wyatt, writing in the 1530s, the word 'proof' must resonate with its new meaning in the realms of bibliography. The indenture between John Palsgrave and the printer Richard Pynson from 1523 sets out the responsibilities of author and printer, including proofreading:

farder more hyt ys agreed that the saide Richard schall vse good fayth in the printing off the saide worke and suffer the said Iohn Palsgraue or hys assignes to correct the proff.[56]

I have made much of this detail because in Rebholz's edition these ambivalences are completely effaced:

> I see the change from that that was
> And how thy faith hath ta'en his flight.
> But I with patience let it pass
> And with my pen this do I write
> To show thee plain by proof of sight
>   I see the change.
>
> I see the change of wearied mind
> And slipper hold hath quit my hire.
> Lo, how by proof in thee I find
> A burning faith in changing fire.
> Farewell, my part. Proof is no liar.
>   I see the change.
>
> I see the change of chance of love.
> Delight no longer may abide.
> What should I seek further to prove?
> No, no, my trust, for I have tried
> The following of a false guide.
>   I see the change.

I see the change, as in this case,
Has made me free from mine avow;
For now another has my place
And ere I wist, I wot ne'er how,
It happened thus as ye hear now.
      I see the change.

I see the change. Such is my chance
To serve in doubt and hope in vain.
But since my surety so doth glance,
Repentance now shall quit thy pain,
Never to trust the like again.
      I see the change.
                              (Rebholz 215)

Now it is true that Rebholz acknowledges, in his note at the back of the
book, that lines 6, 12, 18, 24 and 30 offer a 'pun on "the / thee" in the
refrain. The word "thee" (l. 9) is spelled "the" in the MS' (p. 522). But that
is all he notes. The point is not just that there is a pun in the refrain, nor
that in one particular line 'thee' is spelled 'the'. The point is that the poem
as a whole presents one spelling throughout for these two words and that
spelling is the key to the poem's theme. Indeed, spelling is, I think, the
poem's theme – what you write with the pen is always subject to change;
and when you read you see the change.

In other poems, such as 'Me list no more to sing', 'Lament my loss' and
'Who would have ever thought', relationships of text and reader, speaker
and hearer, are similarly addressed. The plea for correction and emendation
takes on new force in 'Lament my loss' in particular, where the image of
the quaking pen – borrowed from Chaucer's *Troilus and Criseyde* by way
of Lydgate – is pressed into the service not just of a plea for modesty or an
excuse for ineptitude but for a poetics of error itself:

Yet well ye know yt will renue my smarte
Thus to reherse the paynes that I have past;
My hand doth shake, my penn skant dothe his parte,
My boddye quakes, my wyttis begynne to waste;
Twixt heate and colde in fere I fele my herte
Panting for paine, and thus as all agaste
I do remayne skant wotting what I wryte:
Perdon me then rudelye tho I indyte.

And patientlye, o Redre, I the praye
Take in good parte this worke as yt ys mente,
And greve the not with ought that I shall saye,
Sins with good will this boke abrode ys sente

To tell men how in youthe I ded assaye
What love ded mene and now I yt repente:
That musing me my frindes might well be ware,
And kepe them fre from all soche payne and care.

(214.17–32)

What Wyatt, in the 'Defence', called 'mysreportynge and mysvnder-standinge' resonates anew with the conventions of the envoy and the fears of the pen. In this ballad, however, the quaking pen has been transferred to the poet's whole body. The sequence of lines 19 to 21 is a veritable anatomy of a Chaucerian idiom: from hand, to pen, to body, to wits, to heart, the in-securities of writer move from the extremities of writing to the inner site of feeling and desire. By the time we get to the line 'I do remain scant wotting what I write', we can see that the narrator's self-ignorance grows from this fundamental separation of the writing hand from the feeling heart.[57] To grant the writer our 'goodwill' is not, therefore, simply to share in the topoi of modesty but to recognize that those texts inscribed with quaking pens are, quite simply, textually unreliable.

This question of the unreliable text is both a condition of Wyatt's textual transmission and a theme addressed throughout the poetry. When Wyatt concludes the short poem 'Who would haue euer thought' with the lines

But note I wyll thys texte,
To draw better the nexte

(191.17–18)

what he implies is the possibility of endless rescription. The next poem will be better drawn; the scribal lessons of the previous will be incorporated in the next. But this will never happen. What we must see, as Wyatt's readers, is the constantly changing nature of his verse as it is always written, and, in the process, expose how both the poems and their scribes bring out the insecurities of manuscript transmission. From the standpoint of editorial practice, the sacrifices to modernity do not just misrepresent a historical artifact. They censor the controlling ambiguities in the poetry. Crewe's choice of words, then, is uncannily accurate, as Wyatt himself constructs, in the 'Defence', an argument for textual criticism grounded in the language of censorial politics. Repentance is a key word for both the poems I have looked at in detail here, as it is for More and Elyot in their respective meditations on error. The urge to confess remains; indeed, in 'Lament my loss' so does the urge to pray.

And, so, too, does the urge to prove. Pynson's indenture, in addition to offering what may be the earliest use of the word 'proof' in textual terms in English (it predates the *OED* entries by nearly half a century), also deploys the rhetoric of goodwill, error and correction, of responsibility and authorship, explored in all the texts I have discussed here. It reveals something of the habits of the print shop, and Percy Simpson uses this and other contemporary texts to show the ways in which the printer and his employees struggled with error and correction. In another document – a poem written around 1530, describing the principles of selection in Robert Copland's printing house – the exchange between printer and an anonymous customer (called 'Quidam') shows what is going on in language precisely equivalent to Wyatt's.[58] When Copland asks his customer if he has 'any copy' of the work he wants, Quidam replies:

> I haue no boke, but yet I can you shewe
> The matter by herte, and that by wordes fewe.
> Take your penne, and wryte as I do say
> But yet of one thyng, hertely I you praye,
> Amende the englysh somwhat if ye can.
> And spel it true, for I shall tel the man
> By my soule ye prynters make such englysche
> So yll spelled, so yll poynted, and so peuyshe
> That scantly one can rede lynes tow
> But to fynde sentence, he hath ynought to do.

What is the nature of transcription; how can the pen transcribe what the heart knows; and how can printers accurately print those words? True spelling is as much the core of Copland's craft as it is Wyatt's imagination and the modern editor's responsibility. This versified exchange admonishes the modern editor much as it abashes the early Tudor printer: right down to the spelling of the word 'the'. 'For I shall tel the man' really means 'For I shall tell thee, man'. Take your pen, says Quidam. 'My pen, take payn a lytyll space', says Wyatt. But what happens when 'My hand doth shake, my penn skant dothe his parte'?

In the end, it is faith both in heart and hand that leads the printer and the scholar to adjudicate the error. In 1560, summing up not just the personal but the historical situation of all authors, Jasper Heywood complained about the printing of his Seneca translations by no less a hand than that of Richard Tottel:

> For when to synge of Hande and Starre
>   I chaunced fyrst to come,
> To Printers hands I gaue the worke:
>   by whome I had suche wrong,
> That though my selfe perusde their prooues
>   the fyrst tyme, yet ere long

> When I was gone, they wolde agayne
>   the print therof renewe,
> Corrupted all: in such a sorte,
>   that scant a sentence trewe
> Now flythe abroade as I it wrote.[59]

Proof and repentance, admission and control, these are the terms not just of excuse but of identity. The admission of error and the public mark of self-correction stand as the identifying gestures of the humanist subject. In its typographical, political and lyric forms, it represents the transformation of a voice into a text, a body into a book, an artifact into a narrative. As Guillaume Budé put it, in a brilliantly cranky letter to Erasmus in the spring of 1515:

I was wrong, I admit; I cannot seek to avoid the blame, only the penalty and the disgrace, and it is normal to let a man off these if he owns up.[60]

Budé's letter is as much a self-defence as Wyatt's prose and poetry or Elyot's *Dictionary*. It places authorship on trial, makes the admission of error the defining gesture of individual identity, locates the self in history as the historicizer of the text.

Some still hold that academic scholarship should be the search for truth, and, in turn, that editorial practice should purge texts of their errors and corruptions and restore them to the matchless handiwork of the author's hands. And yet, when we review the slips, errata and defences of these figures, we see not the claim of truth but the admission of mistake. The life of scholarship has, from its origins, been immured in the pains of penmanship and the 'errori de la stampa'. It is the admission of error that stands as the mark of the professional. 'I dare warrante ye shall fynde mysreportynge and mysvnderstandinge.' We are always lost on the byways of the text, and any claims for an approach to truth or certitude must be left, instead, to misperceiving judges who would claim correctness as the only virtue and who find no lies in the proof texts of our passion.

But then again, I could be wrong.[61]

NOTES

1. For the origins of pedantry in the literary and intellectual representations of pedagogy in the sixteenth century, see S. L. Sondergard, ' "To Scape the Rod": Resistance to Humanist Pedagogy and the Sign of the Pedant in Tudor England', *Studies in Philology*, 91 (1994), pp. 270–82.
2. J. Crewe, *Trials of Authorship* (Berkeley and Los Angeles, 1990); and E. Pittenger, 'Aliens in the Corpus: Shakespeare's Books in the Age of the

Cyborg', in G. Brahm Jr and M. Driscoll, eds., *Prosthetic Territories: Politics and Hypertechnologies* (Boulder, Colo., 1995), pp. 204–18, quotation p. 214.

3. While there is to my knowledge no sustained history of the errata sheet and of the larger question of the humanist attitude towards error and correction, several recent studies of humanist book making inform my own account here. See, in particular, J. F. D'Amico, *Theory and Practice in Renaissance Textual Criticism* (Berkeley and Los Angeles, 1988); P. Trovato, *Con ogni diligenza correto: La stampa e le revisioni editoriali dei testi letterari italiani (1470–1570)* (Bologna, 1991); A. Grafton, *Defenders of the Text: Traditions of Scholarship in an Age of Science, 1450–1800* (Cambridge, Mass., 1991); D. Carlson, *English Humanist Books: Writers and Patrons, Manuscript and Print, 1475–1525* (Toronto, 1993); L. Jardine, *Erasmus, Man of Letters: The Construction of Charisma in Print* (Princeton, 1993); and B. Richardson, *Print Culture in Renaissance Italy: The Editor and the Vernacular Text, 1470–1600* (Cambridge, 1994). After this essay was substantially completed, I became aware of A. Murphy, ' "Came Errour Here by Myss of Man": Editing and the Metaphysics of Presence', *Yearbook of English Studies*, 29 (1999), pp. 118–37. Murphy's study overlaps in some broader theoretical ways with mine, though he begins chronologically where I end.

4. In this matter, the physical appearance of the early printed book may differ little from that of the medieval manuscript. Much has been made of Chaucer's rhetoric of correction and his own pleas to his readers to correct or emend the texts of his works. For a review of these issues in the making of Chaucerian manuscripts and the history of Chaucer reception in late medieval habits of reading, see my *Chaucer and His Readers: Imagining the Author in Late-Medieval England* (Princeton, 1993). For a survey of the practice of the reader's correction of the printed book from the sixteenth to the twentieth centuries, see H. Widmann, 'Die Lektüre unendlichen Korrekturen', *Archiv für Geschichte des Buchwesens*, 5 (1964), pp. 778–826.

5. For a study of this rhetoric and its accompanying cultural concerns in a later period of European history, see D. Bates, 'The Epistemology of Error in Late Enlightenment France', *Eighteenth-Century Studies*, 29 (1996), pp. 307–27.

6. Elizabeth Eisenstein offers a few brief remarks on the origin and impact of the errata sheet in *The Printing Press as an Agent of Change: Communication and Cultural Transformation in Early Modern Europe* (Cambridge, 1979), pp. 80–1, 85. Elsewhere, she credits the Venetian printer Erhard Ratdolt with the 'innovation' of the 'first list of errata' (pp. 587–8), but I can find no evidence to support this claim.

7. Noted in G. P. Carosi, *Da Magonza a Subiaco: L'introduzione della stampa in Italia* (n.p., 1982), p. 30; see also Trovato, *Con ogni diligenza*, pp. 87–8.

8. Richardson, *Print Culture*, p. 45.

9. See Trovato, *Con ogni diligenza*, pp. 86–93.

10. Horace, *Opera* (Florence, 1482), Huntington Library copy, fols. 265v–266r in the modern pagination.

11. 'Siqui uel desint / uel perperam notati sint in grecis dictionibus accentus: eos eruditi uel restituant / uel emendent pro iudico. Siqua etiam preter hec mendosa lector inuenies / que propera[n]tes oculos nostros subterfugerint / ea quo[que] [pro] tuo iudicio eme[n]dabis; nec [quodcunque] putabis nostrum quod parum sit rectum: Errata aut[em] omnia uel impressoribus adscribes / uel curatoribus: Na[m] si mea esse hic errata ulla credes: tunc ego te credam cordis habere nihil.' Poliziano, *Miscellanea* (Florence, 1489), Huntington Library copy, translation mine. On Poliziano's scholarship generally, see 'The Scholarship of Poliziano and Its Context', in Grafton, *Defenders of the Text*, pp. 47–75, and the comments in D'Amico, *Renaissance Textual Criticism*, pp. 23–7. Problems such as the ones raised in this remark may have arisen from Poliziano's point of having accents printed separately from letters in the first edition of the *Miscellanea* (a fact pointed out to me by both Anthony Grafton and Joseph Dane). For more on Poliziano and printing, see Dane, ' "Si vis archetypas habere nugas": Authorial Subscriptions in the Houghton Library and Huntington Library Copies of Politian, *Miscellenea* (Florence: Miscomini, 1489)', *Harvard Library Bulletin*, new series, 10 (1999), pp. 12–22.

12. See Trovato, *Con ogni diligenza*.

13. For Caxton's remarks, see *The Prologues and Epilogues of William Caxton*, ed. W. J. B. Crotch (London, 1928), *Canterbury Tales* prologue, p. 91, *Eneydos* prologue, p. 109. For the word 'oversee' as specifically meaning proof correcting, see P. Simpson, *Proofreading in the Sixteenth and Seventeenth Centuries* (London, 1935), pp. 1–3. Simpson cites a range of fifteenth- and sixteenth-century examples of the verb 'oversee' as proofread and the noun 'overseer' as the employee of the printer who supervised the correction of proofs during the press run of a book.

14. J. Constable, *Epigrammata* (London, 1520), sig. d4. My attention was drawn to this publication by *Responsio ad Lutherum*, ed. J. M. Headley, in *The Complete Works of St Thomas More*, vol. 5, part 2 (New Haven, 1969), p. 836 n. 3. On the identification of Bercula as Berthelett, see E. G. Duff, 'Richard Pynson and Thomas Bercula', *The Library*, 2nd series, 8 (1907), pp. 298–303.

15. Quoted in Simpson, *Proofreading*, pp. 46–7. I discuss the text of this indenture at the close of this essay. Pynson apparently had a paid corrector of the press as early as 1499, as indicated in a petition (dated 1506) apparently referring to the 1499 publication of the *Abbreuiamentum Statutorum* (see Simpson, *Proofreading*, p. 111).

16. More's books, printed by Pynson and Rastell, are the earliest surviving examples of English books with errata sheets that I can find. The Tyndale Bible of 1526 concludes with three pages of 'The errours comitted in the prentynge'. I suspend discussion of this volume, and of its printing history and contexts, as my primary concern for the remainder of this essay is with English books printed *in England*.

17. W. A. Jackson, F. S. Ferguson and K. F. Panzer, eds., *A Short-Title Catalogue of English Books 1475–1640*, 2nd edn (3 vols., London, 1976–91).

18. *Responsio ad Lutherum*, pp. 832–41, where the complex history of the print-ing of this text is detailed. The work was first published in early 1523, but it was seen as defective; More apparently reworked the text in response to new publications by Luther. A second issue appeared from Pynson proba-bly in December 1523 (according to Headley, the first issue is not in *STC*; the second is, however). It is this second issue which has the errata list. Headley presents evidence and arguments that this list was compiled by More himself.

19. See C. H. Miller, 'The Texts', in *Letter to Bugenhagen, Supplication of Souls, Letter Against Frith*, ed. F. Manley *et al.*, in *The Complete Works of St Thomas More*, vol. 7 (New Haven, 1990), pp. clxi–clxviii. These editions are undated, but are datable on external evidence to before October 1525 (Miller, 'The Texts', p. clxi).

20. *The Apology*, ed. J. B. Trapp, in *The Complete Works of St Thomas More*, vol. 9 (New Haven, 1979), pp. lxxxix–xci.

21. Miller, 'The Texts', pp. clxiv, clxvi.

22. *A Dialogue Concerning Heresies*, ed. T. M. Lawler *et al.*, in *The Complete Works of St Thomas More*, vol. 6, part 2 (New Haven, 1981), pp. 548–87.

23. See Simpson, *Proofreading*, pp. 3–4; and *A Dialogue Concerning Heresies*.

24. See the discussion in *A Dialogue Concerning Heresies*, pp. 556ff.

25. Ibid., p. 571.

26. Ibid., p. 448.

27. Ibid., p. 449.

28. Fisher's sermon against Luther, delivered at St Paul's on 11 February 1526, quoted and discussed in *A Dialogue Concerning Heresies*, p. 440.

29. Ibid., p. 449. More's attentions to the multiple review of his text may also have resonated with the claims of European printers' colophons that touted the high quality of the proofreaders (or correctors of the press) that they employed.

30. This and the following quotation are from *The Confutation of Tyndale's Answer*, ed. L. A. Schuster *et al.*, in *The Complete Works of St Thomas More*, vol. 8, part 1 (New Haven, 1972), p. 36.

31. Anthony Grafton has suggested to me, in a personal communication, that More's presentation of himself as self-corrector smacks of a kind of self-martyrdom: that in his service to truth and to the reader he lowers himself to such tasks as proofreading.

32. Cambridge University Library, shelfmarks H.3.42 and Selden 3.135.

33. Quoted in translation in *Responsio ad Lutherum*, p. 837.

34. Simpson, *Proofreading*, pp. 3–45. This quotation from p. 9, from the printer's advertisement for the 1576 edition of Gascoigne's *The Droome of Doomes Day*.

35. All references to Elyot's *Dictionary* are to the facsimile edition, which repro-duces the copy in the Bodleian Library in Oxford (Menston, 1970).

36. See, for example, *Statutes of the Realm*, 31 Henry VIII (1539), chapter 14, declar-ing anyone a heretic who 'by worde writyng ymprintinge cypheringe or in enye otherwise doe publishe preache' etc. any opinion contrary to articles of the act. For the act concerned with prohibiting the forging of the seal, see 27

Henry VIII, chapter 2. Other acts which deal with legislating what is written or printed include 31 Henry VIII, chapter 14, and 33 Henry VIII, chapter 14. Much of this material is brought to bear on the discussion of Cromwellian control in G. R. Elton, *Policy and Police: The Enforcement of the Reformation in the Age of Thomas Cromwell* (Cambridge, 1972). For the rise of the Privy Chamber and the attendant shifts in Henrician administration and culture, see D. Starkey, 'Representation through Intimacy', in I. Lewis, ed., *Symbols and Sentiments* (London, 1977), pp. 187–244; and Starkey, 'Intimacy and Innovation: The Rise of the Privy Chamber, 1485–1547', in Starkey, ed., *The English Court: From the Wars of the Roses to the Civil War* (London, 1987), pp. 71–118. I have discussed the impact of some of this material on reading and writing in the Henrician period in my *Courtly Letters in the Age of Henry VIII* (Cambridge, 1997), especially pp. 115–16, 133–5.

37. S. M. Foley, 'Coming to Terms: Thomas Elyot's Definitions and the Particularity of Human Letters', *English Literary History*, 61 (1994), pp. 211–30, quotation p. 214.

38. See the accounts in Starkey, 'Representation through Intimacy' and 'Intimacy and Innovation'.

39. Starkey, 'Representation through Intimacy', p. 198.

40. Quoted and discussed in Starkey, 'Representation through Intimacy', p. 207.

41. Foley, 'Coming to Terms', p. 212.

42. *A Dialogue Concerning Heresies*, p. 450.

43. *Opus Epistolarum Des. Erasmi Roterodami*, ed. P. A. Allen (12 vols., Oxford, 1910), vol. 2, letter 325, p. 52. Translation from *The Correspondence of Erasmus*, ed. R. A. B. Mynors and D. F. S. Thomson, in *The Collected Works of Erasmus*, vol. 3 (Toronto, 1976), p. 65.

44. D. Greetham, 'Textual Forensics', *Publications of the Modern Language Association of America*, 111 (1996), pp. 32–51. Material in this section of my essay develops, with substantial change of emphasis, augmentation of detail and correction of error, arguments I made in my *Courtly Letters in the Age of Henry VIII*, pp. 183–201.

45. See the account in K. Muir, *The Life and Letters of Sir Thomas Wyatt* (Liverpool, 1963), pp. 172–8; P. Zagorin, 'Sir Thomas Wyatt and the Court of Henry VIII: The Courtier's Ambitions', *Journal of Medieval and Renaissance Studies*, 23 (1993), pp. 113–41, especially pp. 122–3, 132–3; and S. M. Foley, *Sir Thomas Wyatt* (Boston, 1990), pp. 76–7.

46. The two texts are preserved in British Library MS Harley 78, fols. 5–15, and edited by Muir, *Life and Letters* ('Declaration', pp. 178–84; 'Defence', pp.187–209). The reasons why Wyatt did not deliver these speeches remain unclear, though Zagorin argues that Wyatt 'went through the motions of confession and petitioning for mercy in order to save his life and regain his freedom' ('Sir Thomas Wyatt and the Court of Henry VIII', p. 135).

47. Muir, *Life and Letters*, p. 178. All subsequent references will be cited in the text.

48. See the repeated remarks on letters sent and received in Muir, *Life and Letters*, pp. 179–80.

49. See Grafton, *Defenders of the Text*, pp. 47–75; and Trovato, *Con ogni diligenza*, especially pp. 93–6.

50. I quote from the facsimile edition, *Geoffrey Chaucer: The Works, 1532*, ed. D. Brewer (Menston, 1969). The *OED* cites this passage as the first appearance in English of the word 'collation' used in textual criticism (s.v. 'collation', def. 3). The verbs 'collate', 'confer' and 'compare' are linked together in the example offered next by the *OED*, a 1568 reference to *Love Letters of Mary Queen of Scots*, ed. H. Campbell, appendix 52: 'The originals...were duly *conferred* and *compared*...with sundry other lettres...in *collation* whereof no difference was found' (emphasis added). The *OED* also notes, s.v. 'confer', def. 4: 'to bring into comparison, compare, collate (exceedingly common from 1530 to 1650)', and offers a citation from 1533 as its first appearance. The word 'collation', however, appears in More's 1532 *Dialogue* in precisely these textual-critical terms (uncited by the *OED*): Scripture 'maye be well vnderstanden / by the collacyon...of one texte wyth an other' (*A Dialogue Concerning Heresies*, p. 451).

51. See W. A. Sessions, 'Surrey's Wyatt: Autumn 1542 and the New Poet', in P. G. Herman, ed., *Rethinking the Henrician Era* (Urbana, Ill., 1994), p. 175: 'What Brian Tuke had indicated in his preface to Thynne's 1532 edition of Chaucer – as obvious a place as any to locate the inception of the idea of a new language – the later Tottel and Puttenham knew absolutely: the power of language was nothing if it did not center primarily on that source of all power and finance, the court.'

52. All quotations from Wyatt's poetry are from *The Collected Poems of Sir Thomas Wyatt*, ed. K. Muir and P. Thompson (Liverpool, 1969), cited by number in my text. Reasons for using this old-spelling edition will be made clear in the course of this essay.

53. Crewe, *Trials of Authorship*, p. 22.

54. *Sir Thomas Wyatt: The Complete Poems*, ed. R. A. Rebholz (Harmondsworth, 1978).

55. *Courtly Letters in the Age of Henry VIII*, pp. 191–7.

56. Quoted in Simpson, *Proofreading*, p. 47.

57. Compare Skelton's indictment of Wolsey and king in *Why Come Ye Nat to Courte?*: 'He sayth the kynge doth wryte, / And writeth he wottith nat what' (lines 678–9).

58. Simpson, *Proofreading*, p. 55.

59. Quoted in Simpson, *Proofreading*, p. 5. For discussion of this text in the contemporary context of later, sixteenth-century editorial practice, see Murphy, 'Came errour here by myss of man'.

60. 'Agnosco, fateor, deprecor non culpam sed poenam, sed ignominiam, quae fatenti remitti solet.' *Opus Epistolarum*, letter 403, p. 231. Translation from *Correspondence*, p. 278.

61. Among the many who have commented on this material, I am especially grateful to Joseph A. Dane, Timothy Hampton, Anthony Grafton, David Kastan and Karla Mallette. A more fully developed and somewhat recalibrated version of this material forms the opening chapter of my book *Error and the Academic Self* (New York, 2002).

CHAPTER TWO

Abandoning the capital in eighteenth-century London

Richard Wendorf

Total and sudden transformations of a language seldom happen.
Samuel Johnson[1]

This essay attempts to define a problem concerning printing history and cultural change that has intrigued and often baffled me for the past twenty-five years. I begin by describing a phenomenon that is literally minuscule: the gradual abandonment of pervasive capital letters (majuscules), as well as italics, in English books published during the middle decades of the eighteenth century. I attempt to relate this important change in printing practice to the roles of author, bookseller and printer during this period, to the growth (and diversification) of the reading public in England, and to other cultural phenomena of the 1750s – the publication of Johnson's *Dictionary* and the adoption of the Gregorian calendar, in particular – with which these changes in the printing house might profitably be associated. My research suggests that such a fundamental shift in printing conventions was closely tied to a pervasive interest in refinement, regularity and even cultural conformity at mid-century. But such a change also reveals the conflicting emotions English men and women of the eighteenth century continued to harbour concerning their country's relationship to the rest of Europe. Samuel Johnson noted that 'Our language, for almost a century, has, by the concurrence of many causes, been gradually departing from its original *Teutonick* character, and deviating towards a *Gallick* structure and phraseology, from which it ought to be our endeavour to recal it.'[2] But by 1755, when Johnson published these words – in the new style – in the 'Preface' to his *Dictionary*, the typographical floodgates had stood open for almost twenty years.

I

My first confrontation with what I now realize was a sweeping transformation in the appearance and 'readability' of the printed page in

72

eighteenth-century England occurred when Charles Ryskamp and I began preparing our edition of the poetry of William Collins in the mid-1970s. Collins enjoyed an unusual career as a writer, publishing a number of poems while he was still at Winchester and Oxford, orchestrating a somewhat successful assault on London in his early twenties, and then essentially disappearing from the literary scene in 1747, at the age of twenty-five. In deciding which version of Collins's *Persian Eclogues* of 1742 to accept as copy-text for our critical edition, we discovered that the revised edition of 1757 (entitled *Oriental Eclogues*) contained not only substantive variants but a host of changes in its 'accidentals' as well: nouns other than proper names were no longer capitalized, and many of the words and phrases in italics were stripped of their distinctive styling. The difference between the presentation of the accidentals in these two editions can be gauged in the opening two lines of the poem (see figures 1 and 2):

> 1742: Ye *Persian* Maids, attend your Poet's Lays,
>   And hear how Shepherds pass their golden Days:
> 1757: Ye Persian maids, attend your poet's lays,
>   And hear how shepherds pass their golden days.

Our attempt to account for the changes to be found in the second edition was doubly difficult. We discovered, in the first place, that Collins's modern editors had rejected the later edition's substantive alterations – usually defined as the verbal changes that affect the meaning of the text – because Collins was thought to be insane (and therefore incapable of revising his own poetry) in the 1750s. After looking closely at the surviving evidence, however, I concluded that the poet, despite the vaguely defined illness from which he suffered, was 'able and eager to perform additional revision as late as 1756',[3] and we therefore accepted, for the first time in the long trail of modern textual transmission, the substantive variants as they appeared in the text of the *Oriental Eclogues*.

It proved just as difficult, however, to determine a proper copy-text for a poem that had undergone such significant transformation in the space of only fifteen years. Under normal circumstances, a work with this kind of printing history would have prompted a straightforward editorial decision in the 1970s to follow the first edition as copy-text because that text would be most likely to preserve the author's intentions regarding accidentals (spelling, punctuation and other elements of the formal presentation of the text). The edition would then incorporate authorial revisions from the later printing into the base text, and these revisions would be modified, if necessary, to conform to the presentation of the copy-text. These are the

(5)

ECLOGUE the First.

SELIM; or, the Shepherd's Moral.

SCENE, a Valley near Bagdat.

TIME, the MORNING.

YE *Perſian* Maids, attend your Poet's Lays,
    And hear how Shepherds paſs their golden
        Days:
Not all are bleſt, whom Fortune's Hand ſuſtains
With Wealth in Courts, nor all that haunt the Plains:
Well may your Hearts believe the Truths I tell;
'Tis Virtue makes the Bliſs, where'er we dwell.

  Thus *Selim* ſung; by ſacred Truth inſpir'd;
No Praiſe the Youth, but her's alone deſir'd:
Wiſe in himſelf, his meaning Songs convey'd
Informing Morals to the Shepherd Maid,

          B   Or

Figure 1. First page of William Collins's *Persian Eclogues*, 1742

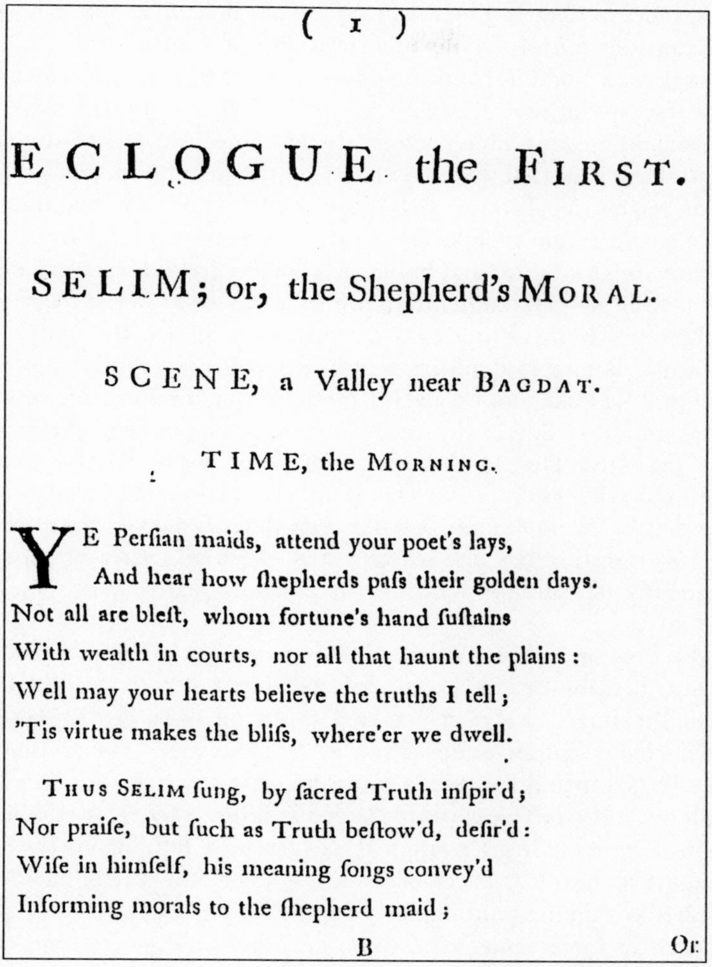

(I)

E C L O G U E the F I R S T.

S E L I M; or, the Shepherd's M O R A L.

S C E N E, a Valley near B A G D A T.

T I M E, the M O R N I N G.

Y E Perfian maids, attend your poet's lays,
　　And hear how fhepherds pafs their golden days.
Not all are bleft, whom fortune's hand fuftains
With wealth in courts, nor all that haunt the plains :
Well may your hearts believe the truths I tell ;
'Tis virtue makes the blifs, where'er we dwell.

T H U S S E L I M fung, by facred Truth infpir'd ;
Nor praife, but fuch as Truth beftow'd, defir'd :
Wife in himfelf, his meaning fongs convey'd
Informing morals to the fhepherd maid ;

B　　　　　　　　　　　　　　　　Or

Figure 2. First page of William Collins's *Oriental Eclogues*, 1757

procedures laid down by W. W. Greg in his classic essay on 'The Rationale of Copy-Text' and subsequently refined and codified by Fredson Bowers and other textual editors and theorists.[4]

But the *Persian* and *Oriental Eclogues* pose a special problem in the modification of accidentals, standing as they do on opposite sides of what Bertrand Bronson has called the 'Great Divide' in eighteenth-century printing practice. In his essay on 'Printing as an Index of Taste', Bronson was the first modern scholar, I believe, to point out that what I have described in the transmission of Collins's text was actually characteristic of printing practices in London from roughly 1745 to 1755: the highly mannered look of the typical English page of the preceding century had rather suddenly become (to impose *my* terms) the less emphatic, less cluttered and less distinctive page that we expect to encounter in books published today. Bronson was aware, of course, that inconsistencies existed within the printing of a single author's works during the first half of the century, and he conceded, in a footnote, that books in a smaller format were more likely to retain their vigorous capitalization. But it was nevertheless clear to him 'that there is a quite abrupt shift of convention just at the midpoint of the century. Before 1750 poetry was likely to be generously capitalized; after 1750 it was likely to be given a modern capitalization. There are exceptions on either side of the line, but they do not conceal the fact that 1750 is the Great Divide.' And prose, he adds, 'seems to have followed roughly the same course'.[5] Given the inherent conservatism of printing as a trade, the phenomenon Bronson first described took place virtually overnight, transforming 'the whole visual effect of a page of type' and consequently demanding a 'change in psychological response' in us, as readers.[6]

In the case of a poet such as Collins, with his heavy investment in allegorical personification, we immediately sense a radical difference in the visual texture of his poetry as well as the dilemma of distinguishing between what is figurative and what is literal in his verse. The decision that Charles Ryskamp and I faced almost twenty-five years ago was therefore a difficult one indeed. If we chose the later text as our copy, we would be both imposing a form of Greg's 'tyranny of the copy-text' by allowing the choice of substantives to rule the accidentals *and* ignoring the careful distinctions established within the printing houses of the early 1740s, when Collins was most active as a publishing poet. If, on the other hand, we returned to the presentation of accidentals in the 1742 edition, we would not be able to suggest – at least not in the text of the poem itself – the major departures in stylistic presentation occurring within the author's own lifetime. We finally decided to retain the accidentals of the *Persian Eclogues* in our eclectic, 'amalgamated' text, and to address the editorial dilemma itself at length in the textual commentary. But this fundamental change in printing practice has continued to haunt me. Why did such a radical transformation take place? Who was responsible for it? How, precisely, did it unfold? And why did such an all-encompassing change occur at this particular moment, roughly at the midpoint of the eighteenth century?

We know that writers and printers had already experimented with the stylistic presentation of their works for at least two hundred years. In the unpublished final chapter of his Lyell Lectures devoted to Pope and the eighteenth-century book trade, David Foxon noted that Ben Jonson abandoned the free use of capitals in preparing his folio *Workes* for publication in 1616. Jonson reserved final polishing for the fine-paper folio copies of his play *Every Man out of His Humour* while also taking a further step towards what Foxon calls 'the classical tradition' by printing the names of the characters in his plays in capitals and small capitals – not just in the scene headings and speech prefixes but in the text itself.[7] John Ogilby, on the other hand, adopted a typographical style later in the century that was abundantly capitalized, and Abraham Cowley invested equally heavily in italics.[8] Perhaps the most systematic of authors, moreover, was Edward Benlowes, whose *Theophila* of 1652 capitalizes every noun (as well as every pronoun relating to God, angels or the soul), generously italicizes words for emphasis, and for even greater stress prints some words in capitals and small capitals, with the deity always printed in full capitals.[9] The result, of course, is a textual page filled with the intricacies of hierarchical differentiation.

We discover a similar concern with 'the visual language of typography' in what D. F. McKenzie has characterized as 'a new and intimate form of teamwork between author or editor, bookseller and printer' at the beginning of the eighteenth century.[10] In revising and reprinting his Restoration plays for a new, collected edition in 1710, William Congreve collaborated with the publisher Jacob Tonson and the printer John Watts to produce classicized texts that attempt to bridge 'the gap between the fleeting image on a stage and the printed words on a page'.[11] Congreve and Tonson did so by carefully choosing capitals and small capitals for headlines and character groupings and by introducing headpieces and other printers' devices to separate act from act and scene from scene – an innovation that enunciated the scenic design of the plays for the first time in print and thereby repudiated the normal presentation of dramatic texts throughout the seventeenth century. In his plays as well as in his novel *Incognita*, McKenzie argues, Congreve was intent on making reading 'a dramatic experience'.[12] Tonson and Congreve did not abandon the capital, however; they simply learned to modulate it.

The distance between the 1710 edition of Congreve's works and the early collected editions of Pope is fairly short – only seven years – and David Foxon has demonstrated, at great length and in painstaking detail, the care with which Pope revised the accidentals of his work 'at least as thoroughly as he revised the words of his text'.[13] Pope's pioneering abandonment of capitals began in his collected *Works* of 1717 and was continued in his miscellaneous *Poems on Several Occasions*, where he imposed this new convention on his fellow contributors. Proof-sheets for the first two volumes of Pope's *Iliad* unmistakably show us, moreover, that it was the poet rather than his printer, William Bowyer, who was responsible for this usage, for we have not only the evidence of Pope's own hand on the proof-sheets but the testimony of Bowyer's other publications of this period, which all follow the traditional style. By the time the *Dunciad Variorum* was published in 1729, Pope had begun to abandon the use of italic type as well, and the so-called 'death-bed' editions of 1743–4 show the entire range of his editorial activity: 'first the abandonment of profuse italic, then of initial capitals for common nouns, and finally the abandonment of italic for proper nouns'.[14] Only John Gay, in Foxon's view, was as bold a typographical revolutionary during the first half of the eighteenth century.

It is worthwhile rehearsing the example of Pope in some detail because of the prominence and prestige of his published work and because of the obvious care he devoted to the presentation of his poetry on the printed page. But Pope is interesting for two other reasons as well. In the first place, we need to realize that, despite Pope's insistence on these pervasive changes in typographical convention between 1717 and his death in 1744, he never followed this system in his own manuscripts.[15] Pope's holographs clearly show that he continued to write his poetry – and even revise it in fair copies – according to the traditional conventions; only in his proof-sheets and in the revised copies of his early editions do we see him actively changing the style of his accidentals. This suggests, among other things, not only that his manuscripts should not automatically be drawn upon as copy-text by modern editors, but that Pope, like writers later in the century, created his work in the old style even as he realized that it would eventually be published in the new. Old habits seem to die hard, even for inveterate innovators.

The second point worth emphasizing about Pope's practice is the fact that, like Ben Jonson before him, he distinguished between different editions or formats of his works. The evidence of most of his publications after 1717 indicates that he wished to classicize or Romanize his verse, even though this practice was in direct conflict with his continuing temptation to use italics to make a point or mark an antithesis. Foxon concludes, however, that Pope consciously decided to employ italics in his trade editions – whether they were original folio publications of his poems or the collected works in octavo – whereas he avoided italics as far as possible in the large formats intended for a 'select circle'.[16] Perhaps Pope felt, Foxon speculates, 'that the vulgar needed help in reading his work correctly, or at least that they should have italics for proper names as they would expect; and if these italics, why not others?'[17]

Given the powerful force of Pope's example, it might seem both natural and inevitable that English publications would move in the direction of Bronson's 'Great Divide' sometime around 1750. My own research indicates, however, that this transformation did not take place as quickly, consistently or completely as we might be led to believe. We need to consider, in the first place, the unusual nature of Pope's role. Pope was a shrewd businessman and a master manipulator as well as a painstaking writer and editor. His influence over Bowyer and his later printer, John Wright, was extraordinary, and it should not be assumed that many other writers of the time could lay claim to equal control of the printed word, although there are interesting exceptions such as Jonathan Richardson.[18] Printing conventions, including the presentation of capitals and italics, firmly fell within the purview of the trade during this period – compositors, correctors, printers and booksellers – and the power of the booksellers in particular only increased during the middle years of the century.[19]

Pope was also, primarily, a poet; and poetry, important as it was, represented a relatively small percentage of the output of the London press during this period.[20] The English reader was assaulted by an astonishing array of literary genres ranging from sermons and histories to plays, political tracts, reference books and the suddenly emerging novel of the 1740s. Many booksellers and printers specialized in a narrow spectrum of work, and there is no reason to believe that they would be unduly influenced by the rarified world of Augustan verse. And there was also, as Foxon's speculation about popular and refined editions suggests, significant variety within the reading public itself. If Pope himself sensed a need for retaining italicized pointing within the trade editions of his own poetry – which would presumably fall into the hands of most of his readers – we can begin to gauge how sophisticated indeed the members of his more select circle probably were. Pope's innovations, in other words, were not directed at his entire reading public, let alone at those readers whose normal choice of text was the ballad, broadside, newspaper or chapbook.

My preliminary research indicates that this general transformation of printing conventions took much longer to complete than Bronson had realized or than the revelations of Foxon's study of Pope might suggest. It is even difficult to define the word 'complete', given the fact that English books are filled with inconsistency and exceptions throughout the century. At what point do we decide that such a change is statistically persuasive? And what do we make of the fact that a change in one convention – the abandonment of capitals for all substantive nouns, for example – could trigger a countervailing change in the opposite direction: the italicization of place names, for instance, or the placement of personified words in small capitals? For an example of this modulation, we need look no further than the opening lines of Collins's *Oriental Eclogues*, where the italicized '*Selim*' of the 1742 edition now appears as 'SELIM'; only 'sacred Truth' retains its original appearance.

The sheer number of books published at mid-century is daunting, moreover, and my observations in this essay are based on an examination of a thousand books, far from the entire complement of books published in London between 1740 and 1760, which the Eighteenth-Century Short-Title Catalog estimates to be 33,000.[21] The books I have examined suggest to me that this transformation was not pervasive, let alone complete, by the close of the 1750s. My research indicates that a majority of books did not appear in the new style until 1765, a full fifteen years after Bronson's 'Great Divide'. The sheer amount of inconsistency is also perplexing, especially when it occurs in the collaborative work of a single writer and bookseller, or even between the prefatory matter and the main text of the same book.

Certain patterns *are* clear, however, and I want to present two firm conclusions as well as one tentative one. My tentative claim is that sermons and other religious publications were just as likely as poetical texts to appear without the capitalization of common nouns in the 1740s. A handful of books published by Joseph Burroughs and Samuel Chandler in 1743, for instance, disclose remarkably modern texts, with italics used for biblical quotations and titles – and occasional emphasis – and with capitalization disappearing to the point where even the word 'christianity' appears without an initial capital in Burroughs's *Defence of Two Discourses*.[22]

I find this to be an especially interesting development, for while the italic still reflects its historical role as 'the typeface of privilege, as the type of quotation, of accuracy, obtrusion, assertion' (as Joseph Loewenstein has forcefully characterized it),[23] hierarchical distinctions involving the complex play among capitals, small capitals, italics, and lower-case letters have significantly disappeared. 'God' and 'Christ' continue to be enshrined in capitals or small capitals, but the rest of creation appears in a much more uniform style, with the result that the visual distinction between the divine and the human or secular is more pronounced than it was formerly. What I have not yet been able to determine is whether the publication of sermons and religious tracts followed denominational lines. John and Charles Wesley, for instance, were continually publishing during this period, and the printing history of the Methodists needs to be traced with these changes in convention in mind.

My second conclusion is much firmer. In addition to examining individual publications as they appeared in the 1740s and 1750s, it is also important to look carefully at the periodical press. The *Gentleman's Magazine*, founded by Edward Cave in 1731, provides a month-by-month digest of information and previously published material throughout this period, and I have found it particularly instructive to follow the fortunes of Cave's monthly instalment of 'Poetical Essays'. The poetry Cave published in 1731 and 1732 vacillates between the old style and the new in the treatment of both capitals and italics. There is a revealing episode in January 1732, for instance, when Cave publishes the text of Colley Cibber's 'Ode for New-Years-Day 1732' with scant capitalization and a matching parody in the old style directly next to it on the same page, with the capitals and italics carefully employed to mark parodic difference (see figure 3).

In 1733, however, matters begin to change abruptly. The January issue employs the new style, February reverts mostly to the old, March includes both, April returns almost completely to the old – and then, in May 1733, the 'Poetical Essays' appear entirely in the new style. There is one exception to this development in June and one in July (perhaps because the poems were already in standing type), but none in August or September, and this virtual abandonment of capitals for common substantives holds throughout the ensuing months and years. Capitalized personifications and poems printed entirely in italic continue to appear in these monthly instalments (perhaps to include more text, perhaps for the sake of visual variety), but a decisive change has clearly taken place. It is worth noting that this development occurs long before mid-century and that the rest of each issue in 1733 – and long afterwards – appears as thoroughly unrehabilitated prose, with every form of distinction imaginable cramming its already crowded columns. Only eleven years later, in his October 1744 issue, would Cave extend this ban on capitalized substantives to the extensive sections of prose in his magazine.

This emphasis on uniformity in the periodical press is similar, moreover, to the third pattern I have discovered, which is that this new house style was likely to be adopted when writers, editors and booksellers issued collections of works written by diverse hands and previously published in diverse styles. This is true of the *Gentleman's Magazine* as early as 1733 and it continues all the way to Johnson's *Dictionary* in 1755, with its 116,000 illustrative

580   *Poetical* ESSAYS *in* JANUARY, 1732.   No. XI

O D E *for New-Years-Day* 1732.   The *Poet Laureat's Ode for N.*
By *C. Cibber*, Efq; Poet Laureat.   *Years-Day* burlefqu'd.

Recit.   *Recit.*

AWAKE with joyous fongs the day   AWake, with *Grub-ftreet* Odes, the D.
    That leads the op'ning year ;   That leads the op'ning Year ;
The year advancing to prolong,   The Year advancing to prolong
Augustus' fway demands our fong,   Great *C--bb--r's* Fame, demands a Song,
And *calls* for univerfal cheer.   Infpir'd by *Gin*, or by *Small Beer*.

Air.   *Air.*

Your antient Annals, Britain, read,   Your Ancient *Ballad-Makers* read,
   And mark the Reign you moft admire ;   And mark the *Fool* you moft admire ;
The *prefent* fhall the paft exceed,   The *prefer* fhall the *paft* exceed,
   nd yield enjoyment to defire.   And yield *Enjoyment* to Defire :
Or if you find the coming year   Or, if you find the coming Year,
   In bleffings fhould tranfcend the laft   In *Nonfenfe* fhould tranfcend the laft,
The diff'rence only will declare   The Diff'rence only will make good
   The prefent fweeter than the paft.   The prefent *duller* than the paft !

Recit.   *Recit.*

But, ah! the fweets his fway beftows,   But ah ! the *Stuff* his *Strain* beftows
Are greater far than Greatnefs knows.   Is duller far than Dulnefs knows ;
With various penfive cares oppreff'd,   With various *lumpifh Loads* oppreft
Unfeen, alas, the Royal Breaft   Unfeen, alas! the Laureat's Breaft
Endures *his many a weight*,   Endures his many a Weigh',
Unfelt by fwains ot humble ftate.   Unfelt by all but *Bards of State.*

Air.   *Air.*

Thus *brooding* on her *lonely* neft,   Thus brooding o'er her lovely Neft,
   Aloft the Eagle wakes,   The *watchful Owl* awakes,
   Her due *delights* forfakes,   Her due Delight forfakes,
Tho' Monarch of the air confefs'd,   Reftlefs to give all others Reft ;
Her *drooping* eyes refufe to clofe ;   Her drooping Eyes refufe to clofe,
   While fearlefs of annoy,   Whilft, fearlefs of Numbers
Her young belov'd enjoy   To threaten their Slumbers,
Protection, food, and fweet repofe.   All around her enjoy much Sleep and Repoft.

Recit.   *Recit.*

What thanks, ye *Britons*, can repay   What Praifes can repay an *Owl*
So mild, fo juft, fo tender fway ?   So flat, fo heavy; and fo dull ?

Air.   His *annual Odes* which he admires,

Your annual aid when he defires,   Lets the *Dunces* than *fool* Lives!
Lefs the King than land requires ;   All the *Strains* which from him flow;
All the dues to him that flow   Are ftill of *noble Ufe* to you ;
Are ftill but Royal wants to you :   Whilft his kindly Sheets enrich
So the feafons lend the earth   Every Bard *to wipe his B——*
Their kindly rains to raife her birth ;   And well the *mutual Labours* fuit
And well the mutual labours fuit,   His the *Glory*, yours the *Fruit*.
His the glory, yours the fruit.

Recit.   *Recit.*

Affift, affift, ye fplendid throng,   Affift, affift, ye warbling Throng,
   Who now the Royal circle form ;   Who now the *Grub-ftreet Corus* form ;
With duteous wifhes blend the fong,   With gen'rous Wifhes blend the Song,
And every grateful wifh be warm.   And ev'ry grateful Wifh be warm.

C H O R U S.   *C H O R U S,*

May *Cæfar's* health his reign fupply,   May *C--bb--r's* Mufe his *Odes* fupply,
  'Till faction fhall be pleas'd, or die ;   Till *Nonfenfe* fhall be pleas'd to die ;
'Till loyal hearts defire his fate :   Till *ftupid Fools* defire his *Place* ;
  'Till happier fubjecks know,   Till happier *Courts* fhall know,
  Or foreign realms can fhow   Or Foreign Realms can fhow,
A land fo blefs'd, a King fo great!   A *Dunce* fo dull, an *Ode* fo low ;
                   What *Thanks* are due to ——s G——!

N B.' *The Words and Expreffions in this Character*
being chiefly carp'd at, are defended by way of
Iro-y in the Grub-ftreet Journal No 105.]

Figure 3.   Colley Cibber's 'Ode for New-Years-Day 1732', *Gentleman's Magazine*, 1732

quotations.[24] The publishing history of Robert Dodsley, however, provides the most interesting example.

Dodsley made a name for himself not just as a shrewd and successful bookseller ('Doddy, you know, is my patron', Johnson told Bennet Langton)[25] but also as an editor and writer. During the 1730s and 1740s, Dodsley's publications almost invariably appeared in the old style; because he employed different printers and was not always his own publisher, it seems reasonable to conclude that he preferred the traditional conventions to the new. By 1757, when he wrote to John Baskerville about the printer's new type specimens ('Your small letter is extreamly beautiful'), we sense a softening of attitude as he chides Baskerville for using 'too many Capitals, which is generally thought to spoil the beauty of printing: but they should never be us'd to adjective verbs or adverbs'.[26] But as late as 1761 we find the poet William Shenstone writing that 'Spence, Burke, Lowth, and Melmoth, advise [Dodsley] to discard *Italicks*. I confess he has used them to a very great excess, but yet I do not think they should be utterly discarded.'[27] Earlier, in 1744, we discover him publishing Mark Akenside's *Epistle to Curio* in the old style and Akenside's *Pleasures of Imagination* in the new, possibly (Foxon speculates) because Dodsley had shown the unknown Akenside's poem to Pope, who may – in approving it – have suggested how it might best be printed.[28]

In 1744, on the other hand, Dodsley also published his *Select Collection of Old Plays* in twelve volumes. This was an ambitious work of scholarship in which Dodsley made the texts of several old English plays available to the eighteenth-century reader for the first time. 'I am, as it were,' he wrote in his extensive preface to the first volume, 'the first Adventurer on these Discoveries.'[29] The preface itself is entirely printed in the old style, whereas the dramatic texts that follow are consistently printed in the new, with the traditional authorial voice thus quickly giving way to the new editorial style. Why should this be so? The answer lies in the nature of the material to be edited, which originally appeared in 'so many Stiles and Manners of Writing' that Dodsley found he had to impose some form of uniformity on behalf of his contemporary readers.[30] At the same time, he was eager to show 'the Progress and Improvement of our Taste and Language', and he therefore decided to retain the 'very original Orthography' of the oldest plays whenever he had recourse to 'first Editions'.[31] The plays that appear in the first volume retain their old-spelling texts, which Dodsley believed would be 'entertaining to the Curious'. But he also realized that such a practice would be 'very disagreeable' to 'the Generality of Readers' and therefore attempted 'to make the Reading as easy as I could in the rest' of the collection by modernizing the spelling and 'privately' (silently) correcting or emending both substantives and punctuation.[32]

At no point in his preface does Dodsley address the issue of typographical style, but it is clear from his discussion of these other editorial issues that the imposition of this new style went hand in hand with his other efforts to modernize what appeared to him to be very unorthodox texts. Even the plays published with their original orthography, moreover, were printed without the traditional capitalization and use of italic. 'The Pointing,' he remarked in his preface, 'is at the same time so preposterous (which, like false Guiding-Posts, are perpetually turning out of the High Road of Common Sense) that one would almost suspect there was as much Malice as Stupidity in these old Editions.'[33] These words are suitably printed in the old style, with each substantive capitalized – a style of printing that was already appearing to many of his contemporaries as a preposterous practice, replete with false guiding-posts and departing from what we might now call the low road of common sense.

Robert Dodsley continued to publish his own work in the old style following the appearance of his *Select Collection of Old Plays* in 1744, but he returned to the new typographical conventions when he edited his influential *Collection of Poems* in 1748, 1753 and 1758 and his popular edition of *Select Fables*, printed by the now lean and spare Baskerville, in 1761.[34] When new English poems and old English plays officially entered the canon in the mid-decades of the century, they therefore did so in the new, uniform, crisper style that we continue to find in our anthologies today. Canonization and modernization went hand in hand.[35] And it is therefore also safe to conclude that editors had more influence on the evolution of the new style than writers did, even those as powerful as Pope. It was Dodsley as editor – rather than as author or bookseller – who was responsible for these changes, or (and this is an important distinction) it was Dodsley as editor responding to the advice of his printers as well as his authors.

It is very difficult, finally, to adjudicate the relative importance of printers and booksellers in the slow evolution of style towards the 'Great Divide'. It is rare, for one thing, for printers to be identified on the title pages of books published during this period, although there are often other sources for establishing their roles. In his *Printer's Grammar* of 1755, James Smith noted that 'before we actually begin to compose, we should be informed, either by the Author, or Master, after what manner our work is to be done; whether the old way, with Capitals to Substantives, and Italic to proper names; or after the more neat practice, all in Roman, and Capitals to Proper names, and Emphatical words'.[36] (In his *Dictionary*, by the way, Johnson defined 'neat' as 'Pure; unadulterated; unmingled'.) Smith's commentary indicates that the distinction between the old manner and the new was quite clear, that a firm choice needed to be made, that the choice did not (normally) lie in the hands of the compositor, and that this question was still lingering as late as 1755. Foxon argues, moreover, that printers themselves did not have a house style which they imposed on their authors: whatever uniformity there was in the eighteenth century, 'the burden must have fallen largely on the reader or corrector of the press'[37] (a judgement that is largely corroborated by Smith).[38]

Was a change as fundamental as this – a change so dramatic and irreversible that it has permanently transformed the look and texture of modern print culture in English – actually determined by the individual or collective decisions of countless and equally nameless eighteenth-century correctors? If so, then the denizens of the Augustan printing house must have been aware of the concerns expressed, in print, over the decisions they were taking, and they must have been equally aware that the size and nature of their reading audience were changing as well.

III

There are a number of interesting signposts along the way. In Guy Miège's *English Grammar* of 1688, for instance, italic is proposed for frequent emphasis 'as if the Reader had not sense to apprehend it, without so visible and palpable a distinction',[39] a practice (as we have seen) that Pope retained in the trade editions of his poems. Similarly, in John Jones's *Practical Phonography* of 1701, we are told that printers generally place capital letters at the beginning of the common names of things, a practice that 'daily gains ground'.[40] Six years later Thomas Dyche, in his *Guide to the English Tongue*, reports that capitals are given to any substantive 'if it bear any considerable stress of the Author's Sense upon it, to make it the more Remarkable and Conspicuous'. But he then adds, in a footnote, that the custom of printing every substantive with an initial capital letter is 'unnecessary, and hinders that remarkable Distinction intended by the Capitals'.[41]

This is where Ephraim Chambers took up the argument in his much reprinted *Cyclopaedia* of 1728. Under his entry for capital letters, he wrote that 'The *English* Printers have carried *Capitals* to a pitch of Extravagance; making it a Rule, to begin almost every Substantive with a *Capital*; which is a manifest Perversion of the Design of *Capitals*, as well as an Offence against Beauty and Distinctness.' 'Some of 'em,' he adds, 'begin now to retrench their superfluous *Capitals*, and to fall into the Measures of the

Printers of other Nations' (vol. 1, p. 154), but not in Chambers's own case, ironically, for his entire diatribe is printed in the old style, with a superfluity of capitals and italics alike. In the second edition of 1738, however, the capitalization disappears with the exception of the word 'Capitals' itself, which remains true to its function until it is finally beheaded in the seventh edition of 1752.

It is significant that this debate involved not just writers and printers but grammarians and encyclopedists as well, for what is at stake here is not just the 'proper' function of various typographical conventions but the necessity of employing these mediating modes of pointing, distinction and emphasis in the first place. Chambers's hostility to the old way of doing things was based on 'Extravagance', perversion of the proper role of capitals, and the abrogation of both beauty and consistency ('Distinctness'), which is another way of arguing that the very conventions which had been cultivated to provide the reader with helpful signposts had become impediments themselves to the comprehension of English poetry and prose.

Such a transformation in thinking about the nature of the conventions, moreover, presupposes a similar transformation in the sophistication of the reading public during the first half of the eighteenth century. And here, of course, we are on notoriously uncertain ground, for the various assessments of literacy, the reading public, and the sale and dissemination of newspapers, magazines and books in the eighteenth century continue to differ from – if not actually contradict – one another. We have only to compare Samuel Johnson's description of 'a nation of readers' in 1781 with his friend Edmund Burke's estimate, ten years later, that the English reading public included only 80,000 persons, less than 10 per cent of the entire population.[42] In his recent survey of the growth and nature of literacy, John Brewer cautions us that the most reliable figures are not very reliable at all, especially given the traditional definition of literacy as the ability to write one's name. He estimates that 60 per cent of men and 40 per cent of women could read at mid-century, although these figures are significantly higher for the inhabitants of London, where female literacy seems to have reached 66 per cent by the 1720s. These figures may have declined, however, late in the century.[43]

Brewer argues that 'the growth in the reading public after 1700 would not have been possible without the gradual spread of literacy' and that without 'readers the spurt in publishing that began in the late seventeenth century would have been impossible'. But he nevertheless concludes that the major transformation that occurred was the change in the supply of printed matter following the removal of constraints imposed by the government and conservative booksellers alike. Such an increase in the amount of printed material 'changed the nature of reading itself', he argues, particularly in the transition from 'intensive' to 'extensive' reading: from the careful perusal and rereading of a few essential and relatively expensive volumes to the more exploratory and occasionally cursory examination of a wide variety of texts, including those that were ephemeral.[44] Brewer concludes that 'Books, print and readers were everywhere. Not everyone was a reader, but even those who could not read lived to an unprecedented degree in a culture of print.'[45]

Each of these factors – the rise in literacy and thus in the size of the reading public, the growth in publishing, the increasing variety of the publications themselves, and the changing nature of reading habits – bears directly on the evolution of the printed page. Type design, Stanley Morison once wrote, 'moves at the pace of the most conservative reader',[46] and much the same can be said of typographical conventions. When Pope stipulated that his works should appear in both popular and elite editions, he was counting on a sophisticated readership that could afford the higher cost of his classicized texts; but he was also acknowledging the fact that the general reading public still needed the typographical pointing to be found in the octavos and duodecimos. England may have been a nation of readers in 1781, but it was clearly a nation of different *kinds* of readers during the first half of the century.

Cautions concerning the nature of this larger reading public were voiced outside the confines of Pope's dunciadic vision as well as within it. Complaining in 1711 about the unfortunate desire of English poets and readers alike for 'extremely *Gothick*' taste, Addison drew on Dryden's invidious distinctions, particularly his contempt of 'the Rabble of Readers', 'Mob-Readers', those who inhabit the 'lowest Form' of the reading public for poetry.[47] In another issue of the *Spectator* Addison playfully referred to his 'Illiterate Readers, if any such there are', as he boasted of the increase in learning in England and the consequent improvement in the art of printing.[48] As late as 1756, in the abridgement of his *Dictionary of the English Language*, Johnson could matter-of-factly recommend his pared-down volumes to 'the greater number of readers, who, seldom intending to write or presuming to judge, turn over books only to amuse their leisure, and to gain degrees of knowledge suitable to lower characters, or necessary to the common business of life: these know not any other use of a dictionary than that of adjusting orthography, or explaining terms of science or words of infrequent occurrence, or remote derivation.'[49] Being able to read, as Ian Watt pointed out decades ago in *The Rise of the Novel*, 'was a necessary accomplishment only for those destined to the middle-class occupations – commerce, administration and the professions'; only 'a small proportion of the labouring classes who were technically literate developed into active members of the reading public, and . . . the majority of these were concentrated in those employments where reading and writing' were vocational necessities.[50]

The distinctions that continued to be made among English readers of the first half of the century thus provide another crucial context in which to place this gradual but steady change in printing history. It is one thing to associate the abandonment of capitals and italics with the growth of literacy, the reading public and print culture; it is another, however, to place it within a rapidly evolving society in which the relative sophistication of readers was still an issue. The printing practices of the 1740s and 1750s suggest to me that, individually and perhaps even collectively, writers, compositors, correctors, printers, booksellers *and* readers agreed that the reading population as a whole could accommodate these new typographical conventions and the change in taste they represented. Year by year, printer by printer, publication by publication, the printed material of mid-eighteenth-century England appeared in a less hierarchical, less differentiated, less heavily textured style.

This pervasive levelling of the text, with its less visually and intellectually mediated form of presentation, in turn placed much more emphasis on the discriminating power of the individual reader. These fundamental changes in printing conventions, in other words, are not only a result (and reflection) of the development of the reading public but also a cause of increased facility and sophistication as readers were faced with a greater uniformity in the presentation of printed texts. Such a revolutionary development did not go unnoticed, of course, and the most vociferous opposition to these changes was voiced – much too late in the century, as it turned out – by Benjamin Franklin. Writing to his son William in 1773, Franklin complained about the reprinting of one of his anonymous pieces, which had been 'stripped of all the capitalling and italicing, that intimate the allusions and marks [*sic*] the emphasis of written discourses, to bring them as near as possible to those spoken'. Printing such a piece 'in one even small character,' he added, 'seems to me like repeating one of Whitefield's sermons in the monotony of a school-boy'.[51] Later still, in a famous letter to Noah Webster of 1789, Franklin repeated his concern about the difficulty of reading modern texts aloud, noting that 'the Eye generally slides forward three or four Words before the Voice' and therefore relies upon distinctions within the visual field in order to modulate one's expression.[52]

But Franklin's principal concern is with the sheer difficulty of understanding a less visually differentiated text. In examining books published between the Restoration in 1660 and the accession of George II in 1727, he observes that 'all *Substantives* were begun with a capital, in which we imitated our Mother Tongue, the German', a practice that was particularly helpful to those who were not well acquainted with English and its 'prodigious Number' of words that are both verbs and substantives. Franklin (and who would know better?) ascribes this change to 'the Fancy of Printers', who believe that the suppression of capitals 'shows the Character to greater Advantage; those Letters prominent above the line disturbing its even regular Appearance'. The 'Effect of this Change is so considerable', he writes, that a learned Frenchman who used to read English books with some ease now found them difficult to understand, blaming the stylistic obscurity of modern English writers because he did not realize that the printing conventions themselves had changed.[53]

IV

By 1789, of course, Franklin was espousing a lost cause. The look of the English page had thoroughly evolved into the form with which we are familiar today – even to the point of tending to drop the traditional long 's' and the ligatures in which it was embedded (another of Franklin's concerns).[54] The fact that these changes intensified at mid-century, moreover, suggests to me that cultural forces were at work which extended far beyond the growth of the reading public or the sophistication of the individual reader. The phenomenon I have been mapping is, by its very nature, an amorphous one, appearing not at a single, distinct moment but in tens of thousands of books over a period of several decades. It is therefore useful to associate these changes with other, more discrete phenomena, keeping in mind Foucault's proviso that such changes did not necessarily 'occur at the same level, proceed at the same pace, or obey the same laws'.[55]

What I specifically have in mind is the desire at mid-century for the rationalization of knowledge and of the formal means by which it is represented. We find this strongly emerging tendency in everything from what Lawrence Lipking has characterized as 'the ordering of the arts' in eighteenth-century England to the publication, in the late 1760s, of Blackstone's *Commentaries*.[56] As Paul Langford has argued, Blackstone's pioneering volumes were designed 'to explain the arcane mysteries of English law to an audience which had the intelligence and interest to grasp its principles, but was too busy serving the diverse requirements of a complex, developing society to put itself through the costly experience of a traditional legal education'. And 'practically every learned and scientific specialism,' Langford adds, 'had its Blackstone in the middle of the eighteenth century, appealing to much the same readership'.[57]

At the heart of these developments was an attempt to codify knowledge and, in so doing, to impose some degree of uniformity on conventions that were widely believed to be inconsistent, capricious and irregular – not to mention out of step with England's neighbours on the continent. Johnson's great *Dictionary*, published in 1755 and seven years in the making, represents an ambitious and complicated attempt to achieve both of these goals. The 'one great end of this undertaking,' Johnson wrote in his *Plan* of 1747 (published by Dodsley and his associates in the new style, by the way), 'is to fix the English language', an undertaking that he eventually realized would be impossible.[58] Our language, he opined, 'now stands in our dictionaries a confused heap of words, without dependence, and without relation'.[59] The chief rule he proposed to follow, however, was 'to make no innovation, without a reason sufficient to balance the inconvenience of change', for 'All change is of itself an evil', he wrote in the *Plan*.[60] But systematic attempts were nevertheless needed to impose coherence on an idiom 'composed of dissimilar parts, thrown together by negligence, by affectation, by learning, or by ignorance'.[61] Orthography, pronunciation, etymology and definitions all had to be established, and Johnson's groundbreaking (and backbreaking) innovation was to balance his own judgement against the collective authority of the best English writers, particularly those before the Restoration, whose works he regarded, as he remarked in his 'Preface', as '*the wells of English undefiled*' (a phrase printed in italics, by the way, to indicate that it is a quotation).[62]

The 'Preface' of 1755 and the dictionary that follows it in two folio volumes reveal the extent to which Johnson was forced to back away from his intention to 'fix' the English language, relenting in the face of what he called 'the boundless chaos of a living speech'.[63] Etymology gave way to usage and uniformity to custom; staunchly held beliefs concerning the evils of change were tempered, in the 'Preface', into commendations of 'constancy and stability', in which one finds a 'general and lasting advantage'.[64] 'I am not yet so lost in lexicography,' he wrote, 'as to forget that *words are the daughters of earth, and that things are the sons of heaven*' (also suitably printed in italics, by the way).[65] Language is only the instrument of science, and yet Johnson could still wish that the instrument itself 'might be less apt to decay'.[66]

At the close of his *Plan*, Johnson confessed that the extent of the project he had so ambitiously surveyed made him feel like Caesar's soldiers, gazing at a 'new world, which it is almost madness to invade'. Perhaps with Dodsley's introduction to his *Select Collection of Plays* of 1744 echoing in his ear, Johnson announced that, even if he did not complete the conquest, he should 'at least discover the coast, civilize part of the inhabitants, and make it easy for some other adventurer to proceed farther, to reduce them wholly to subjection, and settle them under laws'.[67] The opening pages of the 'Preface' are much more muted, but Johnson's accomplishment is no less clear. The lexicographer found 'our speech copious without order, and energetick without rules'; desperately needed were established principles of selection, settled tests of purity, and the suffrages of acknowledged authority.[68] And thus Johnson 'accumulated in time the materials of a dictionary, which, by degrees, I reduced to method, establishing to myself, in the progress of the work, such rules as experience and analogy suggested to me'.[69]

It was, famously, a solitary task completed by a single scholar in the space of seven years, whereas it had taken the forty French academicians forty years to complete their own *dictionnaire*. The counterexample of the French academy and their dictionary – and the great Italian *Vocabulario degli Accademici della Crusca* as well – remained deeply impressed on Johnson's mind as well as those of his contemporaries. We 'have long preserved our constitution', he wrote in the 'Preface'; 'let us make some struggles for our language'.[70] The making of the dictionary was, by definition (so to speak), a nationalistic undertaking, predicated on clearly articulated needs but simultaneously enshrining the most polished of English writers.

This complicated tension between what must be lamented and what can be celebrated is reinforced, moreover, by Johnson's ambivalence towards French culture and the elegance of its language. I have already drawn attention to his remark, in the 'Preface', that 'Our language, for almost a century, has, by the concurrence of many causes, been gradually departing from its original *Teutonick* character [spelled, by the way, with a 'k'], and deviating towards a *Gallick* structure and phraseology, from which it ought to be our endeavour to recal it', primarily by 'making our ancient volumes the groundwork of stile'.[71] At the same time, it is manifestly the purpose of the *Dictionary* to supply for Great Britain what the French and Italians already enjoy. It may do so by canonizing what is most genuinely English – and by avoiding the undue contamination of continental drift – but the example and influence of European models cannot be entirely neglected. Johnson is forced, in the *Plan* of the *Dictionary*, to praise the accuracy of French and Italian pronunciation, which are now 'fix'd', and to refer to them, at least in this context, as 'more polished languages' than his native English.[72]

Johnson's immense project will itself produce a more polished language, but it will do so by supplying the rules, judgement, rationalization and authorities that are historically lacking.

V

Let me suggest one additional counterexample, no less complicated than the first. In 1752, while Johnson was deep in the process of preparing his *Dictionary*, he went to sleep on Wednesday, September 2nd, and woke the next morning on Thursday the 14th. This long sleep was occasioned by an act of Parliament that enabled the British to move from the Old Style Julian calendar to the New Style Gregorian calendar, which had been adopted by Catholic countries in 1582–3 and by most Protestant countries around 1700. The English court had approved such a change as early as 1584, but the Protestant bishops were not eager to adopt a proposal from the pope, and they replied to Sir Francis Walsingham's inquiries with delaying tactics that proved to be effective. By 1735, however, a proposed change was taken up in earnest in the press, and in 1751 an act of Parliament 'for regulating the commencement of the year, and for correcting the calendar now in use' was successfully sponsored by the earl of Macclesfield and by Lord Chesterfield – who served not only as one of the king's secretaries of state but as the undisputed arbiter of polite behaviour as well as the authority on polite linguistic usage to whom Johnson dexterously deferred in his *Plan* of the *Dictionary*.[73]

Although there was some opposition to the adoption of the Gregorian calendar, it was generally muted: the friction between Protestant and Catholic causes was less important, as Paul Alkon has shown, than 'the desire to rationalize timekeeping systems for commercial purposes' as well as for public worship.[74] The only nationalistic rhetoric raised at the time was an appeal to patriotic shame at the way England had lagged behind other Protestant countries in taking such a 'rational step'. This change of calendar occurred, moreover, amid similar debates concerning the rationalization of English weights, measures and coinage, and even the introduction of a national census.[75] And this, it seems to me, is precisely the cultural environment in which printing conventions could also undergo a similar transformation from the old style to the new: in a nation comfortable with the prospect of change, ready to accept uniform standards and conventions, and confident enough to do so in a manner that would no longer place them out of step with most of the Continent. Despite the Jacobite rising in 1745, the Seven Years' War that began in 1756, and a Hanoverian dynasty

on the throne, the English were nonetheless willing to synchronize themselves in their calendars and on the printed page roughly at mid-century,
high Georgian noon.

These analogies obviously have their limits. Johnson, after all, resisted
the Gallic and embraced the Teutonic even as he strove to fix the language
and codify its laws. Writers, including Johnson, continued to capitalize and
italicize their substantives throughout the century, and Johnson continued
to depart from his own orthography at every turn.[76] Like many of his contemporaries, Johnson followed the new-style calendar with its renumbering
of the days of public worship, but reverted to the old style in commemo-
rating personal events: his birthday on September 7th (which he observed
on the 18th) or the death of his wife Tetty, which he also observed eleven
days later.[77] It could be argued, moreover, that the old style of printing
enjoyed its own codification and principles, and that what the new style
offered in terms of evenness and regularity it lacked in precise linguistic
differentiation. This was Franklin's essential objection to what he characterized as 'Improvements *backwards*' ('Improvements' capitalized, by the way,
'*backwards*' in italic).[78]

By the way? My parenthetical asides throughout this essay have a consistent point, of course, which is to register the intentionality of the printed or
written act and the importance of this particular 'bibliographical code'.[79]
No matter how complicated or amorphous these changes in printing conventions may turn out to be, they were anything but accidental, which
Johnson defined as 'Casual, fortuitous, happening by chance'. The *presentation* of substantives directly affects – and may even control – the meaning
as well as the texture of the printed word. When Johnson went on to define
'accidental' as a noun – as a substantive – he referred to it as 'A property
nonessential' and quoted the following sentence from Isaac Watts's *Logick*:
'Conceive, as much as you can, of the essentials of any subject, before you
consider its *accidentals*.' In this essay I have attempted to refute Johnson
(as well as Greg) *thus*, considering the accidentals first in order to demonstrate the ways in which printing history reveals the general impress of
cultural change while also working to generate it. As the American printer
Daniel Berkeley Updike nicely put it, 'we unconsciously govern our printing by the kind of life we approve'.[80] The example of printing history
in mid-eighteenth-century London suggests that Johnson's, Collins's and
Dodsley's contemporaries approved of a renewed emphasis on the discrim-
inatory powers of the individual reader by means of what we, today, would
characterize as a less cluttered, more elegant, more aesthetically polished
text. It also suggests a willingness to accept, if perhaps not quite to embrace,

an insistence on uniformity and regularity well beyond the confines of the printed page.

1. S. Johnson, 'Preface to the English Dictionary', in Johnson, *Poetry and Prose*, ed. M. Wilson (London, 1950), p. 320.
2. Johnson, *Poetry and Prose*, p. 314.
3. *The Works of William Collins*, ed. R. Wendorf and C. Ryskamp (Oxford, 1979), p. 104.
4. W. W. Greg, 'The Rationale of Copy-Text' (1950), in O. M. Brack Jr and W. Barnes, eds., *Bibliography and Textual Criticism: English and American Literature 1700 to the Present* (Chicago, 1969), p. 43: 'We need to draw a distinction between the significant, or as I shall call them "substantive", readings of the text, those namely that affect the author's meaning or the essence of his expression, and others, such in general as spelling, punctuation, word-division, and the like, affecting mainly its formal presentation, which may be regarded as the accidents, or as I shall call them "accidentals", of the text.' The argument of my essay, on the other hand, is that 'formal presentation' directly affects the author's meaning and expression, although it should be kept in mind that Greg himself was empirical rather than prescriptive in his views. For similar arguments to mine on behalf of the role of accidentals, see especially D. F. McKenzie, *Bibliography and the Sociology of Texts* (1986; rev. edn, Cambridge, 1999), and J. J. McGann, *A Critique of Modern Textual Criticism* (1983; repr., Charlottesville, Va., and London, 1992).
5. B. H. Bronson, 'Printing as an Index of Taste', in Bronson, *Facets of the Enlightenment: Studies in English Literature and Its Contexts* (Berkeley and Los Angeles, 1968), pp. 339–40.
6. Ibid., p. 340.
7. D. Foxon, 'Poets and Compositors', unpublished sixth Lyell Lecture, pp. 228–9. Copies of this lecture are deposited in several major libraries, including the British Library. I am grateful to David L. Vander Muelen for providing me with a copy and thereby drawing my attention to this text, which is in many ways a rough draft whose quotations and conclusions need to be verified.
8. Ibid., pp. 238–40.
9. Ibid., p. 235.
10. D. F. McKenzie, 'Typography and Meaning: The Case of William Congreve', in G. Barber and B. Fabian, eds., *Buch und Buchhandel in Europa im achtzehnten Jahrhundert: The Book and the Book Trade in Eighteenth-Century Europe* (Hamburg, 1981), p. 110.
11. Ibid., p. 117.
12. Ibid., p. 116.
13. D. Foxon, *Pope and the Early Eighteenth-Century Book Trade*, rev. and ed. J. McLaverty (Oxford, 1991), p. 153.

14. Ibid., p. 179.
15. Ibid., p. 186 and passim.
16. Ibid., p. 196.
17. Ibid., p. 196.
18. See, for instance, R. Wendorf, *The Elements of Life: Biography and Portrait-Painting in Stuart and Georgian England* (Oxford, 1990), pp. 136–50.
19. For the relative autonomy of the printer, see P. Gaskell, *A New Introduction to Bibliography* (New York and Oxford, 1972), pp. 40–3 and 339 (where note 6 refers to changes in printing practices in the mid-eighteenth century). For a discussion of the book trade, see T. Belanger, 'Publishers and Writers in Eighteenth-Century England', in I. Rivers, ed., *Books and Their Readers in Eighteenth-Century England* (Leicester and New York, 1982), pp. 5–25, and J. Brewer, *The Pleasures of the Imagination: English Culture in the Eighteenth Century* (London and New York, 1997), p. 477.
20. J. Feather, 'British Publishing in the Eighteenth Century: A Preliminary Subject Analysis', *The Library*, 6th series, 8 (1986), pp. 32–46, shows that literature represented about 20 per cent of all titles and that poetry represented 47 per cent of all literary titles.
21. This figure does not include periodicals or later editions of books printed earlier. The *total* figure for all such imprints between 1740 and 1760 is approximately 52,500. I am grateful to John Bloomberg-Rissman of the ESTC for this information.
22. Published by John Noon, *A Defence of Two Discourses* begins entirely in the new style; capitals are used for the occasional important word, such as 'Truth' or 'Saviour'; italics are used for biblical quotations, for titles and for emphasis. For the most part, however, this is a book with very modest capitalization.
23. J. Loewenstein, '*Idem*: Italics and the Genetics of Authorship', *Journal of Medieval and Renaissance Studies*, 20/2 (Fall 1990), pp. 224.
24. This figure is drawn from L. Lipking, *Samuel Johnson: The Life of an Author* (Cambridge, Mass., 1998), p. 117.
25. J. Boswell, *Boswell's Life of Johnson*, ed. G. B. Hill, rev. L. F. Powell (6 vols., Oxford, 1934–50), vol. 1, p. 326.
26. *The Correspondence of Robert Dodsley 1733–1764*, ed. J. E. Tierney (Cambridge, 1988), p. 273.
27. R. Straus, *Robert Dodsley* (London and New York, 1910), p. 291.
28. Foxon, 'Poets and Compositors', p. 256.
29. R. Dodsley, ed., *A Select Collection of Old Plays* (12 vols., London, 1744), vol. 1, p. xxxv.
30. Ibid., p. xxxxvii.
31. Ibid., p. xxxvi.
32. Ibid., p. xxxvi.
33. Ibid., p. xxxxvii.
34. For a full discussion of Dodsley's editorial roles, affecting both substantives and accidentals, see R. Wendorf, 'Dodsley as Editor', *Studies in Bibliography*, 31 (1978), pp. 235–48.

35. I am speaking here of eighteenth-century poetry in particular as it began to be anthologized and thereby placed within the 'modern' canon. For a discussion of canon formation during this period that focuses on the enshrinement of Spenser, Shakespeare and Milton as the exemplars of the English literary tradition, see J. B. Kramnick, *Making the English Canon: Print-Capitalism and the Cultural Past, 1700–1770* (Cambridge, 1998), which essentially argues that the Augustans' early eighteenth-century commodification of politeness and refinement in the canon (as represented by Waller, Denham and even the modernization of Elizabethan texts) was replaced by a mid-eighteenth-century valuation of 'an abstruse, quasi-Latinate vernacular in older, canonical English' and a concurrent disavowal of modern politeness and the novel (pp. 43–4). 'The project of surmounting the difficulty and vulgarity of England's past gives way to one of appreciating the linguistic distance and aesthetic difficulty of Spenser, Shakespeare, and Milton' (p. 44).

　　The changes in typographical conventions that I have been charting in this essay would seem to dovetail with this first, early movement towards refinement and politeness, although it must be kept in mind that this 'modernization' of capitals and italics posed difficulties for readers who were used to relying upon the distinctions and emphasis the older style conveyed. Presumably the conscious valuation of 'the difficulty and vulgarity of England's past' at mid-century flies in the face of attempts such as Dodsley's to rationalize and refine the texts of old English plays.

36. J. Smith, *The Printer's Grammar* (London, 1755), p. 201; elsewhere he refers to the old way as the 'common' way (p. 168) and the new as 'the more modern and neater way' (pp. 201–2).

37. Foxon, 'Poets and Compositors', p. 244.

38. Smith, *The Printer's Grammar*, p. 199: following copy is a 'good law ... now looked upon as obsolete' because authors expect 'the Printer to spell, point, and digest their Copy, that it may be intelligible to the Reader'. The compositor and corrector have joint responsibility for this; both need a 'liberal education' (p. 200). Correctors should revise copy before it goes to the compositor if they suspect any problems, including capitalization (p. 273). Correctors are chosen from compositors 'who are thought capable of that office' (pp. 274–5).

39. Quoted by Foxon, *Pope and the Early Eighteenth-Century Book Trade*, pp. 180–1.

40. Ibid., pp. 181–2.

41. Ibid., p. 182.

42. For Johnson, see G. B. Hill, ed., *Lives of the Poets* (3 vols., Oxford, 1905), vol. 3, p. 19, cited by I. Watt, *The Rise of the Novel: Studies in Defoe, Richardson and Fielding* (Berkeley and Los Angeles, 1957), p. 37; for Burke, see R. Altick, *The English Common Reader* (Chicago, 1950), p. 49. Both Watt and Altick take these statements with a large pinch of salt – and both of their pioneering books are still worth consulting. My own sense is that Johnson was referring to the palpable *growth* in reading of all kinds during the second half of the century as well as the rise of the 'common reader', whereas Burke may have

been drawing a distinction between the educated sector of the public and less sophisticated readers. Johnson would elsewhere refer, satirically, to 'a nation of writers'.

43. Brewer, *The Pleasures of the Imagination*, pp. 167–8.
44. Ibid., p. 169. The model distinguishing between intensive and extensive reading was developed by Rolf Engelsing, a German historian; see R. DeMaria Jr, 'Samuel Johnson and the Reading Revolution', *Eighteenth-Century Life*, 16 (1992), pp. 86–102.
45. Brewer, *The Pleasures of the Imagination*, p. 187.
46. Quoted by Bronson, 'Printing as an Index of Taste', p. 326.
47. *The Spectator*, ed. D. F. Bond (5 vols., Oxford, 1965), vol. 1, p. 269.
48. Ibid., vol. 3, p. 382. By 'Illiterate Readers' Addison may also have been drawing on the traditional definition of literacy, in elite circles, as a knowledge of both Greek and Latin.
49. S. Johnson, *A Dictionary of the English Language*, abridged edn (2 vols., London, 1756), vol. 1, 'Preface'. See A. Reddick, *The Making of Johnson's Dictionary 1746–1773* (Cambridge, 1990), pp. 86–7, for a discussion of this edition.
50. Watt, *The Rise of the Novel*, pp. 39–40.
51. B. Franklin, *Writings*, ed. J. A. L. Lemay (New York, 1987), p. 886.
52. Ibid., p. 1177.
53. Ibid., p. 1176.
54. Ibid., p. 1177. The disappearance of the long 's' in England was greatly influenced by French practices according to J. Mosley, 'S and f: The Origin and Use of the "Long s"' (single sheet, various issues, 1993–9; reprinted in S. Tuohy, *James Mosley: A Checklist of the Published Writings 1958–1995* (Over, Cambridgeshire, 1995), pp. 20–2). For the possible influence of Spanish printers, see Mosley's 'The Disuse of the Long s in Spain' (single sheet, London, 2000).
55. M. Foucault, *The Order of Things: An Archaeology of the Human Sciences* (New York, 1970), p. xii.
56. L. Lipking, *The Ordering of the Arts in Eighteenth-Century England* (Princeton, 1970).
57. P. Langford, *A Polite and Commercial People: England 1727–1783* (Oxford, 1989), p. 2.
58. Johnson, *Poetry and Prose*, p. 127.
59. Ibid., p. 128.
60. Ibid., p. 126.
61. Ibid., p. 130.
62. Ibid., p. 314.
63. Ibid., p. 307.
64. Ibid., p. 304.
65. Ibid., p. 304.
66. Ibid., p. 305.
67. Ibid., p. 138.

68. Ibid., p. 301.

69. Ibid., p. 302.

70. Ibid., p. 322.

71. Ibid., p. 314.

72. Ibid., p. 128.

73. My summary is indebted to E. G. Richards, *Mapping Time: The Calendar and Its History* (Oxford, 1998), pp. 247–56.

74. P. Alkon, 'Changing the Calendar', *Eighteenth-Century Life*, 7/2 (January 1982), p. 7. Alkon's work is corroborated and expanded by R. Poole, *Time's Alteration: Calendar Reform in Early Modern England* (London, 1998).

75. See, for example, J. Hoppit, 'Reforming Britain's Weights and Measures, 1660–1824', *English Historical Review*, 108 (1993), pp. 82–104, and P. Buck, 'People Who Counted: Political Arithmetic in the Eighteenth Century', *Isis*, 73 (1982), pp. 28–45.

    Although I do not have space to draw an extended parallel in this essay, it should at least be noted here that the adoption of printing conventions at mid-century which were generally thought to be more elegant and refined can profitably be compared with a similar development in English prose itself. For a thorough analysis of changes in linguistic usage, see C. McIntosh, *The Evolution of English Prose 1700–1800: Style, Politeness, and Print Culture* (Cambridge, 1998), who charts the movement towards a 'standardization' that encourages 'formality, precision, and abstractness in language', 'a trend towards writtenness and away from the redundancy, sloppiness, and concreteness of speech' (pp. 23–4).

76. Foxon charts the consistency or inconsistency of authors' manuscripts versus their printed texts in 'Poets and Compositors'.

77. S. Johnson, *Diaries, Prayers, and Annals*, ed. E. L. McAdam Jr with D. and M. Hyde, *The Yale Edition of the Works of Samuel Johnson*, vol. 1 (New Haven and London, 1958), pp. 3, 49, 50 (the anniversary of his wife's death), and 309 (his birthday).

78. Franklin, *Writings*, p. 1177.

79. D. C. Greetham, foreword to McGann's *Critique of Modern Textual Criticism*, p. xviii, where he contrasts the 'bibliographical codes' of a text (typography, layout, paper, order) with 'linguistic' ones (the words of the text).

80. Quoted by Bronson, 'Printing as an Index of Taste', p. 326.

PART II

Reading as politics

CHAPTER THREE

'Boasting of silence': women readers
in a patriarchal state

Heidi Brayman Hackel

sixteenth-century treatise on marriage prescribes each spouse's role
armonious household: 'The dutie of the man is, to bee skillfull in
and of the wife, to boast of silence.'¹ Taking this oxymoronic ideal
played silence as emblematic, this essay examines the silence of early
rn women readers – both literal and figurative, prescribed and per-
ed. Certainly, reading in late medieval and early modern England was
en public and social as it was private and silent, and gentlewomen's
ng, in particular, frequently took an oral form. Women's experiences as
rs, however, were nevertheless circumscribed by legal and cultural in-
ions for silence. For women's reading, like women's writing and speak-
aroused controversy and attracted comment throughout the period,²
the pressures of the patriarchal state on female readers can be felt in
statutes, educational practices and conduct books. While legal and in-
tional practices demonstrate the workings of a partriarchal state, early
ern conduct books reveal the assumptions of patriarchy in its 'domestic
', which Kathleen Brown defines as the 'historically specific authority
e father over his household'.³ This essay considers three prescribed
is of female readerly silence – restraint from public reading, limitations
nguistic proficiency and abstention from vocal criticism – as the con-
for women's habitual silence in the margins of their books. As readers'
ginalia have emerged as a central archive for the history of reading in
modern England, that history has focused on goal-orientated, profes-
al and contestatory readings, and it has largely elided women readers.⁴
the cultural and material practices that discouraged women from anno-
ng their books have also made it difficult for modern scholars to write
n into the emerging history of reading. If women as readers are not
emain inaudible, we must shift the fields of evidence and listen very
ely.

n concert with the urgings of conduct books, English laws provided
e room for women's public performance of reading. The application

of benefit of clergy in the sixteenth and seventeenth centuries acknowledged and rewarded the oral performance of reading by men but not by
women. Until 1624, benefit of clergy, which required public oral reading,
was available as a legal loophole only to men (and also, before the Reformation, to professed nuns). By the early seventeenth century, the privilege had
been eliminated for many felonies, including murder, rape, stabbing, piracy,
horse theft and burglary.[5] While serious crimes were increasingly exempted
throughout the period, Cynthia Herrup has demonstrated the widespread
reliance upon this privilege as a compromise between acquittal and capital
punishment for first-time offenders, during a time when all felonies were
punishable by death.[6] Benefit of clergy was granted at startlingly high rates
during the Elizabethan and Jacobean periods – at rates between 80 and
100 per cent of convictions and confessions of clergyable felonies in Sussex.
Even as it was more strictly enforced during Charles I's reign, benefit of
clergy was still extended to well over half of those convicted of or confessing
to clergyable felonies between 1634 and 1640.[7] By contrast, David Cressy
reports that only 29 per cent of people living in Sussex in 1641–4 signed
their names rather than making a mark on state documents.[8] Herrup's
figures, therefore, suggest both the leniency of the test for benefit of clergy
and the possibility of far more widespread reading literacy than studies of
signature literacy have indicated. But not until 1691 could women claim
this privilege for anything beyond petty theft. Pregnant women could exercise benefit of belly, which might be demonstrated by a silent display of
the body, but this privilege merely delayed execution.[9] Whereas benefit of
clergy saved the life of the criminal, that is, benefit of belly saved the life of
the criminal's child.

During this period when the courts did not reward female literacy, Henry
VIII criminalized reading aloud by women with his 1543 Act for the Advancement of True Religion. While cultural ideals of feminine modesty
might demand silence outside the domestic sphere, the reading of the
Bible was so charged that this Henrician act required female readers' silence at home as well.[10] A response to the perceived abuses following the
wide availability of the Bible, this act prohibited the printing, importing,
selling, keeping and using of all Tyndale translations of the Bible, along with
other 'pestiferous and noysoome' books.[11] The act criminalized the reading
of the Bible by most women and by men beneath the rank of yeomen. Gentlewomen were permitted to read the Bible to 'themselves alone' but, unlike
their husbands, they were forbidden from reading Scripture aloud to their
families.[12] All other women were grouped with men of the 'lower Classes'
and prohibited altogether from reading the vernacular Bible. To justify its

rchy of readers, the act points to the varying reception of the vernac-
Bible, which has been used 'to good effecte' by subjects of the 'highest
moste honest sorte' but 'abused' by the 'lower sorte', who 'have therbye
/en and increased in divers naughtie and erronyous opynions'.[13] The
.s revealing for a number of reasons: first, it equates habits of read-
with social status, assigning 'naughtie and erronyous' reading with the
:r ranks; second, it foregrounds gender over class in grouping all women
:ther despite its careful gradations of rank for men and in forbidding
lic reading for all English women, regardless of rank; and finally, it
phasizes the prevalence of aural reading in sixteenth-century England.
the act allows

ye noble man and gentleman being a householder to reade or cause to be red
iny of his famylie or servantes in his house orchard or gardeyne, and to his owne
iylie, any texte of the Byble or New Testament, so the same be doone quietlie
l without disturbaunce of good order.[14]

iis provision extends the scene of devotional reading from the prayer
)set or the great hall out to the grounds of an estate, and it significantly
ows the householder to assign the task of reading to someone – daughter,
fe, servant – who could not otherwise lawfully read the Bible aloud.

While this 1543 act was repealed early in King Edward VI's reign, the
:nder distinction it codified persisted throughout the period both in edu-
itional practices and in conduct manual prescriptions. Eve Sanders argues
iat the Reformation and the humanist educational program issued in a
endering of reading, a departure from the gender-neutral reading prac-
ices of the medieval period. The Reformation eliminated many educa-
ional possibilities for girls and women, closing down both convent schools
ind confraternities.[15] Prohibitions against the admission of girls to grammar schools continued to appear in statutes from the Reformation to the
English Civil War, registering, as Sanders argues, an ongoing debate about
girls' education.[16] While far fewer girls than boys attended school, even
those girls enrolled in schools followed a different curriculum from their
brothers: as boys were taught to read and write and add, girls learned to read,
sew and spin.[17] 'Unlike boys...whose access to education was narrowed
mainly by economic, geographic, and demographic circumstances, girls
of all social backgrounds were the object of purposeful, concerted efforts
at restricting their access to full literacy.'[18] Silenced by a curriculum and
gender ideology that taught them to read but not write, early modern girls
who did not learn to write disappear as readers from the historical record
as well, for it only captures reading accompanied by writing.

The emphasis on reading-only literacy for girls is consistent with the value placed upon silence in contemporary domestic conduct manuals. Like a schoolgirl able to read but not write, the ideal woman constructed in these books listened without speaking, observed without commenting. In their persistence over the course of a century and in the uniformity of their doctrine, these domestic manuals articulated and institutionalized a set of cultural ideals. Beginning with the English translation of Juan Luis Vives's *Instruction of a Christen Woman* (*c*.1529) and continuing until the English Civil War, these manuals advocated the ideals of silence, chastity and obedience with consistency to the point of cliché.[19] Vives encouraged the chaste woman 'in company to holde her tonge demurely. And let fewe se[e] her and none at al here her'; Richard Brathwait, echoing Vives a full century later, asserted that 'all women . . . should be seene, and not heard'.[20] Like the sixteenth-century treatise that assigned to women the duty to 'boast of silence', Brathwait transformed silence into an act of virtuous display: his English Gentlewoman will 'tip her tongue with silence' when in company in recognition that 'Silence in a *Woman* is a mouing Rhetoricke, winning most, when in words it wooeth least.'[21] Citing St Paul's injunction in Corinthians as their authority, domestic manuals equated women's public speech with unruliness, shame and insubordination. Daniel Rogers, for instance, in his *Matrimoniall Honour* (1642) condemns women who display themselves by speaking: 'Such immodesties and insolencies of women, not able to containe themselves within boundes of silence and subjection, I am so farre from warranting, that I here openly defie them as ungrounded, and ungodly.'[22] Rather than subsiding, the pressure on women to be silent seems to have increased in the early seventeenth century.[23]

Though silence was persistently gendered as feminine in domestic manuals throughout the period, these treatises were prescriptive polemics, and, despite their prevalence and consistency, they failed to contain all women's behaviour within the 'boundes of silence'. Many scholars – Ann Rosalind Jones, Barbara Lewalski, Hilary Hinds, Tina Krontiris, Mary Ellen Lamb and others – have documented early modern women's resistance to these patriarchal constructions of femininity.[24] Certainly, there were individual women who did not 'tip their tongues with silence', choosing instead to speak in church, preach in marketplaces, or refute in print the Pauline injunctions for female silence.[25] While many women, therefore, did not internalize these constraints, the treatises nevertheless usefully delineate the dominant view of the accepted scope of feminine behaviour.

The contest between the prescriptions in conduct books and the actions of individual women shows up vividly during the 1650s in an exchange of

ters between a ten-year-old girl, her father and her godfather. Sir Ralph
rney draws upon the rhetoric of contemporary conduct books when he
vises his long-time friend Dr William Denton to exclude from Anne
enton's training both classical languages and shorthand – verbal skills
at would threaten her eventual happiness:

. the pride of taking Sermon noates, hath made multitudes of woemen most
ifortunate . . . if she would learne anything, let her aske you, and afterwards her
isband, *At Home*. Had St. Paul lived in our Times I am most confident hee would
ive fixt a *Shame* upon our woemen for writing (as well as for theire speaking) in
ie Church.²⁶

xpanding upon St Paul, Verney significantly defines virtuous silence to pre-
lude both speaking and writing in public. Taught to write, Anne Denton
vas nevertheless discouraged from learning to write quickly or publicly;
he skill of rapid transcription, especially if used in a church, Verney feared,
vould ruin her. Fast writing, after all, might become fast living. For Verney
hen, like the authors of conduct books, appropriate literacy for women was
ine that was limited in its fluency and its use. His Pauline insistence on the
:ontainment of Anne's education *'At Home'* and Anne's subsequent bold-
iess illustrate the debate about female literacy and learning in the period,
iarticularly as the correspondence moves beyond a discussion of religious
iractice to address secular reading and linguistic proficiency.

Perhaps encouraged by her father's more progressive attitudes towards
girls' education, Anne Denton expresses an interest in learning the classical
anguages. Still orthographically clumsy even by early modern standards,
:he young Anne Denton declares to her godfather her intellectual acquis-
tiveness: 'i know you and my coussenes wil out rech me in french, but
am a goeng whaar i hop i shal out rech you in ebri grek and laten'.²⁷ Not
inly does this young girl aspire to learn Hebrew, Greek and Latin, but she
;eeks to *outreach* her godfather in these skills. The letter also hints at an
awareness on Anne's part that such aspirations will goad her godfather; she
seems to know, that is, on just what grounds to bait him. Such awareness
in a ten-year-old girl suggests that the opposing views on girls' education
were clearly enough drawn as to be accessible to a clever child.

Surprised by the young girl's ambitions, Verney tries to dissuade her by
appealing to the accepted scope of feminine education:

Good sweet hart bee not soe covitous; beleeve me a Bible (with ye Common
prayer) and a good plaine cattichisme in your Mother Tongue being well read and
practised, is well worth all the rest and much more sutable to your sex; I know

your Father thinks this false doctrine, but bee confident your husband will bee of my oppinion.[28]

Invoking Anne's as yet hypothetical husband, Verney alludes to the legal reality that Anne's identity and care will one day pass from her father's to her husband's hands. Verney first parrots the view of contemporary conduct manuals that devotional texts are the most appropriate reading for women, but he goes on to recommend secular French books to the young girl, bribing her with the promise of a small French library and including in its contents precisely those books so often characterized as 'light' and 'undecent':[29]

In French you cannot bee too cunning for that language affords many admirable bookes fit for you as Romances, Plays, Poetry, Stories of illustrious (not learned) Woemen, receipts for preserving, makinge creames and all sorts of cookeryes, ordring your gardens and in Breif all manner of good housewifery. *If* you please to have a little patience with yourselfe (without Hebre, Greeke, or Lattin) when I goe to Paris againe I will send you halfe a dozen of the french bookes to begin your Library.[30]

Verney's offer of seed books for Anne's library is an instructive reminder that the prescriptions of conduct books were not an unbreakable set; rather, someone like Verney might endorse much of the doctrine of feminine conduct literature while ignoring other aspects. For Verney, at least, the modesty that was threatened if Anne Denton wrote in church was not similarly imperilled if she read French plays and romances.

Did Anne Denton settle for a library of French literature and housewifery manuals? How many of the many early modern gentlewomen's libraries of herbals, romances and French New Testaments represent compromises and second choices finally accepted by girls who gave up on their 'ebri grek and laten'? Scholarship does not yet have full answers to the questions raised by the provocative Denton–Verney exchange; however, the frequent presence of French books and the corresponding absence of Latin books in the collections of early modern gentlewomen suggest the dominance of Verney's view that classical learning had no proper place in a woman's life.

Verney's expectation of a girl's silence in church is predictable within the contemporary gender ideologies that equated silence with modesty, piety and femininity. Women's silence in the margins of their books, however, is more puzzling, for manuscript marginalia would seem to offer a place for women's voices uttered silently and privately 'At Home'. But, in general, very little early modern marginalia can be definitively attributed to women readers.[31] Frances Egerton (1585–1636), who catalogued her London library of 241 books, did not annotate any of the surviving copies that bear her marks of ownership on the bindings and flyleaves. Frances Wolfreston (1607–77) wrote 'Frances Wolfreston hor book' on the flyleaves of ninety-five books that have survived, thereby establishing both her ability to sign and her willingness to mark her books, but she almost never annotated her books.[32] Elizabeth Puckering (c.1621–89), whose initials or signature have been identified in nearly one hundred volumes, was 'not in the habit of annotating her books as she read'.[33] Even in a book such as *The Countess of Pembroke's Arcadia*, which was addressed both generically and explicitly to women, no known examples of substantial annotations can be attributed to female readers. In one sample of one hundred copies of Sidney's *Arcadia* printed between 1593 and 1638, for example, 60 per cent of the sample bears readers' marks, yet none of these can be linked paleographically to the women who wrote their names in twenty-two of these books.[34]

The scarcity of women's marginalia poses an obstacle in the recovery of women's reading practices and highlights the methodological limitations inherent in this form of evidence. Many of the early modern readers we know best – such as Gabriel Harvey and John Dee – remain visible and vocal because of their marginalia, which Carol Meale has called the only 'incontestable evidence' of reading.[35] Such a reliance upon marginalia as evidence does, of course, leave many early modern readers invisible: those whose books have not survived, those who never owned books, those who could read but not write, those who simply never felt inclined to annotate their books, and indeed those who read their books to pieces.[36] Of these many invisible readers, I will pursue here the likely reasons behind the silent margins left by women who owned books and wrote their names in them.

While the subject of marginalia is not often addressed in conduct books, a few statements about the propriety of women's writing in books suggest the narrow confines of permissible annotation.[37] Vives counsels the Christian woman to copy religious passages rather than 'voyde verses' as handwriting practice, and Anne Boleyn is said to have scolded a gentlewoman in her household for scribbling 'idle posies' in a prayer book.[38] Boleyn herself reportedly annotated Tyndale's *Obedience of a Christian Man* for the king with her fingernail.[39] The curious nature of such a marking – at once nearly imperceptible and provocatively physical, both demure and bold – suggests an ambivalence towards marginalia. Annotating without a pen, Boleyn makes literal the pointing fists of contemporary manuscript and printed marginalia. Boleyn's fingernail annotations nicely represent

accepted feminine marginalia: non-interpretive (even non-verbal) finger-
ing of key passages in a religious work. And yet while no annotations remain
that we can *read*, Boleyn clearly made a gesture of deep engagement with
this text as she quite literally left her impression upon it.

Anne Boleyn's method of inkless marking is included in a discussion of
annotations in John Brinsley's book of pedagogy, *Ludus Literarius, or The
Grammar Schoole* (1612). Urging schoolmasters to train students to mark
both the difficult and excellent bits in their books, Brinsley suggests three
methods of annotation:

> it is best to note all schoole books with inke; & also all others, which you would
> have gotten *ad unguem*, as we use to say, or wherof we would have daily or long
> practice because inke will indure: neither wil such books be the worse for their
> noting, but the better, if they be noted with iudgement. But for all other bookes,
> which you would have faire againe at your pleasure; note them with a pensil of
> black lead: for that you may rub out againe when you will, with the crums of new
> wheate bread.
>
> The very little ones, which reade but English, may make some secret markes
> thus at every hard word; though but with some little dint with their naile; so that
> they doe not marre their bookes.[40]

Ink, pencil, or the impression of a fingernail: Brinsley characterizes each
method as suitable to a particular reading practice. Both the book *and* the
reader must warrant ink annotations; lesser books and lesser readers should
produce erasable or nearly imperceptible marks. Curiously, Brinsley's use
of the Latin phrase 'ad unguem' (literally 'to the fingernail', figuratively,
'perfectly') works counter to his hierarchy of annotation methods, for it is
imperfect readers who should annotate by nail. As one might expect in a
pedagogical treatise, Brinsley emphasizes the 'use' to be made of reading.
Ink annotations by competent readers, rather than marring a book, will
make it more useful and hence more valuable. Brinsley counsels schoolmasters to 'have the choysest bookes of most great learned men, & the
notablest students all marked through thus, in all matters eyther obscure,
or of principall & most necessary use'.[41]

Unlike the reading of 'schoole books' or devotional works, gentlewomen's secular reading was constructed in opposition to such 'necessary
use' as trivial and passive, though sometimes morally perilous. These notions surely encouraged women's silence in the margins. Further contribut-
ing to this discourse of women's reading as passive was the practice of
aural reading, popular among the elite from the fourteenth to the eighteenth centuries in England.[42] The lack of readers' marks in their books
may, therefore, be a practical consequence of such a reading habit, for the

arrangement sets up a degree of physical and vocal – if not intellectual – passivity. Lady Margaret Hoby, who regularly wrote notes in her Bible, also recorded her habit of listening to a reader, as she did in a diary entry for November 21, 1599: 'after dinner I wrought and h[e]ard Mr Rhodes Read tell all most supper time'.[43] Though she often wrote notes in private, it is needlework, not writing, that accompanied her aural reading. Lady Anne Clifford, too, frequently recorded 'hearing of reading'. In her diary of 1616–19, she writes twenty-three times about a specific moment of reading, nineteen of which are scenes of aural reading. Two records exemplify this practice: 'Mr *Dumbell* read a great part of the History of the Netherlands . . . Upon the 9th I sat at my work and heard *Rivers* and *Marsh* read Montaigne's Essays which book they have read almost this fortnight'.[44] Often only an awareness of this convention establishes Clifford as a participant – rather than a mere eavesdropper – in these readings.

Notations in extant books, both secular and devotional, also document this reading practice and provide further clues about the dynamics between readers and listeners. A careful record of one reading of *Barclay His Argenis* survives from the early seventeenth century: 'I began to reade this booke to yor: Ladiship the xvjth day of January: 1625: and ended it the xxvth of the same moneth.'[45] This now anonymous pair – a reader and a noblewoman – read through the romance, therefore, at the fairly voracious pace of forty folio pages a day. It seems wrong to label as passive a noblewoman who orchestrated such a reading, particularly if we think of the authority given to the householder in Henry VIII's 1543 act, who may 'cause [the Bible] to be read'.[46] Certainly, the arrangement challenges our definition of the term 'reader' itself. While it is the lector of the book not the female listener who has recorded the reading history in this case, the inscription addresses the lady in the second person, thereby suggesting the possibility of scribal annotations. And, indeed, a recently identified set of marginal annotations in a copy of *A Mirror for Magistrates* testifies to precisely this practice in Lady Anne Clifford's household.[47] Written between 1670 and 1673, these marginalia form 'a detailed reading diary' of the octogenarian Clifford's encounter with this volume, which she both heard read aloud and read to herself.[48] Representative annotations record the mix of voices and hands inscribed in the margins of this book: 'some part of this I red over my selfe and rest of [it] Wm. Watkinson read to me the 30: 31st of March 1670 in Brough Castle', 'this I red over in Pendragon Ca: the 15: of May 1670', and 'part of this Chap[ter] was read over by yor La[dyship] and the rest by some of yor mense[r]vants in Pendragon Ca[stle]: in Westmoreland the 20 of May'.[49] A reader needs to handle a book in order to annotate it in her own hand, but, as this extraordinary record of Clifford's reading demonstrates, a listener might dictate marginal commentary or alternate between aural and solitary reading. However, unless a compulsive reader such as Clifford leaves such a reading diary in the margins, scribal annotations disappear into the hand of the scribe.

It was not just aural reading that interfered with and complicated the practice of annotating: the habit of reading away from a desk or table also would have made it difficult to annotate a book during the era of quill pens. Many contemporary literary accounts – both those that satirized and those that solicited female readers – envisioned ladies reading with books in their laps. This imagined posture not only trivialized and eroticized women's reading, but it also made annotation unlikely. Reading with a book in one's lap would have made annotation messy, if not wholly impractical, for in addition to a quill pen, the reader would need to balance a penknife, inkpot and perhaps a sachet of pouncing powder.[50]

For the women constructed in these literary accounts, secular books were diversions, interchangeable with trifles, needlework and lapdogs. This trivialization of women's reading surely discouraged women from marking in their books, an activity, John Brinsley reminds us, that made books useful. In an epistle to the female readers of *Euphues and His England*, John Lyly conjures up a conventional scene of reading and suggests how gentlewomen might treat his book: 'I am content that your Dogges lye in your laps, so *Euphues* may be in your hands, that when you shall be wearie in reading of the one, you may be ready to sport with the other.'[51] The poet Francis Quarles uses language almost identical to Lyly's when he addresses his readers: '*Ladies* (for in your silken laps I know this book will choose to lye) ... my suit is, that you would be pleased to give the faire *Parthenia* your noble entertainment.'[52] In both letters, the female reader is clearly figured as a gentlewoman – a lady holding a lapdog or dressed in silks who is in a position to bestow favours.[53] So too a current of distinctly sexual language moves through both letters as the female reader is solicited to 'sport with' and 'entertain' the book in her fair lap.

While Lyly and Quarles use this sexualized language as prefatory rhetoric, Richard Brathwait participates in the same discourse to dissuade the English gentlewoman from such secular reading: '*Venus* and *Adonis* are unfitting Consorts for a Ladies bosome. Remoue them timely from you, if they ever had entertainment by you.'[54] Like Lyly and Quarles, Brathwait refers to Shakespeare's poem by its title characters, heightening the sense of the physical involvement of the woman's body in her reading, for he imagines the characters themselves – not merely the octavo – at the lady's bosom.[55]

Thomas Middleton eroticizes the female reader even more explicitly in *A Mad World, My Masters*, when his courtesan advises Mistress Harebrain on her reading:

> If [your husband] chance to steal upon you, let him find
> Some book like open 'gainst an unchaste mind,
> And coted scriptures, though for your own pleasure
> You read some stirring pamphlet, and convey it
> Under your skirt, the fittest place to lay it.   (1.2.86–90)

A woman might finger such a 'stirring pamphlet' under her skirt, but she certainly couldn't annotate it. On the one hand, these constructions of women's reading trivialized it so that marginalia would seem ridiculous; however, conduct books also voiced the anxiety that women might be overly attentive to their reading and seek to make use of it. Brathwait, for example, advises the English gentleman to throw any books of love 'to the darkest corner of our studies', and he then imagines women readers attending excessively to such books as they carry 'about them (even in their naked Bosomes, where chastest desires should only lodge) the amorous toyes of *Venus* and *Adonis*: which Poem ... they heare with such attention, peruse with such devotion, and retaine with such delectation'.[56] Attending, perusing and retaining: these habits of reading were urged by humanists and often facilitated by annotation. Brathwait is alarmed, it seems, by the intensity of women readers' attention to love poetry, and he worries that they will read it as one should read a school text or Bible.

Though not in the eroticized language of these prefaces and conduct manuals, entries in women's diaries similarly cast secular reading as a pastime often performed concurrently with another activity, much as Lyly imagines. The context in which Anne Clifford presents much of her reading advances this notion of feminine reading as play and as a diversion. In entries from 1617 and 1619, she wrote: 'The 12th and 13th I spent most of the time in playing at Glecko and hearing *Moll Neville* read the Arcadia ... The 30th and 31st I spent in hearing of reading, and playing at tables with the Steward.'[57] In these diary entries, Clifford presents card-playing and reading as nearly interchangeable (and perhaps concurrent) activities. Even the bibliophile Christina of Sweden, who at one time commanded a royal library of 8,000 volumes, reportedly found Tacitus 'as interesting as a game of chess' and read Plato before picnics and games of charades.[58] For men, too, reading was, of course, sometimes a diversion. But reading as a diversion was generally cast as feminine, and books read in this way were characterized as 'trifles' or 'toyes'.

Conventional early modern portraits present male and female sitters in different relations to books. In a portrait that includes books, a male sitter typically demonstrates an active connection and engagement with the text; often seated in a study, he is frequently surrounded by books, many of them opened, and by other signs of learnedness, and he often marks his engagement by writing. Even in portraits of less scholarly men, the subject often fingers a book, keeping his place as he is interrupted by the gaze of the painter or viewer. This physical contact with the book visually defines the literate man, and it appears in literary accounts as well. Bernard André praises the intellectual accomplishments of a young prince by listing the books that the boy has read and handled by age sixteen: Arthur, the son of Henry VII, 'had either committed in part to memory or had at least *handled* and read ... *with his own hands and eyes* all of the following'.[59] In *The Forrest of Fancy*, the scholarly man is happiest when he has precisely this immediate, physical access to books: 'setled in his study, there to tosse and turne his bokes, perusing the workes of auncient wrighters'.[60]

In his letter to the female readers of *Euphues and His England*, Lyly echoes this gendered convention as he defines his desired female audience: '*Euphues* had rather lye shut in a Ladyes casket, then open in a Schollers studie.' Contemporary portraits of early modern women typically depict closed books as props or mere decoration.[61] Unlike analogous portraits of men, female sitters often do not even make physical contact with the books within the frame. Open books – books in use – are masculine; clasped books, like chaste women, are feminine. The extraordinary portrait of Mary Neville, Lady Dacre, by Hans Eworth plays with this convention by posing its subject much like her male contemporaries: interrupted by our gaze, Lady Dacre pauses with a quill poised over an open book as she holds her place in another book with her left hand. This portrait may be unique in sixteenth-century English portraiture for its depiction of a contemporary woman writing, for 'writing and reading, particularly in a pictorial context, are usually associated with a man'.[62] A significant departure from this convention is the iconographic tradition of the Virgin Mary pictured as a reader, especially in paintings of the Annunciation. Even as Protestant iconography moved away from such depictions of Mary, an Englishwoman's virtue might still be announced – as Middleton's courtesan suggests – by her handling of an open devotional text. Even the solid, manly Lady Dacre holds her place in a devotional book, signified by the illuminated letter visible on the open verso.[63]

Conduct books urged women to be silent, self-contained, 'solitarie and withdrawne'.[64] While such admonitions most directly relate to women's interactions with their husbands and other men, they might also apply to women's interactions with books. Voracious female readers often read on the sly; both Elizabeth Cary and Lucy Hutchinson, for instance, read covertly throughout adolescence, Hutchinson sometimes resorting to 'steal[ing] into some hole or other to read'.[65] It was not only patriarchal conduct manuals and meddling mothers that produced such covert readings; prefaces to women's books also constructed women readers as silent. John Lyly pairs his letter 'To the Ladies and Gentlewomen of England' with one 'To the Gentlemen Readers' of *Euphues and His England*. While the two prefatory epistles are clearly companions, they invite different, gendered readings of the text. Lyly first asks women for their silence as readers:

crauing this only, that hauing read, you conceale your censure, writing your iudgments as you do the posies in your rings, which are alwayes next to the finger, not to be seene of him that holdeth you by the hands, and yet known to you that wear them on your hands.

Lyly encourages his 'Gentlemen Readers', on the other hand, to 'say that is best, which he lyketh best', and he urges them to 'correcte [any errors] with your pennes'. Though Lyly asks both gentlewomen and gentlemen for their complicity as readers, masculine complicity produces collaborative corrections, while female complicity yields silence.

Lyly does not deny that his female readers will form critical opinions of his work, nor does he discourage them from 'writing [their] iudgments'. He begs of them only to conceal these opinions. In doing so, he continues to eroticize female readers and their responses as he casts the woman as promiscuous, presumably concealing the posies of one lover from the one who holds her hand. While only an analogy, this passage offers the tantalizing prospect that early modern women did record their reactions to their reading, but that they kept them, like the engraving inside a gold ring, hidden from public view, hidden indeed even from those who held their hands. If so, we must learn to turn these rings inside out, as it were, by searching for records of women's private responses in their correspondence and in their journals. Alternatively, we might stop looking for engraved records of reading and turn our attention instead to the rings themselves – that is, towards records of consumption.

As Lyly's attention to concealment suggests, the margins of early modern books may not have been the private spaces we might suppose they were. Perhaps, instead, as books circulated within households, the margins were a fairly public space, inviting the marks of many hands, but also putting those hands on display. Certainly, the palimpsests of ownership marks so common in early modern books indicate the many hands through which books passed. One 1627 copy of the *Arcadia*, for example, bears sixteen contemporaneous signatures on its flyleaves and in its margins (along with lines of poetry, resolutions of debts, school exercises, mottos, drawings, even a legal summons and a laundry list).[66] Marginalia, therefore, like personal letters, may never have been fully private. In a letter urging her daughter to 'keep your resolutions with silence', Margaret Clifford counseled her daughter, Anne, to be cautious when writing: 'Dear heart be very wary what you say but most wary what you write.'[67] This wariness that Margaret Clifford urged upon her daughter and that conduct books insisted upon may well have discouraged women from writing in their books. Annotations, after all, leave evidence not just for the modern historian of reading but also for a reader's contemporaries in a household where books circulated through many sets of hands.

The women whose traces I have tried to uncover may seem to have been passive and silent if we assume that active reading requires a written record or response, but women often demonstrated otherwise that books played an important role in their lives. Many gentlewomen displayed the importance of their book ownership in elaborate bindings, careful catalogues, commissioned portraits, gift exchanges and final bequests. Frances Egerton passed many of her books to her son, the future earl of Bridgewater; Anne Clifford allowed her servants to choose books from a small collection quarterly and commissioned a portrait of herself flanked by books;[68] and Anne Boleyn dinted a copy of Tyndale's devotional work and gave it to the king. Frances Wolfreston, who inscribed her books 'Frances Wolfreston hor book', arranged for the continued integrity of her collection even after her death. In her will, Wolfreston makes the bequest of her books to her son conditional upon his willingness to loan books to his siblings and then return them 'to their places againe'.[69] For many women, it was perhaps in their physical control of books (what we might call their consumption) – in their organizing, cataloguing and bestowal – that they demonstrated to others their engagement with the world of books. Books, after all, may have been accommodated more easily as household objects than as discursive texts. Anne Clifford's eulogist offers an insight to the modern historian of reading when he asserts that books do reveal something about their owners: 'She much delighted in that holy Book, it was her Companion, and when persons, or their affections, cannot so well be known by themselves, they may be guessed at by their Companions.'[70] Like this seventeenth-century clergyman, I would argue that the books that women inscribed and stamped and catalogued were their 'Companions', and that they tell us about their 'persons' and 'their affections'. And what we may 'guess' is that books and reading were central and serious matters for these women – not to be exchanged on a whim for a lapdog and not to be slipped under one's skirt.

NOTES

I am grateful to Kevin Sharpe and Steven Zwicker for providing the initial occasion for this essay and for arranging such a productive, exciting exchange of ideas at the Huntington Library. For their careful readings of an early version of this essay, I am indebted to Frances Dolan, Ian Moulton, Eve Sanders, Katherine Scheil, and Steven Zwicker.

1. R. Cleaver, *A Codly* [*sic*] *Form of Householde Governement* (London, 1598), p. 169.
2. For analyses of reading as a contested activity, see M. Ferguson, 'A Room Not Their Own: Renaissance Women as Readers and Writers', in C. Koelb and S. Noakes, eds., *The Comparative Perspective on Literature* (Ithaca, 1988), p. 115; M. E. Lamb, *Gender and Authorship in the Sidney Circle* (Madison, Wisc., 1990), p. 19; F. E. Dolan, 'Reading, Writing, and Other Crimes', in V. Traub, M. L. Kaplan and D. Callaghan, eds., *Feminist Readings of Early Modern Culture: Emerging Subjects* (Cambridge, 1996), pp. 142–67; J. Pearson, 'Women Reading, Reading Women', in H. Wilcox, ed., *Women and Literature in Britain, 1500–1700* (Cambridge, 1996), p. 80; K. Walker, *Women Writers of the English Renaissance* (New York and London, 1996), pp. 15–20; and E. R. Sanders, *Gender and Literacy on Stage in Early Modern England* (Cambridge, 1998), p. 3.
3. K. Brown, *Good Wives, Nasty Wenches, and Anxious Patriarchs: Gender, Race, and Power in Colonial Virginia* (Chapel Hill, N.C., 1996), p. 4. In their studies of patriarchy in early modern England, Margaret J. M. Ezell (*The Patriarch's Wife: Literary Evidence and the History of the Family*, Chapel Hill, N.C., 1987, pp. 3–8) and Anthony Fletcher (*Gender, Sex, and Subordination in England, 1500–1800*, New Haven, 1995, pp. xv–xvi) usefully insist upon the historical specificity of this subject.
4. For the most important work in this field centred on marginalia, see L. Jardine and A. Grafton, ' "Studied for Action": How Gabriel Harvey Read His Livy', *Past and Present*, 129 (1990), pp. 30–78; W. H. Sherman, *John Dee: The Politics of Reading and Writing in the English Renaissance* (Amherst, Mass., 1995), and 'What Did Renaissance Readers Write in Their Books?', in J. Andersen and E. Sauer, eds., *Books and Readers in Early Modern England: Material Studies* (Philadelphia, 2002), pp. 119–37; and S. N. Zwicker, 'Reading the Margins: Politics and the Habits of Appropriation', in K. Sharpe and S. N. Zwicker, eds., *Refiguring Revolutions: Aesthetics and Politics from the English Revolution to the Romantic Revolution* (Berkeley and London, 1998), pp. 101–15. Kevin Sharpe, whose study relies instead upon some sixty manuscript volumes,

provides an efficient survey of this emerging field (*Reading Revolutions: The Politics of Reading in Early Modern England*, New Haven and London, 2000, pp. 274–7). See also H. J. Jackson, *Marginalia: Readers Writing in Books* (New Haven and London, 2001) for a learned survey of the practice from 1700 to 2000.

5. C. B. Herrup, *The Common Peace: Participation and the Criminal Law in Seventeenth-Century England* (Cambridge, 1987), p. 48; Dolan, 'Reading, Writing, and Other Crimes', pp. 145–56; *Statutes of the Realm*, vol. 3 (London, 1817), passim. For a discussion of the unequal application of the privilege both before and after the closure of the convents, see Sanders, *Gender and Literacy on Stage*, p. 17.

6. Herrup, *The Common Peace*, p. 48.

7. Ibid., p. 49, table 3.5.

8. D. Cressy, *Literacy and the Social Order: Reading and Writing in Tudor and Stuart England* (Cambridge, 1980), p. 201.

9. Dolan, 'Reading, Writing, and Other Crimes', pp. 145–6; Herrup, *The Common Peace*, p. 143.

10. 34 and 35 Henry VIII, chapter 1, *Statutes*, pp. 894–7.

11. Ibid., pp. 894–5.

12. Ibid., p. 896.

13. Ibid.

14. Ibid.

15. Sanders, *Gender and Literacy on Stage*, pp. 18–19. Margaret Ferguson has characterized recent feminist work as demonstrating that 'if women did not have a Renaissance, they did at least have a Reformation' ('Moderation and Its Discontents: Recent Work on Renaissance Women', *Feminist Studies*, 20 (1994), p. 352).

16. Sanders, *Gender and Literacy on Stage*, pp. 21–2.

17. M. Spufford, *Small Books and Pleasant Histories: Popular Fiction and Its Readership in Seventeenth-Century England* (Cambridge, 1981), pp. 22, 34–5.

18. Sanders, *Gender and Literacy on Stage*, p. 170.

19. Jacques Du Bosc, in a late example, identifies the three perfections of *The Compleat Woman* (London, 1639) as 'Discretion, Silence, and Modesty' (p. 18). Suzanne W. Hull names her useful book on prescriptive literature after this triad: *Chaste, Silent, and Obedient: English Books for Women, 1475–1640* (San Marino, Calif., 1988). For more on the ideal of silence, see L. Jardine, *Still Harping on Daughters: Women and Drama in the Age of Shakespeare* (New York, 1983), pp. 37–67, 106–13; M. P. Hannay, ed., *Silent but for the Word: Tudor Women as Patrons, Translators, and Writers of Religious Works* (Kent, Ohio, 1985), pp. 1–14; K. U. Henderson and B. F. McManus, eds., *Half Humankind: Contexts and Texts of the Controversy about Women in England, 1540–1640* (Urbana, Ill., 1985), pp. 53–5; P. Stallybrass, 'Patriarchal Territories: The Body Enclosed', in M. W. Ferguson, M. Quilligan and N. J. Vickers, eds., *Rewriting the Renaissance: The Discourses of Sexual Difference in Early Modern Europe* (Chicago, 1986), pp. 126–7; and Walker, *Women Writers*, pp. 8–15.

20. J. L. Vives, *A Very Frutefull and Pleasant Boke Called the Instruction of a Christen Woman*, trans. R. Hyrd (London, 1529?), facsimile edn in D. Bornstein, ed., *Distaves and Dames: Renaissance Treatises for and about Women* (Delmar, N.Y., 1978), sig. E2v; R. Brathwait, *The English Gentlewoman* (London, 1631), p. 41.

21. Brathwait, *The English Gentlewoman*, pp. 89–90.

22. D. Rogers, *Matrimoniall Honour* (London, 1642), p. 285.

23. A. R. Jones, 'Nets and Bridles: Early Modern Conduct Books and Sixteenth-Century Women's Lyrics', in N. Armstrong and L. Tennenhouse, eds., *The Ideology of Conduct: Essays on Literature and the History of Sexuality* (New York, 1987), pp. 60–1.

24. Jones, 'Nets and Bridles'; B. K. Lewalski, *Writing Women in Jacobean England* (Cambridge, Mass., 1993), p. 3; H. Hinds, *God's Englishwomen: Seventeenth-Century Radical Sectarian Writing and Feminist Criticism* (Manchester, 1996), pp. 38–42; and T. Krontiris, *Oppositional Voices: Women as Writers and Translators of Literature in the English Renaissance* (London, 1992). For women's resistance as readers specifically, see Mary Ellen Lamb, who characterizes the constructions of female readers in these manuals as 'finally only caricatures, distorted by ideological functions' ('Constructions of Women Readers', in S. Woods and M. P. Hannay, eds., *Teaching Tudor and Stuart Women Writers*, New York, 2000, p. 32); and S. Roberts, 'Reading in Early Modern England: Contexts and Problems', *Critical Survey*, 12/2 (2000), pp. 2–5. For other compelling accounts of the disjunctions between such prescriptions and practice, see Sanders, *Gender and Literacy on the Stage*, pp. 6–7; A. L. Erickson, *Women and Property in Early Modern England* (London, 1993), p. 236; and Fletcher, *Gender, Sex, and Subordination*, pp. 101–25.

25. Hinds discusses a pamphlet written by two Quaker women in jail, *To the Priests and People of England* (London, 1655), which explicitly refutes the Pauline injunctions for silence (*God's Englishwomen*, pp. 182–4).

26. M. M. Verney, *Memoirs of the Verney Family*, vol. 3: *During the Commonwealth, 1650 to 1660* (London, 1894), p. 72.

27. Ibid., p. 73.

28. Ibid., pp. 73–4.

29. Thomas Salter excludes books of love and 'undecent bookes' from the reading list of virtuous women (*A Mirrhor Mete for All Mothers, Matrones, and Maidens*, London, 1579, sig. C3r), as do Vives (*Instruction of a Christen Woman*, sig. B2v, sig. F2r), H. Bullinger (*The Christen State of Matrimonye*, Antwerp, 1541, sig. K4v), and Brathwait (*The English Gentlewoman*, p. 139; *The English Gentleman*, London, 1630, p. 28) in their conduct manuals.

30. Verney, *Memoirs*, vol. 3, p. 74, emphasis mine.

31. I draw here on my surveys of early English printed books in the British Museum and the Huntington, Folger and Bodleian libraries, and I exclude non-verbal marks that cannot be dated or attributed. For an analysis of a more general survey and a lucid discussion of methodological challenges, see Sherman, 'What Did Renaissance Readers Write?'. His study focuses on 'more substantial

annotations', providing figures for the presence of 'early manuscript notes' rather than ownership marks and non-verbal markings (pp. 120, 122).

32. For a description and edition of Frances Egerton's library catalogue, see my essay 'The Countess of Bridgewater's London Library', in Andersen and Sauer, eds., *Books and Readers*, pp. 138–54. The ninety-five books signed by Wolfreston have been identified by Morgan as remnants of what may have been a library of more than 400 volumes. A few of Wolfreston's books carry brief appraisals or summaries on the flyleaves, and four tracts have been inscribed with her verses on the blank pages, but most of the located copies have no annotations (P. Morgan, 'Frances Wolfreston and "Hor Bouks": A Seventeenth-Century Woman Book-Collector', *The Library*, 6th series, 11 (1989), pp. 204, 207). In contrast, Lady Margaret Hoby frequently recorded in her diary that she 'wrett my notes in my testement' and transcribed bits from a sermon 'in my Comune place book' (*Diary of Lady Margaret Hoby, 1599–1605*, ed. D. M. Meads, London, 1930, pp. 70, 144, and passim). Hoby's practice, which is unusual in the survival of its careful documentation, is notably part of her religious reading. For an astute analysis of her diary, see M. E. Lamb, 'Margaret Hoby's Diary: Women's Reading Practices and the Gendering of the Reformation Subject', in S. King, ed., *Pilgrimage for Love: Essays in Early Modern Literature in Honor of Josephine A. Roberts* (Tempe, Ariz., 1999), pp. 63–94.

33. D. McKitterick, 'Women and Their Books in Seventeenth-Century England: The Case of Elizabeth Puckering', *The Library*, 7th series, 1 (2000), p. 372.

34. Contemporary ownership signatures appear in forty-five of these books, of which twenty-two are signed by at least one woman. Sixty-two books contain contemporary readers' marks of some kind; twenty of these are substantial. This sample, which consists of copies at twenty-five archives, is part of my ongoing survey of contemporary owners' and readers' marks in copies of the *Arcadia* printed between 1590 and 1674. For a discussion of readers' marks in thirty-two copies printed by 1739 and now held by the Folger Shakespeare Library, see P. Lindenbaum, 'Sidney's *Arcadia* as Cultural Monument and Proto-Novel', in C. C. Brown and A. F. Marotti, eds., *Texts and Cultural Change in Early Modern England* (Basingstoke and London, 1997), pp. 84–7.

35. C. M. Meale, ' "...alle the bokes that I haue of latyn, englisch, and frensch": Laywomen and Their Books in Late Medieval England', in Meale, ed., *Women and Literature in Britain, 1150–1500* (Cambridge, 1993), p. 134. Other indisputable forms of evidence survive as well for the early modern period in women's diaries, letters and translations.

36. Sherman speculates that the practice of annotation 'must have been more widespread' than his figures suggest because readers' handling of books contributes to their deterioration and because later readers and booksellers often effaced early marks ('What Did Renaissance Readers Write?', p. 122).

37. For a more general statement of the anxieties prompted by women's writing, see Walker (*Women Writers*, pp. 20–5), who points to conduct books' collapsing of the distinction between immodest speech and writing.

In *The French Academie*, for example, de La Primaudaye asserts that 'the same rules and precepts that belong to speaking, agree also to writing' (*Women Writers*, p. 21).

38. Vives, *Instruction of a Christen Woman*, sig. E2r, discussed by V. Wayne, 'Some Sad Sentence: Vives' Instruction of a Christian Woman', in Hannay, ed., *Silent but for the Word*, pp. 21–2. For Boleyn, see J. Boffey, 'Women Authors and Women's Literacy in Fourteenth- and Fifteenth-Century England', in Wilcox, ed., *Women and Literature*, p. 174.

39. M. Dowling, 'Anne Boleyn and Reform', *Journal of Ecclesiastical History*, 35 (1984), p. 36.

40. J. Brinsley, *Ludus Literarius, or The Grammar Schoole* (London, 1612), pp. 46–7.

41. Ibid., p. 45.

42. J. Coleman, *Public Reading and the Reading Public in Late Medieval England and France*, (Cambridge, 1996); R. Chartier, 'The Practical Impact of Writing', *A History of Private Life*, vol. 3: *Passions of the Renaissance*, trans. A. Goldhammer (Cambridge, Mass., 1989), pp. 147–52.

43. *Diary of Lady Margaret Hoby*, p. 85.

44. *The Diary of the Lady Anne Clifford*, ed. V. Sackville-West (London, 1923), p. 41. See also *The Diary of Anne Clifford, 1616–1619: A Critical Edition*, ed. K. O. Acheson (New York, 1995).

45. Huntington Library Rare Book 97024. On the basis of paleographic analysis and a comparison with the notes and hands in the Orgel volume discussed below, I have since identified her 'Ladiship' as Anne Clifford. For a full discussion of this volume and its annotations, see my forthcoming book on early modern readers.

46. Pearson characterizes listening as 'passive reading' ('Women Reading', p. 82), and she argues persuasively that women were not encouraged to be active readers or writers (p. 84). Alberto Manguel reports a modern version of the reader as chauffeur when he recounts his job as a reader to the blind Borges (*A History of Reading*, New York, 1996, pp. 17–19).

47. Stephen Orgel owns this copy of the 1610 *Mirror*, which he very kindly allowed me to examine. A preliminary description of the volume and several reproductions appear in Orgel, 'Margins of Truth', in A. Murphy, ed., *Renaissance Text: Theory, Editing, Textuality* (Manchester, 2000), pp. 95–9. Orgel's revised interpretation of the marginalia, some of which he has now identified as Clifford's own hand, will appear in a forthcoming essay entitled 'Marginal Maternity: Reading Lady Anne Clifford's *Mirror for Magistrates*'.

48. Orgel, 'Margins of Truth', pp. 95–6.

49. Ibid., pp. 95, 97.

50. Michael Finlay discusses the range of tools used in conjunction with the quill pen, including the pounce-pot or sander, advised particularly for the preparation of margins of printed books for the more fluid ink used in writing (*Western Writing Implements in the Age of the Quill Pen*, Wetheral, Carlisle, 1980, pp. 32–4).

51. J. Lyly, 'To the Ladies and Gentlewomen of England', *Euphues and His England* (London, 1586).

52. F. Quarles, *Argalus and Parthenia* (London, 1629), sig. A3v.

53. Women below the rank of gentry are more often described – and satirized – as readers than addressed directly. See, for example, Thomas Overbury's portrayal of 'The Chambermaid' in his collection of characters, *A Wife, Now a Widowe* (London, 1614).

54. Brathwait, *The English Gentlewoman*, p. 139.

55. Sasha Roberts juxtaposes the popular trope of the eroticized female reader of *Venus and Adonis* with records of seventeenth-century female owners of this poem in 'Shakespeare "Creepes into the Womens Closets about Bedtime": Women Reading in a Room of Their Own', in G. McMullan, ed., *Renaissance Configurations: Voices/Bodies/Spaces, 1580–1690* (New York, 1998), pp. 39–52.

56. Brathwait, *The English Gentleman*, p. 28.

57. *The Diary of the Lady Anne Clifford*, pp. 76, 112.

58. C. I. Elton, 'Christina of Sweden and Her Books', *Bibliographica*, 1 (1895), pp. 14–15.

59. Cited and translated in D. R. Carlson, 'Royal Tutors in the Reign of Henry VII', *Sixteenth Century Journal*, 22 (1991), p. 256, emphasis mine. The original text is in Latin: 'vel memoriae partim commendasse, vel certe propriis manibus oculisque tum volutasse tum lectasse'.

60. H. C., *The Forrest of Fancy. Wherein Is Conteined Very Prety Apothegmes, and Pleasaunt Histories, Both in Meeter and Prose* (London, 1579), dedicatory epistle.

61. In his study of seventeenth-century Dutch 'images of domestic virtue', Wayne E. Franits discusses portraits of women in the context of domestic manuals, which like their English counterparts celebrate the feminine virtues of chastity, silence, obedience and diligence (*Paragons of Virtue: Women and Domesticity in Seventeenth-Century Dutch Art*, Cambridge, 1993, p. 19). For an overview of eighteenth-century portraits of women novel readers, who are represented as deeply engaged in their books, see W. B. Warner, 'Staging Readers Reading', *Eighteenth-Century Fiction*, 12 (2000), pp. 391–416.

62. E. Honig, 'In Memory: Lady Dacre and Pairing by Hans Eworth', in L. Gent and N. Llewellyn, eds., *Renaissance Bodies: The Human Figure in English Culture, c. 1540–1660* (London, 1990), pp. 62 and 250 n. 7.

63. Ibid., p. 61.

64. Cleaver, for example, distinguishes between male and female gender roles: 'The dutie of the husband is, to deale with many men: and of the wiues, to talke with fewe. The dutie of the husband is, to be entermedling: and of the wife, to bee solitarie and withdrawne' (*A Codly Form of Householde Governement*, p. 169).

65. L. Hutchinson, 'The Life of Mrs Lucy Hutchinson', *Memoirs of Colonel Hutchinson*, ed. J. Hutchinson (London, 1965), p. 14.

66. Folger STC 22547, copy 3.

67. Dated 22 September 1615, this letter is excerpted in Lewalski, *Writing Women*, pp. 134–5.
68. For discussions of Anne Clifford's commissioned portrait, see M. E. Lamb, 'The Agency of the Split Subject: Lady Anne Clifford and the Uses of Reading', *English Literary Renaissance*, 22 (1992), pp. 347–68; G. Parry, 'The Great Picture of Lady Anne Clifford', in D. Howarth, ed., *Art and Patronage in the Caroline Courts* (Cambridge, 1993), pp. 202–19; and Sanders, *Gender and Literacy on Stage*, pp. 188–94.
69. Morgan, 'Frances Wolfreston and "Hor Bouks" ', pp. 200–1.
70. E. Rainbowe, bishop of Carlisle, *A Sermon Preached at the Funeral of the Right Honorable Anne Countess of Pembroke, Dorset, and Montgomery . . . with Some Remarks on the Life of That Eminent Lady* (London, 1677), p. 61.

CHAPTER FOUR

Reading revelations: prophecy, hermeneutics and politics in early modern Britain

Kevin Sharpe

I

The histories of reading and the book have largely been written in two, very different, ways. Early research concentrated on the long *durée* of publications and reading habits – on the shift in the quantities, materials and genres of books over several centuries, and on the move from the intensive study of a few titles to the extensive reading of a myriad of print. Changes in habits of reading, that is, have been viewed as changes in the types and availability of books: we write of reading revolutions effected by print, the penny pamphlet or the novel. Alternatively, specialized case studies have focused on the reading habits of particular individuals who brought to the often familiar books of their culture a radical new hermeneutics which was sometimes personal, as with Menocchio the Friulian miller of Carlo Ginzburg's study, and sometimes, as with Jean Ranson, the mark of shifting cultural sensibilities, in this case what we characterize as Romanticism. What neither approach offers is an understanding of how books with a continuous history were read, interpreted and deployed in different communities and in a variety of very different and changing circumstances over long historical periods. What, in other words, did it mean to read the same texts – the classics, Scripture, legal treatise or fable – through the upheavals of Reformation, Civil War, Hanoverian Succession, Scientific Revolution and Romantic movement? Any such history must endeavour attention to local circumstance and moment, but, for all the difficulties, it is study of the reception of a text over the long historical arc that elucidates the relationship of cultural and political to hermeneutic change and brings the history of reading to where we argue it belongs: at the centre of all histories, of History.

This, of course, is, as most histories of reading are, a history based on writings, some of which have been studied before. My approach here differs in foregrounding these texts not simply as arguments but as readings of

Scripture, and re-viewing these as texts that bring to attention and priority acts of reading and readers. The sketch that follows, therefore, is not just a history of biblical interpretation – though we still need that; it discloses the ways in which readers read and were thought to read Scripture and it charts the endless negotiations between the efforts of authors and exegetes to impose and control readings and of readers to follow their own mind and faith. In so doing it offers an exemplar of that larger negotiation that we call the exercise of authority, be it textual or governmental.

For early modern English men and women the most important book was the Bible. The Bible was for all classes the book they first heard and read, and the text they reread most often. Scripture was the only text regularly expounded to the illiterate and the foundation text in any training in literacy received in the school, parish or household. The Bible was also the platform on which the whole edifice of early modern religious, social and political institutions was built. Robert Browne, the separatist, (for once) stated nothing controversial when he told Lord Burleigh, that 'the word of God doth expressly set down all necessary and general rules of the arts and all learning'.[1] Early modern educators, churchmen and governors regarded it as their Christian duty to come as close as possible to realizing the word in the world. They sought, that is, to restore fallen man and society to the state of grace and to frame a government that fulfilled not only Aristotle's goal of the good life but Augustine's model of the godly commonweal.

Almost no one in early modern England disputed the centrality or authority of the Bible. Differences, therefore – over matters of faith and liturgy, indeed over social codes and political programmes – arose from variant interpretations of what Scripture 'meant'. Disputes about the meaning of Scripture were ideological and political disagreements.

From the beginning of Christianity the meaning of Scripture had been disputed and contested. The ambiguity of Scripture was explained as a consequence of the fall which had separated sinful man from God's revealed truth. The quest to return to knowledge of that truth (to the reason of the first man created in God's image) was the goal of the Christian life and society. A true understanding of the word of God would both restore fallen man to grace and unite all Christians in harmony. Efforts were therefore made to find a perfect text of Scripture and a perfect understanding of biblical language. Though historians have tended to emphasize its importance for classical texts, Renaissance philological scholarship was concerned first with the recovery of a pure biblical text and with the lost language of Adam. Even before the rent of Christendom in the sixteenth century, scholarship failed to resolve all the textual and hermeneutic problems concerning the

Bible and its meaning. Nor was scholarship the only road taken to reveal God's truth. Throughout Christian history there have been mystics, visionaries and prophets who have claimed personal revelation of God to them and, under the guidance of the spirit, special understanding of his word. At every period authorized interpretations of the Bible have been open to scholarly disagreement and subject to challenge by personal revelation.

The Reformation compounded both problems. In the first place, the attack on the Vulgate Bible and the proliferation of vernacular Bibles exposed the problems of scriptural translations and variations, and made explicit the relationship between different texts and contesting sects and churches. Secondly, the Protestant emphasis on the household and on individual Bible reading promoted and legitimized a personal interpretation of the meaning of Scripture, one unmediated by clerical authority. If these were the logic of Protestant scripturalism and solifidianism, Protestant churches and countries proved no less concerned than their Catholic counterparts to insist on religious orthodoxy and obedience to the magistrate. That is to say, they were no less concerned to secure an authorized and agreed text and interpretation of Scripture. Beza's Geneva Bible was the first to order Scripture by arrangement of the text into verses; and the Geneva Bible bore printed marginal notes included to direct the reader, to delimit the potentially boundless possibilities of personal interpretation. Moreover, the Protestant emphasis on godly preaching and upon the sermon as the core of worship arguably rendered the service a more didactic and less participatory experience. From the pulpit elevated above the altar, the word of God was expounded and determined.

In addition to the differences between Protestant confessions – Lutheran, Zwinglian, Calvinist – there were tensions within the heart of Protestantism: tensions concerning the authority of the word and its expositors, between the community of the visible church and the elect, between clerical authority and the freedom of the godly, and between conscience and obedience. In large part all these issues came down to the question of which Bible was valorized and who had the ultimate right to teach and interpret God's word – that is, to the authority of the text and authority over the text.[2]

In early modern Britain, the tensions and ambiguities were exacerbated by the peculiar nature and chronology of its reformations. As we know, the church of England was a mix of Erasmian, Lutheran, Zwinglian and Calvinist theologies blended with traditional Catholic ritual, which could be (and often was) viewed as tempering Protestant doctrine. And within the small confines of Britain, where Wales remained for most of the sixteenth century a dark corner of Catholic conservatism, Scotland underwent a radical reformation which to many hotter Protestants presented a model for further reform. Even within England, we have learned, reformation proceeded at a very different pace in different parts of the country, and authority permitted a wide variety of practice and belief.[3]

But if we have long appreciated that in early modern Britain God's word meant many different things to different people, we have paid inadequate attention to the question of which Bible was favoured and read and how Scripture was interpreted and expounded. There were, of course, a number of Bibles available throughout the sixteenth and seventeenth centuries: Hebrew, Greek and Latin editions as well as vernacular Bibles – Erasmus's New Testament, Coverdale's Bible, the Geneva Bible, the Bishops' Bible, the Rheims–Douai translation and the Authorized King James Bible. In each case, new editions not only came in varying formats and typographies, but also introduced 'improvements' to the translation – that is, further changes to the meaning.[4] Among English Protestants, the Geneva Bible increasingly gained popularity over the great Bible, but even talk of the Geneva Bible oversimplifies a complex textual history. For although the 1560 Geneva Bible was widely available in England, the first English edition appeared in 1575, the year of Grindal's elevation to the see of Canterbury. Thereafter there were not only myriad different formats of the Bible, some bound with a Puritan revision of the Prayer Book, some in roman type, some in black letter, some with maps and illustrations, but also editions with very different marginal notes. In 1576, for example, an English edition was published with notes by the Cambridge divine Richard Thomson, fuller than those of 1560. Then, in a 1602 edition, Thomson's notes were in turn replaced by those of Franciscus Junius, which constituted a 'massive and violently antipapal diatribe' by a scholar and polemicist who had 'experienced the horrors of the French wars of religion'.[5] The notes attracted immediate attention and notoriety. If Thomson's annotation avoided some of the more contentious glosses of the 1560 edition, Junius's excited 'vivid apostolic expectations'.[6]

It was not least concern about the Geneva notes that led Archbishop Whitgift, the opponent of further godly reformation, to endeavour to enforce use of the Bishops' Bible, and subsequently impelled James I to commission a new English Bible free of all marginal annotation or gloss. But neither the Bishops' Bible nor the Authorized King James Bible supplanted the Geneva editions. Indeed, Thomas Fuller maintained that some complained specifically about the removal of marginal notes on the ground that 'they could not see into the sense of the Scripture without the spectacles of those Geneva annotations'.[7] Even after 1611 Robert Barker, printer to the king, continued to publish 'cum privilegio regiae majestatis' new editions of the Geneva Bible with Thomson's and Junius's notes. In an edition of 1616, the preface to the 'Christian reader' acknowledged that 'some translations read after one sort and some after another' and advertised that 'we have in the margent notified the diversity...of reading'.[8]

The Bible itself, therefore, was, in early modern England, a varied and variant text which in its varying forms and translations, its editions and annotations, offered a variety, indeed a multiplicity, of reading experiences. Within these books, moreover, were other 'books' of the Bible which themselves differed generically, some being history, some prophecy or gospel. And beyond the text, early modern English people encountered a growing literature of interpretive guides, ranging from thousand-page scholarly exegeses to brief paraphrases and pulpit expositions. We know too little about which Bible, still less about which commentaries, were favoured by particular religious or social groups, let alone by individuals. That is to say, we have scarcely begun to ask the question of what it meant to read the Bible in early modern England. The full answer to such a large question, of course, lies beyond the scope of this essay. What I endeavour is some examination of various attempts to read and interpret one book: a sketch not just of the different interpretations but of the hermeneutic principles they recommend to readers and apply – or do not apply – themselves, and a glance at the contemporary reading practices they disclose and often seek to change.

II

The book of Revelation was widely held to be the most important and the most difficult of all biblical books. 'Not one necessary point of belief,' wrote John Bale, 'is in all the other Scriptures that is not here also'; 'he who knoweth not this book, knoweth not what the church is'.[9] Yet, Arthur Dent admitted, 'it is so dark and hard to understand'; 'in manner riddle like', Augustine Marlorate described it.[10] From the first age of the church there had been many attempts to decode and appropriate its message. Where St Jerome found in Revelation 'as many sacraments as words' and that 'in every of the words are hid manifold understandings', other commentators divided into those such as Irenaeus, who approached it literally, and those who interpreted it, with Augustine, as spiritual allegory.[11] Politically, while followers of Joachim of Fiore seized on the emperor Frederick II as the fulfilment of millenial hope, Hussites and Anabaptists looked to apocalypse in a communist utopia.[12]

Erasmus questioned the authorship and authority of the book, as at first did Luther. But Luther's mounting conviction under pressure that the pope was the biblical Antichrist refocused attention on Revelation and emphasized its polemical importance in the struggle against Rome.[13] In Revelation, too, the Protestants were to find a history which enabled them to answer the charge of innovation and prophecy of a triumphant future to sustain them during the dark days of persecution. From the sixteenth century Revelation was inextricably linked to reformation and the apocalyptic with the political.[14] Despite Calvin's reticence on the subject, the sixteenth century saw an outpouring of paraphrases and commentaries on the text. They constitute a hermeneutic history which charts and crosses the ecclesiastical and political history of early modern Europe.

In early modern England, as we have seen, the text appeared in different forms, Revelation being the book to which annotations were heaviest, most revised and most controversial.[15] Some texts of the Geneva Bible introduced the complex book with a summary of 'the argument', others with a historical 'order of time', 'whereunto the contents of this book are to be referred'.[16] Where all editions with notes tried to assist the reader with the general structure of the book and with the elucidation of difficult passages, some were more philological and historical while others were more concerned with applications and prophecies of the future. The language and tone of the annotations differed markedly: the word 'reprobate' used to gloss chapter 9 verse 2 in the 1602 edition does not appear in the 1560 Bible. Interestingly, the 1560 gloss on chapter 21 verse 24, noting that 'kings are partakers of the heavenly glory if they rule in fear of the Lord', did not appear in many later editions.

Variations in the text were only the first of the problems that confronted the reader of Revelation. From the start the book seemed to announce both its openness and impenetrability. The first chapter promises that 'blessed is he that readeth and they that heareth the words of this prophecy'; in chapter 5, by contrast, the reader confronts the sealed book that none could open. Revelation was also generically indeterminable. Was it history or prophecy? Were some chapters narrative of church history, others moral allegory? Were the visions, figures and tropes to be interpreted literally or parabollically? As early modern readers used to a textual culture in which meaning was encoded in genres grappled to assign Revelation to generic classification, they only encountered more problems and disagreements. What some took as history, others read as 'epistle monitory' to the church, and others still as 'heavenly drama' or interlude.[17] Edward Waple was not alone in his inability to decide what it was. Even those who concurred in viewing it as 'a prophetical drama' could not agree about the subclassification of its dramatic form – whether comedy, 'truly tragical' or 'tragical comedy'.[18] Given the textual instabilities, generic uncertainties, complex structure and difficult language of Revelation, it is not surprising that there was an industry of commentaries and evidently a market for them.

The many commentaries also evidenced a number of authors with a wish to advance an interpretation and a cause. That involved steering and persuading the reader to adopt a particular approach or interpretive strategy towards the biblical text. As we shall see, several commentaries explicitly outline a reading method in epistles dedicatory or addresses to the reader; in other cases, the method unfolds in the course of interpreting the text. What all have in common is a need and endeavour to make sense of the book by explicating it within cultural contexts and language familiar to the early modern reader. Bernard, Pareus and others discuss the prophecy as if it were a piece of theatre, while William Perkins tries to make Revelation into an early modern book with its 'proem', epistles dedicatory and 'an entrance to the vision'.[19] Several commentators describe Christ and his kingdom in the language of earthly kings, with their 'chamber of presence'.[20] John Tillinghast domesticated scriptural mystery by writing of Christ gaining the 'outshires and suburbs' of the Antichrist's city,[21] and in a quotidian reference Dent compared the drying up of the Euphrates (Revelation 16.12) with the draining of 'great fish ponds'.[22] Such cultural referents, of course, as well as rendering Revelation more familiar, also situated the text in the midst of contemporary debates and polemics – that is, outside the author's control.

The forms of commentaries differed as authors endeavoured to reach different audiences at different times. Some were learned exegeses of hundreds of pages, others short octavos or revised sermons. In some, Scripture was carefully separated from paraphrase or comment, in others Revelation, comment and annotation became hard to distinguish. The tone in some cases was didactic, even authoritarian; others, especially in the 1640s, took the form of a dialogue which invited the reader's participation. But in every case the independence of the reader was, implicitly or explicitly, acknowledged. Nearly all commentaries open with self-justificatory or apologetic addresses to the reader; John Napier closed with an appeal to 'the misliking reader' whom he feared he had not persuaded.[23] As authors recognized, each reader, in each moment of reading, brought to the commentary, as did the writers themselves, the concerns of their personal circumstances and time. From the lines – sometimes between the lines – of commentaries, therefore, we may not only read the efforts to interpret Revelation in changing circumstances but also discern the negotiations between authors

and readers and the shifting strategies deployed to delimit and direct interpretation. We may, that is, trace the contest for ecclesiastical and political
authority which was (and is) never separable from the struggle to control
interpretation of valorizing but ambiguous texts.

In the late sixteenth century, English commentators on Revelation were
undoubtedly preoccupied with the threat of Catholicism, domestic and foreign, and with the need to establish Protestant doctrine in a church which
had in 1559 left much open to interpretation and preference. In 1574 the
English translation of the Huguenot Augustine Marlorate's *Catholic Exposition upon the Revelation* voiced anxiety about the continuing attractions
of 'gorgeous' Catholic churches, feasts and holidays and about the persistence of a good-works theology of salvation.[24] His solution was to gloss
Revelation as an unequivocally Protestant text. Accordingly, Marlorate and
his translator use the language of 'election' and 'reprobation' to paraphrase
the text, and in lengthy passages of explanation denounce Catholic practices and pilgrimages, pardons and images.[25] Marlorate is at pains to make
Revelation 'simple, plain and clear' to the faithful, who, as they follow
the exposition, affirm their Protestant commitment and their hostility to
Rome.[26] Marlorate does not pause to weigh scholarly debates or ponder
difficulties. Yet for all his clear purpose and straightforward exposition ('his
meaning is this'), he in passing acknowledges the 'university' of interpretations, both the textual variants ('some copies have it') and exegetical disputes
('as many expositions as there are expositors').[27] Marlorate's concern was
that the reader might be drawn to approaches less 'to the advancement
of Christ's glory'.[28] As Arthur Golding put it in dedicating his translation
to Mildmay, the devil worked all the mischief he could; to counter him
Revelation had to be read with 'a Christianly mind of being edified to
salvation'.[29] Paradoxically, just as faith was built upon the word, so the
right reading of Scripture depended upon faith.

The threat from Spain and defeat of the armada in 1588 unquestionably
heightened English interest in the apocalypse as events appeared to confirm an English history foretold in biblical prophecy. Some went to the
lengths of identifying the woman clothed with the sun in Revelation 13 as
Queen Elizabeth.[30] But even amid the euphoria of English victory, Revelation did not simply applaud authority. Martin Marprelate infamously
identified the bishops as the beast and made interpretation of apocalypse
central to the conflict between the church and the Presbyterians.[31] We
have another window onto the relationship of hermeneutic to ecclesiastical contest in George Gifford's sermons on Revelation published in 1596.[32]
Gifford, deprived of his living in 1584 for his nonconformity, had other

goals than the celebration of armada victory. In a dedication to the earl of Essex, champion of the Protestant cause, he wrote of the need to recruit 'noble warriors' for Christ at home and abroad.[33] For Gifford, exposition of Revelation was part of the war against the papists who sought to 'drive men from the reading and study of it because it pointeth out great Babel'.[34] However, the expositors he favoured were not the bishops, but the 'pastors'; 'there is,' he added in words freighted with Elizabethan controversy, 'a great matter depending upon this ministry'.[35] While he was at pains to distance himself from radical extremists such as Anabaptists, Gifford's whole exegesis of Revelation focused on the importance of godly ministry to teach the errors of the Antichrist and the glad tidings of the gospel. He closed his commentary with a denunciation of 'dumb dogs' and of those who persecuted the true preachers of the word: 'the state of every church,' he maintained, 'is set forth under their pastor'.[36] Gifford placed little emphasis on the capacity of the common reader to interpret Scripture – he was scathing about those who came to church with their Bibles but had no understanding of their faith.[37] He stressed the godly preacher rather than the individual believer or the church as the expositor of the word. In his hands Revelation became a godly treatise for a preaching ministry.

The openness of Revelation to readings and groups critical of the establishment in church and state was not lost on Elizabeth's fellow sovereign James VI of Scotland, who succeeded amidst the civil war that followed reformation in Scotland. In 1588 the king took the unusual step of writing an interpretation of the text – in a meditation on chapter 20 and in a 'paraphrase' of the whole book.[38] Because he knew that 'of all the Scriptures the book of the Revelation is most meet for this our last age', James sought to impose his own interpretation upon the text, and to support his authority with biblical prophecy.[39] Indeed, in his paraphrase James erased the distinction between text and commentary and wrote in the first person pronoun of St John.[40] When he paraphrases verse 8 of chapter 10 as 'that voice which I heard spoke to me from heaven', he is claiming divine inspiration for himself as exegete as well as for the apostle.[41] James even denies the place of commentary, claiming that Scripture is its own interpreter: 'we are taught,' he writes in the meditation, 'to use only Scripture for interpretation of Scripture'.[42] But in practice he does deploy other texts. And, while claiming merely to ventriloquize the word, James rewrites Revelation for his own purposes. In his paraphrase there are no notes, no references to textual differences or alternative meanings, no epistles dedicatory or prefaces to the reader. The impression given is of Scripture 'laid open' without gloss. Yet James outlines the structure of the book and the 'argument' of each chapter. And in the course of 'paraphrasing' he in fact makes a number of important polemical and political points. The comment, for example, on chapter 20, that between election and hell 'there is no midway', was obviously directed against the doctrine of purgatory,[43] as the gloss on the 'grasshoppers' (chapter 9) skilfully avoided naming the bishops as had the Geneva Bible. One even wonders whether his comparison 'as the phoenix revives of her own ashes' (chapter 13) was intended to compliment Queen Elizabeth, who had begun to adopt the phoenix as her emblem.[44]

At the close of his paraphrase James's final words seek to foreclose other interpretations than his own: 'whosoever,' he writes in a loose rendering of the original, 'in coping or translating this book adulterateth any ways the original or in interpreting of it wittingly strays from the true meaning of it . . . to follow the fantastical invention of man or his own preoccupied opinions shall be accursed'.[45] The language bears witness to a nervousness. For all his robust exposition, James knows that the text is open to other readings, as his own authority is subject to debate and dispute. James claimed to resolve doubts about Revelation through privileged access to God's meaning, just as he claimed divine right for his rule. But there were others who regarded even royal exegesis as 'of man' rather than God; and some would also come to view monarchy as of mere human constitution.

By the time James, now king of Great Britain, published his *Meditation* and *Paraphrase* as the first items in his folio works of 1616, several other commentators had tackled the mysteries of Revelation. Some were undoubtedly encouraged by the king's own exposition; John Napier dedicated his *Plaine Discovery* to James VI and published 'cum privilegio regali'. But even the loyal Napier's treatise opened up other ways of interpreting apocalypse. Napier was readier than James had been to draw attention to obscure and ambiguous passages and his identification of different translations, of irony and figure, opened the text. More importantly, Napier's statement that 'one hour of prayer took me further than a thousand days of inquisition' ultimately passed exegetical authority to, as he put it, the 'auditor'.[46] In his valedictory remarks to the 'misliking reader', Napier acknowledged that since 'infinite and repugnant interpretions do arise', 'we shall greatly differ'.[47] Ultimately he knew and accepted that he could not exercise sovereign interpretive powers, but had to fall back on 'brotherly admonition'.[48] James I and his successors were to find that, in large part, the same was true for their proclamations and their rule.

One of the outcomes of James's meeting with Puritan critics of the church at the Hampton Court conference was the Authorized Version of the Bible. The team of translators entrusted with the task included conservative divines such as Lancelot Andrewes as well as those of godly sympathies such as Lawrence Chadderton, John Reynolds and Richard Thomson. If the project was to produce a text that put an end to 'infinite and repugnant interpretations' of Revelation, it was very soon shown to have been a failure. One of the most popular expositions of Revelation in early seventeenth-century England was that of the Puritan divine Arthur Dent. In the preface to his *The Ruine of Rome* Dent freely admitted that many held it dangerous to expound apocalypse to the people, with all its 'uncertain conjectures' obscuring the 'true meaning'.[49] Dent, however, believed it should be 'openly preached' and read by 'all the Lord's people', there being nothing that ordinary men could not understand 'with prayer and humility'.[50] Indeed, Dent continued, the times made it easier for a man of mean learning to comprehend than it had ever been before. He did not deny the value of study or the knowledge of Old Testament prophets, antiquities and histories as aids to understanding. But in the end, he assured readers, God would open Revelation to all who 'are earnest and humble suitors... for the illumination thereof'.[51]

Here, authoritative and authorized interpretation gives way to an exegetical democracy of the godly. This, of course, was the hermeneutic version of the Puritan plan for the church and state, and much of Dent's language encourages us to link textual with social argument.[52] As he proceeded through the text, Dent's reading was not particularly radical. For the most part he avoids controversy, draws back from close application to the times, and expresses a willingness to refer all 'to the judgement of the church, and such therein as are indued with the spirit of God'.[53] But the 'and' in that quotation reads as conditional as well as conjunctive: the church may exercise judgement only if it consists of those 'indued with the spirit of God' – the elect. Here Dent's church appears to be not the institution but the invisible community of the chosen who, as readers of Revelation, will, like Dent, 'set down that which God hath given me to see and which in mine own conscience... I suppose to be the truth'.[54] Whereas to Dent (as well as to a preaching ministry) the freedom of each to come to his own knowledge of God's word was 'the felicity of the elect',[55] to James VI the appeal to individual conscience represented a threat to the authority of monarch as well as church.

No less popular than Dent's exposition were the lectures and commentaries on Revelation preached by the ardent Calvinist William Perkins and published from 1604. In his *Godly and Learned Commentarie* on Revelation, Perkins offers us insights into the concerns of those whom historians have labelled Calvinist conformists and the relation to those concerns of reading and interpreting the word of God.[56] Perkins stressed the importance of Revelation. Because 'the author is Jesus Christ', the 'author of truth', he maintained, the book was 'certain and in plain terms delivered'.[57] Yet Perkins granted that it did not always appear plain and certain: 'it is hard for any to set down certainly what the Holy ghost intendeth'.[58] Translation, he accepted, could not always do justice to holy writ and led to misunderstandings. Beyond that, there was 'such diversity of opinions', 'yea of the Scriptures themselves', that certainty eluded the reader.[59] Perkins's answer to the problem was to return to the very text that appeared opaque. The key to finding Christ in Revelation lay in reading and rereading. Reading, he explained it, was an active process that involved 'searching out the knowledge' of God and his word.[60] To read aright a man needed a humble, believing heart and to live the message of the gospel; he needed the 'light of the spirit'.[61] Perkins feared there were few right readers who spent time searching out the word: 'nay men will not be at a cost to buy a bible and if they have one they will not take pains to read the same'.[62] The Protestant faith depended on reading, but people, it seemed, could not be trusted to read.

Perkins's solution was the central platform of the godly programme: preaching. 'The duty of those which cannot read the Scripture,' he asserted, was 'to procure others to read to them.'[63] He did not refer only to the illiterate – 'all . . . are bound . . . to frequent sermons'.[64] Preaching, of course, required the right kind of preachers. Perkins urged that 'every good minister should be a good text man'.[65] Ministers, he insisted, should not overemploy themselves in ancient writings, the Fathers, philosophers and poets, but focus on Scripture. And rather than obscure Scripture with witty, rhetorical conceits and 'vain delivery' (was he attacking the court preachers such as Andrewes?), they should expound the word 'in a plain, easy and familiar kind'.[66] Preaching was to teach men and women how to read aright so as to come to faith. But preaching presented its own problems. Not only were there too few preachers of the best sort, too many inclined to take pride in their own words; congregations did not sufficiently value preaching: their manner was 'to be snorting and sleeping at sermons'.[67] After all, they retorted, there was no need for sermons when men had 'their bible . . . than which no minister can preach better'.[68] Perkins grappled with the central problem for the godly. Protestant belief depended upon the reading of the word but ultimately the reading of the word was an act that required the reader to be imbued with faith. The success of reformation rested not on hermeneutics but, we might say, within a hermeneutic circle.

It may be ironic, then, but it is not surprising that though he condemned ministers who did not confine themselves to the plain word,
Perkins himself deployed his commentary on Revelation to reassert core
Protestant doctrines which he feared were undermined by those who
mocked 'preciseness'.[69] In the course of expounding Revelation, Perkins
rearticulates Protestant doctrine on works, the sacraments, the Sabbath
and the theology of election. Quite a lot of space, for example, is given
over to proving that the elect cannot fall from grace, a doctrine 'oppugned
earnestly not only by the church of Rome but also by some churches...
of the Protestants'.[70] Concern to reassert such positions arose from the
persistent hold of Catholic beliefs 'among our people who call it the
old religion' and from the 'abundance of atheists' 'in the midst of our
congregations'.[71]

Perkins deployed Revelation to try to persuade men to Calvinist orthodoxy. He endeavoured to lead them attentively to hear the word preached
and diligently to read the Scripture. He sought to exercise influence, even
wield authority. But the dilemma that faced the champions of the godly
was ultimately inherent in Protestantism; and it was a problem for all who
sought to exercise authority in a Protestant polity. Perkins put it well himself: 'no man in the world,' he wrote, 'hath authority over this book', neither
preacher nor prince.[72] Ultimately, at least in this world, the meaning of the
book lay with the reader.

That tension between instruction, authority and the freedom of all to
find their own way to God's truth plays across the prefatory pages of
Richard Bernard's *A Key of Knowledge for the Opening of... Revelation* (1617).
Bernard, a godly preacher of Batcombe, Somerset, opens his book with a
series of epistles dedicatory that map the ecclesiastical and secular order of
Jacobean England. In the first to his bishop, Arthur Lake, Bernard praises
the episcopal office as protector of the church against Brownist schism. In
an address to the judges Bernard praises the laws that preserve his mother
church and the 'prerogative royal' and supremacy; Revelation, he tells them,
authorizes them to act against the Lord's enemies, and to frame laws against
the locusts.[73] In a third epistle Bernard calls on the Justices of the Peace
to be vigilant against church papists in an age of plots and conspiracies.
Penultimately, he summons 'martial men' to avenge the saints and secure
England against the Antichrist. Last, but in this case far from least, Bernard
addresses the 'Christian reader' whom he seeks to persuade to truth and
right understanding of the word.[74]

Having addressed the authorities in church and state, Bernard catalogues
the interpretive authorities that direct right understanding. He cites all the

major commentators on Revelation – Bale, Bullinger, Beza, Napier, not least James VI's 'learned pen' – and he advises readers against 'going by themselves without respect of others' in interpreting the text.[75] Understanding, he counselled, may require knowledge of histories and biblical commentaries, as well as the skills of rhetoric, grammar, logic and philosophy.[76] Yet just as he would seem to confine Revelation to the learned and restrict interpretation to established humanistic scholarship, Bernard identifies the limits to traditional learning. For one, learned men had been known to err; after all, papists were learned but failed to probe the secrets of God's kingdom.[77] Learned men also disagreed – to the point where 'their discord may seem to withdraw us from the study of this book'.[78] Exposition of Scripture, then, by 'mere wit and only human learning' was an unreliable path to truth.[79] Knowledge of God's word came from revelation and the spirit: 'the author must be the revealer, even the holy spirit without which we cannot conceive the things here delivered'.[80] And rather than following learned authorities, 'the spirit enlighteneth whom he pleases', enabling him to 'find out the true sense' amid 'all the variable interpretations', or, rejecting them all, 'go almost alone'.[81] For all the address to authorities and all the citation of authorities, Bernard, *in fine*, gives the key to Revelation to the godly reader, to open the secrets of God 'almost alone'.

Bernard's oxymoron concisely expresses the tensions we are examining not only between public church and private believer, but between godly preaching and teaching and the priesthood of each believer. As a preacher, aware of the false teaching of Rome, Bernard desires to instruct and direct his flock. The elaborate engraved title page to his *Key of Knowledge* structures the story of Revelation in a comic strip of scenes, each with explanatory verse, culminating in the day of judgement. Within his treatise he guides the reader, advising him to lay out the whole text in its 'principal parts' analytically, then the contents of each chapter so as to grasp the 'coherence'.[82] He urges frequent rereading of Revelation and comparison with other biblical books, and provides cross-references to passages that elucidate the meaning, as he discerns it. However, in the end even Bernard's own directions took second place to the reader's personal determination. Each reader, he conceded, must 'gather rules for himself to help the interpreting of this book', and each must follow 'the guiding of the spirit in his own order, word for word'.[83]

'The guiding of the spirit in his own order'. Rather than pursuing the radical hermeneutic and political consequences of this principle, Bernard, we have seen, sought to reconcile it to the established authorities – educational, ecclesiastical and political. There were, however, others more willing to take further the implications of autonomy and to apply their own radical readings of Revelation to the times.

The Baptist John Wilkinson published his *Exposition of the Thirteenth Chapter of the Revelation of Jesus Christ* in Amsterdam in 1619. He had, the preface made clear, intended an exegesis of the whole book, but the 'malice of the prelates' had prevented him by detaining him in prison, leaving his friends to 'set forth this little treatise from his own papers'.[84] Wilkinson graphically illustrates not only the inefficacy of early modern censorship when publication abroad remained easy, but, more important for our purposes, the dangers presented by the freedom to interpret Scripture when it was practised by sects hostile to the established church. For sure, his denunciations of the pope and Catholic church were, if more strident than most, innocent enough. But whereas for James and others it was the church of England that was the citadel of the true faith and bulwark against the Antichrist, for Wilkinson the church and its governors were themselves the handmaids of the beast. The church of England, he proclaimed, was not a true church, nor did it have powers to 'make laws in matter of religion'.[85] The 1603 canons, he continued, had no authority from Christ; the Book of Common Prayer was full of 'absurdities and blasphemies'; the copes and rituals prescribed were but 'foolish ceremonies', commanded by a 'lordly prelacy' who were the 'dragon's ministers', the 'mark of the beast'.[86] 'This church of England,' Wilkinson asserted, glossing his text, 'still remaineth under the bondage of antichrist and is ruled and governed by the image of the beast'.[87] Though in a placatory gesture he allowed for the authority of godly kings in matters ecclesiastical, Wilkinson's diatribe against the bishops, as James was quick to recognize, was also an assault upon the royal supremacy.[88] Indeed, Wilkinson's reference to convocation as the Presbyterians' preferred 'national synod' makes his threat explicit.[89] Ministers may have the duty to teach; but the saints, those called 'precisians or puritans', had the ultimate right to determine all for themselves, to separate.[90] The way to the word for Wilkinson lay outside the church with the separated congregations, and ultimately with each believer. We may be familiar with assaults on the church such as this; what we need to appreciate is how radical ecclesiology developed from an individual and radical hermeneutic.

Given the views of exegetes such as Wilkinson, it is not surprising that there appears to have been some wariness about publishing on Revelation. Even Thomas Brightman, whose exposition was far from radical, was published posthumously and abroad. Brightman had addressed his *A Revelation of the Revelation* of 1615 to the 'holy reformed churches' of Brittany, France and Germany, telling them that the last act had now begun and 'thy husband is about to arise even now for the avenging of thy grief'.[91] Within three years the Thirty Years' War erupted across Europe, signalling to many that the last age had come and that the final war between Christ and Antichrist had commenced. James I, anxious to keep out of the war and fostering closer relations with Spain, was concerned to cool rather than enflame millenarian fervour and became equivocal about the identity of the pope with the Antichrist.[92] Charles I, especially after 1629, endeavoured to suppress the millenarian hopes excited by the victories of Gustavus Adolphus of Sweden. At home, his archbishop, William Laud, emphasizing the continuity of the church of England with the pre-Reformation church rather than its affinity with continental reform, questioned whether the pope was the Antichrist and was accused of expunging such references to Rome from books he licensed for the press.[93] As Anthony Milton writes, 'the doctrine of the papal antichrist was clearly on the retreat in the 1630s'; and divines such as Joseph Mede held back from publishing English editions of their expositions of the apocalpyse 'for fear of . . . an overpotent opposition'.[94] Like Mede's, other expositions of Revelation remained untranslated or were published abroad.[95]

But, while official disapproval discouraged commentaries and exegeses of Revelation, events in Europe and Britain stimulated millenarian expectations and prophecies – in popular as well as elite circles. Corantos, newsbooks and almanacs increasingly deploy apocalyptic language, as each victory or setback was seen to herald the last days.[96] Puritan émigrés to New England and the Netherlands also found 'apocalyptic significance' in their flight and became acquainted with radical literature on Revelation which found its way back to England through the networks of the godly.[97] By the late 1630s, as the disputes over the Scottish Prayer Book flooded England with radical Presbyterian pamphlets, the Covenanter Andrew Ramsey issued from Edinburgh *A Warning Come out of Babylon*.[98] In England, John Lilburne denounced the bishops as the 'work of the beast' and called upon his readers to study Revelation and separate from the church.[99] The book of Revelation had, in the sixteenth century, provided an arsenal for all Protestants against Rome. But its openness to interpretation had always rendered it a text that could be deployed against authority. By 1640 it had become the manifesto for Puritan opposition to church and state, and justification for their destruction and for the rule of the spirit.

Civil war, as we have learned, polemicized and rendered overtly partisan all the literary forms and genres – epic, pastoral and play.[100] What we need to appreciate is how conflict and the opening of *arcana imperii* to popular debate transformed traditional genres, such as biblical exegesis, in similar ways. During the 1640s and 1650s commentaries on Revelation echo with the noise of battle and skirmish as protagonists looked for signs of the Lord in unfolding events. Sancroft may have mocked the radical preacher 'puzzling his geography to find Armageddon about Preston and Warrington bridge', but none could afford to disregard the signs of divine providence which might herald the final victory or defeat.[101] Millenarian hopes and fears pervade the language and literature of civil war across genres and forms, popular as well as elite.[102] As well as the first English commentaries hitherto deemed too radical or risky (such as Mede), a different genre of exegesis – shorter, more polemical and often in the form of a dialogue – emerged to address the new audiences created by the pamphlet and the newspaper. The new genres fostered as well as reflected changing habits of reading as well as writing.[103] With the collapse of authority, the proliferation of print and the daily exchange of arguments, readers were faced with the need to choose and discriminate. Milton, it has been argued, deliberately promoted the independence of the reader as the key to successful revolution.[104] The reading of Scripture, especially Revelation, led some readers beyond the reform of constitution favoured by Milton, even further than regicide, into advocacy of the end of all government and social order. Having originally united the godly cause, Revelation, once again, became the text which fractured and destroyed it. In expositions of Revelation during civil war and commonwealth we may read not just another chapter in the long contest for biblical validation, but a larger story of struggle – for hermeneutic authority and control.

Two early examples of the impact of events on interpretations of Revelation may be taken from the eve of conflict in 1641. *Napier's Narration, or An Epitome of His Book on the Revelation* and *A Revelation of Mr Brightman's Revelation* were both short, punchy comments on the learned treatises published by John Napier in Edinburgh in 1593 and by Thomas Brightman in Amsterdam in 1615. *Napier's Narration* takes the form of a colloquial dialogue between Napier and 'Rollock', with simple, direct questions (about, for example, how long the world would continue) answered as simply and straightforwardly. There is nothing newly radical in the content of the exposition. Rather it is the form that is striking, with 'Rollock' having the last word – 'I take leave of you for this time' – and indicating his right to ask more when he pleases.[105] The *Revelation of Mr Brightman's Revelation* similarly stages a dialogue, very much reminiscent of contemporary pamphlet literature, between a minister and a citizen of London. Here the tone as well as the form make this tract a radical attack on the church. The minister, having fled persecution by the bishops, invokes Brightman to declaim against the inadequacies of 'lukewarm' reformation in England. Castigating the bishops as agents of the Antichrist, the minister praises the Scottish kirk for triumphing over prelacy. The citizen is persuaded – 'we shall have great cause to thank the Lord for their [the Scots'] coming into England' – and awaits further fulfilment of Brightman's prophecy: 'he speaks of our times'.[106] In a text that replicates the social role of the ministers in driving men to radical beliefs, a reading of Revelation is itself reread and polemically appropriated for altered times.

When Joseph Mede's *Clavis Apocalyptica* of 1627 appeared in translation in 1643, it was the circumstances of reading rather than the writing that made it a treatise of radical politics. Mede, in most church matters a conservative ceremonialist, had penned a cautious and historical interpretation of Revelation based on his rule of synchronisms between one set of visions and another. He had concluded his commentary leaving 'the whole matter to the church to be determined'.[107] By 1643, however, there was no established church in existence, and Mede's editor, William Twisse, prolocuter of the Westminster assembly, felt more inclined to 'let the reader judge' and to stress the prophetic elements in both Revelation and Mede's *Key*.[108] The translator, Richard More, Puritan champion of the parliamentary cause in Shropshire, similarly urged the reader to be guided by the spirit to the 'course of all prophecies'.[109] Another writer, John Trapp, minister of Weston-super-Mare, found new and different meanings in Revelation in the 1640s from what his master had preached in his childhood at Evesham. Indeed, he came to believe that it was the role of ministers 'by reading and meditation' to 'digest the holy scriptures that . . . they may draw out new and old for the use of the church'.[110] When he published his commentary on Revelation in 1647, therefore, he pointed up the fulfilment of the prophecy of the red horse in 'our late battle of Edgehill' and the downfall of the Antichrist at Naseby.[111]

Though he thus associated the Royalists with the Antichrist, Trapp, a scholar divine, drew back from the most revolutionary apocalypticism, leaving his readers to 'ruminate what ye read' and 'stay for the explication by the event'.[112] Others were less circumspect. After 1647, as Charles I was characterized as a 'man of blood', so increasingly was he identified as a servant of

the Antichrist.[113] The prophetess Eleanour Douglas, performing a radical
act in essaying biblical commentary as a woman, published *The Revelation
Interpreted* in which she detected the rise of the beast in the beginning of
Charles's reign.[114] In ways that still await elucidation, regicide was advanced
and defended in apocalyptic language and literature which radicalized the
hermeneutic as well as the political process. Another woman, the prophetess
Mary Cary, associated radical politics with a radically gendered hermeneutics when she predicted in 1648 that not only would Christ 'bring down
the power of the beast' but that 'women shall prophecy'.[115] Those who
would interpret God's word would be 'not only superiors but inferiors; not
only those that have university learning but... servants and handmaids'.[116]
After the regicide, in commentaries on apocalypse which she dedicated to
Elizabeth Cromwell and Bridget Ireton, Cary showed how 'the late king's
doom and death was... predeclared' and how prophecy was fulfilled when
the royal beast ceased to prevail.[117] In his prefatory remarks, Hugh Peter
appeared somewhat uneasy about a female exegete who taught her sex that
'they that will not use the distaff may improve the pen'. 'Doubtless,' he
concluded in language that returned her to her place in the patriarchy, 'she
had good help from above in her travail for this birth'.[118] Yet it was as much
in that claim of help from above as in female authorship that the radicalism
of Cary's commentary was manifested. For though she gestured to praise
of Oliver Cromwell, 'the great Lord General of the army of saints,' Cary
ultimately bowed to the authority of none, claiming personal direction
from God.[119] 'All saints,' she argued, 'have a spirit of prophecy'.[120] God
was her 'sufficiency' to prophesy that Christ would soon appear to raise the
saints to reign with him. And when that day came, she knew, there would
be no division and no other authority, either hermeneutic or political, as
the saints would recover the 'spiritual language' of Christ, direct access to
the word and the Lord.[121]

   The logic of Cary's claims was made manifest by the activities of the
millenarians in the Barebones' assembly of 1653.[122] As we shall see, it was
to be a turning point in the history of biblical hermeneutics as well as interregnum politics. For, when he set up the Protectorate, Cromwell sought
some form of established church and a measure of ecclesiastical authority
against the claims of the individual spirit. His move did not go unchallenged; and not for the first or last time, a reading of Revelation provided
the script for opposition. In 1654, to take a case, the rector of Trunch,
Norfolk, and Fifth-Monarchist John Tillinghast dedicated the third part of
his *Generation Work*, an exposition of Revelation 16, to the Lord Protector.
If the dedication appeared a conventional gesture to authority, it quickly

became clear that Tillinghast wrote to admonish rather than praise. 'If what is written be truth,' Tillinghast warned, 'it is your duty to hear it'.[123] The word, he instructed Cromwell, was sovereign over all others. Scripture provided the example of Asa, who turned away from God to oppress the prophets: 'that it may never be our highness's case is my prayer'.[124] In no uncertain terms Cromwell was warned not to persecute the saints – those who have 'the signs of the times grounded upon the word'.[125]

Scripture, Tillinghast argues, was the property of the godly reader. In an epistle to the reader he explains the method of interpretation he has followed and recommends. Though he had read other commentators, he advised that it was best to 'take the naked Scripture and read it over and by some distinguishing marks made in the bible to sever those Scriptures... which treat of the last times'.[126] The choice of passages was for each reader to make himself: to read the Bible 'diligently thyself', Tillinghast counselled, 'and mark them out will do thee much more good'.[127] James I, we recall, had removed from the Authorized Version the marginalia of the Geneva editors. In 1654 Tillinghast granted to every reader the right to 'mark out' holy writ. Such authority over the holy writ, as Cromwell understood no less than James, implied power in church and state too. 'I greatly rejoice... to see so much power in saints' hands,' Tillinghast writes, 'and believe more will be every day.'[128] Indeed, in a final address he appears willing to surrender his own authority and to give literally the last word to his readers. Listing the printer's errors, Tillinghast desired the reader 'with thy pen to amend' them. As for punctuation and orthography, he closed, 'let thine own reason be thy monitor'.[129]

The course of politics was soon to remove power from the saints' hands. Nor will we be surprised to discover that increasingly there was a reaction against the hermeneutic freedom of the individual and renewed emphasis upon authorized and authoritative interpretation of God's word and will. The backlash against millenarian fervour came early from expected quarters. In 1650, for example, Joseph Hall, former bishop of Norwich, published a 'polemical discourse against the tenets of the millenaries' in *The Revelation Unrevealed*.[130] Hall's title epitomized his interpretive strategy – or rather his argument against interpretation itself. Surveying some of the many interpretations and applications of the book of Revelation in recent times, Hall dwelt on the 'obscurity' and 'multiplicity of sense' in the biblical text and the 'multiplicity of judgement amongst learned and Christian interpreters'.[131] Rejecting the claims of the spirit to probe God's meaning, he asked: 'which reader doth not find himself lost in this wilderness of opinions?'[132] Too many exegetes, Hall protested, 'strained [Scripture] to the defence of their assertion'; the millenarians in particular 'put a merely literal construction upon the prophecies', which were better spiritually understood'.[133] Hall dismissed their false confidence and urged readers to beware their 'errors of opinion'.[134] Amidst uncertainty he advised all to 'a safe suspension of judgement in a matter so abtruse and *altogether indeterminable*'.[135] Only the course of events would disclose the meaning of prophecy; till then it 'will become modest Christians . . . to leave the unlocking of the secret cabinets of the Almighty'.[136] Coming from a former bishop, Hall's denunciation of prophetic politics may seem unworthy of remark. But we should note that his book was licensed in 1650 as a 'learned and judicious work' by John Downham, Puritan divine and licenser of the press.[137]

A sense that radical reading of Revelation was again causing concern in official circles is confirmed by Samuel Hartlib's English translation of Comenius's *Clavis Apocalyptica* in 1651. Comenius himself, unlike Hall, may have recommended Revelation to all 'such as know what the communion of saints doth mean', but the preface to the English edition both qualified millenarian expectations and denounced radical politics.[138] In his prefatory address to Hartlib, the former royal chaplain John Durie, condemning those sects who 'dethrone God and Christ in their ranting and blasphemous imaginations', proceeded to cautionary remarks about the interpretation of prophecy.[139] Durie did not deny Comenius's learning. But where Comenius's purpose had been to relate Revelation 'unto our present times' and to encourage 'every rational man' to 'make the application' for himself, Durie 'confessed himself, though once drawn by such arguments, now to be sceptical of the predictions . . . and unhappy with the whole method' of exegesis.[140] He had come to consider historical exegesis and direct application neither 'certain' nor 'obvious', nor 'proportionate to the capacity of all sincere professors'.[141] Durie argued instead that the kingdom of Christ was manifested not in 'particular concernments' but in 'the nature of man'.[142] In an explicit rebuke to those who applied biblical prophecy to contemporary events, Durie italicized his counter-hermeneutic rule: '*no prophecy is of particular application*'.[143]

After 1653 the shift to more conservative politics was progressively accompanied by efforts to delimit hermeneutic freedom and to exercise that control over the interpretation of Scripture that Hobbes had argued was essential to order and government.[144] Towards the end of the Protectorate, in 1658, James Durham, a confidant of Cromwell, published a *Commentary upon the Book of Revelation* which may be revealing of the shifting times. Durham did not discourage the reading of apocalypse – 'it is a good thing,' he wrote, 'soberly and humbly to read and to seek to understand it'.[145] The problem, as he identified it, stemmed from the wrong sort of readings and readers. In a section subtitled 'Of Reading and Readers,' therefore, Durham expressed his conviction that readers could not 'be left to arbitrariness' in interpreting Revelation.[146] For too many manifested 'lightness... in the practice of reading', still worse, an 'itching after some new doctrine and a... discontent with sound doctrine'.[147] Re-emphasizing informed judgement over personal inspiration, Durham insisted that 'seeing every one hath not that ability to discern poison from good food, there must therefore be a necessity that people regulate their Christian liberty in this'.[148] In reading, that is, Christians should be guided by what the most learned commentators had written and what the most judicious preachers expounded.

In a move that explicitly connected hermeneutic to political authority, Durham proceeded to discuss 'church government and discipline', and to stress the necessity for regulation here too: 'authority,' he proclaimed, in language that had become unfamiliar, 'lies in God's appointing such to rule and such others to obey'.[149] The individual had no more 'Christian liberty' to determine his own church than to make his own meaning of Scripture. Enacting his belief that Christians needed to be told and taught, Durham published a series of lectures on Revelation, nearly 800 pages in length, the very size and form of his book announcing the authority upon which the author insists. Durham displays formidable learning; he identifies but resolves difficulties and interpretive differences; his tone is didactic, in places authoritarian. What he eschews is application. Asserting against the familists that events 'cannot be expected from the text', Durham denounces those who 'expect too great a temporal kingdom or an absolute universal freedom to come'.[150] Christ, he maintained, against Tillinghast especially, would not reign with his saints on earth.[151]

Durham, like James VI, closed his exegesis with a warning to other commentators. 'God,' he admonished, 'will preserve this piece of sovereignty to himself to decide what shall be accounted his revelation and will have no other meddle with it.'[152] It is no coincidence that within two years another Stuart, claiming, with the approbation of his readers, to be God's lieutenant on earth, would again assume 'sovereignty' and assert once more that in 'his word' his 'supremacy doth especially consist'.[153]

IV

During the interregnum the millenarians had turned the world upside down. We might therefore expect that the Restoration marked the demise of apocalyptic hermeneutics as well as millenarian politics; Christopher Hill has indeed asserted the 'rapid disappearance' of the Antichrist after 1660.[154] The story is not so simple, however; and it is one of change rather than termination.[155] Revelation remained a text too fundamental to ignore. In the so-called age of science and reason, we now know that Newton laboured to calculate the day of the Second Coming. Rather than abandoning Revelation, in the changed and changing circumstances of Restoration England, old and new readers read the book differently and devised different, and competing, hermeneutic methods to make apocalypse speak to their situation and for their cause. As the radicals confronted defeat, as the church faced the revived threat of resurgent Catholicism and the new challenge of atheism, all looked to Revelation, for solace and ammunition. When the 'great deliverer' William III arrived to rescue Protestantism from the beast of Rome, millenarian languages and images were heard and seen again, to underpin rather than undermine authority.[156] Far from it marking the end of scriptural politics, Jonathan Clark has argued for eighteenth-century England as a theocratic state.[157] In any such state, Revelation remained a text that all needed to read, own and appropriate.

Amid the euphoria of Restoration, with Charles II heralded as a returning David, those who had expected God's rule on earth were forced to review their course. In 1661 the Fifth-Monarchist preacher Thomas Venner led a last desperate rising to set up Christ's kingdom. Milton, contemplating a paradise lost, sought the ways of God in epic. The visionary London tailor Lodovick Muggleton penned *A True Interpretation of... the Revelation*. Muggleton's reading had certainly led him to reject kings; he was sure that the red horse of apocalypse represented 'kings and magistrates who do ride upon the people'; even Protestant monarchs had shed the blood of the faithful.[158] Bishops, too, he saw, were guilty of superstition and persecution.[159] But Muggleton had no more time for the sects who had ruled during interregnum. Baptists, Ranters and Quakers he dismissed as 'all superstitious'; Presbyterians and Independents had been the 'two anti-angels' of the church.[160] Muggleton rejected all their claims to authority as the voice of the beast. Articulating a revolutionary epistemology as well as a radical theology, Muggleton denounced the authority of reason as that of the devil. As he glossed Revelation, he found the bottomless pit to be the 'imagination of reason in man' and the devil's work most in evidence when 'the imagination of reason is exercised upon a religious account'.[161] In his preface to his readers Muggleton explained that the right interpretation of Revelation necessitated the experience rather than the rational understanding of vision – 'visions are hard to be interpreted by one that never had them'.[162] It was the revelation of faith in vision that opened 'the interpretation of the chief things'; to those to whom the faith had not been revealed the mysteries were 'hard for me to explain in words'.[163] In place of preachers and learning Muggleton proclaimed the sole authority of the 'spirit of faith' to open the mysteries and 'hard sayings'. 'God hath given us,' he assured his readers, 'the chosen witnesses of the spirit, more knowledge in the Scriptures than all the men in the world... the gift of revelation and interpretation of many visions and revelations.'[164]

Though he stopped short of revolutionary action, Muggleton made dangerous claims for the hermeneutic authority of the visionary witness at a time when the church, like the king, was trying to regain control. Not surprisingly, therefore, conservative commentators wrote to dampen the flames of millenarian passion and to narrow the scope for radical interpretation of Scripture, just as the Royal Society was established to promote the authority of reason over enthusiasm and of logic over the anarchic ambiguity of words.[165]

In *The Meaning of the Revelation* (1675) the Oxford theologian Richard Hayter poured scorn on all the recent attempts to apply Revelation to the times – 'what is it,' he asked, 'that one may not find there?'[166] To rein in interpretive freedom, Hayter denied that prophecy had already been realized and observed that it was anyway 'written unto Asia and not unto Europe'.[167] More generally, he argued forcefully against mystical interpretations which led to 'absurdity'; 'the literal sense of Scripture is... the only rule both of faith and manners'.[168] Mystical reading, he explained, 'subjects the Scripture to our vain lusts and humours and gives everyone liberty to interpret as his humour leads him'; 'it makes men,' he continued, in language that resonates with recent history and conflict, 'interpret the Revelation... of themselves or of their own party'.[169] We may not, he took it as a rule, 'make of the Scripture a nose of wax and turn it wither we please'.[170] But while firmly denying the freedom of readers to apply and deploy Revelation as they chose, Hayter certainly had his own agenda – and one for the times. In the first place, he evidently did not regard Rome as the threat other commentators had feared and was sceptical about the identification of the pope with the Antichrist. In consequence, he maintained, 'we may not begin a war with papists, thinking thereby to fulfil the prophecies of Revelation'.[171] Rather, the text suggested that Christians should 'live peaceably' with all men and leave battles against false religion to the day of judgement.[172] Indeed, it was not Catholics but separatists and visionaries whom Hayter took to be the principal threat. In language that directly answers Muggleton, Hayter affirmed that 'men have reason to guide them' and reason was the best interpreter of Scripture.[173] In his exegesis of Revelation Hayter argued that the structure of the text (which many others had found confused and disordered) expressed the rational order that he desired in church and state. Denying that holy writ could possibly be a 'confused chaos', and rejecting Mede's synchronisms, he found that Revelation 'set down things in order, as a chronicle doth'.[174] Dismissing the 'vain hopes' of millenarians, Hayter reread Revelation, and counselled others to read it, as a book that revealed the rational order of the world and taught peace and patience to all Christians. 'On earth peace,' he closes with a prayer for the healing of dispute, 'and good will towards men'.[175]

As time passed and the threat of revolutionary millenarian politics subsided, the Restoration church faced other challenges. In general, a mood of scepticism became fashionable among the court and coffee-house wits, leading to fears of atheism and unbelief.[176] More particularly, Charles II's foreign policy and most probably private faith had fostered closer relations with France and a greater tolerance towards Catholics. We can hear contemporary concern about both developments in Henry More's *Apocalypsis Apocalypseosis, or The Revelation of St John the Divine Unveiled*, a work published in 1680 amid the paranoia of the Popish Plot. More, one of the so-called Cambridge Platonists, had written before in defence of the church against both Rome and the sectaries. In 1680 his commentary was directed first and foremost at the 'profane Hobbians and Spinozians' who dismissed Revelation as imagination and who did 'laugh at anyone for a fool that pretends the endeavouring to understand prophecies'.[177] Scepticism about Revelation was, More feared, the first step to atheism: 'the pretending to understand the Apocalypse seem[s] a fanciful ridiculous thing to the wits of this age that are ready to sneer and flear at any such profession, and indeed at the serious profession of any religion at all, as if it were an indication of but mean parts and wit, and in great ignorance of matters of philosophy'.[178] Against them, More argued that it was Revelation that revealed the truth of natural religion and confirmed the existence of God.[179] As well as defending Christian belief, More was concerned to read Revelation as support for the church of England and to discourage other interpretations. Against those who had claimed that a man may 'make [of the text] quidlibet ex quolibet as he pleases', he affirmed that 'there is but one right sense', the elucidation of which was not for ordinary men.[180] 'And therefore,' he argued, 'enthusiasts that attempt any exposition of this book without carefully consulting the most likely interpreters before them, it is no inspiration of the spirit in them but a blind puff of pride and vanity of mind.'[181] Understanding required careful scholarly exegesis, and More himself favoured learned commentary, detailed annotation and historical method based on extensive research. Such scholarship revealed the 'right sense' of Revelation to be a justification of Protestant separation from Rome and celebration of the church of England as the fulfilment of prophecy.[182] That Rome was the whore and the church of England the true church More was 'as well assured of and as little doubt of as I do any demonstration in Euclid'.[183] The next year More returned to the apocalypse at a time when he feared that 'but dough baked Protestants' were in 'great peril to be kneed again into the old sour lump of popery'.[184] In circumstances where there was 'strong effort by the popish party to bring their religion again here in England', he frankly stated that his first duty as an exegete of Revelation was to 'defend the established religion'.[185] Far from abandoning Revelation, the church took it up as a principal weapon against critics and foes.

Within a few years, as we know, realizing all More's fears, the popish party brought their religion to the very throne of England. Interestingly, few commentaries on Revelation were published in England during the reign of James II – apart from anonymous supplements to More.[186] Revelation had become a Protestant text in England and no attempt appears to have been made to publish a Catholic exposition. Rather, during the 1680s, apocalyptic language was the discourse of opposition and apocalypse the theme of virulently anti-papal cartoons as well as pamphlets and squibs.[187] No less than the repulsion of the armada in 1588, the invasion of William of Orange in 1688 was viewed as a national deliverance, a victory over the Antichrist foretold in Revelation. As Tony Claydon has shown, William III was lauded as the angel of the apocalypse and depicted as the saviour riding the white horse, restoring the word and rescuing the realm from the bottomless pit.[188]

In retrospect the 1688 Revolution may appear an inevitable success. But the outcome of William's invasion, planned in that summer, hung in the balance until James II fled in December. During those anxious months, the Baptist émigré who had returned to London, Hanserd Knollys, undertook an *Exposition of the Whole Book of Revelation* which would advance the cause of William and Protestantism. Knollys's book was licensed – we know not by whom – in September 1688, when the French attacks on the Palatinate led William to embark for England, and was clearly intended to help secure him a welcome.[189] Throughout his exposition Knollys rereads Revelation as the demonstration of 'antichristian papal power', but this time his emphasis is also on the allies of the beast.[190] The 'sun' of chapter 16 he instructed readers now to understand as the emperor and king of France, the 'lights of Rome'. But Revelation foretold deliverance, and, Knollys comforted his readers, 'if the historians say true we may conjecture that the ending time of the beast's forty two months...will be about 1688'.[191] From that 'conjecture' came a deduction very much for the moment. Knollys closed his treatise 'with an invitation to all the people of God to come out of Babylon'. 'Leave going to and worshipping in...popish temples', he admonished, or face the plagues of Revelation 18.8 – famine, fire and death.[192]

England responded to his call. By November William was on his way to his 'spiritual Jerusalem', London, where he was heralded as a second Elizabeth, who had rescued the kingdom from darkness.[193] Amid the celebrations, Walter Garrettt, vicar of Titchfield, Hampshire, reread his Bible and found 'the Church of England...particularly described' in the fourth and fifth chapters of the book of Revelation.[194] Garrett prefaced his *Essay* of 1690 with a dedication to William and Mary, expressing 'rapturous excess of joy and gratitude for [our] late wonderful deliverance'. His design in writing, he informed them, was 'to make it evident to your majesties, and to all the world, in my way (that is by Scripture prophecy) what a heavenly church...your Majesties have saved from ruin'. 'You are,' he told the royal pair, 'the chosen servants of Christ.'[195]

As he proceeded to explain the 'main strokes' of the chapters, Garrett pointed up the resemblance of the sitter with the sealed book (Revelation 5) to kings of England who enjoyed the title 'Defender of the Faith'.[196] God had throughout history chosen as protectors of his church kings whose laws had proved 'thunders' against Rome.[197] And now he presented William as the heir to Elizabeth, who had checked 'the deluge of popery'.[198] In a new and at first reading surprising departure, Garrett, in his catalogue of kings, singled out Charles I 'of blessed memory' as a godly ruler, the lion of the tribe of Juda who, in fulfilment of prophecy, had been slain, as indeed the representative of Christ. Charles, Garrett continued, was 'the root of David', father of that 'so glorious monarch king Charles the second who carried in his life and reign so intimate a resemblance to the patriarch David' and who again brought back the ark of the lord.[199] As he read on in his Revelation, Garrett became certain that 'the wonderful work of God in restoring both king and church in the year 1660...are things worthy to be *made* the subject of this prophecy'.[200]

As Garrett makes plain, the succession of William had restored the historical bond between church and monarchy which James II had ruptured but which Charles I, in the loyal rhetoric of Restoration, had come to symbolize no less than the Protestant Deborah, Elizabeth.[201] For Garrett, it was now fitting not only to read but to 'make' Revelation a prophecy of recent English history and 'not applicable to any other king and church in the whole world'.[202] The church of England, Garrett concluded, transmuting radical millenarian prophecy into conservative polemic, was the Fifth Monarchy: 'there seems to be no fear that the church of England should ever be destroyed another time'.[203] It now remained only for God and his exegetes to illuminate the minds of others, so that 'both the erroneous may come over to the communion of this excellent church [and] the wavering may be established in it'.[204]

In a short, revolutionary year, readings of Revelation had shifted from fearful anxiety to confident celebration. As William prepared to lead his armies in Europe, Revelation was quickly mustered to support his cause on the international stage. In a sermon on Revelation 2.11 of 1692 Thomas Beverley saw foretold in the rising of the witnesses 'the great works that will...show forth themselves so as to be completed by 1697'.[205] For the kingdom of Christ was approaching, and 'why,' he asked, 'may not this be this summer', as William moved to rescue the oppressed Protestants in Piedmont.[206] Reading with a 'sound sober mind', not indulging fantasy or enthusiasm, Beverley instructed his flock to 'compare what I declare to you from the word of God and what you see come to pass'.[207] Thence they would see the 'undertaking of Protestant princes and their arms', which signalled the arrival of God's kingdom.[208]

At home, as the Revolution settlement in church and state looked more established, the political emphasis shifted to healing and settling and the alleviation of bitter exchange and party division. In his preface to his paraphrase of *The Book of the Revelation* of 1693, Edward Waple explicitly connected biblical exegesis to contemporary politics when he advised that 'a man who would understand the will of God in this prophecy must... renounce parties and prejudices'.[209] The 'prejudice' Waple seemed most concerned about in 1693 was no longer Catholicism but an overzealous Protestantism. While he would not subscribe to a jejune formality in religion, Waple felt his nation too 'prone to enthusiasm'.[210] And in an excellent demonstration of the relationship of textual form to ideological position, he promised that in his own writing 'bare imagination hath not been the least indulged but in the annotations where it is lawful to pose conjectures to the learned world and to give the reins of fancy but under the curb and restraints of Reason and Prudence'.[211] Waple's text was what he wished his church to be: inspired but restrained, divine but rational, fervent but prudent, a church (and text) that restricted theological quarrels to the learned and promoted the core of Christian belief to the people.

In his long treatise, Waple cross-referenced to all the Scriptures, closely examined difficult passages and drew on a wide range of earlier

commentators, such as Mede, Grotius, Hammond, Beverley and others.[212]
Like several post-Restoration commentators, he claimed Revelation as the
'most illustrious proof for the being of a God' against the 'atheists', and as
demonstration that 'the papacy is the antichrist'.[213] What is novel in his exegesis is his finding in the text the lessons of unity and tolerance. Waple even
half apologizes to Catholics, whom he asks to take no offence at the sometimes 'harsh expressions' he has used.[214] When he turns to the Protestants,
his message is clear: the divisions among them evidenced the imperfection
of the Reformation, which had, in England, been tarnished since Elizabeth's
reign by 'the contrary strugglings of two parties' through whose 'mutual
animosities and immoderate opposition... things have sometimes rather
gone back than forwards'.[215] Division was the obstacle, Waple argued in
the language of politeness, 'to all noble and peaceable designs'.[216] Revelation, as he read it, taught Christians that since all churches were imperfect,
the best 'ought to bear with the worst'; for there was 'scarce any erroneous
persuasion in religion that hath not some truth mixed with it'.[217] Pointing
out that even the Quakers, the most feared of the sects, taught the duty of
Christian patience, Waple argued for toleration of all confessions as both
the message of Scripture and the interest of the state.[218] It was, he posited,
right for the church to 'consider what is good' in other sects rather than 'to
confute them', and 'of greater benefit to the state to amend the faults which
occasioned them than to prosecute them with rigour'.[219] Now that Protestantism was secure, Revelation, once the text for civil war and sectarian
strife, was being reread and rewritten as a script for unity and toleration.

The 1688 Revolution produced a stable settlement not least because the
Whigs secured a cultural as well as political dominance. It was the Whig
view of the constitution, of history and of the law that became the 'national'
view.[220] No less was it a Whig reading of church history and Scripture
that underpinned the more latitudinarian church of England that emerged
after the Toleration Act of 1689. For thirty years Walter Garrett continued
his series of chapter-by-chapter expositions of the book of Revelation.[221]
Garrett discussed various approaches to Revelation and engaged with some
other commentators. But his own view was clear: Revelation told the history
of two churches – that of Rome until the reign of Queen Elizabeth and that
of the church of England thereafter. From that hypothesis he interpreted
every vision, showing that Elizabeth, Charles I and Charles II represented
God the creator, Christ the martyr and Christ the resurrected. Though
'pseudo-Protestant' popish persecutors had brought down Charles I, the
Lord had restored his church in 1660, as indeed he again saved it from
the 'serpentine practices' of papists under James II and of sectaries under

William III.[222] Garrett saw 1697 as the fulfilment of biblical prophecy. When William led the gallant army of the fifth trumpet to victory at Ryswick, and so forced the French to recognize his legitimacy, he finally extirpated the Antichrist. Here, Garrett opined, was 'the greatest revolution that ever befel this powerful nation', one that secured at last both the church of Christ and 'that admirable constitution that we... by the singular favour of our good God are blessed withall'.[223] 'No man,' Garrett concluded, 'can have a right understanding of the Revelation but he must have a more than ordinary esteem and veneration for the church of England, which questionless is thus singled out by the spirit of prophecy.'[224] The Revolution had brought to England the end of Revelation.

Garrett's became the official, even the established, view. But it was by no means the only view of the church in the past or present. Queen Anne's reign again witnessed fierce argument and bitter division as high Anglicans attempted to regain control of the church and prosecute dissent.[225] And the voices of millenarian prophets were still heard, not least through the writings of the Quaker Jane Lead and of John Lacey, who published his *Prophetical Warnings*, 'a pseudo-biblical rant', as they have been described, in 1707.[226] During the last years of the seventeenth century and the early years of the eighteenth, Paul Korshin writes, 'the church establishment stayed aloof from the contemporary debate over millenialism and the genuineness of prophetical inspiration about the apocalypse'.[227] But official disengagement from millenarian controversy by no means signalled the end of the exegesis of Revelation, in the parish or in print. In his dedication to the archbishop of Canterbury of his guide to Revelation, Edward Wells, rector of Cotesbach, Lincolnshire, emphasized the vital need 'to find out the true meaning of this... book', though it was 'the most difficult in the whole canon of Scripture'.[228] In a very learned tome, Wells printed the original Greek text alongside a translation and textual notes, and with, on the facing page, a full commentary. Here, Wells identified and discussed textual variants, reviewed other interpretations and deployed philological and historical analysis. His tone appears scholarly, judicious and unpolemical throughout. Rather than pointing up differences, Wells writes to mitigate the 'great and unhappy difference of opinions which is now in the church'.[229] In this case, in a move that speaks to a new literary as well as political culture, the polemic lies in the denial of polemic and partisanship, and in the form as much as in the content of Wells's treatise. The form of the text with its layers of commentary, with variation and disagreement displaced to the notes, not only made Revelation a learned work; it made its, indeed all, religious ambiguities and variations the subject of textual rather than ecclesiological or political dispute.[230] Just as in the wider culture violent conflict transmuted into party rivalry and propaganda, in Wells we discern an attempt to move religious controversy from the parish to the scholarly page.[231]

We have learned, however, that if civil war and revolution civilized political engagement, they also fully politicized society and culture. That is to say, while politics became increasingly a battle of books and words, all texts and textual performances participated in and were marked by political contest. After 1642, as Steven Zwicker has demonstrated, all literary forms and genres were rendered partisan; even those that seemed to eschew engagement, like Walton's *Compleat Angler*, were no less polemical than those which embraced it.[232] We need to appreciate that this is true for other texts which critics have yet fully to examine: travel writing, medical and scientific treatises, histories – and scriptural exegeses. Dryden, Swift and Pope were not only immersed in political as well as literary skirmish; they all devoted time and space to mocking and satirizing millenarian beliefs and prophecies, just as the scientific establishment increasingly characterized them as insane.

Yet we should not take the *Dunciad* as the death knell for apocalypse: mockery and charges of madness express anxiety about the persistent force of heterodox beliefs. The new aesthetic of reason, wit and ridicule discloses an enduring fear of enthusiasm and the broadest cultural moves to contain it. We may also discern them in the last of the commentaries on Revelation we shall consider, Charles Daubuz's *A Perpetual Commentary on the Revelation*, published in 1720. Daubuz, the son of a French émigré and vicar of Brotherton, Yorkshire, had little time for those who dismissed prophecy in a 'sceptical and inquisitive age'.[233] He regarded Revelation as the best commentary on the history and destiny of the church and therefore held it imperative to 'convince all men' of its importance and meaning.[234] Like Wells, Daubuz eschewed the interpretational war over the text in which 'each endeavours to draw it to his side'.[235] He sought rather a 'full account of this prophetical enigma' which was 'able to bear itself out with such clearness as to convince all men that the whole is understood'.[236] Daubuz's desire for agreement was not new. But the language and strategies he deployed in making his case open interesting windows onto the textual and political culture of eighteenth-century England. In the first place, Daubuz found the unity and harmony he sought in the world within the text of Revelation itself. The key to the book, he argued, 'depends upon the admirable conjuncture of its parts and their mutual relation', the 'harmony and correspondency' of the parts together.[237] Secondly, he insisted that the key to understanding was knowledge of the symbolic system from which it emerged, a 'system of principles to understand the prophetic language'.[238] But as he turned to explicate the symbols by reference to Egyptian and Jewish antiquities, poetry and dreams, Daubuz read his Scripture, as perforce all exegetes did (and do), as a text of his own culture, with its own signifying forms and systems.

To assist readers with mysterious symbols, Daubuz advised them to consider the contemporary blazons or imprese which were an essential part of aristocratic and heraldic culture: 'the visions of St. John,' he advised, '*are* emblems or prophetical impressas, having figures exposed to the sight and mottoes to explain the precise meaning of the symbol'.[239] If here Revelation becomes a book of eighteenth-century aristocratic society, Daubuz proceeds to read it as a text of Augustan aesthetics – as a piece of theatre and painting. Some commentators, such as Mede, he pointed out, had passed over certain passages of Revelation as mere decoration. But, he asked a society in which scene had recently become vital to drama, 'is not the decoration of a theatre and the preparation of the scenes as necessary to the full representation of the actions as words?'[240] So, he continued, 'without these decorations of the theatre and particular scenes of the actions in these apostolical visions, they would be inexplicable'.[241] Similarly, to a society in which the decorative and visual arts had become part of polite culture, Daubuz explicated the form of Revelation as if he were a critic analysing a canvas. For, he explained, 'a prophecy is a picture or representation... in symbols'; so 'as in a picture, which is a kind of human invention... the principal and fairest part of the object for the sight and to strike in the spectator the greatest attention, is placed in the fairest light... so it is the method of the holy ghost'.[242] To win the attention of his own 'spectators', Daubuz did not confine his analogies to the visual and performative arts. Though he admitted to a sceptical age that he could not provide 'philosophical demonstrations' of his case, Daubuz stressed the 'reasonableness' of the Holy Ghost and the rationality of his 'system of principles' that enabled his exposition to be 'as certain and evident as that of geometrical theorems'.[243] In Daubuz's hands, Revelation folds into the scientific and aesthetic culture of Augustan England, to become a set of symbols and representations rather than a script for millenarian action.

V

Daubuz, like all the commentators we have encountered, read and interpreted the book of Revelation in and for his own age. The elucidation of the meaning of Scripture was, and is, always an act of interpreting and commenting on the exegete's own time. That is to say, of course, that it was always an ideological and political act, intended to validate a view or position. Scriptural exegesis, therefore, is a genre that historians cannot afford to ignore and to which they need to pay greater attention. In commentaries on Revelation we have seen a set of contemporary perceptions of faith and church, society and state, which have revised as well as complemented the traditional picture. In most of the expositions of the text we have discerned ambivalencies and anxieties which take us to the heart of early modern society and the early modern psyche – anxieties about faith and reason, order and chaos, certainty and indeterminacy, authority and individual freedom.

These anxieties have been disclosed in contemporary readers' encounters with the prime text of their culture, the Bible. In other words, as we are beginning to appreciate from other disciplines and perspectives, the historical processes that determined the institutions of church and society, self and state, were predominantly textual, hermeneutic processes. To put it boldly, the history of early modern England was (as our telling of it is) a hermeneutic history, a series of successive, and contested, acts, in particular and changing circumstances, of reading and interpretation. The fortune of Mede's *Clavis Apocalyptica* provides a good example of the way an interpretation of Scripture could be read in different times by different groups as learned biblical scholarship, script for revolution and Anglican apologia. Expositions and commentaries, that is, were as unstable and as open to multiple interpretations as Scripture itself.

Indeed, what all the works we have examined also suggest is that, with varying degrees of approval, our readers and commentators on Revelation recognized that their own readings would be reread, and that their endeavours to establish authoritative interpretations would be frustrated. The often elaborate and plaintive epistles to readers, the form and arrangement of texts, with (or without) careful charts and detailed notes, witness both the authors' quest to determine meaning and their recognition that ultimately it lay outside their control – with printers who introduced changes and errata, with licensers, most of all with readers. Beyond a history of biblical exegesis, then, we are led to the reception of expositions and to the occasional traces of individual readers who marked up their text, scribbled in the margins or bound their books together, as did the late seventeenth-century antiquaries Ashmole and Wood, in ways that disclose how they interpreted and valued and engaged with books.[244] While that next move lies beyond the scope of this essay, one cannot help but ponder Robert Kelsey's references to classical pagan texts as he read Gifford's sermons on

Revelation, or the pen that marked the passage of Knollys that foretold the end of the beast in 1688. Such marks of reading are inconsistent and hard to interpret, just like Scripture itself. But far from telling us nothing about the past, they graphically underline how textual, hermeneutic and political authorities were, and remain, in a continuous but shifting process of debate and exchange – one we might even call the human condition.

NOTES

1. Quoted in C. Hill, *The English Bible and the Seventeenth-Century Revolution* (London, 1993), p. 31. I wish to thank Chris Haigh, Peter Lake and Steve Zwicker for helpful comments on this essay.
2. See A. Manguel, *A History of Reading* (London, 1996), pp. 270–6; and G. Cavallo and R. Chartier, eds., *A History of Reading in the West*, trans. L. G. Cochrane (Oxford, 1999), chapters 8, 9.
3. See C. Haigh, *English Reformations* (Oxford, 1993).
4. See A. C. Partridge, *English Biblical Translation* (London, 1975); and B. F. Westcott, *A General View of the History of the English Bible* (London, 1905).
5. M. Betteridge, 'The Bitter Notes: The Geneva Bible and Its Annotations', *Sixteenth Century Journal*, 14 (1983), pp. 41–62, quotation p. 45. I owe this reference to the kindness of Diarmaid McCulloch.
6. Ibid., p. 53.
7. Ibid., p. 48.
8. 'Barker's Bible', 1616, University of Southampton Rare Books Library.
9. Hill, *The English Bible*, p. 299; see also A. Williamson, *Scottish National Consciousness in the Age of James VI* (Edinburgh, 1979), p. viii.
10. A. Dent, *The Ruine of Rome, or An Exposition upon the Whole Revelation* (London, 1602), sig. A3v; A. Marlorate, *A Catholic Exposition of the Revelation of St John* (London, 1574), fol. IV.
11. See M. Forey, 'Language and Revelation: English Apocalyptic Literature, 1500–1660' (Ph.D. dissertation, University of Oxford, 1993), p. 65; K. Firth, *The Apocalyptic Tradition in Reformation Britain, 1530–1645* (Oxford, 1979), chapter 1; and N. Cohn, *The Pursuit of the Millenium* (London, 1970), chapter 1.
12. See Cohn, *The Pursuit of the Millenium*, chapters 6, 11.
13. See Firth, *The Apocalyptic Tradition*, pp. 9–10.
14. See R. K. Emmerson, *Antichrist in the Middle Ages* (Seattle, 1981), pp. 204–36; Firth, *The Apocalyptic Tradition*, passim.
15. See Firth, *The Apocalyptic Tradition*, p. 122.
16. See the Geneva Bible of 1579 and the Barker edition of 1616.
17. E. Waple, *The Book of the Revelation Paraphrased* (London, 1693), p. 504; for Waple, see below, pp. 149–50; D. Pareus, *A Commentary upon the Divine Revelation of the Apostle John* (London, 1641), p. 20.
18. Pareus, *Commentary*, pp. 20, 26; R. Bernard, *A Key of Knowledge for the Opening of the Secret Mysteries of St John's Mystical Revelation* (London, 1617),

p. 130; cf. J. Tillinghast's description of Revelation as 'doleful tragedy', *Generation Work: The Second Part* (London, 1654), p. 159.

19. W. Perkins, *A Godly and Learned Commentarie upon the Three First Chapters of the Revelation* (London, 1607), sig. A4v.
20. Dent, *The Ruine of Rome*, p. 47.
21. Tillinghast, *Generation Work*, p. 264.
22. Dent, *The Ruine of Rome*, p. 217.
23. J. Napier, *A Plaine Discovery of the Whole Revelation of St John* (Edinburgh, 1593), p. 270.
24. Marlorate, *A Catholic Exposition*, fols. 192r–193r.
25. Ibid., fols. 49v, 236r.
26. Ibid., fol. 1v.
27. Ibid., fols. 61v, 181v, 183r, 201r.
28. Ibid., fol. 89r.
29. Ibid., sig. q3v.
30. See B. Capp, 'The Political Dimension of Apocalyptic Thought', in C. A. Patrides and J. Wittreich, eds., *The Apocalypse in English Renaissance Thought and Literature* (Manchester, 1984), pp. 93–124, especially pp. 97–8. See also E. S. Richey, *The Politics of Revelation in the English Renaissance* (Columbia, Miss., 1998), p. 7.
31. See M. Forey, 'Language and Revelation', p. 41.
32. G. Gifford, *Sermons . . . on the Whole Book of the Revelation* (London, 1596).
33. Ibid., sig. A3v.
34. Ibid., sig. A8v.
35. Ibid., p. 30.
36. Ibid., pp. 85, 445.
37. Ibid., p. 105.
38. James VI and I, *A Paraphrase upon the Revelation* and *An Fruitful Meditation Containing a Plaine and Easie Exposition . . . of the Twentieth Chapter of the Revelation* (Edinburgh, 1588), both in *The Workes of the Most High and Mighty Prince James* (London, 1616). See D. Fischlin, '"To Eate the Flesh of Kings": James VI, Apocalypse, Nation, Sovereignty', in D. Fischlin and M. Fortier, eds., *Royal Subjects: Essays on the Writings of James VI and I* (Detroit, 2002), pp. 388–420.
39. James I, *Workes*, p. 73.
40. See K. Sharpe, 'The King's Writ: Royal Authors and Royal Authority in Early Modern England', in Sharpe, *Remapping Early Modern England: The Culture of Seventeenth-Century Politics* (Cambridge, 2000), chapter 3.
41. James I, *Workes*, p. 32.
42. Ibid., p. 80.
43. Ibid., p. 66.
44. Ibid., p. 40.
45. Ibid., p. 72.
46. Napier, *A Plaine Discovery*, sig. A6, p. 49.
47. Ibid., pp. 270–2.

48. Ibid., p. 272.
49. Dent, *The Ruine of Rome*, 'The Epistle to the Christian Reader'.
50. Ibid.
51. Ibid.
52. Ibid., pp. 47, 74.
53. Ibid., p. 89.
54. Ibid., p. 89; cf. p. 192.
55. Ibid., p. 283.
56. For Calvinist conformists, see P. Lake, *Moderate Puritans and the Eliza-bethan Church* (Cambridge, 1982); Lake, 'Calvinism and the English Church, 1570–1635', *Past and Present*, 114 (1987), pp. 32–76; and P. Collinson, *The Religion of Protestants* (Oxford, 1982).
57. Perkins, *A Godly and Learned Commentarie*, p. 2.
58. Ibid., p. 55.
59. Ibid., p. 18.
60. Ibid., pp. 10, 18, 48, 69.
61. Ibid., pp. 11, 18.
62. Ibid., p. 195.
63. Ibid., p. 9.
64. Ibid., pp. 127–8.
65. Ibid., p. 42.
66. Ibid., pp. 19, 42, 70.
67. Ibid., p. 181.
68. Ibid., p. 127.
69. Ibid., p. 27.
70. Ibid., p. 82; see also pp. 42–5, 51, 63.
71. Ibid., pp. 116–18.
72. Ibid., p. 3.
73. R. Bernard, *A Key of Knowledge for the Opening of the Secret Mysteries of St John's Mystical Revelation* (London, 1617), sigs. A5–A8v.
74. Ibid., sig. C7.
75. Ibid., pp. 16, 105.
76. Ibid., pp. 9, 79, 100, 123, 153, 155.
77. Ibid., pp. 100, 103.
78. Ibid., pp. 92, 237.
79. Ibid., p. 79.
80. Ibid.
81. Ibid., pp. 92, 105–7.
82. Ibid., pp. 112–13.
83. Ibid., pp. 155, 120.
84. J. Wilkinson, *An Exposition of the Thirteenth Chapter of the Revelation of Jesus Christ* (Amsterdam, 1619), verso of title page.
85. Ibid., p. 29.
86. Ibid., pp. 32, 36.
87. Ibid., p. 36.

88. Ibid., pp. 30, 31.
89. Ibid., p. 29.
90. Ibid., p. 35.
91. T. Brightman. *A Revelation of the Revelation* (Amsterdam, 1615), sig. A3.
92. See K. Fincham and P. Lake, 'The Ecclesiastical Policy of King James I', *Journal of British Studies*, 24 (1985), pp. 169–207; Fincham and Lake, 'The Ecclesiastical Policies of James I and Charles I', in Fincham, ed., *The Early Stuart Church, 1603–1642* (Basingstoke, 1993), pp. 23–50; and A. Milton, *Catholic and Reformed: The Roman and Protestant Churches in English Protestant Thought* (Cambridge, 1995), part 1.
93. See Milton, *Catholic and Reformed*, pp. 118–127; and C. Hill, *Antichrist in Seventeenth-Century England* (Oxford, 1971), p. 37 and chapter 1, passim.
94. A. Milton, 'The Church of England, Rome and the True Church: The Demise of a Jacobean Consensus', in Fincham, ed., *The Early Stuart Church*, pp. 187–210, quotation p. 199.
95. See Hill, *Antichrist*, pp. 38–40.
96. See K. Sharpe, *The Personal Rule of Charles I* (New Haven and London, 1992), pp. 646–7, 683–90; B. Capp, *English Almanacs, 1500–1800* (London, 1979); and D. Freist, *Governed by Opinion: Politics, Religion and the Dynamics of Communication in Stuart London, 1637–1645* (London, 1997).
97. See Capp, 'The Political Dimension of Apocalyptic Thought', pp. 107–8. In particular the circles of Lords Saye and Brooke, who wrote on Revelation, *Persecutio Undecima* (London, 1648).
98. See Capp, 'The Political Dimension of Apocalyptic Thought', p. 107; and Sharpe, *The Personal Rule of Charles I*, pp. 813–24.
99. J. Lilburne, *A Work of the Beast* (London, 1638), pp. 17–18.
100. See S. N. Zwicker, *Lines of Authority: Politics and English Literary Culture, 1649–1689* (Ithaca, 1993).
101. Quoted in Capp, 'The Political Dimension of Apocalyptic Thought', p. 113.
102. See Forey, 'Language and Revelation', passim.
103. See chapter 6 below.
104. See S. Achinstein, *Milton and the Revolutionary Reader* (Princeton, 1994); K. Sharpe, *Reading Revolutions: The Politics of Reading in Early Modern England* (New Haven and London, 2000), pp. 291–2.
105. *Napier's Narration, or An Epitome of His Book on the Revelation* (London, 1641), sig. C4v.
106. *A Revelation of Mr Brightman's Revelation* (London, 1641), pp. 19, 34.
107. J. Mede, *The Key of the Revelation* (London, 1643), p. 125; for Mede, see M. Murrin, 'Revelation and Two Seventeenth-Century Commentators', in Patrides and Wittreich, eds., *The Apocalypse*, pp. 125–46.
108. Mede, *The Key of the Revelation*, sig. A3, p. 20; see Firth, *The Apocalyptic Tradition*, p. 228.
109. Mede, *The Key of the Revelation*, p. 26.
110. J. Trapp, *A Commentary or Exposition upon All the Epistles and the Revelation of John the Divine* (London, 1647), pp. 512, 530.

111. Ibid., pp. 514, 553.
112. Ibid., p. 597.
113. See P. Crawford, 'Charles Stuart, That Man of Blood', *Journal of British Studies*, 16 (1977), pp. 41–61.
114. Lady E. Davies (Douglas), *The Revelation Interpreted* (London, 1643), chapter 13; Davies, *The Day of Judgements Model* (London, 1646); E. Cope, *Handmaid of the Holy Spirit: Dame Eleanor Davies, Never soe Mad a Ladie* (Ann Arbor, Mich., 1992); and M. Matchinske, 'Holy Hatred: Formations of the Gendered Subject in English Apocalyptic Writing, 1625–1651', *English Literary History*, 60 (1993), pp. 349–77.
115. See Hill, *Antichrist*, p. 107.
116. Ibid.
117. M. Cary, *The Little Horns Doom and Downfall* (London, 1651), title page.
118. Ibid., sig. a1v, a3.
119. Ibid., p. 179.
120. Ibid., p. 106.
121. Ibid., p. 267, sig. A8. For Cary, see C. F. Otten, ed., *English Women's Voices* (Miami, 1992), pp. 100–3.
122. For the best account, see A. Woolrych, *Commonwealth to Protectorate* (Oxford, 1982)
123. Tillinghast, *Generation Work*, 'To His Highness the Lord Protector', sig. A6v.
124. Ibid., sig. a7v.
125. Ibid., sig. A8v.
126. Ibid., sig. b3v.
127. Ibid., sig. b3v.
128. Ibid., p. 215.
129. Ibid., closing address to the 'courteous reader'.
130. J. Hall, *The Revelation Unrevealed* (London, 1650). Note on title page by John Downham: 'I have perused this polemical discourse against the tenets of the millenarians and find it to be … learned and judicious.'
131. Ibid., pp. 11, 49.
132. Ibid., pp. 63–4.
133. Ibid., pp. 102, 180.
134. Ibid., p. 209.
135. Ibid., p. 66, my italics.
136. Ibid., p. 273.
137. See note 130 above.
138. S. Hartlib, *Clavis Apocalyptica, or A Prophetical Key by Which the Great Mysteries in the Revelation … Are Opened* (London, 1651), fol. 3v; Firth, *The Apocalyptic Tradition*, pp. 242–5.
139. Hartlib, *Clavis Apocalyptica*, p. 9.
140. Ibid., pp. 13–20; Firth, *The Apocalyptic Tradition*, p. 243.
141. Hartlib, *Clavis Apocalyptica*, pp. 13–15.
142. Ibid., pp. 17, 18, 22.
143. Ibid., pp. 33–4.

144. T. Hobbes, *Leviathan*, ed. R. Tuck (Cambridge, 1991), p. 378.
145. J. Durham, *A Commentary upon the Book of Revelation* (London, 1658), p. 3.
146. Ibid., p. 64.
147. Ibid.
148. Ibid., p. 65.
149. Ibid., p. 100.
150. Ibid., pp. 709, 711.
151. Ibid., p. 715.
152. Ibid., p. 781.
153. Durham, *A Commentary*, p. 781.
154. Hill, *Antichrist*, p. 154; and Hill, *The English Bible*, p. 243 and chapter 18, passim.
155. See P. Korshin, 'Queuing and Waiting: The Apocalypse in England, 1660–1750', in Patrides and Wittreich, eds., *The Apocalypse*, pp. 240–65.
156. See T. Claydon, *William III and the Godly Revolution* (Cambridge, 1996).
157. J. C. D. Clark, *English Society, 1688–1832*, 2nd edn (Cambridge, 2000).
158. L. Muggleton, *A True Interpretation of All the Chief Texts and Mysterious Sayings and Visions… of the Revelation of St John* (London, 1665), pp. 56, 200.
159. Ibid., p. 57.
160. Ibid., pp. 57, 105.
161. Ibid., pp. 91, 125.
162. Ibid., sig. A3, p. 30.
163. Ibid., pp. 199, 226.
164. Ibid., p. 230, sig. A3.
165. The Royal Society took as its motto 'Nullius in verba'.
166. R. Hayter, *The Meaning of the Revelation, or A Paraphrase with Questions on the Revelation* (London, 1675), 'To the Reader'.
167. Ibid., p. 30.
168. Ibid., pp. 201, 243; cf. pp. 74, 200.
169. Ibid., p. 201.
170. Ibid., p. 66.
171. Ibid., p. 236.
172. Ibid., pp. 223–4, 238.
173. Ibid., p. 74.
174. Ibid., pp. 95, 96–7.
175. Ibid., p. 249.
176. See M. Hunter and D. Wootton, eds., *Atheism from the Reformation to the Enlightenment* (Oxford, 1992), chapter 8; and J. Redwood, *Reason, Ridicule and Religion: The Age of Enlightenment, 1660–1750* (London, 1976).
177. H. More, *Apocalypsis Apocalypseosis, or The Revelation of St John the Divine Unveiled* (London, 1680), pp. ix, xvi.
178. Ibid., p. 357.

179. Ibid., pp. xvi–xvii and passim.
180. Ibid., p. 347.
181. Ibid., pp. 249–50.
182. Ibid., pp. xxff., 250–2, 339, 356.
183. Ibid., p. 357.
184. Henry More, *A Plain and Continued Exposition* (London, 1681), p. lxxxvii. The exposition was of both Daniel and Revelation.
185. Ibid., p. lxxx.
186. For example, *An Illustration out of Those Two Abstruse Books in Holy Scripture... Framed out of the Exposition of Dr Henry More* (London, 1685); *Paralipomena Prophetica: Containing Several Supplements and Defences of Dr H. More* (London, 1685). Of course, the staunchly Protestant exegesis by Increase Mather, *A Discourse upon the Day of Judgement*, published in Boston, was read in England.
187. The opposition to James II awaits full study; for illustrations of cartoons against the king and Catholics, see Huntington Library, Richard Bull Granger, collection of engravings, vol. 18.
188. Claydon, *William III*.
189. H. Knollys, *An Exposition of the Whole Book of Revelation* (London, 1689). The title page indicates that the book was licensed on 12 September 1688. See J. Carswell, *The Descent on England: A Study of the English Revolution of 1688 and Its European Background* (London, 1969).
190. Knollys, *An Exposition*, p. 106.
191. Ibid., p. 144.
192. Ibid., pp. 243–4.
193. Ibid., p. 138, for the reference to the 'spiritual Jerusalem'.
194. W. Garrett, *An Essay upon the Fourth and Fifth Chapters of the Revelation... Showing That the Church of England Is Particularly Described in Those Chapters* (London, 1690).
195. Ibid., sig. A2.
196. Ibid., p. 3.
197. Ibid., pp. 4–5.
198. Ibid., p. 5.
199. Ibid., p. 9.
200. Ibid., p. 9, my italics.
201. See K. Sharpe, ' "So Hard a Text?": Images of Charles I, 1616–1700', *Historical Journal*, 43 (2000), pp. 395–404.
202. Garrett, *An essay*, p. 11.
203. Ibid., p. 13.
204. Ibid., p. 14.
205. T. Beverley, *A Sermon upon the Revel. II, 11* (London, 1692), p. 1.
206. Ibid., p. 3.
207. Ibid., pp. 6, 12.
208. Ibid., p. 13.

209. E. Waple, *The Book of the Revelation Paraphrased* (London, 1693), sig. A3v.

210. Ibid., sig. A4v.

211. Ibid., sig. A5v.

212. Ibid., sig. d3, pp. 5, 6, 453, 470.

213. Ibid., sig. b1v, p. 389.

214. Ibid., sig. b4v.

215. Ibid., pp. 194, 196.

216. Ibid., p. 196.

217. Ibid., p. 192.

218. Ibid., p. 193: 'Even the behaviour of the Quakers may put Christians in remembrance of the duties of patience.'

219. Waple, *The Book of the Revelation*, p. 194.

220. See Sharpe, *Remapping Early Modern England*, chapter 1.

221. Garrett first published on the Antichrist in 1680 and was writing commentaries on various books of Revelation until 1714. See Garrett, *Of the Usefulness of the Prophecy of Revelation* (London, 1711).

222. W. Garrett, *An Exposition of Rev. VII* (London, 1702), pp. 6–9, 20 and passim.

223. W. Garrett, *An Exposition of Rev. XI* (London, 1703), pp. 14, 26.

224. Ibid., p. 26.

225. See G. Holmes, *British Politics in the Age of Anne*, 2nd edn (London, 1987); Holmes, *The Trial of Dr Sacheverell* (London, 1973).

226. See J. Lead, *The Revelation of Revelations* (London, 1683); Lead, *The Signs of the Times* (London, 1699); Korshin, 'The Apocalypse in England', pp. 246–7.

227. Korshin, 'The Apocalypse in England', p. 249.

228. E. Wells, *An Help for the More Easy and Clear Understanding of the Holy Scriptures, Being the Revelation of St John* (London, 1717), sig. a2.

229. Ibid., p. 83.

230. For the ideology of annotation, see A. Grafton, *The Footnote: A Curious History* (London, 1997).

231. Steven Zwicker also makes this point about marginalia. See S. N. Zwicker, 'Reading the Margins: Politics and the Habits of Appropriation', in K. Sharpe and S. N. Zwicker, eds., *Refiguring Revolutions: Aesthetics and Politics from the English Revolution to the Romantic Revolution* (Berkeley and London, 1998), pp. 101–15. I am grateful to Steve Zwicker for discussions of his forthcoming book on marginalia.

232. Zwicker, *Lines of Authority*, chapter 3 and passim.

233. C. Daubuz, *A Perpetual Commentary on the Revelation of St John* (London, 1720), p. 53; *DNB*.

234. Ibid., p. 17.

235. Ibid., p. 16.

236. Ibid., p. 17.

237. Ibid., pp. 17, 20, 24.

238. Ibid., p. 29.

239. Ibid., p. 35, my italics.
240. Ibid., p. 49.
241. Ibid., p. 50.
242. Ibid., pp. 44, 56.
243. Ibid., pp. 50, 53, 57.
244. I am grateful to Michael Mendle, who is working on collectors, for discussions of this subject.

PART III

Print, politics and performance

CHAPTER FIVE

Performances and playbooks: the closing of the theatres and the politics of drama

David Scott Kastan

2 September 1642 is perhaps the best-known date in the history of the English theatre. On that day, Parliament ordered the theatres closed:

whereas Public Sports do not well agree with Public Calamities, nor Public Stage-plays with the Seasons of Humiliation, this being an Exercise of sad and pious Solemnity, and the other being Spectacles of Pleasure, too commonly expressing lascivious Mirth and Levity: It is therfore thought fit, and Ordained by the Lords and Commons in this Parliament assembled, That while these sad causes and set Times of Humiliation do continue, Public Stage Plays shall cease, and be forborn.[1]

While this has often been taken as the order that ended playing for the eighteen years of the interregnum, in truth it neither accomplished that nor intended to. Parliament in September of 1642 ordered a *temporary* stay of playing, not unlike those that followed the deaths of Prince Henry or of King James, when it was similarly held 'that these tymes doe not suit such playes and idle shewes'.[2] No doubt many who voted for it hoped that the injunction would permanently remain in effect, but the explicit intent of the bill before Parliament was to stop playing at a particularly charged moment, one that demanded 'sad and pious Solemnity' rather than public sport, and that proposed, 'instead of playgoing', determined efforts to effect 'Repentence, Reconciliation, and Peace with God'. The king had raised his standard at Nottingham on 22 August, eleven days before the bill was approved, and, with civil conflict inevitable, fasts and prayers had been ordered to appease and avert the wrath of God that seemed already to be in evidence. The deteriorated political situation and the public worship mandated in response were the 'sad causes' and the 'set Times of Humiliation' that the bill spoke of. In 1642, the decision to prohibit playing was undertaken in the name of propriety at least as much as in that of politics.

Playing, of course, did not end with the 1642 ordinance ('ordinance' being the formal term used, until the king's execution, for acts passed without royal consent). The players 'persevering in their forbidden Art', as an issue of the *Weekly Account* put it in 1643, led the next year to the inclusion of an article in the Treaty of Uxbridge demanding the king's assent to an act 'for the suppressing of interludes and stage playes' (a suppression that its proponents hoped would be 'perpetual'), and, indeed, the continued inability to eliminate playing forced Parliament in both 1647 and 1648 to renew its own prohibition.[3] Nonetheless, the 1642 injunction has usually been understood as the 'closing of the theatres' and as the victory of the parliamentary Puritans, the triumph of their anti-theatricality by legislative means. Certainly, Francis Rous, the author of the injunction, was a committed Calvinist, who turned to government service precisely (in every sense of the word) to help effect a further reformation. The language of the order in places reveals his scruple, mainly in its obvious discomfort with the 'lascivious Mirth and Levity' produced by the theatre's 'Spectacles of Pleasure'.

But if the wording of the 1642 act and, perhaps even more unmistakably, its reiteration in February 1648 reflect the influence of a godly rigour (the 1648 ordinance noting that plays, which have tended 'to the high provocation of Gods wrath and displeasure', are not to be 'tolerated amongst Professors of the Christian Religion'),[4] it is still too simple to see the ordered closing as the revenge of a precise puritanism over those who would still enjoy their cakes and ale. 'Puritan', as we have come to see, is a label too inexact to do as much work as it is often asked to (it is notoriously 'ambiguous', as Giles Widdowes observed in 1631, or indeed 'offensive', as John Yates said five years earlier, calling for 'some statute' both to 'define it and punish it');[5] and certainly the familiar homology between puritanism and anti-theatricality is, in any case, unsustainable.[6] Not all Puritans were opponents of the theatre, and neither were all opponents of the theatre Puritans. Men such as Milton or Marvell, or Leicester and Walsingham, for that matter, who by most definitions must be regarded as Puritans, were obviously sympathetic to, even fascinated by, theatrical activity. William Herbert, the third earl of Pembroke, whom the Venetian ambassador identified as the 'head of the Puritans' in the government of James I,[7] annually gave Ben Jonson twenty pounds to buy books, and was, along with his brother, the dedicatee of Shakespeare's first folio. Henry Hastings, the fifth earl of Huntingdon, of radical Protestant background and belief, was the patron of John Fletcher. Indeed, Cromwell himself patronized the theatre in the 1650s, allowing Davenant's operas to be performed at court.

Conversely, though voices plausibly identified as 'Puritan', such as John Stockwood, William Perkins and William Prynne, were indeed loudly heard in the choruses of anti-theatricality, equally strong anti-theatrical attitudes were held by those, such as Robert Anton or Richard Brathwait, who were well known for their anti-Puritan sentiments. Archbishop Laud, a regular target of Puritan hostility, himself worked in 1637 to prevent the re-opening of the theatres after they had been closed for fifteen months on account of a severe plague outbreak.

It is impossible to assent to the familiar notion that an ever-growing Puritan hostility to the theatre resulted finally in the prohibition against playing. The anti-theatrical tracts themselves belong to an earlier genera-tion of polemic, being far more numerous in the last part of the sixteenth century than in the years immediately before the theatres' closing. Though there were a number of anti-theatrical tracts in the 1620s, Prynne's vitu-perative *Histrio-Mastix* was less the culmination of the attack on the stage, as Jonas Barish and others have argued, than an anachronism at the time of publication and one that had no immediate successors. Prynne's anti-theatricality echoed the anxieties of an earlier generation of Englishmen (though it was in fact responding to a different theatrical environment: not the new commercial theatres but the court theatricals). Sermons were preached against plays and play-goers in each of the last four years of the 1570s – that is, the years immediately following the erection of the theatre in Shoreditch – but none of the Paul's Cross sermons published between 1630 and 1642 mentioned the theatre or theatre-going among London's proliferating vices.

But if Puritan opposition can at most explain the tone of the prohibition order rather than the fact of it, what was its actual motivation? The timing of the order certainly suggests that considerations were more pragmatic than precise. Although Herbert Grierson confidently asserted that 'when the Long Parliament meets, one of its earliest acts is to close the theaters',[8] the truth is far otherwise. The Long Parliament did immediately begin dismantling the royal bureaucracy when it first sat in November of 1640, but almost two years passed before it acted to prohibit stage plays. And then it did so not with the consolidation of the power of the parliamentary Puritans in January of 1642 – when in fact a bill for the theatres' closing was introduced by a moderate Puritan, Edward Partridge, the baron for Sandwich, but quickly defeated, opposed by, among others, Pym, on the grounds that playing was a 'trade' enhancing the economy of the capital and therefore should not be inhibited[9] – but much later in 1642, at the end of August, after the king had raised his standard.

What Milton said of Catholics was, then, perhaps more true of the theatres in 1642: 'if they ought not to be tolerated, it is for just reason of

State, more then of religion'.[10] But when the political issues have been
examined, both political and literary historians have tended to reproduce
rather than analyse the Royalist narratives of the mid-century culture wars.
The closing of the theatres, we are regularly told, if not merely a puritanical
reflex, was a calculated attack on a Royalist institution; Philip Edwards,
for example, claims that 'the central motivation (in which religion had a
share) was antagonism to the monarchy and all its works'.[11] And, certainly,
some contemporaries did see the legislation against stage plays as a form of
opposition to the king. '[N]ever rebel was to arts a friend', wrote Dryden
scornfully in *Absolom and Achitophel* (line 873), and John Denham claimed:
'They that would have no KING, would have no Play: / The *Laurel* and the
Crown together went, / had the same *Foes*, and the same *Banishment*.'[12] As
the common joke had it, Parliament had turned Westminster into the only
playhouse: 'we perceive at last why plays went down,' Samuel Butler later
noted acidly, 'to wit, that murders might be acted in earnest. Stages must
submit to Scaffolds, and personated Tragedies to real ones...No need of
heightening Revels, these Herods can behead without the allurements of a
Dance.'[13]

But this explanation will not quite do. In 1646, the acting company that
had played at the Globe and the Blackfriars, the King's Men, petitioned
Parliament for the salary that was owed them, and on 24 March the House
of Lords 'specially recommended to the House of Commons that they may
have their Monies paid them'.[14] If the prohibitions against playing were
directed primarily at the king, this parliamentary scrupulousness would be
virtually inexplicable, especially if, as James Wright claimed in 1699, most
of the actors 'went into the King's Army, and like good men and true, Serv'd
their Old Master, tho' in a different, yet more honourable, Capacity'.[15]

And, in any case, in spite of their royal patronage, the theatres had
often proved themselves ungrateful clients. As Margot Heinemann, Martin
Butler and others have convincingly shown, the drama was neither servile
nor escapist but often critical, regularly subjecting royal policies to scrutiny
and challenge. In the period of the personal rule, wilful and unpopular
monarchs regularly blustered on the stage, and loyal subjects – there, at
least – were allowed to admit, like Suckling's Brennoralt, that they were
'angry / With the King and State sometimes' (*Brennoralt*, 3.2.38–9; the play
was written about 1639 and first published in 1646). Though criticism was
most apparent in the plays of the public amphitheatres, even in the private
theatres the narrow self-interest of the court was displayed, and the criticism
was sometimes felt to be too pointed to ignore. In 1640, William Beeston

was removed from the directorship of the King's and Queen's Boys company and imprisoned for performing Richard Brome's *Court Beggar*, which, in Henry Herbert's phrase, 'had relation to the passage of the [king's] journey into the Northe', but was clearly a more general attack, as Butler has shown, upon 'the bankruptcy of the personal rule'.[16]

Why then should Parliament seek to close the playhouses late in the summer of 1642 when a critical theatre might well have proved a powerful weapon of propaganda in the war against the king? (It may perhaps be useful to state at this point that Parliament is here imagined not as a monolith but as being itself marked by disagreement and division along economic, regional and sectarian lines; nonetheless, Parliament, however much its coherence was compromised by the various allegiances of its membership, increasingly served as the focus for effective opposition to the monarch, if not the monarchy.) While this is not the place to argue the case at length, I would suggest that the actual motivation for the injunction against playing was neither Puritan anti-theatricality nor parliamentary anti-royalism but a pragmatic response to the spreading public discontent and disorder in the summer of 1642.[17]

As early as 1640, the populace of London had begun to prove itself an effective political agent, willing, if not yet to contest oligarchical control aggressively, at least to insist that its desires and expectations be heard. After Henry Burton and William Prynne were released from prison, thousands of men and women accompanied them into the city, 'the people flocking together to behold them, and receiving them with acclamations, and almost adoration, as if they had been let down from heaven'.[18] This unprecedented popular response was correctly perceived as an attack upon the authority of the Star Chamber and the High Commission – indeed, as an assault on the king's authority itself. Clarendon called the orderly display of support an 'insurrection (for it was no better) and frenzy of the people';[19] but if Royalist anxiety rather than reportorial accuracy shapes Clarendon's judgement of the event, the demonstration was, in Peter Heylyn's phrase, 'generally esteemed the greatest affront that ever was given to the courts of Justice in England'.[20] Clarendon believed that it was at this moment that the Civil War was both begun and lost:

without doubt, if either the Privy Council, or the judges and the king's learned counsel, had assumed the courage to have questioned ... the seditious riots upon the triumph of these ... scandalous men ... it had been no hard matter to have destroyed those seeds and pulled up the plants, which, neglected, grew up and prospered to a full harvest of rebellion and treason.[21]

What was perceived as dangerous was precisely the expression of popular will, as even Thomas May recognized, lamenting 'actions of that nature, where the people, of their own accords, in a seeming tumultuous manner, do express their liking or dislike of matters in government'.[22]

Increasingly, however, the people did begin to 'express their liking or dislike of matters in government'. 'The multitude' began to assemble and demonstrate, insisting upon the exercise of their voices. Fifteen thousand Londoners signed a petition for the abolition of episcopacy in November of 1640, and, when the petition was at last accepted, the intervention by the people was as much the issue as the reform of church government. Lord Digby was one of the many who objected to 'the manner of bringing' the petition, considering it reason enough for its rejection:

what can there be of greater presumption, than for petitioners, not only to prescribe to a Parliament, what, and how it shall do; but for a multitude to teach a Parliament, what, and what is not, the government, according to God's word.[23]

But the popular will demanded to be heard ever more insistently. Sir John Coke reported that 'there is a petition preparing in the City with 20,000 or 30,000 subscribed ... to demand justice against the Earl of Strafford'.[24] On 3 May 1641, a huge crowd (Nehemiah Wellington estimated it as 15,000 people) assembled at Westminster in support of the petition, promising they would 'never rest from petitioning, till not only the Lieutenant's matter, but also all things else that concern a Reformation be fully perfected'.[25] The next day a larger and more sullen crowd assembled which dispersed, according to the Venetian ambassador, only 'upon the condition that inside this week the Lieutenant should be condemned to death, otherwise they promise more violent action'.[26] On 12 May, Strafford was beheaded, and though the populace greeted the event with 'the greatest demonstrations of joy, that could possibly be expressed',[27] the king, the army and even many members of Parliament who had opposed Strafford were obviously apprehensive at the evidence of the power of the multitude. Popular opinion had forced the king's hand. 'My Lord of Strafford had not died,' wrote a troubled London citizen, 'if the people had not pressed the Lords in a tumult as they did.'[28]

In the ensuing years, popular demonstrations and disturbances intensified – 'the people ... press[ing] ... in a tumult' – as did levels of anxiety among the gentry who observed them. Citizens, often armed with swords and staves, assembled ominously before Parliament, as on 28 November, when Robert Slingsby reports that 'the factious citizens begin to come again to the House with their swords by their sides, hundreds in company'.[29]

The parliamentary cause was no doubt advanced by the demonstrations, which at once showed popular support for their policies and which could also be used to demonstrate the king's inability to rule and to justify the extension of legislative powers. If, however, Parliament learned how to exploit popular disruption (as the Venetian ambassador claimed, noting how 'members of the lower house ... encourage disturbance with all their might, in the assurance of raising their own estate upon the ruins of the sovereign's authority'),[30] it always remained aware of the danger to its own authority in releasing the radical potential latent within the unstable social and political environment.

Parliament increasingly came to realize that 'prudent men', as John Corbet observed, should tolerate popular political energies 'no further than themselves can over-rule and moderate'.[31] With growing evidence of the danger of 'Tumults and insurrections of the meaner sort of people', in Pym's phrase, Parliament began to take measures to ensure their control, among them the ban on 'publike Stage-Playes'. Significantly, the order to prohibit playing was formally published in tandem with a proclamation 'for the appeasing and quietting of all unlawfull Tumults and insurrections in the severall Counties of England'. Though a determined 'Puritan' hostility to playing no doubt contributed to the desire to close the theatres, the bill to do so was finally passed in the late summer of 1642 largely to prevent disorder, attempting to stabilize the political situation even as Parliament sought to replace the Crown as the source of political stability. The popular unrest that had previously aided the parliamentary cause now had to be controlled, and Parliament, aiming more at the popular energies they themselves had released than at the king, acted to close the theatres that had become notorious 'places of common assembly' and disorder.

Plays, however, continued to be published.[32] The impressive Beaumont and Fletcher folio, for example, appeared in 1647. And other smaller format collections were issued: some of Suckling's plays were included in *Fragmenta Aurea* (1646); Cartwright's *Comedies, Tragi-Comedies, with Other Poems* appeared in 1651; a collection of Marston's *Comedies, Tragi-Comedies and Tragedies* was published in 1652; a collection of Chapman's plays also appeared that year. Volumes of *Six New Playes* by Shirley (1653), *Five New Playes* by Richard Brome (1653), *Three New Plays* by Massinger (1655), *Two New Plays* by Middleton (1657), and *Two New Playes* by Lodowick Carlell (1657) also found an eager market.

And publishers brought forth numerous editions of individual plays for the consumption of readers, some clearly designed to be bound with the previously published collections, such as Humphrey Moseley's publication of *The Wild-Goose Chase*, which, as he had lamented in his preface to the 1647 folio, was the only previously unprinted play he could not acquire, and which he printed in 1652 in folio form to allow it to be bound with the earlier collected edition. Similarly, in 1655 Moseley published two plays by Shirley, *The Politician* and *The Gentleman of Venice*, issuing each simultaneously in quarto and octavo formats to allow owners of the octavo collection of 1653 to bind them in should they wish to. But also a remarkable number of discrete editions were published, 168 issues of individual playbooks appearing in the years of playing's official prohibition.

With the theatres closed, the appetite for drama was satisfied by a willing book trade. Richard Brome's prefatory poem to the Beaumont and Fletcher folio (1647) remarked that the political situation worked '*to th' Stationers gaines*', and shall so continue '*till some After-age / Shall put down* Printing, *as this doth the* Stage' (sig. g1v). But the government, in spite of its concerns about playing, seemed unconcerned about playbooks. 'We shall still have Playes', wrote Aston Cockayne, even as he noted the 'precise Ignorance' that banned them from the stage; 'though we may / Not them in their full Glories yet display; / Yet we may please ourselves by reading them'.[33] The prologue to *Craftie Cromwell* (1648), one of a number of political pamphlets adopting play form,[34] sarcastically acknowledged the government's tolerance of printed drama, even as the attack on the theatres was intensified:

> An Ordinance from our pretended State,
> Sowes up the Players mouths, they must not prate
> Like Parrats what they're taught upon the Stage,
> Yet we may Print the Errors of the Age.   (sig. A1v)

Indeed, printed drama thrived. Playbooks were readily available in the bookstalls, and readers were directed to them not only by the title pages that were still displayed on the bookstalls as advertisements for specific volumes, but increasingly by booksellers' notices and catalogues that often appeared in their published books. James Shirley's *The Court Secret* (1653) includes below the 'Names of the Persons' a list of three 'Plays newly printed for Humphrey Moseley': *The Wild-Goose Chase*, *The Widow* and *The Changeling* (sig. A4r). Similarly, all of the playbooks published by William Leake, including two of the three Shakespeare quartos that were published during the interregnum (*The Merchant of Venice* and *Othello*), include lists of books 'Printed or sold by William Leake, at the signe of the Crown in Fleetstreet, between the two Temple Gates'. Jane Bell's editions of *Friar Bacon and Friar Bungay* and of *King Lear* include an advertisement of books 'Printed and are to be sold by Jane Bell at the east end of Christ-Church'. More remarkable are the comprehensive catalogues appearing in two plays of 1656. The title page of Thomas Goffe's *The Careless Shepherdess* reads:

THE / Careles Shepherdess. / A / TRAGI-COMEDY / Acted before the King & Queen, / And at the *Salisbury-Court*, with great / Applause. / Written by T. G. Mr. of Arts. / . . . With an Alphabeticall Cataloguue of all such Plays / that ever were Printed. / [ornament] / LONDON, / Printed for *Richard Rogers* and *William Ley*, and are to be sould at *Pauls* Chaine / nere Doctors commons, / 1656.

Various things are interesting here, not only a play advertised as acted 'before the King and Queen' (one of seventeen plays so advertised between 1643 and 1660) but also the very mention of the catalogue of plays on the title page, an impressive list of somewhat over 500 titles. The same year *The Old Law* (1656) appeared with its own catalogue (this of over 650 titles), also claiming to include 'all the plaies that were ever printed' and available for purchase either 'at the Signe of *Adam and Eve*, in little Britain; or, at the *Ben Johnson's* Head in Thredneedle-street, over against the Exchange'.

Though many would have agreed with Richard Baker that 'a Play *read*, hath not half the pleasure of a Play *Acted*'[35] (Baker, however, writing in 1662, with the theatres recently re-opened), before the legalized resumption of playing readers eagerly sought the dramatic pleasures that were available to them. James Shirley, in a prefatory epistle in Humphrey Moseley's folio edition of Beaumont and Fletcher's plays (1647), rehearses the familiar attack upon Parliament for the closing but reverses the familiar valence of stage and page, recommending that the

Reader in this Tragicall Age *where the* Theater *hath been so much out-acted* congratulate thy owne happinesse, that in this silence of the Stage, thou hast a liberty to reade these inimitable Playes . . . which were only shewd our fathers in a conjuring glasse, as suddenly removed as represented. (sig. A3r–v)

For Shirley, the enforced 'silence' of the stage at least ensured that plays were presented in forms more enduring than performance. And, similarly, Thomas Stanley's commendatory verse turns the loss of the stage into cultural gain:

> They that silenc'd Wit
> Are now the authors to Eternize it;
> Thus Poets are in spite of Fate reviv'd,
> And Playes by Intermission longer liv'd.
> (sig. B4v)

Paradoxically, the closing of the theatres helped to preserve the plays that made up the dramatic repertoire (and arguably even ensured the successful transformation of drama into a literary form) by intensifying the market for published playbooks. Publishers and booksellers clearly felt no fear of government displeasure in supplying these, advertisements for printed plays appearing even in pamphlets published directly under parliamentary authority and the plays themselves, as we have seen, conspicuously proclaiming their royal favour. Parliament, however, was not concerned about people reading plays, even though it could not easily have mistaken the manifest royalism of much of what was published, perhaps most notably the Beaumont and Fletcher folio. In the forty-one pages of prefatory material to that volume, the dead Fletcher is repeatedly remembered and mourned explicitly in a language of royalty: 'King of Poets' (sig. f1v); 'abs'lute Sovereign'; 'sole Monarch' of 'Wits great Empire' (sig. f4v); 'Imperiall FLETCHER'; 'FLETCHER the people cry! / Just so when kings approach' (sig. f1v). The volume itself is a 'Kingdome' (sig. A3v). One contributor even worried that his praise of Fletcher 'might raise a discontent / Between the Muses and the _____' (sig. a2v). The absent rhyme would not have been difficult to supply. And lest the overall point be missed, Shirley ends his contribution, capping the collection of thirty-four commendatory poems: 'A Balme unto the wounded Age I sing / And nothing now is wanting but the King' (sig. g1v).

Blair Worden, in a useful account of political censorship in early modern England, includes among his list of 'questions concerning the extent of censorship that have yet to be properly answered' that of 'whether the performance or the publication of plays was viewed as the more – or the less – dangerous'.[36] At least in the interregnum the answer seems clear. Reading plays, even those presented as unmistakably Royalist in sentiment, does not appear to have been regarded as at all dangerous. Although the playbooks themselves often pointed explicitly at their politics – such as John Quarrel's prefatory poem to Robert Baron's *Mirza* (1653), which boasts that 'Text and Time doe suit' and that readers will therefore 'easily find a Parallell' (sig. A3v) – even after a censorship process was re-established with the passage of the licensing act in June of 1643, it seems that no play was ever censored.

It was not that Parliament was unaware of the political risks of print. Initially buoyed by the support for its position mobilized by the radical press, which was operating without any restraints with the abolition of Star Chamber and the Court of High Commission, Parliament quickly came to recognize the danger to its own position that existed in the absence of licensing provisions, and as early as February 1641 a subcommittee was established 'to examine all abuses in printing'.[37] Little was done at that time, however, and over a year passed before Commons, on 7 April 1642, irritably ordered the subcommittee to 'bring in Tomorrow, the Order they are appointed to prepare, to hinder this liberty of printing'.[38] In August, as the polemics on all sides became more outrageous, both houses finally approved, in the absence of a comprehensive bill for the control of the press, a temporary order to control the 'great Disorders and Abuses by Irregular Printing', designed to inhibit the publication of anything 'false or scandalous to the Proceedings of the Houses of Parliament'.[39] In June 1643, the final form of the licensing order was agreed to, an order 'for suppressing the great late abuses and frequent disorders in Printing...to the great defamation of Religion and Government' that provided both for licensing and for the 'diligent search' for and seizure of unauthorized publications.[40]

Like most English efforts to regulate printing, this gave primary responsibility for enforcement to the Stationers themselves, who had petitioned Parliament in April of 1643 for the reinstatement of restrictions. 'The main care,' they had argued, was 'to appoint severe Examiners for the licensing of things profitable, and suppressing of things harmful', and they offered themselves as the vehicle of enforcement, since 'in manners of the Presse, no man can effectually prosecute, as the Stationers themselves'.[41] (It was this petition that Milton described contemptuously in *Aeropagitica* as 'the fraud of the same old *patentees* and *monopolizers* in the trade of bookselling'.) With the passage of the 1643 act, Parliament had successfully transferred to itself the powers previously held by the Crown (and many angrily observed that this act was, in Milton's phrase, 'the immediat image' of the pre-revolutionary licensing act of 1637).

Further legislative efforts to control printing followed: one in September 1647, which gave temporary control to the army, another in January 1649, another that September, yet another in January 1653 and the most stringent of all in September 1655. These last two are of particular interest, as, in spite of the increasing rigour of control, over 100 play titles appeared in the decade of the 1650s, the third largest number in any decade of the sixteenth and seventeenth centuries.

What is apparent is that as Parliament sought to bring the unruly press to heel, instituting severe penalties and punishments for authors, printers, publishers, booksellers and even buyers (who could be fined £2 an item for failing to turn in an unlicensed publication and say where it was purchased), the printed drama was not its concern. Parliament's focus in its reiterated licensing acts was on the increasingly violent pamphleteering, some of which did assume play form, but the publication of plays written before the official closing drew no explicit comment nor caused any apparent alarm.

Plays, however, were insinuated into the political struggle. Pamphlets repeatedly used allusions to the pre-Civil-War drama for controversial ends. Royalists regularly turned to the closing of the theatres as the sign of Parliament's moral failing. 'We need not any *more Stage-playes*', wrote one critic in the anonymous *Key to the Cabinet of Parliament* (1648):

> we thanke them for suppressing them, they save us money; for Ile undertake we can laugh as heartily at *Foxley*, *Peters*, and other of their godly Ministers, as we ever did at *Cane* at the *Red Bull*, *Tom: Pollard* in the humorous Lieutenant, *Robins* the Changling, or any humorist of them all. (p. 8)

But it was not merely Royalist propagandists that made use of theatrical allusions; even zealous Parliamentarians so commonly used references to well-known plays that one Royalist critic wrote of his imagined Puritan opponent:

> Nor can we complain that *Playes* are put down while he can preach, save only his *Sermons* have worse sense, and lesse Truth. But he blew down the *Stage* and preach'd up the *Scaffold*. And very wisely, lest men should track him, and find where he pilfers all his best *Simile's*.[42]

But in spite of the fact that allusions to plays became a significant part of the rhetoric of Civil War propaganda, the government seemed unconcerned about play publication. Since there was no obvious venue for playing, it is understandable that few new plays were being written; and the old plays that were now being published had been previously licensed and were at least arguably without contemporary political relevance. Not incidentally, as their rights belonged to members of the Stationers' Company, commercial considerations outweighed political concern as they were offered for sale. But, perhaps more simply and as importantly, the official indifference to printed plays stemmed mainly from the fact that their reading was not thought to be of any political consequence. Clearly what Parliament thought dangerous was not plays but their playing; and that was what was carefully controlled. A surreptitious performance after the ordered closing was stopped and the actors arrested, according to *Mercurius Melancholicus*, 'to prevent such dangerous assemblies',[43] and, indeed, the Venetian ambassador later observed that the government has 'absolutely forbidden plays, suspecting that these gatherings of the people might occasion some disadvantage to the present state of affairs'.[44]

And what made the theatre threatening to Parliament was not merely that crowds assembled. Other places of public assembly continued to function unchallenged. Indeed, the actors in January 1644 protested that they had been unfairly singled out: 'Stage-playes, only of all publike recreations are prohibited,' they complained, while 'other publike recreations of farre more harmful consequence [are] permitted still in statu quo prius, namely that Nurse of barbarisme and beastlinesse, the Beare-Garden.'[45] But the theatres did represent a unique threat. Unlike the bear-baiting houses, theatres were places where private people not only came together but came together as a public. In the theatres people congregated, were provided with a political vocabulary that served to construct and clarify their interests, and were endowed, by the theatres' commercial logic, with an authority over its representations. The audience was thus not merely a public assembly but *a public* constituted as a domain of political significance, and it was this that made playing unacceptable to Parliament in 1642.

The reading of the plays that had been performed was, however, thought to be an innocuous activity. 'Is it unlawfull since the stage is down / To make the press act?' asked one of the commendatory poems in *The Queene* (1653), its title page advertising it as 'An excellent Old play', the poem then predictably concluding that it is not unlawful for plays to be published, purchased and read: 'the guiltles presse' dresses plays in 'its own innocent garments' (sig. A3r). No doubt 'R. C.', the unidentified author of the poem (Robert Cox?), protests too much, but many were eager to assume the printing of plays 'innocent' and the press 'guiltles' in the effort.

Play reading could be thought innocent precisely because it was not public. Unlike the charged readings of the Bible in the 1530s and 1540s, which both took place in public and were part of a process by which a godly community was constituted, the reading of drama a century later was increasingly a private activity and often (at least imaginable as) a gentrified female one. 'Make then your Chamber your priuate Theatre', urges Richard Brathwait in *The English Gentlewoman*, instructing women to read devotional works in the privacy of their closet, but his very metaphor expresses a truth about play reading, as gentlewomen did read plays in their book closets and bedchambers, precisely turning those spaces into their private theatres.[46] Aston Cockayne's *Obstinate Lady* (1657) does 'nothing all day but read little comedies' (sig. B4r), and though Lorece refuses to see this a fault – 'Houswifry is the Superficies of a gentle Female, and the parenthesis of a Lady, which may well be left out' – the play clearly marks the interest as at best trivial. Nonetheless, there is unmistakable evidence of enthusiastic female play readership. Frances Wolfreston was an eager collector of

playbooks, as was Frances, Countess of Bridgewater. In 1639, Ann
Merricke, disappointed by her inability to meet a friend in London and go
with her 'to see the Alchmyst, which I hear this tearme is revis'd', lamented:
'I must content my selfe here, with the studie of Shackspeare, and the historie of woemen, All my countrie librarie.'[47] At least ten of the Folger copies
of the Shakespeare first folio have ascriptions from their women owners, the
most assertive being that of Elizabeth Brockett, who on the opening page,
in addition to her signature, wrote out Mary, Lady Chudleigh's poem, 'To
the Ladies', which calls on women to 'Value you selues and Men despise'
and to eschew marriage because 'Wife and seruant are the same / And only
differ in the name.'[48]

Yet however aggressively women might have read the plays they purchased, their increasing presence as consumers in the marketplace of print
was carefully noted by publishers (and perhaps as much to assert publicly
that this was the fact as to provide actual evidence that might prove it so).
In 1647, Moseley justifies his decision to include only the previously unpublished plays in the folio of Beaumont and Fletcher on the grounds that
a complete edition of the work would have been too large: '*Gentlewomen*
would have found it scarce manageable, who in Workes of this nature
must be first remembered' (sig. A5r). Gentlewomen are first remembered
by Moseley; 'gentlemen' come next, whom Moseley felt might well already
own texts of the published plays and be reluctant to 'pay twice for the same
book'. Certainly the readership Moseley imagines for his expensive folio, if
not restricted to women alone, conspicuously includes females and equally
conspicuously excludes all but the gentry.

Although unmistakably Royalist in sympathy, the book overtly appealed
to polite society rather than to the popular energies once evident in the
audiences of the commercial theatre in which the plays had been performed,
and it could therefore be tolerated. Plays, in a sense, were acceptable as they
became literature (the polemical play-pamphlets never did, of course, and
so were not tolerated); and plays became literature precisely as they left
the stage and found their way into print. 'Though *Johnson, Shakespeare,*
Goffe, and *Devenant*, / Brave *Sucklin, Beaumont, Fletcher, Shurley* want /
The life of action, and their learned lines / Are loathed, by the Monsters
of the times', the 'Prologue to the Gentry' in *The Famous Tragedie of King*
Charles I (1649) complains – one of those unlicensed play-pamphlets that
Parliament *did* worry about – 'Yet your refined Soules can penetrate /
Their depths of merit' (sig. A3r). Even if the implication is that careful
reading of these playwrights will reveal support for political positions that

the government would find odious (and obviously a reading made possible only by their appearance in print), the gentry readers, who can 'penetrate' the surface of the printed texts to the Royalist politics beneath, did not congregate in public – or at least did not form themselves as a public – and so did not worry Parliament, who were content to let them exercise their interpretive skills.

As play reading became a private act for 'refined Soules', or at least could easily be so imagined, it was allowed to fall below the radar of an anxious government. The political charge of the drama that had been established – or at least confirmed – by the very ban against its playing passed not to printed plays but to the innumerable pamphlets that circulated, many of which pointedly used theatrical form and language for their polemical ends. In September 1648, Francis Bethan was authorized to apprehend 'all Persons as sell, sing or publish, Ballads or Books, scandalous to the Parliament... and to suppress Playhouses, and apprehend the Players'.[49] The authorization performs a revealing linkage: not plays and playing, but pamphlets and playing. It is these that were dangerous; printed plays were not. If the publication of plays and the privatization of their reading were part of the process by which the drama climbed the cultural ladder to become respectable, even (may we say it?) literary, they were also the conditions that marked its isolation from a public sphere and determined how limited a role it would play in the wrenching historical drama of its time.

NOTES

1. C. H. Firth and R. S. Rait, eds., *Acts and Ordinances of the Interregnum, 1642–1660*, vol. 1, pp. 26–7.
2. Quoted in E. K. Chambers, *The Elizabethan Stage* (4 vols., Oxford, 1930), vol. 4, p. 341.
3. *Weekly Account* quoted in G. E. Bentley, *The Jacobean and Caroline Stage* (7 vols., Oxford, 1948), vol. 6, p. 174; the provision of the Treaty of Uxbridge in S. Rawson Gardiner, ed., *Constitutional Documents of the Puritan Revolution* (Oxford, 1906) p. 277; for the ordinances of 22 October 1647 and 11 February 1647/8, see Firth and Rait, eds., *Acts and Ordinances*, vol. 1, pp. 1027 and 1070–2.
4. Firth and Rait, eds., *Acts and Ordinances*, vol. 1, p. 1070.
5. G. Widdowes, *The Schysmatical Puritan* (London, 1631), sig. A3r; J. Yates, *Ibis ad Caesarem* (London, 1626), sig. Eee4v.
6. See M. Heinemann, *Puritanism and Theatre: Thomas Middleton and Opposition Drama under the Early Stuarts* (Cambridge, 1980), passim.

7. R. Brown *et al.*, eds., *Calendar of State Papers Venetian* (hereafter *CSPV*), vol. 14, p. 245.

8. H. C. Grierson, *Cross Currents in English Literature of the Seventeenth Century* (1929; repr., London, 1965), p. 69.

9. John Moore, 26 January 1641/2, in W. H. Coates, A. Steele and V. P. Snow, eds., *The Private Journals of the Long Parliament, 3 January to 5 March 1642* (New Haven, 1982), p. 182.

10. J. Milton, *A Treatise of Civil Power in Ecclesiastical Causes* (London, 1659), sig. B12v.

11. P. Edwards, 'The Closing of the Theatres', in P. Edwards, G. E. Bentley, K. McLuskie and L. Potter, eds., *The Revels History of Drama in English, 1613–1660* (London, 1981), p. 63.

12. J. Denham, 'The Prologue to His Majesty', in *The Poetical Works of John Denham*, ed. T. H. Banks (New Haven, 1928), p. 94.

13. [S. Butler], *The Loyal Satyrist, or Hudibras in Prose* (London, 1682), sig. E4r.

14. *Journals of the House of Lords* (hereafter *LJ*), vol. 5, p. 234.

15. J. Wright, *Historia Histrionica* (London, 1699), sig. B4r. It should, however, be remembered that Wright is not above special pleading; cf. *Mercurius Britannicus*, 11 August 1645: 'the Players, who now in these sad times, have most of them turn'd Lieutenants, and Captains, as their fellowes on the other side, have turn'd *Deacons*, and Lay-elders'.

16. Herbert quoted in N. Bawcutt, *Control and Censorship of Caroline Drama: The Records of Henry Herbert, Master of the Revels 1623–1673* (Oxford, 1996), p. 208; M. Butler, *Theatre and Crisis, 1632–1642* (Cambridge, 1984), p. 200. Bawcutt notes that Butler and others perhaps assume too confidently that Herbert's comment refers to *The Court Beggar*.

17. For a fuller account, from which much of the first half of this essay was drawn, see my *Shakespeare after Theory* (London, 1999), pp. 201–20. See also Martin Butler's compact and convincing treatment in his *Theatre and Crisis*, pp. 136–40; and a fine essay by Rick Bowers, 'Players, Puritans, and Theatrical Propaganda, 1642–1660', *Dalhousie Review*, 67 (1987–8), pp. 463–79.

18. T. Hobbes, *Behemoth, or The Long Parliament*, ed. F. Tönnies (Chicago and London, 1990), p. 64.

19. E. Hyde, earl of Clarendon, *The History of the Rebellion and Civil Wars in England*, ed. W. D. Macray (6 vols., Oxford, 1888), vol. 1, p. 269.

20. *The Diurnall Occurances, or Dayly Proceedings of Both Houses... from the Third of November 1640 to the Third of November 1642* (London, 1641), sig. B4v.

21. Clarendon, *The History of the Rebellion*, vol. 1, p. 270.

22. T. May, *The History of the Parliament in England* (London, 1647), p. 79.

23. *The Third Speech of the Lord George Digby, to the House of Commons* (London, 1641), sig. B1v–B2r.

24. Quoted in B. Manning, *The English People and the English Revolution* (London, 1976), p. 58.

25. Quoted in Manning, *The English People*, p. 64.

26. *CSPV*, vol. 25, p. 148.

27. Sir P. Warwick, *Memoires of the Reigne of Kinge Charles I* (London, 1701), p. 163.

28. Quoted in Lindley, 'London and Popular Freedom in the 1640s', in R. C. Richardson and G. M. Ridden, eds., *Freedom and the English Revolution* (Manchester, 1986), p. 120.

29. *Calendar of State Papers Domestic, 1641–1643* (hereafter *CSPD*), p. 188.

30. *CSPV*, vol. 25, p. 84. The Venetian ambassador, of course, cannot be thought to offer an entirely objective account of the events he reported, and here, as always with his dispatches, his oligarchical bias must be taken into account.

31. J. Corbet, *An Historicall Relation of the Military Government of Gloucester* (London, 1645), sig. B3v.

32. See L. B. Wright, 'The Reading of Plays during the Puritan Revolution', *Huntington Library Quarterly*, 6 (1934), pp. 73–108.

33. A. Cockayne, 'A Praeludium to Mr RICHARD BROMES playes', R. Brome, *Five New Playes* (London, 1653), sig. A4r.

34. Polemical pamphlets in play form appeared with increasing regularity. For this aspect of what Dale Randall calls the 'paper war', see Randall, *Winter Fruit: English Drama 1642–1660* (Lexington, Ky., 1995), pp. 70–92; L. Potter, *Secret Rites and Secret Writing: Royalist Literature, 1641–1660* (Cambridge, 1989), pp. 90–3; N. Smith, *Literature and Revolution in England, 1640–1660* (New Haven and London, 1994), pp. 70–92; and S. Wiseman, *Drama and Politics in the English Civil War* (Cambridge, 1998), pp. 19–79.

35. R. Baker, *Theatrum Redivivum, or The Theatre Vindicated* (London, 1662), sig. D1v.

36. A. B. Worden, 'Literature and Political Censorship in Early Modern England', in A. C. Duke and C. A. Tamse, eds., *Too Mighty to Be Free: Censorship and the Press in Britain and the Netherlands* (Zutphen, 1987), p. 60.

37. *Journals of the House of Commons* (hereafter *CJ*), vol. 2, p. 84. For a lucid account of the regulation of printing in this period, see F. S. Siebert, *Freedom of the Press, 1476–1776* (Urbana, Ill., 1952), especially pp. 165–91.

38. *CJ*, vol. 2, p. 514.

39. *CJ*, vol. 2, p. 739; see also *LJ*, vol. 5, p. 322. See *Complete Prose Works of John Milton*, vol. 2, ed. E. Sirluck (New Haven, 1959), pp. 159–64.

40. Firth and Rait, eds., *Acts and Ordinances*, vol. 1, pp. 84–5.

41. *To the High Court of Parliament: The Humble Remonstrance of the Company of Stationers* (London, 1643), sig. A1v.

42. J. Birkenhead, *The Assembly-Man: Written in the Year 1647* (London, 1663), sig. C1v.

43. *Mercurius Melancholicus*, 4 Sept 1647; quoted in Bentley, *The Jacobean and Caroline Stage*, vol. 7, p. 176.

44. *CSPV*, vol. 30, p. 165. See also *The State Papers of John Thurloe*, ed. T. Birch (7 vols., London, 1742), vol. 4, pp. 107–17, where district commanders are instructed to forbid public gatherings, including plays, because 'treason and rebellion is [sic] usually hatched and contrived against the state on such occasions'.

45. *The Actors Remonstrance*, in W. C. Hazlitt, ed., *The English Drama and Stage under the Tudor and Stuart Princes 1543–1664* (London, 1869), pp. 259, 261.

46. R. Brathwait, *The English Gentlewoman* (London, 1631), sig. G4v.

47. *CSPD*, vol. 13, p. 342.

48. Folger Library, Shakespeare folio no. 3.

49. *CJ*, vol. 6, p. 20.

CHAPTER SIX

Irrational, impractical and unprofitable: reading the news in seventeenth-century Britain

Joad Raymond

I

When Gabriel Harvey sat at his desk, his copy of Livy before him, surrounded by other works with which he intended to compare the Roman history, he did so with a clear sense of purpose: he wished to contrive practical advice for policymakers, and thereby to make himself a useful reader. John Dee studied his occult manuscripts and books with an objective in mind: to furnish himself with a better understanding of nature and providence, to further his insight into the Magus's arts, to draw closer to the philosopher's stone. When John Milton read Euripides, it was perhaps for pleasure, but also to acquire the solid learning of a gentleman, and to tool himself the better to achieve his literary ambitions. When Thomas Hobbes read Thucydides, he sought knowledge of history and good government.[1] In the most everyday of reading encounters, readers consulted the Bible, seeking comforting words, the advice of their maker or his Son, and surer knowledge of salvation or the paths that led to it.[2]

Historians of the practices and interests of early modern readers have shown the centrality of reading to early modern history, especially but not exclusively cultural and intellectual history. They have emphasized the importance of *ratio* and *utilitas* in the conscious intentions of readers, and the sophistication of readers and their interpretive strategies. Reading, we are told, was 'utilitarian or preparatory' and radically analytic. Texts were anatomized and fragmented, individual words were subjected to perspicacious scrutiny. Comparison was diligently undertaken between passages within a text and between different texts: the book-wheel has been proposed not only as a practical means of accomplishing this, but as a metaphor for the intertextual habits of early modern readers. Texts were not speculatively explored so much as ruthlessly mined for florilegia and *loci communes*, for the purpose of confirming existing beliefs and contradicting the expressions of others.[3]

Many early modern readers and writers expressed anxiety about the potentially deleterious effects of reading certain kinds of publication, particularly printed pamphlets and periodicals of news. A piece of government propaganda printed in 1594 regretted that 'friends and enemies on either side, according to their owne humors do feede the worlde with diuersitie of Reportes agreable to their owne affections and passions'.[4] The surge of news publications during the 1590s caused several writers, including Samuel Daniel and Gabriel Harvey, to express fears that readers 'eagerlie longed' for news publications above the literary excellencies of Spenser and Sidney, and that pamphlets and libels animated 'confused tumults of the minde'.[5] They could be worse than romances, another source of distraction and pleasure.[6] John Bunyan, portraying his youthful and immoderate enthusiasm for idle reading, lumped news with romances and fables:

the Scriptures thought I, what are they? a dead letter, a little ink and paper, of three or four shillings price. Alas, what is the Scripture, give me a Ballad, a Newsbook, *George* on horseback, or *Bevis* of *Southampton*, give me some book that teaches curious arts, that tells of old fables; but for the holy Scriptures I cared not.[7]

Though the number of pamphlets of news and politics published annually was still quite small in 1614, that year several authors suggested that many readers' appetites were not governed by reason. One news pamphlet, *True and Wonderfull. A Discourse Relating a Strange and Monstrous Serpent, or Dragon, Lately Discouered*, blamed both credulous readers and the excesses of the 'Pamphleteering presse' for the disbelief with which sensible men regarded even true news. George Chapman's masque *Andromeda Liberata*, celebrating the marriage between Robert Carr, earl of Somerset, and Lady Frances Howard, warned that the 'ungodly Vulgars' would not 'heare / Of any newes, but what seditious were'. The same year Richard Brathwait singled out 'the understanding Reader' as his intended audience, complaining that 'So many idle Pamphleters write to Thee now a daies, as thy understanding (in my judgement) seemes much disparaged.'[8]

In the increasingly commercialized marketplace of print the mass of injudicious readers threatened to engulf the studied and disciplined few. Writers blamed the invention of the printing press, or of movable type, for the dissemination of news and pamphlets that threatened to promote sedition and to corrupt popular morals and good understanding. Reading pamphlets of news and popular polemic, they said, was both unprofitable and liable to result in the uncontrolled expression of enthusiasm rather than deliberation, reflection, or the increase of knowledge. One clause in the 1640 'Root and Branch' petition against episcopacy complained of 'The swarming of lascivious, idle and unprofitable Books and Pamphlets,

Play-books and Ballads... in disgrace of Religion, to the encrease of all Vice, and withdrawing of People from Reading, Studying and Hearing the Word of God, and other good Books'.[9] The fault lay partly with the press, and its availability to 'every ignorant, empty braine'; but mainly with the 'Humour' of natural 'Curiosity' among readers, which flattered the vanities of potential authors.[10] During the 1640s London and populous areas of Britain witnessed a dynamic culture of reading and debate; yet in 1647 a pamphleteer described the times as 'this lazie age, wherein no man will take paines to read a Pamphlet that containes above a Sheet, though it comprehend never so much seasonable truth'.[11]

Fault could be found with all kinds of reading matter. 'Bookes are de-lightfull,' reflected the keeper of a seventeenth-century commonplace book, 'but if by continuall frequenting them, we in ye end loose both health & cheerfulness (our best parts) let us leave them. their fruit can no way coun-tervaile this loss.'[12] Thomas Hobbes suggested that reading 'the glorious histories and the sententious politics of the ancient popular governments of the Greeks and Romans' had prompted university men to rebel against their rightful king in the late war (a verdict in which recent writers have found some truth).[13] Others said that the proliferation of poor histories would weary and mislead even diligent readers.[14] Pride in book learning was also a temptation; John Wilkins warned that it was 'in it self a very specious part of learning, making oftentimes a more pompous shew then the knowledge of things'.[15] Excessive and immoderate reading had dangerous consequences; like all activities, reading should be governed, it was argued, by a principle of temperance and moderation, according to a personal regimen.[16] But the fears expressed over the reading of news pamphlets and periodicals sup-plemented and exceeded these concerns. The peculiar status and nature of news added a further and troubling factor into the dynamic, and one which did not fit a 'goal-oriented' mode of reading: passion.

The place of passion was not unrecognized in seventeenth-century ac-counts of reading, and philosophers did not view it entirely as the antagonist of right reason.[17] Hobbes warned that 'the *Understanding* is by the flame of the Passions, never enlightened, but dazled', but he was peculiar in his very literal belief in this connection.[18] An Italian polemical pamphlet, translated by Titus Oates, who benefited from a more intimate relationship with news and news publications, offered a physiological account of the impression made by literary style upon different readers:

there are certain *Occult Attractives* in all *Treatises* which will captivate the Minds of those men who are prepared with a Correspondent Gust; and all this results from the various *idiopathies* in lapsed Mankind, which are apt to Incurvate the

Choice of Right Reason, and to transport them in their Choice, by Impulses from peculiar Springs in the inferiour partial Faculties of the Soul, whether there fixed by Nature, Education, Providence, or Chance.[19]

According to the author, or translator, passion was a condition of post-lapsarian reading: the truth of any text was more important than the emotional responses it provoked; but the two elements of the reading experience were not incompatible. Yet the passion for news, and the passions aroused in reading it, were commonly seen as disruptive and deleterious, an enemy to reason. Thomas Wright, explaining in 1604 the working of the passions, thought that these lightweight and ungodly books were therefore an impediment to virtue:

I must confesse, that these books and exercises corrupt extreamely all good manners, and with a silent perswasion insinuate their matter unto all the chief affection and highest part of the Soule, and in all good Commonweales, are either wholy prohibited, or so circumcised [sic], that no such hurt followeth, as some by stealth purchase, and by a wilfull theft rob their owne soules of grace and goodnesse.[20]

I want to suggest that there is an underlying significance and perhaps coherence in the aspersions cast upon the judgement of those who read pamphlets and news periodicals in the late sixteenth and seventeenth centuries. This was not just the conventional rhetoric of prefaces, which sought to capture goodwill and create an intimate atmosphere by differentiating the author from an increasingly crowded marketplace, or by flattering the reader that while the general may be foolish, credulous and vulgar, he (or sometimes she) was all the more distinguished for rising above the commonality in the exercise of judgement and discrimination. Cheap print was read for sub-utilitarian purposes, not for profit or for the augmentation of reason or even, perhaps, of knowledge; it was approached without purpose, through a sense of compulsion or for pleasure. Moreover, some of the traces left by readers in their encounters with inexpensive, topical publications suggest they were charged with precisely the kind of emotional intensity that critics suspected. Reading the news could be the enthusiastic pursuit of appetite, inutile and unreasoned.

II

A veil will always remain between the historian and the reader in history: it is possible to reconstruct the circuits through which words moved from writers to readers, the modulations that texts underwent in being turned into books, and how their manufacture influenced their reception; it is possible to deduce who read what, where and sometimes why, and even how that reading was conducted; but it is not possible to recreate in depth the *experience* of reading, what passed through the reader's mind, the experiences – and passions – that he or she felt. The evidence for impressions is refracted and perhaps transformed by the media through which it survives.

Is it possible to write about historically distant reading – as opposed to readers – at all? Or even about individual readers and their experiences? Reader-response criticism and reception theory rely on the concept of a structured reading experience.[21] The reader in the theories of Wolfgang Iser, Hans Robert Jauss and Stanley Fish is an ideal reader, a notional amalgam of a collection of individuals, whether real or imagined; the reader here, however historically grounded, is not a real reader, but a figure deployed in a critical exercise, a figure intrinsic to the text if inferred beyond it.[22] Though these exercises have been edifying and inspiring, they reveal little about the individual readers whose practices can sometimes be reconstructed. It has been doubted, moreover, whether studies of individual readers can contribute to the history of reading: the experience of reading is contingent, in time, beyond communication; it is by definition apolitical and asocial because intangible; readers are heterogeneous, defined by difference, and thus resistant to being forced into a mould labelled 'reading'.[23]

Sceptics of attempts to reconstruct reading practices underestimate the social elements of reading: the degree to which responses to texts are shaped by education, and by collective experience, by shared social spaces, such as coffee houses and classrooms, by reading aloud, by critical discussion; and they neglect the role of the media, from the seventeenth century onwards, in co-ordinating responses. Recent empirically driven work has demonstrated how we can unearth that history and what the historicity of reading means for other fields of history, and it has profound implications for attempts to theorize reading and aesthetic reception.[24] Reading the news – and the passions implicated in it – contributes a new layer of difficulties. News was the object of a series of anxieties and debates about popular access to privileged matters of state.[25] Despite the fact that the exchange of news was for many an everyday activity, the discourse that surrounds news was peculiarly charged; it is even more imperative that we consider not just what readers said they did, but what they actually did.

It is a premise of this essay that the history of reading has to be written not from the perspective of the implied or ideal readers of printed texts, nor even solely from diaries and retrospective narratives, but from a full range of printed and manuscript evidence of real readers encountering texts. Marginalia have proved a particularly valuable source in recent years,[26] though the study of marginalia is doubtless fraught: first, with the immediate difficulty of identifying and dating the reader; and second, with the beguiling illusion that it offers a direct window onto a reading encounter. Marginalia are not always a transparent medium for detecting the reader's first impression: some readers can be seen to self-consciously construct their appearance in the margins. I have in my possession a book formerly owned by a lecturer who taught me as an undergraduate; his strident annotations bear a striking resemblance to the comments he placed on my essays. Some readers read and annotate as if conscious of an audience. Though marginalia may be the most direct evidence available, such evidence is by no means unmediated. For news publications, however, there is a shortage of this kind of evidence. While scholarly readers variously left marks in notebooks and margins, dense and significant marginalia are particularly rare in pamphlets and newsbooks. The archives are curiously reticent on the matter of news reading. Readers usually read a short topical work once, without anticipating a second reading and without stopping to record their reactions. They turned the page leaving few traces to posterity.

Nevertheless, extensive examination of newsbooks and news pamphlets yields enough evidence to reveal patterns in readers' experiences of and responses to these texts. Marks on the printed page can also be supplemented by other sources implicated close to the original scene of reading, including diaries, commonplace books, correspondence, habits of collecting and binding, and printed responses and reactions to reading. I will begin by surveying correspondence, marginalia and commonplace books for practical and systematic reading of newsbooks, then consider diaries and autobiographical accounts expressive of appetites, before turning to marginalia and other evidence that suggests emotionally charged responses. From these I will infer a congeries of approaches to reading news that in their diversity indicate that readers brought to news publications a spontaneous and improvisatory spirit that owed at least as much to desire as to schooled discipline.

III

Readers of news publications rarely left vestiges of their purposes or responses. When they did mark pages, most frequently they underlined a passage, or made a vertical line or a cross in the margin; or they drew a hand pointing to a passage of interest, or wrote 'marke' or 'observe'. A few corrected spellings or dates, and a disgruntled minority wrote 'false' against paragraphs or comments.[27] One possible reason for the paucity of marginalia was the absence of any textbook giving instructions on how to read news publications. No one was trained in reading news. Preachers and auditors of sermons were given at least rudimentary interpretive tools. Thus John Wilkins, in *Ecclesiastes, or A Discourse Concerning the Gift of Preaching as it Fals under the Rules of Art*, first published in 1646 with many subsequent editions, noted that he wrote in English rather than Latin 'because in some respects it may be usefull for the hearers as well as the Preacher'.[28] Wilkins provided guidelines on the organization of sermons and on decorum, and recommended plain and unaffected styles as the most effective. There were also guides to reading history, including (in the vernacular) Thomas Blundeville's *The True Order and Methode of Wryting and Reading Hystories* (1574), Degory Wheare's *De Ratione et Methodo Legendi Historias* (1623), translated by Edmund Bohun as *The Method and Order of Reading Both Civil and Ecclesiastical Histories* (1685), Mathias Prideaux's *An Easy and Compendious Introduction For Reading All Sorts of Histories* (1648) and others. These works outlined both a systematic reading programme and a set of interpretive aids, recommending the slicing of periods into digestible sizes, and the compilation of chronologies.[29] Studies of poetry, and of poetics, from George Puttenham's *Arte of English Poesie* (1589), through Sir Philip Sidney's *Defence of Poetry* (1595), to Sir William Davenant's *Preface to Gondibert* (1650) and Thomas Hobbes's *Answer* to the same, offered techniques for the appreciation and interpretation of poetry and drama.[30] Even the popular stage came with some instructions in the form of a tradition of self-conscious metatheatre embedded within plays. In the eighteenth century Addison and Steele would instruct readers of the *Tatler* and the *Spectator* in how to read the periodical press, as part of a wider project to describe the cultural and intellectual life of polite society. Prior to this the reader of news was obliged to extemporize.

Readers brought with them reading strategies learned at school, or from other kinds of books, and adapted them to different kinds of publication. A handful of exceptional readers introduced the reading practices of scholarly humanism into their encounters with news pamphlets and periodicals. They corrected and schematized newsbooks, adding apparatus, as if preparing for subsequent readings. One reader of the *Moderate Intelligencer*, who collected at least two volumes of the weekly newsbook, amended spellings, added punctuation and inserted words, changed dates and issue numbers, and drew in typographical markers, placing boxes around headings; she or he also noted when there was a interruption in publication. On the title page of the first issue of the first volume she or he marked 'a whole year', and every eighth issue is marked '8 weeks'.[31] A similar attempt to systematize a newsbook was undertaken by a reader and collector of *Mercurius Politicus*, who constructed a series of haphazard indices, dispersed among empty spaces throughout the copies. The same reader was probably responsible for inserting manuscript foliation and for correcting dates.[32] Another reader of *Politicus* noted at the top of one page: 'this belongs to loose pap[er]s a litle after yt. 41', suggesting that it fitted into a system.[33] A collector and reader of another volume of various newsbooks headed it 'Newes Bookes from ye. 10th of December 1653. to the 28th Sept 1655', inserted pointing hands throughout the text, and added an index headed 'The table of most remarkable passages contained in the Booke'.[34] We cannot know the motivations of these readers; their markings look spontaneous, but they follow the tendencies of purposeful reading.

The bookseller George Thomason, who collected around 22,000 ballads, books, newsbooks and pamphlets during the period 1641–60, annotated the title pages of the majority of them with the date on which he purchased them, the approximate date of their publication, or the date to which the contents pertained. He also compiled separately a list of the dates on which he bought each item. Thomason's purpose seems to have been both to document the dynamic arena of writing and reading during the troubles that beset Britain during those decades, and to build a collection that would be of considerable value in later years.[35] Another reader with a specific purpose in mind – he planned to write a history of his times – was John Rushworth. He compiled apparatus to help him navigate through his collection of newsbooks from 1641–4, frequently underlining headings, inserting place names and dates, identifying an interruption in publication, but also noting important page numbers in the endpapers of his books. The leaf commencing one volume reads: 'Beginning Aug: 9. 1642. unto June: 6th. 1643 – & on to August. 16th – 1644'. His marks were placed to assist him in locating items in future readings, and to clarify the disorganized typography common in speedily printed serial publications.[36]

Another mode of annotation intended to assist in future readings, perhaps to aid other readers of the same copy, involved the decoding or identification of allusions. Readers of John Dryden's *Absalom and Achitophel* (1681) interpreted the allegorical names in the margins.[37] A reader of William Lilly's *Monarchy or No Monarchy* (1651) glossed a reference to '*English* Merchants' with 'Tompson', presumably referring to the merchant Maurice Thompson; he or she added to the relation that Frances Howard was 'uncapable of *Coition*' for the last twelve years of her life, 'an Impostun\<me\> in her womb\<e\>'.[38] Other annotators offered evaluations: one reader of a pamphlet by Sir John Birkenhead commented in the margin on the persons mentioned in the text: Colonel Pride was 'a Drayman at first', Harrison was 'Major Gen: Harrison / a fift Monarchy Man / Hangd & Quartred', Alderman Atkins is glossed 'beshitt himself'.[39] These commentaries suggest the tendency to interpret while reading, even when reading for pleasure rather than profit.

Readers of history were instructed to draw up chronologies and to make politic observations on the characters and actions described. News material seems to have been intractable to such a use. While dates were corrected, I have not seen a reader of a news pamphlet or serial draw up a chronology to assist in interpreting its contents. Politic observations are scarce but not unknown: a copy of a 1657 foreign news publication, describing the progress of the commonwealth's war with Spain, has an unusual example of a political apothegm. An annotator – perhaps from later in the century – wrote: 'all Rebelli[on] proceeds from pretences of Religion and Reformation. Necessity is their sanctuary for sin, wch themselves make', and continued in a like vein.[40]

This may reflect the utilitarian acquisition of practical information, also implied by advertisements, common in news publications from the late 1640s onwards. Samuel Hartlib expressed pleasure that a work by Comenius was being printed, a fact he learned by reading a newsbook. Notices in newsbooks were used as a means of identifying and catching criminals.[41] Readers could put news publications to other, less predictable uses. Among them we might number Sir Samuel Luke, governor of Reading: his interest, despite mutual political antipathy, in the Royalist newsbook *Mercurius Aulicus* and his efforts in distributing it to other Parliamentarians suggest that he and his correspondents read it in a professional capacity.[42] The many Royalists in exile from England during the 1650s who read the republican *Mercurius Politicus*, despite its obnoxious opinions, were evidently both purposeful and pragmatic. One living in Holland in 1654 was inspired by a report of a reward offered for the killing of an enemy; he advised 'C. Stuart his master to do the like to any that would kill the protector'.[43] This was both a practical reading, and against the grain. *An Impartial Account of the Nature and Tendency of the Late Addresses* (1681) advised the reader to check the gazettes to find out which counties had not sent addresses to the king endorsing the succession rights of his brother; this suggests a labour of comparing sources derived from other kinds of work. Sir Samuel Luke recommended to his correspondents that *Aulicus* should be compared with London publications.[44] Numerous commentators suggest that oral reports were confirmed by printed ones, and vice versa. Another occasion upon which topical pamphlets were read specifically for an intended action was when the reader intended to write a response; though presumably this was usually a form of rereading that took place after an initial encounter.[45] Reading provoked writing, and in preparation for this the disputatious reader might mark reflections and criticisms in the margin.[46] When this resulted in publication, sometimes the original text would be printed, in fragments or whole, together with the reader's response, a genre known as animadversion.[47]

Nevertheless, the difficulty in utilizing news reading is indicated by its absence from the handbooks that readers compiled for future application. Young scholars were advised to compile commonplace books, to assist learning and memory.[48] These they filled with flowers of eloquent speech, *sententiae*, historical anecdotes, satires, poems, parliamentary speeches, pleasing passages of prose; commonplace books were private repositories for organizing knowledge which might then be put to public use. Contemporary news items are strikingly rare in commonplace books and other notebooks. Nehemiah Wallington's habit of transcribing fragments of news into his notebooks, and binding pamphlets with them, was unusual.[49] A few examples of commonplace books and notebooks which do refer to printed news suggest the ways in which those sources could prove recalcitrant. The physician John Ward compiled many notebooks, one of which he entitled 'A Book on purpose <for> such things as are of common use and observat<ion> not in physick nor in Divinitie but promiscuous'. News was, of course, part of this 'common' and 'promiscuous' social exchange, and in the volume, covering the 1660s through to 1681, Ward included without discrimination historical notices – including some taken from Rushworth's *Historical Collections* (1659–1701) and Hobbes's *Behemoth* (1679) – and recent news stories. The only note explicitly derived from a printed news publication concerns the Popish Plot: 'Roger Le'Strange says, y^t ye whole number of priests wch have been pickt up since this plott brake forth is not above five and thirtie or thereabouts.' Ward doubtless kept up to date with the news, and read prolifically, but did not write about printed news; his reason for including this stray fact is suggested by the comment immediately preceding it: 'Hobbs has a prettie expression thus: if a mans understanding were not dazled by ye flames of his passions.'[50] The critique was evidence of mass delusion caused by the impassioned and credulous reading and spreading of news, and Ward's note reflects on the capacity of news to delude and misinform when read without due scepticism. It was the passion and not the news itself that intrigued him.

The notebook of Brian Cave, dating from *c*.1625, is a collection of manuscript separates, a not uncommon genre. It contains letters, speeches and manuscript pamphlets, including James's speech to Parliament on 26 January 1620 and Francis Bacon's response; Thomas Scott's 'Vox populi [or] Newes from Spaine'; Thomas Alured's 'Memento Mori A Letter sent unto the right hono^ble the Marquesse of Buckingham about the match wth Spaine. Anno Domini 1620'; and the Commons' Protestation of 18 December 1621.[51] Cave's was a collection of public historical documents, brought together probably not because of any connections between them but because they were what he could lay his hands on. A similar notebook kept by Thomas Medcalfe from the early 1620s included a prison letter by Walter Ralegh, the arraignment of the same, the marriage contract between the elector palatine and the Princess Elizabeth in 1612, and some poetry.[52] Another typical commonplace book from the 1650s contains an account of the trial of the king, a common topic, with fragments of verse and notes on Roman historians.[53] In these and other notebooks and commonplace books the pieces are transcribed not for their newsworthiness but because they retained, or developed, new significance as time passed. They had achieved an historical and literary status. Their value was precisely that they had ceased to be topical.

A particularly interesting set of commonplace books and notebooks containing detailed notes on news items consists of seven volumes compiled by Roger Whitley during the 1650s. Further volumes are probably no longer extant, or await identification. Of these seven two contain chronologically organized notes on current affairs, three are organized under conventional commonplace headings, and two combine elements of both. The formal commonplace books reflect indirectly on current affairs. Under the heading 'Desire of Government', Whitley observed: 'ye Passionate desire of Governm^t: doth often p[re]tend feares & jealousies, as a cloake, for to hide theire wicked and ambitious designes'. Elsewhere he observed that Parliament is always at odds with passion because 'Passions disturbe ye Judgements'.[54] Whitley is a useful example of the development of Machiavellian political thought in resistance to the Protectorate: his observations suggest a complex interpretation of the turbulent parliaments of the 1650s. The commonplace books also contain several reflections on tyranny, plainly moved by anti-Cromwellian sentiment; they spill over into the notebooks of current affairs.[55] Whitley's interest in current affairs is manifest in the notebooks, which include lists of Royalist gentry, accounts of the proceedings in the West Indies, an abridged summary of the Instrument of Government, articles of the 1654 treaty with Sweden, and other items of public news.[56] The news was gathered from printed sources: there is at least one explicit reference to *Mercurius Politicus*, and other scraps probably derived from this useful source; this was necessary when Whitley spent some time overseas.[57] Whitley was unusual in his interest in deriving general political principles from the news, and in interpreting the news according to specific political theory; he brings into focus the failure of most compilers of commonplace books to make these links. Even Whitley, however, does not introduce contemporary news into the more formal commonplace books.

Why should this be? Though news publications may not have been read using the book-wheel – metaphorically or literally – to compare them with other texts, this does not mean that they were kept separate from other books. Many periodicals and pamphlets bear ink stains on the title pages. This suggests that they were present on readers' desks while other books were being read and annotated; this is evidently the case when a circular stain reveals that a pot of ink has been set down on the title page on a crowded table.[58] But commonplace books and notebooks were meant for future use; while news publications might be read carefully, their content, and the satisfaction gained from reading them, had only transient applications. Francis Bacon, in his essay 'Of Studies', advised: 'Read not to contradict and confute; nor to believe and take for granted; nor to find talk and discourse; but to weigh and consider.'[59] News was, however, above all a currency of social exchange.[60] The brief life-expectancy of news meant that notes to aid memory were unnecessary. News, the proverb went, was like fish, because after three days it stank.

The most practical use for a pamphlet or periodical of news may not have been reading at all. There were fish to wrap, or, as one pamphlet attack on newsbooks from 1652 proposed: 'This will serve to put under Pies, to lap Tobacco in, and keep Roast-meat from burning.'[61] Or, as was widely intimated, news pamphlets supplied other necessities in the area of personal hygiene.

IV

The silence or reticence of readers of news does not indicate disinterest. It is significant in itself. The most eager reader might be quiet about his ardour. The diary of Richard Stonley, a teller in Queen Elizabeth's Exchequer of Receipt, reveals the frequency with which he read, but has little to say about the nature of that reading, what he thought and how he felt about it. Throughout the extant volumes of his diary (extending over 1581–2, 1593–4 and 1597–8), most of the daily entries report that for some part of the day 'I kept at home at my books with thankes to God at night', or 'passed the tyme at my Books', or 'spent the Afternoone at my books'.

Comparison between his uses of these and other phrases suggests that in some instances 'books' designates his accounts, and in others reading matter. Only occasionally did Stonley specify what he read, and that was when he read the Bible on Sundays. Books are sometimes indirectly implicated. For example, on Sunday 23 July 1581 he reported, after his reading in Scripture, a rumour of the arrest of Edmund Campion: 'And this day report was made that one Campion a Jesuyt was brought through Cheapside & so to the Tower & viij others, wth a paper vpon his hatte. Writtne this ys Campion the Chef Capten of the Jesuytes.' Then on Friday 4 August he registered a purchase: 'For Books & Ballads touchinge Campion & Ducket iiij d'. Over the following months he noted the trials of Campion and other Jesuits accused of treason, once leaving blank spaces for the retrospective addition of details. Stonley followed the news story using a mixture of printed and oral sources.[62] Elsewhere his reading matter is indicated in his fragmentary accounts: on Friday 11 August 1581 he purchased, for two pence, 'a little book of the joyfull entry into the Dukedom of Brabant'. He subsequently stopped at the mayor's house for a drink, and then 'kept home at my Books all the Afternoone & so ended this day'.[63]

Judging by the evidence of the extant volumes of his diary, Stonley only infrequently purchased books, despite the frequency with which he read. Fortunately there is further documentation for his reading habits. In 1597 he was arrested for the embezzlement of more than twelve thousand pounds, and his goods were seized and inventoried. Among his possessions was a library of several hundred volumes, and the clerks who compiled the inventory helpfully listed the titles of many. The list shows that Stonley's interests were educated and eclectic, ranging from scriptural commentaries and theological treatises to the classics, histories, legal works, Spenser's *Shepheardes Calendar* and Shakespeare's *Venus and Adonis*, Philip Stubbes's *Anatomy of Abuses*, writings by Thomas Hooker and Justus Lipsius, a handful of news pamphlets, and several items labelled 'bundles of pamphlets', numbering up to fifty items in each.[64] Stonley was evidently a passionate reader, avid to consume news publications and printed poetry as well as religious works. Books were an everyday part of the high living which his embezzlement brought him. He remained occupied with them after his imprisonment: the diary for 1597–8 records him keeping 'at my Chamber at my Books', on one occasion paying for the clasp of his Bible to be mended, on another purchasing a copy of *Jack of Newberry* for four pence.[65]

Books not only amused Stonley; they absorbed him. They were not a passing interest, but something that enthralled him daily, on which he laid out his stolen money. Yet in his diary they received only passing notice.

In the first volume the only notes he made on the contents of his reading were derived from Scripture. In the second and third volumes he added the classics, frequently quoting Cato, and making an occasional politic observation. Though his diary indicates how much time he spent reading, it does not reveal how he spent that time, nor give any clue as to how he read. His reserve is far from indifferent: it implies that his passion was not for any particular purpose, but for the pleasure in itself.

Other readers testify to an appetite not dissimilar to Stonley's. Nehemiah Wallington, a Presbyterian wood-turner in mid-seventeenth-century London, was scarcely in a position to afford many books; yet his journal refers to over three hundred printed items.[66] He was above all excited by the 'little pamphlets of weekly news', and felt compelled to read and purchase them against his perceived will and reason; they 'were so many thieves that had stolen away my money before I was aware of them'.[67] After undergoing a bleary-eyed self-examination on 29 November 1654 (by coincidence the birthday of the printed newsbook), he wrote: 'I find,' inserting 'at 3 a Clocke in morning' above the line, 'many wayes that Sathan doth gule me, delude me and begile mee as . . . some time in bying Books that are scarse giveing above my ability & bying more then I need haveing.'[68] The books which most attracted him were not the most meritorious, demanding or godly, but topical works. Occasionally he found comfort in reading books, and felt pressed to make some record of this, so his posterity could benefit from his reading. The materials he transcribed included godly reflections, but also historical narratives and passages of news found in printed newsbooks and pamphlets. Wallington's remarkable documentation of his experiences of reading and writing reveals a craving for news that was beyond what he felt to be reasonable, and, like Stonley, contrary to economic prudence.

Another eager consumer of books was Ralph Josselin, the vicar at Earl's Colne in Essex; like Wallington, Josselin found his appetite for buying was sometimes greater than his self-control. In January 1645, for example, he wrote in his diary:

Wheras a supply of bookes is necessary for mee, and my meanes but small to purchase them, I have layd downe a resolucion. to buy but few, and those of choice and speciall concernment, and to allott towards the same a moity of all those moneyes, that providence doth by guift or otherwise unexpectly and freely supply mee withall; and to purchase them at the second hand, out of libraries that are to bee sold.

Later, in 1648, he complained of 'multitudes of base bookes written to stirre up to sedicon'; entries in his diary that mention his reading suggest that for the most part he restricted himself to serious theological and historical works, though he was anxious to read news, and to have oral rumour confirmed by printed pamphlets of news.[69] Both Josselin and Wallington were possessed of a strong sense of what they should read; but they also testify to their compulsion to read less erudite and godly, topical publications.

v

There is evidence not only for the craving for reading news matter, but for the emotions aroused by that reading. Books maligned the plague of pamphlets. Correspondence amply testifies to the irritation felt at printed books of news. Thomas Holdsworth wrote to William Sancroft in August 1653: 'Newes and I must still be at odds. Would it not vexe one to be rackt by a sort of Pamphlets? S^r you would wonder to see how we are boxt with their variety and contradictions.'[70] It was probably *Mercurius Politicus* that troubled him. Edward Rainbowe wrote from Oxford in January 1646 that he would not pen any news 'whilst the pennyworth from the presse may out-doe me', but wrote facetiously of a proposal 'the Moderat intelligencer... insinuats' in the previous issue.[71] News publications *insinuated* – a word Thomas Wright and others used – when they should have explicated.

Stronger forms of antipathy can sometimes be found in the margins of controversial pamphlets. This form of marginalia is known as adversaria: this term can be applied to an unsystematized memorandum book, but is more commonly applied to annotation inscribed upon and engaging with a text.[72] Some readers prepared for a response, perhaps by animadversion, others retorted with extemporaneous recriminations of foolishness or factual error. A vitriolic reader of Rachel Speght's *A Mouzell for Melastomous* (1617), a pamphlet defending women's virtue, scattered in the margins misogynistic expressions of outrage.[73] A reader of Lilly's *Monarchy or No Monarchy* (1651) took objection to the phrase 'those rude *Scots*', deleted the pejorative qualifier and added in the margin 'religious and resolute'.[74] A reader of a petition printed in *A Perfect Diurnall* in 1645 tirelessly wrote 'false' against clause after clause.[75] A reader of Hamon L'Estrange's *The Reign of King Charles* (1655), objecting to a reference to a report based on 'fame' (i.e. common rumour), noted in the margin, 'a better Poet than Historien'.[76] The antiquarian and book collector Anthony Wood sporadically registered his irritation at pamphlets by scribbling on the title pages 'Nothing but fooleries & rascallitiy', or 'Merch. Nedha[m] published this meerly to curry favour.'[77]

Other extremes of emotion were provoked by reading the news. Democritus Junior, the bibliophile anatomist of Robert Burton's *Anatomy of Melancholy*, professes to have had both his unmethodical reading habits and his melancholic disposition nourished by a daily diet of news pamphlets: the experience was probably not solely fictional.[78] Robert Overton responded with righteous anger to an unsympathetic account of his politics in a newsbook. Under arrest in the Tower of London, he wrote in January 1655:

The newsmongers and others, I perceive, report me to be a leveller and a discontented person ... if a leveller be one, who bears affection to anarchy, destroying propriety or government, then I am none. But if upon account of New-market and other engagements, for the settling of a well grounded government, redress of grievances, civil, ecclesiastical, or military, or inflicting condign punishment upon capital offenders, &c. if this be levelling, I was and am a leveller.[79]

A report of the sudden death of the 'Roman King' in *Mercurius Politicus* in August 1654 listed a series of prodigies that had preceded it; one reader drew a hand in the margin pointing at these, and added: 'W[ill] more of them die suddenly.' The same reader, against a report of new ordinances regarding the jurisdiction of the court of chancery, added 'change laws'.[80] On the title page of a copy of *Politicus* covering the week ending 29 January 1652 a contemporary wrote in the margin: 'ffriday Janu: 30th 1651'.[81] Dates might be written for a range of reasons, but this one is unlikely to have been guileless; it commemorates the anniversary of the regicide, and suggests a Royalist act of remembrance, coupled with an objection to the republican editorial with which the issue began. Lord Hatton, a reluctant reader of *Politicus*, called the newsbook or its editor a 'base rogue' for its treatment of Charles Stuart.[82] Another Royalist reader wrote to a friend in February 1648, describing his bemusement that a declaration of the then imprisoned king had been printed as a pamphlet; he added: 'Indeed in my Judgm[t] it can be no other Pen but his owne by the Phrase and Spirrit, And suer I thinke a Counterfeite would never have had that power of my Passion that this had.'[83] Passion had even greater summits: in 1646 the Lord Keeper of Oxford read an account of the king's imprisonment in the *Moderate Intelligencer* and burst into tears.[84]

Readers of news commonly sought reassurance. John Fitz James, a reader of *Politicus*, wrote to Marchamont Nedham, its editor: 'I perceave by y[r] Thursdayes Booke w:[t] is to be done wth y[e] Citizens, & then I hope our feares of Plott over.'[85] Samuel Trotman wrote to his brother in November 1648 enclosing a news pamphlet and expressing the optimism and partial relief he had felt in reading it: 'the best newes wee hope and longe for is to heare of a happy conclusion of the treaty there'.[86] Brian Duppa wrote of the tumults of 1653 with more than a hint of scandal but also with a genuine sense of the excitement which reading the news offered: 'every day unfolds new wonders, which I beleive your diurnalls ar full of'.[87] Both Duppa and his correspondent had other sources of news, but they scoured printed newsbooks and pamphlets seeking confirmation of rumour. This was a common practice. In his 1620 masque *Newes from the New World Discover'd in the Moone*, Ben Jonson identified a paradox in the reception of news. A scrivener declares: 'it is the Printing I am offended at, I would have no newes printed; for when they are printed they leave to bee newes; while they are written though they be false, they remaine newes still'. A printer responds: 'It is the Printing of 'hem makes 'hem newes to a great many, who will indeed believe nothing but what's in Print.'[88] With the expansion in the market for printed news in the 1640s the printer triumphed over the scrivener. Though many readers were (often justifiably) sceptical of the veracity of printed news, they nonetheless treated it as a reliable means of verification.

Responses to news were refracted through a degree of identification. As readers might be moved by the depiction of emotions in play in a romance or on the stage, so they could be stimulated by representation of emotions in the news. Rushworth read his substantial collection of newsbooks and pamphlets diligently, intending to write a history of the war and its origins, but his extensive marginalia from 1641–2 capture some of the flavour of reading for the news itself. Most commonly he drew a symbol in the margins of his newsbooks meaning 'observe'. More provocatively he noted in shorthand, 'fears'.[89] Most of the passages thus marked are not descriptions of the actions of participants in the crisis that led to the Civil War, who might themselves be feeling emotions including fear, but references to documents of various kinds: letters, petitions, bills of Parliament. The earliest instance concerns letters from Hull describing the mayor's refusal to admit John Hotham in his attempt to take the magazine into custody.[90] Later marks accompany votes concerning the rebels in Ireland, those who accompanied the king to Westminster on 4 January, and the right of Parliament to dispose of the militia.[91] Rushworth detected 'fears' expressed in these documents, printed as news, because he sensed history unfolding in the pages before him. The arousal of 'fears and jealousies' became a central element in his interpretation of the origins of the civil wars.

Rushworth underlined extensively in his newsbooks covering the year 1641–2. For the most part he drew attention to names and dates; yet on a few occasions he underscored phrases that indicated not the matters of fact that would subsequently be useful for writing his history, but subjective responses. Thus in one issue of *Speciall Passages*, a newsbook he seems to have preferred in late 1642, the phrases he underlined included 'I want language to expresse our sad condition about *Dublin*', and 'help bleeding Ireland'.[92] He was not unique. Similar underlining was made by a reader of the *Moderate Intelligencer* (1646–8) and the *Publick Intelligencer* (1655), emphasizing such expressions as 'as gallant a man as ever fought', 'but that we see so many rocks, as are able to split the Royall Soveraign' (and here the reader added in the margin 'and so did'), and 'and {happily} to conferr by word of mouth', where the adverb is further emphasized by the insertion of brackets.[93]

Finally, and perhaps most importantly, a providential interpretation of the news stirred passions while reading. This explains the attraction that news had for the godly. Prior to the transformation in the news market during the 1640s, much of the domestic news available in print catered for a taste for the sensational, emphasizing its providential significance. A pamphlet of 1617, *A Wonder Woorth the Reading*, describing a monstrous birth in London, warned 'and yet for all this (O *London*) art thou misled by the malice of Sathan, and thyne owne corruption, miserably deceiued with the pleasures of sinne, which last but for a moment: and still doest thou lift vp thy heeles & hands against God'. Readers were told to interpret the news as a sign that directly related to them and to their community. The child was 'A monstrous Message *sent from the* King of Glorie'.[94] A pamphlet of 1613 on the severe weather of the preceding winter apologized for mixing domestic and foreign news, 'contrary to true method in writing', and proceeded to report news gathered among merchants at the Exchange, 'of the overflowing & drowning of townes in the Low-countries, where many hundreds have perished in their owne houses, by the merciles seas, driven in by these late windes, oh heart breaking newes: especially to that country people there borne, and here dwelling in London'. The news was meant to affect émigrés, but also to inspire feelings in fellow Protestants, to remind them of 'Gods anger purposed against us, by many variable and unusuall accidents, happening in these our latter daies, to moove sinful mankind to repentance and newnesse of life'.[95] John Vicars wrote in 1643 that divine displeasure with the king's party was manifest in 'the admirable providence of God in stirring up (besides the whole Nation of our loyall brethren of *Scotland*) the whole Kingdome of *Swethland*, to fall furiously and fortunately on the Kingdome of *Denmarke*, a most admirable providentiall piece, mightily to crosse and curbe our *English Malignants* hopes and designes against us'.[96] Providence gave form and meaning to the news, for those who were prepared to read it attentively. This in part explains the powerful interest of foreign news.

Protestant fellow-feeling was at the heart of much of the interest in Stuart foreign policy and the progress of the Thirty Years' War, but foreign news also weighed directly upon a much more local sense of identity. Looking back in around 1654, Nehemiah Wallington recorded perspicacious insights into the experience of reading foreign news pamphlets in the reign of Charles I, which are worth quoting at length:

Now to make some use of these three ferefull Judgments of God Warr. Famin and pestilence First to my selfe even now while I am writting the Serious thought of their troubls & miserys being compared with my owne (discovers to me my corruptions &) Shews to me my great Sinnes as my unthankfulnes my murmurings. my impatienc that if I have not my hearts desier but suffer a littel that distasts mee I am ready waspishly to break out as though God had dealt very hardly with mee . . .

2 Secondly this discovers Gods Marcys to mee in giveing me an heart to Simpothize & morne as though I were in the same body which gives to me some evidence that I am a lively member of Christs body because I am a feeling member for whre there is sence there is Life

3 Use Is the gracious Loving kindnesse of God towards our nation is duely to be obsarved and with praise for ever to be acknowledged because he hath given us peace and plenty & Liberty and hath taken all from them whose sinns were not gratter then ours, nor their provications more grevious then ours

4[ly] I may see the Lot of Gods dearest Sarvants who are not previledged from bloody and firye trialls and this may warne us to prepaire and lay up store of graces against the day of our visitation and not to be dejected when his hand lies upon us as though Correction were signe of disertion

Fiftly Wee may examin our selves whither wee have not been wanting to them in their wants and warres. Whether wee have prayed for them in their troubls and sorrows

Sixtly Wee may examine whether their miserys were not warnnings and forerunners of our miserys O how hath Ierland drunk of this bitter Cuppe of the Lord and the church of Scotland tastted of it also All giveing warnning to Sinfull England (which hath had yet but a smack of it) to take heed of their Sinns Lest we (drinke the dreges and) be destroyed with their plauges.[97]

The account was prepared for public consumption: Wallington was explicit about his refusal to have any of his works printed, but nonetheless intended certain manuscripts to be read by his family and friends. Wallington wanted them to think providentially. His remarks are not unmediated evidence of a reading experience, but do reveal a set of associations actively made by, and in a sense required of, a group of readers. One reason why news was moving was because it required these readers to reflect upon their own fortune and responsibilities.

Despite the scarcity of evidence for the experiences of readers of news in the seventeenth century, there is enough to suggest that many readers read not studiously but with emotion. Perhaps this was not solely prompted by the content: the medium of cheap, printed news itself might have been disposed to induce excitement. Readers felt a compulsion to read the news, against the better powers of their reason, and while reading they encountered anger, amusement, wonder, relief and anxiety. The experience of reading the news may have been, as many writers disparagingly suggested, associated with the passions more than with the rational faculties.

VI

Any quantity of marginalia, commonplace books and correspondence could not claim to be representative of a universal structure of common experiences. The account of news reading does suggest, however, that this very ordinary reading matter required a improvisatory and makeshift attitude, and involved expectations and interests divergent from those emphasized in accounts of pragmatic reading. A handful of conclusions can be drawn about specific practices, and about the range of responses that could be encompassed in the encounter between reader and news publications.

Pamphlets and periodicals of news were approached with diligence: this is shown by the careful interpretations sometimes placed upon the news and by a handful of attempts to systematize or place editorial frameworks around assembled volumes of news publications, as well as by the degree of awareness of the recent history of news publications.[98] Yet this reading was rarely 'goal-oriented'; readers were interested in the news, but only exceptionally for any specific purpose. Knowledge of recent events was not ordinarily acquired in order to be put into practice.

Pamphlets and periodicals of news were read with fervour. This can be seen in three ways. Some of the more introspective diarists of the seventeenth century suggest the compulsion they felt to read the news – their narratives confirm Thomas Wright's claim that popular books could 'with a silent perswasion insinuate' into reason and the affections. Secondly, readers were interested in emotions, as recounted in the news. Reports of reactions – of participants and writers – to events could provoke curiosity as much as matters of fact. Thirdly, an emotional response to news was not uncommon.

We may be unable to reconstruct the contours of those emotions, but we can smoke out a reaction in excess of the dispassionate and abstract intelligence of the pragmatic and utilitarian reader.

Hobbes, Wright and others understood the emotions to have a largely disruptive effect upon the practice of reading. A different view was offered by the dramatist James Shirley in his preface to the 1647 folio edition of the *Comedies and Tragedies* of Francis Beaumont and John Fletcher. Shirley wrote:

You may here find passions raised to that excellent pitch and by such insinuating degrees that you shall not chuse but consent, & go along with them, finding your self at last grown insensibly the very same person you read, and then stand admiring the subtile Trackes of your engagement.[99]

This affective model of reading, applied to literary works, resembles Wallington's thanks to God for making him sensitive to news reports, and for 'giveing me an heart to Simpothize & morne as though I were in the same body'. Both relate understanding to being moved by an insinuating sympathy, followed by a cathartic reflection upon the more immediate or local condition of the reader.

The numerous critics of news reading (and readers) may have been right to suggest that it had a compulsive dimension, that it was guided by passion and confused the understanding. It was not the pragmatic, utilitarian, analytic exercise prescribed for the study of scholarly books. Though the critics of cheap print may have underestimated the diligence, self-consciousness and savviness of its readers, news culture was, in a sense, irrational, impractical and unprofitable. Or alternatively – and this would have been even more liable to provoke anxiety – the culture of news reading may have transgressed these boundaries with its complex, quotidian and messy character.

NOTES

With particular thanks to Tony Grafton, Nick Jardine, Lauren Kassell, Lori Humphrey Newcomb, Kevin Sharpe, Steve Zwicker and the Folger Shakespeare Library.
1. L. Jardine and A. Grafton, '"Studied for Action": How Gabriel Harvey Read his Livy', *Past and Present*, 129 (1990), pp. 30–78; L. Jardine and W. H. Sherman, 'Pragmatic Readers: Knowledge Transactions and Scholarly Services in Late Elizabethan England', in A. Fletcher and P. Roberts, eds., *Religion, Culture and Society in Early Modern Britain: Essays in Honour of Patrick Collinson* (Cambridge, 1994), pp. 102–24; W. H. Sherman, *John Dee: The Politics of Reading and Writing in the English Renaissance* (Amherst, Mass., 1995); *Complete Prose Works*

of John Milton, ed. D. M. Wolfe *et al.* (8 vols., New Haven, 1953–82), vol. 1, pp. 344–513; R. Mohl, *John Milton and His Commonplace Book* (New York, 1969); an interesting discussion of Milton's use of Euripides is D. Norbrook, 'Euripides, Milton, and *Christian Doctrine*', *Milton Quarterly*, 29 (1995), pp. 37–41; T. Hobbes, *The Life of Mr Thomas Hobbes of Malmesbury. Written by Himself in a Latine Poem. And Now Translated* (London, 1680).

2. The major study of reading the Bible in seventeenth-century England remains C. Hill, *The English Bible and the Seventeenth-Century Revolution* (London, 1993), though Hill understates the importance of soteriology in readers' relationships with Scripture. There is a growing literature on the history of reading, useful guides to which include J. Raven, H. Small and N. Tadmor, eds., *The Practice and Representation of Reading in England* (Cambridge, 1996); A. Manguel, *A History of Reading* (London, 1996); A. Bennet, ed., *Readers and Reading* (London, 1995); G. Cavallo and R. Chartier, eds., *A History of Reading in the West*, trans. L. G. Cochrane (Oxford, 1999); and K. Sharpe, *Reading Revolutions: The Politics of Reading in Early Modern England* (New Haven and London, 2000).

3. E. R. Kintgen, *Reading in Tudor England* (Pittsburgh, 1996), quotation p. 181; for the book-wheel, see Jardine and Grafton, 'Studied for Action', pp. 46–8.

4. *A True Report of Sundry Horrible Conspiracies* (London, 1594), sig. Aiir.

5. G. Harvey, *Foure Letters* (London, 1592), in *The Works of Gabriel Harvey*, ed. A. B. Grosart (3 vols., n.p., 1884–5), vol. 1, p. 191; S. Daniel, *Musophilus: Containing a General Defence of All Learning* (1599; facsimile edn, West Lafayette, Ind., 1965), p. 73; J. D.[avies] and A. H.[olland], *A Scourge for Paper-Persecutors... with a Continu'd Just Inquisition* (London, 1625), p. 4.

6. L. H. Newcomb, *Reading Popular Romance in Early Modern England* (New York, 2002).

7. J. Bunyan, *A Few Sighs from Hell* (1658), in *The Miscellaneous Works of John Bunyan*, vol. 1, ed. T. L. Underwood with the assistance of R. Sharrock (Oxford, 1980), p. 333.

8. A. R., *True and Wonderfull. A Discourse Relating a Strange and Monstrous Serpent, or Dragon, Lately Discouered* (London, 1614), sig. A3r; G. Chapman, *Andromeda Liberata* (London, 1614), sig. Br; R. Brathwait, *The Schollers Medley* (London, 1614), sig. A4v; for the publications and contexts of 1614, see J. Raymond, '"The Language of the Public": Print, Politics and the Book Trade in 1614', in S. Clucas and R. Davies, eds., *The Crisis of 1614 and the Addled Parliament: Literary and Historical Perspectives* (Aldershot, 2003), pp. 98–117.

9. J. Rushworth, *Historical Collections*, part 3 (2 vols., London, 1691), vol. 1, pp. 93–4.

10. *Calendar of the Correspondence of Richard Baxter*, ed. N. H. Keeble and G. Nuttall (2 vols., Oxford, 1991–2), letter 11; *Modern History, or A Monethly Account*, no. 1 (October 1687), sig. A2r.

11. [M. Nedham?], *A Paralell of Governments* (London, 1647), p. 16. For reading in the 1640s, see S. Achinstein, *Milton and the Revolutionary Reader* (Princeton, 1994); D. Norbrook, '*Areopagitica*, Censorship, and the Early Modern Public Sphere', in R. Burt, ed., *The Administration of Aesthetics: Censorship, Political Criticism, and the Public Sphere* (Minneapolis and London, 1994), pp. 3–33; N. Smith, *Literature and Revolution in England, 1640–1660* (New Haven and London, 1994), passim.

12. Folger Shakespeare Library, MS V.a.281, fol. 18v.

13. T. Hobbes, *Behemoth, or The Long Parliament*, ed. F. Tönnies (Chicago and London, 1990), p. 23; cf. Hobbes, *Leviathan*, ed. R. Tuck (Cambridge, 1991), pp. 129–30; D. Norbrook, *Writing the English Republic: Poetry, Rhetoric and Politics 1627–1660* (Cambridge, 1999); A. B. Worden, 'Classical Republicanism and the Puritan Revolution', in H. Lloyd-Jones *et al.*, eds., *History and Imagination: Essays in Honour of H. R. Trevor-Roper* (London, 1981), pp. 182–200.

14. F. Bacon, *The Advancement of Learning and New Atlantis*, ed. A. Johnston (Oxford, 1974), p. 73; J. Raymond, 'John Hall's *A Method of History*: A Book Lost and Found', *English Literary Renaissance*, 28 (1998), pp. 267–98, at p. 296.

15. J. Wilkins, *Ecclesiastes* (London, 1646), p. 23.

16. For the dangers of excessive reading, see A. Johns, 'The Physiology of Reading in Restoration England', in Raven, Small and Tadmor, eds., *The Practice and Representation of Reading*, pp. 138–61; Johns, 'The Physiology of Reading', in M. Frasca-Spada and N. Jardine, eds., *Books and the Sciences in History* (Cambridge, 2000), pp. 219–314; Johns, 'The Physiology of Reading and the Anatomy of Enthusiasm', in O. Grell and A. Cunningham, eds., *Religio Medici: Religion and Medicine in Seventeenth-Century England* (Aldershot, 1996), pp. 136–70; R. Porter, 'Reading Is Bad for Your Health', *History Today*, 48/3 (March 1998), pp. 11–16.

17. S. James, *Passion and Action: The Emotions in Seventeenth-Century Philosophy* (Oxford, 1997). The *OED* entry for 'Passion', sb., III, contains several contemporary uses of the word in the senses in which I employ it throughout this essay.

18. Hobbes, *Leviathan*, p. 131.

19. T. Oates, *An Exact Discovery of the Mystery of Iniquity* (London, 1679), p. 36; this postscript does not appear in all copies.

20. T. Wright, *The Passions of the Minde in Generall* (London, 1604), p. 334.

21. J. Culler, *On Deconstruction: Theory and Criticism after Structuralism* (London, 1983), p. 82; see also V. B. Leitch, *American Literary Criticism from the Thirties to the Eighties* (New York, 1988), pp. 211–37, 252–9.

22. W. Iser, *The Act of Reading: A Theory of Aesthetic Response* (Baltimore, 1978); H. R. Jauss, *Toward an Aesthetic of Reception*, trans. T. Bahti (Brighton, 1982); S. Fish, *Is There a Text in This Class? The Authority of Interpretive Communities* (Cambridge, Mass., 1980). See also J. Rose, 'Rereading the English Common

Reader: A Preface to a History of Audiences', *Journal of the History of Ideas*, 53 (1992), pp. 47–70.

23. For example, P. de Man, *Allegories of Reading: Figural Language in Rousseau, Nietzsche, Rilke, and Proust* (New Haven, 1979); J. Derrida, *Of Grammatology*, trans. G. C. Spivak (Baltimore, 1976). Accounts of the resistance to reading share some of these propositions; see J. Fetterly, *The Resisting Reader: A Feminist Approach to American Fiction* (Bloomington, Ind., 1978).

24. R. Darnton, *The Kiss of Lamourette: Reflections in Cultural History* (New York, 1990), chapter 7; K. Flint, *The Woman Reader, 1837–1914* (Oxford, 1993); Sharpe, *Reading Revolutions*; S. N. Zwicker, *Producing Passions: Habits of Reading and the Creation of Early Modern Literary Culture*, (forthcoming); J. A. Secord, *Victorian Sensation: The Extraordinary Publication, Reception, and Secret Authorship of Vestiges of the Natural History of Creation* (Chicago, 2001).

25. F. Levy, 'The Decorum of News', in J. Raymond, ed., *News, Newspapers, and Society in Early Modern Britain* (London, 1999), pp. 12–38; D. Zaret, *Origins of Democratic Culture: Printing, Petitions, and the Public Sphere in Early-Modern England* (Princeton, 2000); J. Raymond, *The Invention of the Newspaper: English Newsbooks, 1641–1649* (Oxford, 1996).

26. H. J. Jackson, *Marginalia: Readers Writing in Books* (New Haven and London, 2001); Zwicker, *Producing Passions*; W. H. Sherman, *Used Books: Reading Renaissance Marginalia* (forthcoming).

27. These habits are described, and examples given, in Raymond, *The Invention of the Newspaper*, pp. 264–8.

28. Wilkins, *Ecclesiastes*, sig. A2r.

29. Raymond, 'John Hall's *A Method of History*'; E. R. Kintgen, 'Reconstructing Elizabethan Reading', *Studies in English Literature*, 30 (1990), pp. 1–18.

30. G. G. Smith, *Elizabethan Critical Essays* (2 vols., Oxford, 1904); B. Vickers, ed., *English Renaissance Literary Criticism* (Oxford, 1999); *The Preface to Gondibert, an Heroick Poem Written by Sir William D'Avenant: With an Answer to the Preface by Mr Hobbes* (Paris, 1650).

31. Copies of the *Moderate Intelligencer* in New York Public Library; see also Raymond, *The Invention of the Newspaper*, pp. 265–6.

32. Library of Congress, DA411.M6; see no. 285 (29 November 1655) and no. 293 (24 January 1655[6]), for example. See also *Mercurius Politicus*, no. 230 (9 November 1654), p. 3865, and no. 264 (5 July 1655), p. 5452, both in Cambridge University Library, R.10.41.

33. *Mercurius Politicus*, no. 148 (14 April 1653), p. 2365, in Cambridge University Library, R.10.39.

34. Library of Congress, DA411.S5, *Weekly Intelligencer*. For evidence of discriminating readers, see Raymond, *The Invention of the Newspaper*, pp. 244–68.

35. G. K. Fortescue, ed., *Catalogue to the Thomason Tracts* (2 vols., London, 1908); L. Spencer, 'The Professional and Literary Connections of George Thomason', *The Library*, 5th series, 13 (1958), pp. 102–18; Spencer, 'The Politics of George Thomason', *The Library*, 5th series, 14 (1959), pp. 11–27; S. J. Greenberg, 'Dating Civil War Pamphlets, 1641–1644', *Albion*, 20 (1988), pp. 387–401;

M. Mendle, 'The Thomason Collection: A Reply to Stephen J. Greenberg', and Greenberg, 'Rebuttal', *Albion*, 22 (1980), pp. 85–98; Raymond, *The Invention of the Newspaper*, pp. 256–8.

36. Bodleian Library, Arch. H e. 108 (formerly Fairfax Newsbooks 1), fol. 143v; Arch. H e. 109 (formerly Fairfax Newsbooks 2), first leaf. See also Sherman on Dee's marginalia, *John Dee*, pp. 81–3, also chapter 3, passim.

37. J. Dryden, *Absalom and Achitophel* (London, 1681); Bodleian Library, Ashm. G16; Cambridge University Library, Hib.7.692.1.[16]; and Magdalen College Library, K.11.9.

38. The marginalia are cropped. Folger Shakespeare Library, Accession no. 138195.

39. [Birkenhead], *Two Centuries of Pauls Church-Yard* (London, 1653), Folger Shakespeare Library, Wing B2973, pp. 3, 15, 52.

40. *A Book of the Continuation of Forreign Passages* (London, 1657), Folger Shakespeare Library, B3716 (bound with V306).

41. *The Diary and Correspondence of Dr John Worthington*, ed. J. Crossley, Chetham Society, 13 (1847), p. 56; J. Raymond, 'The Newspaper, Public Opinion, and the Public Sphere in the Seventeenth Century', in Raymond, ed., *News, Newspapers, and Society*, pp. 109–40.

42. References to *Aulicus* appear throughout Luke's correspondence: see *The Letter Books of Sir Samuel Luke 1644–1645*, ed. H. G. Tibbutt (London, 1963).

43. *A Collection of the State Papers of John Thurloe*, ed. T. Birch (7 vols., London, 1742), vol. 2, p. 319.

44. *The Letter Books of Sir Samuel Luke*, p. 322.

45. In *Rereading* (New Haven, 1993), Matei Calinescu argues that all reading is secondary, a form of rereading, and that there is no transcendent, primary reading.

46. For a preparation for a response, see, for example, Cambridge University Library, Adv. d.50.9, annotated copies of T. Goodwin, P. Nye, S. Simpson, J. Burroughes and W. Bridge, *An Apologeticall Narration* (London, 1643) and *Reformation of Church-Government in Scotland, Cleered* (London, 1644).

47. For animadversion, see J. Raymond, *Pamphlets and Pamphleteering in Early Modern Britain* (Cambridge, 2003).

48. An excellent account of the place of these in Renaissance education appears in A. Moss, *Printed Commonplace-Books and the Structuring of Renaissance Thought* (Oxford, 1996). See also Peter Beal, ' "Notions in Garrison": The Seventeenth-Century Commonplace Book', RETS/Newberry Lecture, 2 April 1987; published in typescript and deposited at the Bodleian Library and elsewhere; M. T. Crane, *Framing Authority: Sayings, Self, and Society in Sixteenth-Century England* (Princeton, 1993); Sherman, *John Dee*, pp. 61–5; Sharpe, *Reading Revolutions*, pp. 277–82; A. F. Marotti, *Manuscript, Print, and the English Renaissance Lyric* (Ithaca and London, 1995).

49. 'I did write my XXX Booke... a terrible booke of sudden Iudgements upon wicked livers... I did bind up a printed booke called The Thunder bolt of Gods

wrath against hard hearted sinners and Another… [three others] Of which
many of them I had taken notis off And then I did goe over every particqler
Commandement with places of Scripter.' Folger Shakespeare Library, MS
V.a.436, p. 145. Other manuscript volumes that include printed news items
can be found in British Library, Add MS 46375, and Bodleian Library, Tanner
MSS 66–59.

50. Folger Shakespeare Library, MS V.a.299, fol. 128r; for Rushworth, see especially fol. 6v but also fol. 79r–v; for *Behemoth*, see fols. 141r–143r; *Leviathan* is discussed at fols. 119r–141r, passim.
51. Folger Shakespeare Library, MS V.a.402.
52. Folger Shakespeare Library, MS V.a.130; cf. Cambridge University Library, Add MS 79.
53. Bodleian Library, MS Rawl. D. 1372.
54. The volumes are Bodleian Library, MSS Eng Hist. e.308–14; these references MS Eng Hist. e.312, pp. 1, 77.
55. MS Eng Hist. e.309, pp. 67–9; MS Eng Hist. e.311, p. 10; MS Eng Hist. e. 312, pp. 25, 104, 124.
56. MS Eng Hist. e.309, pp. 1–58; MS Eng Hist. e. 308, pp. 4, 34–5, 45–6.
57. MS Eng Hist. e.308, p. 21; MS Eng Hist. e.311, front board.
58. For example, *Mercurius Politicus* in Cambridge University Library, R.10.41, no. 220 (31 August 1654) and no. 228 (19 October 1654), and Sel.5.164, no. 321 (7 August 1956) and no. 604 (26 January 1660).
59. *Collected Works of Francis Bacon*, ed. J. Spedding *et al.* (1879; repr., 12 vols., London, 1996), vol. 6, pp. 497–8.
60. For news and oral exchange, see A. Fox, 'Popular Verses and Their Readership in the Early Seventeenth Century', in Raven, Small and Tadmor, eds., *The Practice and Representation of Reading*, pp. 125–37, and Fox, 'Ballads, Libels and Popular Ridicule in Jacobean England', *Past and Present*, 145 (1994), pp. 47–83; Raymond, *The Invention of the Newspaper*, pp. 1–2.
61. S. S.[heppard], *The Weepers* (London, 1652), p. 12.
62. The diaries are Folger Shakespeare Library, MS V.a.459–61; the quotations and other notices appear in V.a.459, fols. 10v, 12v, 30v, 31r, 33v.
63. Folger Shakespeare Library, MS V.a.459, fols. 13v–14r.
64. L. Hotson, 'The Library of Elizabeth's Embezzling Teller', *Studies in Bibliography*, 2 (1949–50), pp. 49–61; the inventory is Public Records Office, Exch. K. R. Memoranda Roll, E159/412/435.
65. Folger Shakespeare Library, MS V.a.461, fols. 6v, 6r, 27r.
66. British Library, Add MS 21935; N. Wallington, *Historical Notices of Events Occurring Chiefly in the Reign of Charles I*, ed. R. Webb (2 vols., London, 1869), vol. 1, pp. 142ff., and vol. 2, passim.
67. P. S. Seaver, *Wallington's World: A Puritan Artisan in Seventeenth-Century London* (London, 1985), p. 156.
68. Folger Shakespeare Library, MS V.a.436, p. 261.
69. *The Diary of Ralph Josselin 1616–1683*, ed. A. Macfarlane (London, 1976), pp. 53, 125, 155.

70. Bodleian Library, MS Tanner 52, fol. 34r.

71. Bodleian Library, MS Tanner 60, fol. 354r.

72. For adversaria, see H. J. Jackson, 'Writing in Books and Other Marginal Activities', *University of Toronto Quarterly*, 62 (1992–3), pp. 217–31; Sherman, *John Dee*, pp. 65–75; see also volume 6 of the Cambridge University Library printed catalogue of manuscripts.

73. The copy is held at the Beinecke Library, Yale (Ih Sp 33 617m); the annotations are reproduced in *The Polemics and Poems of Rachel Speght*, ed. B. K. Lewalski (New York and Oxford, 1996), pp. 91–106.

74. Folger Shakespeare Library, Accession no. 138195.

75. Bodleian Library, Hope adds 1128(41); *Perfect Diurnall*, no. 85 (17 March 1644[5]).

76. Folger Shakespeare Library, Wing L1189, p. 21.

77. *A Description of the Passage* (London, 1641), Bodleian Library, Wood 366(11); M. Nedham, *The True Character of a Rigid Presbyter* (London, 1661), Bodleian Library, Wood D26(10). See N. Kiessling, *The Library of Anthony Wood*, Oxford Bibliographical Society, 3rd series, 3 (2002), for more on Wood's annotations.

78. R. Burton, *The Anatomy of Melancholy*, vol. 1, ed. T. C. Faulkner, N. K. Kiessling and R. L. Blair, introduction by J. B. Bamborough (Oxford, 1989), pp. 4–5.

79. *The State Papers of John Thurloe*, vol. 3, pp. 110–11.

80. *Mercurius Politicus*, no. 216 (3 August 1654), pp. 3664, 3668, in Cambridge University Library, R.10.41.

81. *Mercurius Politicus*, no. 86 (29 January 1652), in Cambridge University Library, R.10.38.

82. *The Nicholas Papers: Correspondence of Sir Edward Nicholas, Secretary of State*, vol. 1: *1641–1652*, ed. G. F. Warner, Camden Society, new series, 40 (1886), p. 190.

83. Bodleian Library, MS Tanner 58, fol. 695r.

84. F. J. Varley, *The Siege of Oxford: An Account of Oxford During the Civil War, 1642–1646* (London, 1932), p. 147.

85. British Library deposit: Northumberland MSS, vol. 552, fol. 22v.

86. Bodleian Library, MS Rawl. Letters 47, fol. 56r (letter 15).

87. *The Correspondence of Bishop Brian Duppa and Sir Justinian Isham 1650–1660*, Northamptonshire Record Society, 17 (1955), p. 77.

88. *Ben Jonson*, ed. C. H. Herford, P. Simpson and E. Simpson (11 vols., Oxford, 1925–52), vol. 7, pp. 514–15.

89. Raymond, *The Invention of the Newspaper*, pp. 296, 306, and chapter 6, passim; for Rushworth's marginalia, see also F. Henderson, 'Posterity to Judge John Rushworth and His Historical Collections', *Bodleian Library Record*, 15 (1996), pp. 246–59.

90. Bodleian Library, Arch. H e. 108, fol. 56v; *A Continuation of the True Diurnall*, no. 2 (17–24 January 1642), p. 12. This was followed by a horizontal figure of eight, meaning 'good'.

91. Bodleian Library, Arch. H e. 108, fols. 60v, 61r, 126r.

92. *Speciall Passages*, no. 7 (27 September 1642), p. 49; Bodleian Library, Arch. H e. 109.

93. Copies in New York Public Library: *Moderate Intelligencer*, no. 53 (12 March 1646), p. 338; *Moderate Intelligencer*, no. 54 (19 March 1646), p. 339; *Publick Intelligencer*, no. 1 (8 October 1655), p. 3; see also Raymond, *The Invention of the Newspaper*, p. 267.

94. *A Wonder Woorth the Reading* (London, 1617), sigs. A3r, A1v. For providence and news pamphlets, see A. Walsham, *Providence in Early Modern England* (Oxford, 1999).

95. *The Wonders of This Windie Winter* (London, 1613), sigs. C2r, A3r; a similar statement is made in *The Windie Yeare. Shewing Many Strange Accidents* (London, 1613).

96. J. Vicars, *A Looking-Glasse for Malignants* (London, 1643), pp. 5–6.

97. Folger Shakespeare Library, MS V.a.436, pp. 27–9. For interest in foreign policy and news, see R. Cust, 'News and Politics in Early Seventeenth-Century England', *Past and Present*, 112 (1986), pp. 60–90; T. Cogswell, 'The Politics of Propaganda: Charles I and the People in the 1620s', *Journal of British Studies*, 29 (1990), pp. 187–215.

98. For this last point, see Raymond, *The Invention of the Newspaper*, chapter 4.

99. F. Beaumont and J. Fletcher, *Comedies and Tragedies* (London, 1647), 'To the Reader'.

PART IV

Reading physiologies

CHAPTER SEVEN

Reading bodies

Michael Schoenfeldt

We are oppressed with [books], our eyes ache with reading, our fingers
with turning.

Robert Burton

Those who would apply the analysis of Revolutions to the Positive
study of Society must pass through the logical training given by the
simpler phenomena of Biology.

Auguste Comte

Reading initially seems like the most disembodied of processes. It requires
a minimum of physical activity. The eyes move imperceptibly over the
page, the hands turn pages; the body occasionally stretches and fidgets, but
only to avoid the aches of inactivity. In the framework of early modern
ethical physiology, however, reading entailed a profound intensification
of the perpetual agon between disease and health, between passion and
reason. A highly risky activity, reading imports into the self forces that may
either improve or contaminate it. It can stir the emotions to virtue or to
vice, but even the excitation to virtue is hazardous, since the emotional
medium of such excitation is an inherently unruly and unhealthy arena,
preternaturally subverting the precarious rule of reason. In this essay I want
to think about what was imagined to happen in the embodied self of the
reader. I also want to ask why the quiet hazards of reading were so frequently
likened to the metabolic processes of digestion. I want, finally, to use this
investigation of the physiological processes underpinning early modern
reading to trouble a cliché about political organization (and, to some degree,
medical knowledge) that distorts, I would argue, an inordinate amount of
past and present thinking: that of the body politic. Arguing that there is no
indigenous link between the principles of political order and the tenets of
physiology, I hope in this essay to put some pressure on this sometimes
perverse historical collocation of an incoherent notion of bodily process
and a tendentious attitude to political organization. I am interested, finally,

215

not only in the ethical and medical understandings of reading but also in the reading of politics in medical terms. I hope thereby to demonstrate the ways in which a frequently deleterious physiology conspired with a decidedly hierarchical politics to produce a great ideological chain which captivated the minds and bodies of the disenfranchised and the embittered.

READING AND PHYSIOLOGY

In a famous phrase, Franz Kafka suggested that 'A book must be the axe for the frozen sea within us.'[1] In early modern England, however, the self was not imagined as the frozen sea of alienation that Kafka posits but rather a seething cauldron of destructive passions. A book could either stir the cauldron, applying heat and pressure to an already unstable system, or help to cool the cauldron by the addition of maxims drawn from the realm of cool reason. Kafka's frozen sea would probably offer a compelling image of self-control to many early modern readers, worried by the capacity of reading to upset a delicate moral and physiological equilibrium inside the self. We can measure some of the differences between the early modern regime of the self and our own in the strikingly different internal topographies they idealize.

Adrian Johns has recently explored the 'physiology of reading' in seventeenth-century scientific discourse. Reading was, as Johns demonstrates, as likely to 'facilitate the creation of a new philosophy' as 'to generate error and injury, both to the reader's own body and, by extension, to the body politic of the state'.[2] Reading in particular was dangerous because it could stir the passions, those internal agents of insurgency that the well-regulated individual always worked to master. Martha Nussbaum has recently termed the passions 'geological upheavals of thought'.[3] Reading is a process that puts immense pressure on a self traversed by faultlines dividing the claims of reason from the urgencies of passion.

In *The Passions of the Minde in Generall*, a work dedicated to the manipulation of emotion in oneself and others, Thomas Wright describes well the political and theological fissures that the well-regulated self must withstand:

The flesh molesteth us in the service of God, with an army of unruly Passions, for the most part, withdrawing from goodnes, and haling to ilnesse, they toss and turmoile our miserable soulls, as tempests & waves the Ocean sea, the which never standeth quiet, but either in ebbing or flowing, either winds doe buz about it, or raines alter it, or earthquakes shake, or stormes tyrannize over it: even so our soules are puffed up with selfelove; shaken with feare: now they be flowing with concupiscences and desires, and presently ebbing with desperation & sadnesse: joy altereth the mind, and ire tyrannizeth and consumeth both body and mind.[4]

Reading puts immense pressure on this fragile and unstable edifice, always in danger of collapsing under the weight of its unending appetites and urgent passions. In this moral and physiological dynamic, reading proves a particularly vexed activity. Indeed, according to Wright, among the most significant and seductive impediments to virtue are 'corrupted bookes', which

leadeth us to sinne, not onely, by training us up viciously, and inticing us by wicked examples, but also, by suggesting unto us many occasions of ill, by obscenous and naughty Bookes, as light and wanton Poets, as Machivellian policies, the Art of Conjuring, and such other dregges of mens wits, and off-springs of ungodly affections.[5]

Books are risky because they 'with a silent persuasion insinuate their matter unto the chiefe affection and highest part of the Soule'.[6] Amid this concern over the seductive power of books, we should remember the final words of Marlowe's Dr Faustus: 'I'll burn my books.'[7] For Wright, as for Faustus, the potentially pernicious impact of books makes the exercise of censorship as logical and necessary as the practice of quarantining the sick in a plague: 'in all good Common-weales,' remarks Wright, immoral books 'are either wholy prohibited, or so circumcised, that no such hurt followeth'.[8]

Dante's story of Paolo and Francesca in the *Inferno* epitomizes one aspect of the danger of reading: its capacity to stir mimetically the passions. Francesca remembers that as they read

how love constrained [Lancelot] ... one point alone it was that mastered us; when we read that the longed-for smile was kissed by so great a love, he who never shall be parted from me all trembling, kissed my mouth. A Galeotto [pander] was the book and he that wrote it; that day we read in it no further.[9]

Reading here not only excites the passions but also models the pleasures of acting on unconstrained desire. Francesca terms the book they read and the author who wrote it panders; reading is to subject oneself to their passionate seductions. It melts the frozen sea within them, to their eternal peril.

In *The Anatomy of Melancholy*, Robert Burton complains of books such as those read by Paolo and Francesca, 'by which [the reader] is rather infected than anyway perfected'.[10] Censorship is the effort to develop a prophylactic against such infections. Moreover, as J. F. Senault notes in *The Use of Passions*, poetry tends to make a much better job of portraying vices than it does of virtues, in the process appealing dangerously to the passions of the reader:

it unfortunately falls out (the which I rather attribute to the disorder of Nature, than to the like of Poetry) that Chastity appears not so beautiful in Verse as does uncleanness; and that the obedience of the Passions seems not so pleasing as their rebellion. Men betake themselves more usually to violent affections, than to such as are answerable to Reason; And as the Poets do express them with greater eloquence, their auditors listen unto them with more delight.[11]

It is the capacity of literature to move the reader, combined with the endemic attractions of literary vice, that is at once prized and feared. The bodies and minds of individual readers were imagined as battlegrounds between the corollary forces of good and evil, and of health and illness.

Thomas Wright describes the contrary forces that pull on human conduct from within and without:

Man in this world standeth in the middest betwixt God and the devill. Both pretend to win him to their Kingdomes; God to eternall pleasure, Satan to eternall paine ... the Devill immediately by his suggestions allureth us to sin, he being a spirit, by secret meanes can enter into the former part of our brain, and there chop and change our imaginations: hee can represent pleasures with a goodly shew; he can propound Vertue as a most bitter object; he can make us sloathful in the way of God, by stirring humours, altering the blood, which cause a tedious loathsomenesse in us. His craft is admirable, his malice extreme, his experience long, his forces mighty, his darts invisible, and indeed, so strong, that if wee were not assisted by Gods providence, and the ministery of his holy Angels, it were not possible to resist him.[12]

Suspended between God and the devil, the early modern reader was required to exercise a hermeneutics of suspicion as a bulwark against the admirable craft of the devil. At stake was not just the development of a convincing interpretation but rather the eternal status of the soul.

As a result, readers interacted aggressively with texts. They marked passages for later memorization, entered significant passages in commonplace books under signal headings, identified covert political allegories, sought out analogies and glossed difficult passages in the margins. As Bruce Smith reminds us, a common marginal mark of the period is that of a hand with the index finger (the adjective here is meaningful, linking a part of the body to a section of a book) pointing to some memorable passage: 'the reader's hand "members" the text, divides it into parts, so that the parts can be remembered on the reader's own terms'.[13] In a variety of ways, reading was as much a moral and physiological phenomenon as it was a mental activity.

In his rich and suggestive account of seventeenth-century reading practices, Kevin Sharpe emphasizes the extent to which William Drake frequently recorded 'adages warning against the heat of passion'.[14] Believing that 'Corrupt books produced corrupt manners', Drake repeatedly searched his library for tools to bridle his passions:

What men most needed to learn was what Drake most endeavoured to teach himself: control of the passions. 'Most of the disorders of our lives proceed from the darkness of our understanding or from the command or sway that our passions have over our reason.' The English were especially prone to passions and needed to study to control them, 'moderate passions' being 'the certain signes of a strong and well composed mind' ... For Drake, self-regulation meant men should govern themselves by rules and maxims, learned from reading and experience.[15]

Drake, then, not only emphasized the need for rigorous self-regulation, but also developed a particular form of that regulation in his specific reading practices: the culling of exemplary stories and *sententiae*.

Indeed, one of the most popular methods of dealing with the potential dangers of reading was the careful and deliberate separation of that which is ethically beneficial from that which is morally treacherous. This is a process whose similarity to the physiology of digestion was remarked and exploited continually by contemporaneous commentators. Just as eating involved the necessary separation of nutritive matter from dross, so did proper reading entail the continued discrimination of what is harmful from what is beneficial. As Mary Carruthers remarks, 'Metaphors which use digestive activities are so powerful and tenacious that "digestion" should be considered another basic functional model for the complementary activities of reading and composition, collection and recollection.'[16] Sir Francis Bacon's famous aphorism in his essay 'Of Studies' suggests that 'Some books are to be tasted, others to be swallowed, and some few to be chewed and digested.' In *Areopagitica*, Milton develops the comparison in order to put necessary ethical pressure on the free reader:

For books are as meats and viands are; some of good, some of evill ... Wholesome meats to a vitiated stomach differ little or nothing from unwholesome; and best books to a naughty mind are not unappliable to occasions of evil. Bad meats will scarce breed good nourishment in the healthiest concoction; but herein the difference is of bad books, that they to a discreet and judicious Reader serve in many respects to discover to confute, to forewarn, and to illustrate.[17]

For Milton, the analogy is so compelling that he is drawn to extend it to the point where it begins to break down, since bad meats will make even a healthy constitution sick while bad books will not necessarily harm the well-disciplined individual. As Sharon Achinstein has demonstrated, Milton aspired to a readership that would subject to critical and rational scrutiny the appeals to passion employed by texts defending monarchy and popery. Books, Milton argues, 'are not temptations, nor vanities; but usefull drugs and materials wherewith to temper and compose effective and strong med'cins, which mans life cannot want'.[18] Rather than imagining books as agents of infection and seduction, Milton sees them as powerful but ultimately salutary drugs necessary to achieve moral and physiological health.

But just as drugs need to be refined, so do books need to be redacted. The commonplace book possessed by nearly every serious early modern student (including Milton) was a very literal form of a reader's digest. As Edward Vaughan recommends in his 1594 textbook on reading the Bible, *Ten Introductions*, the careful reader 'must digest in a writing booke of two quires, after the manner of common places'.[19] According to William Sherman, the three main directives in scholarly reading were 'digesting, cross-referencing, and correcting'.[20] The successful reader participated in a deliberate process of vigilant assimilation. Robert Burton describes the creative assimilation of his omnivorous reading into the book that is *The Anatomy of Melancholy* as a metabolic process modelled directly on digestion:

I have laboriously collected this cento [*The Anatomy of Melancholy*] out of divers writers... The matter is theirs most part, and yet mine... *aliud tamen quam unde sumptum sit apparet* [yet it becomes something different in its new setting]; which nature doth with the aliment of our bodies incorporate, digest, assimilate, I do *concoquere quod hausi* [assimilate what I have swallowed], dispose of what I take.[21]

Digestion, the necessary separation of that which is useful from that which is harmful, becomes a very literal metaphor for the proper act of reading.

'Knowledge is as food', Raphael tells Adam in response to human queries about the order of the universe,

> and needs no less
> Her Temperance over Appetite, to know
> In measure what the mind may well contain,
> Oppresses else with Surfet, and soon turns
> Wisdom to Folly, as Nourishment to Winde.
> (*Paradise Lost*, 7.126–30)[22]

Both the acquisition of knowledge and the ingestion of nutrition require the discriminating processes of digestion, and both demand full acknowledgement of the ineffable but critical boundaries set by temperance. In both realms, more becomes less, converting sustenance into flatulence. The body of the inquiring reader was always in danger of taking in what was not good for it, or of taking in too much. The body of the reader, then, required the internalization of the principles of order that governed states.

An internal politics, with reason as a rightful ruler threatened continually by insurgent passions from within and infection from without, governed the language of self-regulation. Reading, then, was deeply enmeshed in notions of physiology and of political order.

THE MEDICAL READING OF POLITICS: FROM *CORPUS MYSTICUM* TO BODY POLITIC

States, too, were imagined entities whose delicate order could be threatened from within or without. As such, they were frequently used to shape the understanding of biology. Thomas Wright, for example, uses politics to explain moral psychology:

By two wayes the subjects of every Commonweale, usually disturbe the State, and breede civill broyles therein: the first is when they rise up and rebel against their King: the second is, when they brawle one with another, and so cause riots and tumults: the former is called Rebellion, the latter Sedition. After the same manner, Passions either rebel against Reason their Lord and King, or oppose themselves one against another ... almost continually inordinate passions contradict right reason.[23]

Here the imagined order of the state glosses the principles of biology and psychology.

The widespread analogy between the state and the body emerges from early modern habit of mind that continually sought out analogy between micro- and macrocosmic systems. The sixteenth and seventeenth centuries are, moreover, a period in which the search for analogy and resemblance was a primary strategy for making sense of the world and its myriad texts. The analogy cuts both ways – ineffable state organizations were understood as versions of physical bodies, and bodies were understood in political terms. In both realms, a premium was placed on the discovery and the sustenance of order. By looking at what physiology and politics were imagined to share, we can see how a system intended to stabilize meanings in another realm is itself wildly unstable. Where physiology allowed politics to assume the mantle of nature, politics bestowed upon the messy complexities of bodies the solemn dignity of deliberate social order. The body politic entailed not the agreed-upon series of inert meanings that it is often imagined to be but a vibrant and highly contested discourse. It is an arena from which obedience, and certain forms of resistance, would derive a vigorous vocabulary. The analogy is most effective, and most dangerous, in relation to what it made difficult or impossible to conceive – the deposition of a monarch, and rule by the many. What emerged from the various attempts to justify political order through physiological analogy was a body of sloppy but supple discourse that aspired to be a true political science.[24]

One of the reasons for the long life of the analogy is the remarkable malleability of medical doctrine, which made the body a metaphoric resource capable of defending almost any political position. Even the function and the relative importance of central organs were in dispute. Where Plato held that the rational part of the soul was located in the brain, Aristotle bestowed dominion over motion and sensation on the heart, imagining the brain as a kind of cooling tower for the body. Galen in turn proposed that the brain was sovereign in such matters, giving the brain the priority it would frequently sustain in political ideology.[25] What is at stake in this debate is not simply medical doctrine but two different notions of priority; where Aristotle opts for priority based on the heart's centrality, Plato and Galen propose that the brain's verticality is a mark of its superiority. As we will see, the imagined organizations of the body could be bent to defend absolute monarchy, or to emphasize the covert importance of apparently subsidiary regions and organs, although the former certainly becomes the predominant application in Western political philosophy.

Galenic physiology, moreover, could be turned to a variety of contradictory purposes. Theorizing that health was achieved by the balance of humoral and temperamental opposites – hot and cold and wet and dry – this physiology could have produced a particular model of creative tension in the body politic, stressing the gentle harmonies of *concordia discors*.[26] Just as easily, though, one could emphasize the harsh remedies that Galenic medicine prescribed, most of which were designed to rid the body through violent excretion of harmful elements. Under the Galenic paradigm, that is, one can stress either the mutual interdependence of parts, or the necessary purgation of deleterious matter. These possibilities multiplied in the seventeenth century, with the rise of Paracelsian medicine, which imagined disease as an invasion by an outside agent rather than as an imbalance of humoral fluid. Jonathan Gil Harris has recently described how Paracelsian physiology could underpin cultural xenophobia, rendering foreign bodies such as Jews, Catholics and witches as threats that need to be expelled.[27] Galenic physiology could in turn be used to encourage trade with such outside forces, particularly since trade was compared to the necessary flow of salutary nourishment, both within the body, and between the body and the outside world. As Sir Francis Bacon writes in 'Of Empire', merchants are the 'vena porta', the central artery, of the body politic, 'And if they flourish not, a Kingdome may have good Limmes, but will have empty Veines, and nourish little.'[28]

Ironically, the analogy that was used most frequently in Renaissance England to underpin absolutist politics seems to have derived, at least in the West, from the comparatively democratic society of Athenian Greece, and its effort to express the unity of disparate members. In the *Timaeus*, Plato suggested that the state is an organism and its citizens are members of this larger organism. Aristotle invokes the analogy in the *Politics* to show that 'the whole must be prior to the parts. Separate hand or foot from the whole body and they will no longer be hand or foot.'[29] The analogy passes through the works of Cicero and Seneca, offering an increasingly elaborate justification for the idea that it is in the interest of each member to behave in ways that benefit the whole. But something significant and wonderful happens to the analogy when it enters the vocabulary of St Paul in his effort to explain his developing notion of the *corpus mysticum* (1 Corinthians 12.12–27, AV):

For as the body is one, and hath many members, and all the members of that one body, being many, are one body: so also is Christ. For by one spirit are we all baptized into one body, whether we be Jews or Gentiles, whether we be bond or free ... For the body is not one member, but many. If the foot shall say, Because I am not the hand, I am not of the body; is it therefore not of the body? And if the ear shall say, Because I am not the eye, I am not of the body; is it therefore not of the body? If the whole body were an eye, where were the hearing? If the whole were hearing, where were the smelling? But now hath God set the members every one of them in the body, as it hath pleased him. And if they were all one member, where were the body? But now are they many members, yet but one body. And the eye cannot say unto the hand, I have no need of thee: nor again the head to the feet, I have no need of you. Nay, much more those members of the body, which seem to be more feeble, are necessary: And those members of the body, which we think to be less honourable, upon these we bestow more abundant honour; and our uncomely parts have more abundant comeliness. For our comely parts have no need: but God hath tempered the body together, having given more abundant honour to that part which lacked: That there should be no schism in the body; but that the members should have the same care one for another. And whether one member suffer, all the members suffer with it; or one member be honoured, all the members rejoice with it. Now ye are the body of Christ.

Paul takes an image whose primary directive had demanded that citizens foreground their duty to the state, and asks this analogy to justify the existence and needs of even the most unseemly parts of the body politic. He also takes an image that could be used to distinguish cultures – our body versus theirs – and asks it to deny the central ethnic distinction of his culture – that between Jew and Gentile. For Paul, then, the image of the mystical body politic united in Christ undoes earthly hierarchies, and emphasizes an ethic of mutual interdependence. The suffering of even one member entails the suffering of all. An idea that had been devoted to the sacrifice of individual interest on behalf of the larger organism is in Paul's sometimes radical hands used to justify and to honour the least honourable parts of the body.

Despite the enormous importance of Paul in the political and ethical development of western Europe, this vision of the subtle interdependence of related parts is not the predominant meaning of the image of the body politic in the Middle Ages and the Renaissance. As William Sherman suggests, the term frequently employed to describe the English national body – commonwealth – was 'often used to advocate the maintenance of an ordered society through the cooperative striving of every particular member, in his or her ordained capacity, for the common good'.[30] John of Salisbury, for example, assigns hierarchical value to different regions of the body in order to underwrite an organic image of political organization:

The place of the head in the body of the commonwealth is filled by the prince... The place of the heart is filled by the Senate, from which proceeds the initiation of good works and ill. The duties of eyes, ears, and tongue are claimed by the judges and the governors of provinces. Officials and soldiers correspond to the hands. Those who always attend upon the prince are likened to the sides. Financial officers and keepers... may be compared with the stomach and intestines, which, if they become congested through excessive avidity, and retain too tenaciously their accumulations, generate innumerable and incurable diseases, so that through their ailment the whole body is threatened with destruction. The husbandmen correspond to the feet.[31]

This kind of political allegory of the body, in which meanings and roles are assigned to various body parts, will make possible both the baroque elegance of Spenser's Castle of Alma in book 2 of *The Faerie Queene* and the obscene mystifications of inequity in Agrippa's fable of the belly in Shakespeare's *Coriolanus*.[32]

Just as the imagined order of the body is thought to explain the disposition of duties in society, different political systems become involved in the medical dispute about the role that different parts of the body play in health. This manifests itself most frequently in proto-medical discussions over whether the sovereignty of the body inheres in the brain, the heart, or the belly. Edward Forset, for example, holds out in *A Comparative Discourse of the Bodies Natural and Politique* (1606) for the sovereignty of the heart because nothing apparently feeds it, a phenomenon that demonstrates its independence, as well as the dependence of the rest of the body upon it. The heart, observes Forset, is of all other the firmest flesh, yet not fed with bloud by any vaynes; and from it all other flesh deriveth by veynes his borrowed living. I have heard it argued, that a King in like sort is alone formely and absolute stated, in and to the lands of his realme, and that all other owners take from him by the veynes and conveyances which he passeth to them.[33]

This reading of the implicit politics of the body accomplishes exactly the opposite point of Agrippa's famous fable of the belly (which we will look at presently): there consumption defines superiority, but here the heart, like Milton's God, is the great unfed feeder. Indeed, Forset proceeds to draw a close parallel between the physiological assimilation of nourishment and the political practices of sovereignty:

Who seeth not that it belongeth to the office of Soveraigntie, to provide for the nourishing and maintaining of the state with necessaries, to amplifie the dominions thereof, for profit and dignitie, to spread abroad the encrease of the people by Colonies, in the nature of generating or propagating, to cherish in the subjects an appetite of acquiring of commodities; to graunt to them places of Mart and Market for the digesting of the same unto all parts of the Realme . . . to give order for the holding and retaining of that which is then become their well agreeing and naturall sustenance, and for the expelling as well of the hurtfull overcharge, as the unprofitable excrements of the weale publique.[34]

Forset's use of the organic metaphor makes the disposition of societal goods and the removal of political opponents processes as natural, and as necessary, as eating and defecation. Political violence is made all the more convincing because it is based on a physiology in which almost all illness is imagined to derive from some failed excretion. That is why the primary therapies – bloodletting, vomiting, defecation – are designed to mimic and encourage the body's own processes of purgation.

William Harvey's famous dedication of *De Motu Cordis* to King Charles likewise sees the heart as the central organ of the body, and praises the king as the very literal heart of his nation:

Most Serene King! The animal's heart is the basis of its life, its chief member, the sun of its microcosm; on the heart all its activity depends, from the heart all its liveliness and strength arise. Equally is the king the basis of his kingdoms, the sun of his microcosm, the heart of the state; from him all power arises and all grace stems.[35]

Fascinatingly, Harvey shows no evidence that his new reading of the body entailed a scientific revolution conceptually akin to a political revolution, dethroning an ancient intellectual regime. Rather than demystifying the *corpus mysticum* of both realms, Harvey assures Charles that in the following treatise the reader will 'be able to contemplate simultaneously both the central organ of man's body and the likeness of your own royal power'.[36] For Harvey, even revolutionary physiology underpins the text of a conservative political vision.

In hierarchical readings of bodily organs, moreover, the belly is normally linked to the lower classes, while the upper classes are aligned with the heart or brain. In the marginalia of Phineas Fletcher's *Purple Island, or The Isle of Man* (1633), for example, the commentator assigns clear hierarchical meanings to the three central regions of the body:

The whole body may be parted into three regions: the lowest, or belly; the middle, or breast; the highest, or head. In the lowest the liver is soveraigne, whose regiment is the widest, but meanest. In the middle the heart reignes, most necessarie. The brain obtains the highest place, and is as the least in compasse, so the greatest in dignitie.[37]

Fletcher's *Purple Island*, itself an extended version of Spenser's Castle of Alma in book 2 of *The Faerie Queene*, is involved not just in reading the political hierarchy of the body but in covertly articulating political strategy. As Tom Healy argues, 'one of Fletcher's designs is to provide supposed scientific evidence for Stuart political policy... the body combats vices in the same way James's policies do... *The Purple Island* constantly urges that a maintenance of native purity is best achieved by not engaging with the outside world.'[38] Engaging in the proto-medical explanation of the order of the body, then, can be a way of flattering power or of offering political advice.

The hierarchies of the body, though, are far from obvious, and can be manipulated for various ideological goals. The stomach, for example, was a conflicted region, possessing a physiological centrality that belied the low political values it is usually assigned. In *Historia Vitae et Mortis*, Sir Francis Bacon, an author attentive both to politics and to science, asserts that the stomach is 'the master of the house as they say, upon whose strength all the other digestions depend'.[39] Digestion was indeed not a process confined to the stomach, but imagined to occur throughout the entire organism. If the stomach failed to do its work of concocting food into nutritive fluid capable of being assimilated by the rest of the body, then the other digestions would inevitably go awry, and the entire organism would suffer.

In this gap between politics and physiology, between the stomach's physiological centrality and its political marginality, emerges perhaps the most notorious use of the organic metaphor to produce a politics, Agrippa's fable of the belly. First narrated by Aesop and developed by Livy, this fable achieves fame in the Renaissance not just for its ingenious employment of the organic reading of the body politic but also for the stunning act of persuasion it entails. That is why it is given a prominent place in Sidney's *Defence of Poetry*. As an angry mob is quieted by Agrippa's assignation of particular corporeal functions to different elements of society, we see how political metaphor alters the conduct of the very society it purports to describe. The meanings of this fable, though, are far from obvious, and could be turned to a range of uses.[40] John of Salisbury retells the fable, indicating that its moral is that 'in the body of the commonwealth, wherein, though the magistrates are most grasping, yet they accumulate not so much for themselves as for others'.[41] It is this kind of trickle-down dietary economics that Shakespeare's Agrippa defends in *Coriolanus*. Indeed, Agrippa's fable depends for its effect on the revelation – politically stunning but physiologically unsurprising – that the stomach is not the passive receptacle it appears to be but rather the central processing unit of food for all the body's parts. Agrippa is thus able to quiet the rebellion of a hungry and angry mob by means of the brilliant but unexpected comparison of a privileged group of aristocrats to the belly they serve. One would not normally defend a voracious aristocracy in a subsistence society by likening it to the organ of digestion.

Agrippa's fable of the belly works as a piece of political persuasion because it is a moment when physiology is allowed to trump politics, when a hierarchical expectation linking the belly with the lower orders is defied, not in a Pauline effort to reveal the covert importance of these lower orders, but rather to justify the appetites of a ravenous aristocracy. Agrippa strategically replaces a hierarchy based on the distinction between low and high with one based on the distinction between centre and periphery, and so underscores the vast importance given to the digestion and distribution of food in the physiological maintenance of the individual body. When the belly is accused of idleness, that 'only like a gulf it did remain / I' th' midst a' th' body, idle and unactive, / Still cupboarding the viand, never bearing / Like labor with the rest', the belly responds by conceding

> That I receive the general food at first
> Which you do live upon; and fit it is,
> Because I am the store-house and the shop
> Of the whole body...
> I send [food] through the rivers of your blood,
> Even to the court, the heart, to th' seat o' th' brain,
> And, through the cranks and offices of man,
> The strongest nerves and small inferior veins

> From me receive that natural competency
> Whereby they live...
> . . . .
>   ...all
> From me do back receive the flour of all,
> And leave me but the bran.[42]

Fantasizing that a society's resources must pass through its most privileged members in order to get to its most indigent figures, just as food must pass through the stomach before it can be dispersed to the various parts of the body, Agrippa uses the physiological centrality of the stomach to mystify a doctrine of social inequality. He manages, moreover, to obscure the actual labour that produces and distributes provisions, and to render the gluttonous consumption of goods and services as a necessary cultural labour. When aristocratic voracity is praised as a social exigency, it is easy to see how the indigent could come to hate the guts of society.

Indeed, as Margaret Healy has recently shown in a wonderful book on the political understandings of disease in early modern England, the very imagery used by Agrippa to defend aristocratic consumption could become the matter of a powerful political critique in the charged political landscape of England in the 1620s. It was a world, she argues, 'in which some English bodies, including many highly placed "paunches", were engaging in frenzies of consumption, whilst the commonwealth, denied the "blood and nourishment" necessary for her survival, was languishing with "weakness and consumption [wasting disease]" '.[43] She cites in particular the warning to Charles I issued by Thomas Mun, which sounds like a deliberate attempt to turn the fable of the belly on its head: 'A Prince...is like the stomach in the body, which if it cease to digest and distribute to the other members, it doth no sooner corrupt them, but it destroys itself.'[44] Here, the greedy prince is the central affliction of what Healy terms a 'glutted, unvented body', a political entity veering on disease, decay and death.

The metaphor of the body politic and the cultural work of consumption receive a unique reading in the thought of Thomas Hobbes. Absorbing both Descartes's interpretation of the body as a machine and Harvey's discovery of the circulation of the blood, Hobbes rewrites the body politic in terms of the new sciences. His version of the body politic draws not on organicism but rather on machinery; body parts are for Hobbes like 'Engines that move themselves by springs and wheeles as doth a watch'. He offers a redaction of the fable of the belly, using the new idea of the circulation of the blood to explain the economic distribution of resources:

By Concoction, I understand the reducing of all commodities, which are not presently consumed, but reserved for Nourishment in time to come, to some thing of equall value...And this is nothing else but Gold, and Silver, and Mony...and the same passeth from Man to Man, within the Common-wealth; and goes round about, Nourishing (as it passeth) every part thereof; In so much as this Concoction, is as it were the Sanguinification of the Common-wealth: For naturall Bloud is in like manner made of the fruits of the Earth; and circulating, nourisheth by the way, every Member of the Body of Man.[45]

'Hobbes,' suggests Leonard Barkan, 'barely sees man as an organic being... Hobbes's body is an actual working machine, and his commonwealth is an actual political machine.'[46] The famous title page of *Leviathan* (1651) shows not a biological being composed of interdependent organs but a herd of individuals conformed rather artificially to the shape of a body and made to look at the head of the sovereign. As Hobbes asks in the opening,

For seeing life is but a motion of limbs, the beginning whereof is in some principal part within; why may we not say that all automata...have an artificial life?.. For by art is created that great LEVIATHAN called a COMMONWEALTH, or STATE, in Latin CIVITAS, which is but an artificial man.[47]

The point for Hobbes is that states are founded by design, not by nature. Hobbes does employ the idea of the body politic to develop parallels between diseases of the body and what he terms 'the Infirmities...of a Common-wealth'.[48] He claims that 'one of the most frequent causes' of 'Rebellion in particular against Monarchy...is the Reader of the books of Policy, and Histories of the antient Greeks, and Romans'.[49] When exposed to such books,

young men, and all others that are unprovided of the Antidote of solid Reason... receive withal a pleasing Idea, of all they have done...From the reading, I say, of such books, men have undertaken to kill their Kings, because the Greek and Latine writers, in their books, and discourses of Policy, make it lawfull and laudable, for any man so to do.[50]

He compares the venom injected via these classical republican texts to

the biting of a mad Dogge, which is a disease the Physicians call Hydrophobia, or fear of Water. For as he that is so bitten, has a continuall torment of thirst, and yet abhorreth water...So when a Monarchy is once bitten to the quick, by those Democraticall writers, that continually snarle at that estate; it wanteth nothing more than a strong Monarch, which neverthelesse out of a certain Tyrannophobia, or feare of being strongly governed, when they have him, they abhorre.[51]

Books, then, stir in the body politic the same kinds of unhealthy passions they generate in the individual reader.

There were, of course, possibilities beyond the defence of monarchy available in the project of using physiological principles to articulate monarchical notions, although it sometimes took some ingenuity to find them. In *The Law of Freedom in a Platform*, Gerrard Winstanley cunningly concedes an elemental linkage between human biology and politics in order to dispute the hierarchical disposition of goods that the organic metaphor was employed to subtend:

True *Freedom* lies where a man receives his nourishment and preservation, and that is in the use of the earth: For as Man is compounded of the four Materials of the Creation, *Fire*, *Water*, *Earth*, and *Ayr*; so is he preserved by the compounded bodies of these four, which are the fruits of the Earth; and he cannot live without them: for take away the free use of these, and the body languishes, the spirit is brought into bondage, and at length departs, and ceaseth his motional action in the body.[52]

For Winstanley, the fact that the human body is a little world made cunningly of the four elements gives each individual an equal right to the elements of that world. Winstanley, then, does not so much use the organic metaphor as turn its intellectual source against its common meanings.

The image of the body politic proves in the middle of the seventeenth century a handy resource of Royalist lament at the violent disturbances of the body politic. In *The New Distemper* (1645), Francis Quarles warns his country, beset with civil war, to 'Take heed while ye goe about to cure a Fever, you run not the Body Politick into a Dropsie, with too much Phlebotomie.'[53] For Richard Lovelace, the execution of Charles means that

> Now *Whitehalls* in the grave,
> And our *Head* is our slave
>> Now the *Thighs* of the Crown,
>> And the *Arms* are lopp'd down,
> And the *Body* is all but a *Belly*.[54]

The organic metaphor of the state, then, provided an effective vehicle for dramatizing the loss and disruption of civil war. It also conveniently rendered those who criticized the current order as foolish disturbers of a salutary harmony.

The metaphor, though, could also be made to signal limitations on the power of monarchs. Sidney's King Euarchus in the *Arcadia* behaves like an ideal monarch,

vertuouslie and wisely acknowledging, that he with his people made all but one politike bodie, whereof himselfe was the head; even so cared for them, as he woulde for his owne limmes: never restrayning their liberty, without it stretched to licenciousnes, nor pulling from them their goods.[55]

Here we have a fictional ruler articulating the organic metaphor as a check on his own political conduct. When writing to Queen Elizabeth to warn her of the dangers of a French marriage, Sidney similarly invokes a physiological metaphor to underpin his advice: as sudden changes are dangerous to health, so 'in this body politick wherof you are the onely head, it is so much the more as there are more humours to receave a hurtfull impression'.[56]

Sometimes, though, the very use of the metaphor showed how effectively it could preclude certain kinds of political thought, and silence certain kinds of resistance. Indeed, John Ponet's *Short Treatise of Politick Power*, written in exile under Queen Mary, is forced to push the analogy into realms in which physiology completely breaks down:

Common wealthes and realmes may live, whan the head is cut of, and may put on a newe head, that is, make them a newe governour, whan they see their olde head seke to muche his owne will and not the wealthe of the hole body, for the which he was onle ordained.[57]

The Jesuit Robert Parsons was driven, from the opposite side of the theological and political situation, to suggest that

The Body Natural, if it had the same ability that when it had an aking or sickly Head, it would cut it off and take another. I doubt not but it would so ... rather than all the other parts should perish or live in pain and continual torment.[58]

In responding to Parsons, Thomas Craig re-invoked physiology to suggest the absurdity of Parsons's position:

A noble Metaphor indeed, which I thus retort upon himself. For seeing without the Head, the Body is only a dead Carcass, and can do nothing of itself without the Head, which is the seat of all the Animal Sense, therefore the Body can do nothing against the Head, seeing without the body it is dead neither had it Power over any Member, but with the consent of the Head. Who could endure such a Metaphor, that a Body may cut off its own Head, that it may remain a Body.[59]

In 1650, William Hickman wrote to Cromwell suggesting that the Protectorate had not found a sufficient substitute for the organicism that underpinned monarchical power:

Hetherto in the chandge of our Government nothinge materiall as yet hath bin done, but a takinge of the head of monarchy and placing uppon the body or trunck of it, the name or title of a Commonwealth, a name aplicable to all forms of Government, and contained under the former.[60]

While the organic metaphor could be used to indicate to monarchs their responsibility to the rest of the body politic, then, it did not prove of great facility in defending the forced change of rulers. As John Rawlinson asserts, with apparently unassailable logic: 'as in the natural body, so it is in the body politic, if the body be without a head it presently falls to the ground'.[61]

The organic metaphor, then, successfully mystified domination as the tender and self-interested care of a head for its body, and rendered resistance or rebellion unthinkable and suicidal. It also managed to make other forms of government appear monstrous, deformed, or diseased. The analogy, in other words, did enormous ideological work, work which was all the more coercive because covert, and buttressed by a pernicious blend of common sense and medical 'fact'. Indeed, many writers attempting to articulate resistance discovered that it might be easier to get rid of the metaphor altogether, because the analogy of the bodies natural and political inevitably emphasized the need for political unity under the rule of a single head.[62] Herbert Palmer, for example, wanted to throw out the organic analogy altogether: 'The natural body can do nothing but by the guidance of the head', Palmer argues, 'But a body politic is a company of reasonable men, whose action may be divided from their politic head, and yet be rational and regular... the members of a politic body may resist the politic head.'[63] Similarly, Samuel Rutherford asserts in the *Lex Rex, or The Law and the Prince*: 'The head natural is not made a head by the free election and consent of arms, shoulders, legs, toes, fingers, etc... but the members of a politic body may resist the politic head.'[64] When Sir John Maynard claimed that even those who do not vote are represented in the elections, just as 'in case a man's hand moves, it is the man that moves, or [when] his eye sees a colour, it is the man that sees', John Wildman responded by arguing: 'I hope the gentleman will please to confess a vast difference between a body natural and a body politic... If [not], if one in the City commit treason all the City are traitors.'[65] Even Cromwell was not immune from those who would attempt to turn the organic metaphor against those in power. A mid-century republican, John Streater, uses the metaphor to suggest that the ruler – here Cromwell – fetters his own power when he puts down those below him: 'It is a madness for the head to chain the Foot. I pray if it doth, how much liberty hath the head more than the foot?'[66] In order for the revolution to succeed, it seems that partisans needed to slay not only the body of the king but also the metaphor of the body politic.

But the head regularly chained, and even threatened with violence, the foot on which it theoretically stood. In a speech to Parliament, 21 March 1609, King James had used his frequent comparison of himself as the head of the body to justify his own application of harsh remedies to the unruly members of that body:

the head hath the power of directing all the members of the body to that use which the judgement in the head thinkes most convenient. It may apply sharpe cures, or cut off corrupt members, let blood in what proportion it thinks fit, and as the body may spare.[67]

In this use of the metaphor, the king becomes a physician who heals himself, applying harsh but necessary remedies to the body of which he is the head and sovereign.

We need to remember that St Paul, whose own doctrine of the *corpus mysticum* had opened up an imaginative space for a dazzlingly interdependent social body, had also sanctioned the surgical removal of unwanted elements: 'I would they were even cut off which trouble you' (Galatians 5.12, AV; legend suggests that Origen read this passage with painstaking literalism, and castrated himself). The passage was interpreted as a licence to remove political opponents by whatever means necessary for the health of the larger body. In such a physiological politics, the amputation of political opponents could be rendered an act of mercy, one absolutely necessary for the health of the larger organism.

In the preface to *Absalom and Achitophel*, Dryden uses the image of the body politic with great cunning, suggesting that the satirist is like a physician to the body politic:

The true end of *Satyre*, is the amendment of Vices by correction. And he who writes Honestly, is no more an Enemy to the Offendour, than the Physician to the Patient, when he prescribes harsh remedies to an inveterate Disease: for those are only in order to prevent the Chyrurgeon's work of an *Ense rescindendum* [something to be cut out in order to prevent infection of the whole organism], which I wish not to my very Enemies. To conclude all, If the Body politique have any Analogy to the Natural, in my weak judgment, an Act of *Oblivion* were as necessary in a Hot, Distemper'd State, as an *Opiate* would be in a Raging Fever.[68]

Dryden argues that his kinder, gentler remedy of political satire is designed as a purgative that would ideally make unnecessary the harsher remedies of the surgeon's amputations. His own pose of moderation works well with a Galenic medical ethos which imagines health in terms of balance, and disease as extremity. Dryden also strategically uses physiology to suggest that an 'Act of Oblivion' like that by which several members of Cromwell's government were forgiven their crimes against the monarchy would only exacerbate the diseased state it intends to cure. Another act of state mercy would put the patient to sleep but not touch his raging fever. The implication is that while 'a bit of judicious bleeding' might have been enough in

1660, now the fever rages, and the surgeon's knife is needed if the patient is to be saved.[69]

Yet another trajectory of a physiological politics can be traced in the work of John Milton. In *Of Reformation*, Milton 'pounced' upon the fable of the belly, argues Annabel Patterson, 'and filled it with disruptive enthusiasm'.[70] Milton rings several significant changes on the fable, making it nearly unrecognizable in the process; he substitutes 'a huge and Monstrous Wen', or tumour, for the clamorous and complaining common people. The wen, by which Milton apparently intends to represent the Anglican bishops, wants 'dignities and rich indowment' worthy of the head, until 'a wise and learned Philosopher' tells the Wen that it is 'but a bottle of vitious and harden'd excrements'. Where Agrippa had revealed the immense usefulness of a gluttonous stomach, Milton's philosopher exposes the covert repulsiveness of a vainglorious cancer. The philosopher then promises to 'cut thee off, and open thee', in order to show 'all men' that this grandiloquent tumour is indeed 'a foul disfigurment and burden' to the head. Excision and anatomy – Milton's own equivalent, forty years earlier, of Dryden's '*Ense rescindendum*' – will reveal the excremental truth of the presumptuous protuberance that is episcopacy.

As Patterson points out, it is ironic that Milton here leaves the sovereignty of the head unchallenged, since it would not be many years before he was arguing that not just episcopacy but also monarchy was 'a foul disfigurment' to the people, and worthy of being removed. *Of Reformation* exploits other aspects of a medicalized politics. Milton has recourse to a near-Pauline sense of the community of disparate parts when he writes:

And because things simply pure are inconsistent in the masse of nature, nor are the elements or humors in Mans Body exactly *homogeneall*, and hence the best founded Common-wealths, and least barbarous have aym'd at a certaine mixture and temperament, partaking the several virtues of each other State, that each part drawing to it selfe may keep up a steddy, and eev'n uprightnesse in common.[71]

As David Norbrook remarks, here Milton

sees the state not as a descending hierarchy but as a dynamic interaction of component parts which share a common interest. This is a commonwealth in which all the parts are subordinated to the whole rather than the body's being subordinated to the monarchical head. The parts are seen in terms of functions rather than individuals.[72]

In *Areopagitica* (1644), Milton turns to the image of the body politic to celebrate the right of the reader to see, and know, and yet abstain from the kinds of textual temptations explored in the first part of this essay. Envisioning political ferment not as the national sickness that Quarles and Lovelace mourn but rather as a sign of the nation's ethical and intellectual vitality, Milton boldly links physiology to political controversy:

For as in a body, when the blood is fresh, the spirits pure and vigorous . . . it argues in what good plight and constitution the body is, so when the cherfulnesse of the people is so sprightly up, as that it has, not only wherewith to guard well its own freedom and safety, but to spare, and to bestow upon the solidest and sublimest points of controversie, and new invention, it betok'ns us not degenerated, nor dropping to a fatall decay, but casting off the old and wrincl'd skin of corruption to outlive these pangs and wax young again.[73]

This image of corporeal vigour leads Milton to envision his nation as a waking hero, giving a particularly poetic edge to a stale metaphor: 'Methinks I see in my mind a noble and puissant Nation rousing herself like a strong man after sleep, and shaking her invincible locks.'

Despite the immense power of this vision, Milton's subsequent political prose only sporadically employs the idea of the body politic, probably because of the deep limitations of the metaphor for articulating a non-monarchical polity, and turns instead to a language of contract.[74] Humans are joined together not out of transcendental organicism but out of rational, mutual agreement that keeps them from 'do[ing] wrong and violence' to each other: 'Forseeing that such courses must needs tend to the destruction of them all,' writes Milton in *The Tenure of Kings and Magistrates*, humans 'agreed by common league to bind each other from mutual injury, and joyntly to defend themselves against that grave disturbance or opposition to such agreement.'[75] Except for Milton's deliberate refusal to centre that contract on a sovereign, we are not far from the political vision of Hobbes's *Leviathan*, published in the same year.

In *Paradise Lost*, Milton completes the turn away from the nation as a significant unit of social or political organization. Indeed, it is only in the founding of Hell that Milton attends at all to the issue of a nation in his epic.[76] In the epic, the notion of the body politic makes only sporadic but nonetheless significant appearance. When Satan claims he is a 'faithful leader' (4.933) of his troops, Gabriel asks: 'Faithful to whom? To thy rebellious crew? / Army of fiends, fit body to fit head' (4.952–3). In the War in Heaven, Abdiel invokes the idea of the body politic to correct Satan's misreading of the dispersal of benefits in heaven. Abdiel tells Satan that with the exaltation of the Son, God intends not 'to make us less, bent rather to

exalt / Our happie state under one Head more neer / United' (5.829–31).
Abdiel then describes how all are exalted with the Son: 'since he the Head /
One of our numbers thus reduc't becomes, / His Laws our Laws, all honour to him done / Returns our own' (5.841–5). As Mary Ann Radzinowicz
argues, Abdiel has an 'intuition of the organic collective ideal' which allows
him to imagine heaven as 'an evolving, organic, unified totality'.[77] Here
Milton's monism, which as John Rogers has shown is a kind of democratic
materialism, is allied with his Pauline sense of the *corpus mysticum*.[78] It is
telling, though, that this *corpus* is not incarnated on earth as it is in heaven.
On earth, rather, we meet the repeated story of the one just man in a world
of woe, isolated from any notion of a meaningful political community. In a
letter to Peter Heimbach, Milton endorses the Stoic sentiment that 'One's
Patria is wherever it is well with him [*patria est, ubicumque est bene*].'[79]
It is Milton's signal achievement in *Paradise Lost* to compose an epic that
assimilates the lessons of individual liberty to a genre normally dedicated
to the founding of empires. Adam and Eve exit Paradise to found not a
nation but a race.

Milton's God does describe the end of time as an occasion of incorpo-
ration, when 'God shall be All in All' (*Paradise Lost*, 3.341). It is hard to
say, though, whether this is a consummation devoutly to be wished, or a
threat to the hard-won autonomy of the post-lapsarian individual.[80] In his
epic Milton focuses not on the redemptive nation that he had articulated
so powerfully in the *Areopagitica* and in the first and second *Defences of
the English People* but rather on a paradise within the individual, independent of national affiliation. Milton, that is, supplants a concern with the
body politic for a fascination with the processes by which the order of the
state is internalized in the individual subject. As Sharpe and Zwicker argue, *Paradise Lost* exemplifies how 'The creation of the self... is a process
of interiorizing all the instability and incoherence of society and state.'[81]
For Milton, the Fall inaugurates a regime of radical interiority, one that
re-situates the political strife of the outside world within the individual
subject. Rather than the body politic, we have a highly politicized body as
the primary unit of political organization. The Fall transforms the passions
and emotions from obedient citizens to unruly rebels in the state of the
self. The overarching effect of the Fall, according to Michael, is that humans lose 'true Libertie', and surrender the control of their passions. Thus
the story of Nimrod, the first tyrant, who 'affect[s] to subdue / Rational
Libertie', issues not just in a political warning against monarchs but also in
the following lesson in post-lapsarian psychology:

Since thy original lapse, true Libertie
Is lost, which alwayes with right Reason dwells
Twinn'd, and from her hath no dividual being;
Reason in man obscured, or not obeyed,
Immediately inordinate desires
And upstart passions catch the government
From reason, and to servitude reduce
Man till then free.   (12.82–90)

This moral psychology is what makes reading such an arduous and volatile enterprise.

Indeed, the last two books of *Paradise Lost* dramatize the enormous difficulty of reading biblical history well. Even with an angelic tutor, Adam must continually be corrected in his interpretations of sacred history. As a spectator at the tragicomedy of human history, Adam in turn reels from despair at his first vision of death, to false joy at the union of the Sons of Seth with the 'Beavie of fair Women' (11.582), to tearful sadness at the story of Enoch, to despair at the Flood, to rejoicing at the survival of Noah and his family, to disgust at Nimrod, to delight at Moses, to overwhelming jubilation at the story of Jesus.[82] The body of the reader, suffused with upstart passions, reads the truths of Judaeo-Christian history through a glass darkly. The confidence expressed in *Areopagitica* that the truth will always win in open contest with falsehood has been replaced by the urgent but ineffable imperatives of internal discipline. As Jesus remarks in *Paradise Regained* to the temptation of earthly power, 'who reigns within himself, and rules / Passions, desires, and fears, is more a king' (2.465–6). Integrity of the well-regulated individual becomes for Milton a bulwark, however fragile, against the infections and usurpations of a corrupt body politic. Where the image of the body politic had frequently been bent to justify the absolutist state, we see in Milton how a well-governed self internalizes politics in order to produce the parameters of possessive individualism.[83]

In this essay I have asked why bodies and politics were read in conjunction with each other. I have wondered why the mysterious phenomena of corporeal order were so frequently used to explicate the inscrutable structures of political organization. Politics and medicine are not reservoirs of transcendent truths but rather arenas of contested and inconsistent meanings. Even in a culture trained to think that right reading involved discovering parallels between the microcosm and the macrocosm, there is nothing whatsoever obvious or logical in the application of biological metaphors to matters of political organization. I have in this essay also explored the myriad ways that reading was imagined to be involved in both physiology and politics. I have suggested that the physiology of an individual reader was linked to ways in which society was itself imagined to function. In both realms, emotional insurgency threatened an apparently transcendent order. A misguided model for how bodies were thought to function was used to articulate political polemic. Distorting both medicine and politics, the body politic offers an instructive fable in the immense power of metaphor to shape and delimit the imagination.

In *Refiguring Revolutions* Sharpe and Zwicker suggest that 'the French Revolution not only marks the death of the body politic, it also stains the romantic landscape and its political vision with the blood of violence and terror'.[84] It is hard to say, though, whether the body politic does not regularly emerge from the grave to walk the earth. We can perhaps hear its ghostly presence rattling around in that particularly twentieth-century pursuit of ethnic cleansing. It is through a particularly pernicious use of the fiction of a body politic that cultures, at least in part, are able to render one group of people the epitome of hygiene and another group the essence of pollution. The image of the body politic has survived long after the political theology on which it was based was rendered obsolete. As Michel Foucault remarks, 'The representation of power has remained under the spell of the monarchy. In political thought and analysis, we still have not cut off the head of the king.'[85] Still a bottomless reservoir of elusive meaning, the image of the body politic can at once contain the exquisite interdependence that Paul articulated in his lengthy account of the *corpus mysticum* and sanction violent action against any group imagined as unhealthy or unclean. 'Society as a corporate Body,' suggests Slavoj Žižek, 'is the fundamental ideological fantasy.'[86] As we see its spectre in the past and present practices of the political collectives that imagine themselves as animate and integral communities and nations, we might want to think about whether the new ways of reading bodies that medical science is now making available will offer more productive metaphors for political order.[87] Or we might just want to jettison the entire project of reading politics biologically.

NOTES

1. Cited in A. Manguel, *A History of Reading* (London, 1996), p. 93.
2. A. Johns, *The Nature of the Book: Print and Knowledge in the Making* (Chicago, 1998), pp. 442, 379.
3. M. C. Nussbaum, *Upheavals of Thought: The Intelligence of Emotions* (Cambridge, 2001), p. 90.

4. T. Wright, *The Passions of the Minde in Generall (1604)*, ed. T. O. Sloan (Urbana, Ill., 1971), p. 334. For this congenitally inconstant self, and the premium on order it enjoins, see my *Bodies and Selves in Early Modern England: Physiology and Inwardness in Spenser, Shakespeare, Herbert, and Milton* (Cambridge, 1999).

5. Wright, *The Passions of the Minde*, p. 333.

6. Ibid., p. 334.

7. C. Marlowe, *Dr Faustus*, ed. R. Gill (New York, 1990).

8. Wright, *The Passions of the Minde*, p. 334.

9. Dante, *The Divine Comedy*, vol. 1: *Inferno*, trans. J. D. Sinclair (New York, 1939), p. 79.

10. R. Burton, *The Anatomy of Melancholy*, ed. H. Jackson (2 vols., New York, 1977), vol. 1, p. 23.

11. In J. F. Senault, *The Use of Passions*, trans. Henry Cary, earl of Monmouth (London, 1649), pp. 170–1.

12. Wright, *The Passions of the Minde*, pp. 329–31.

13. B. R. Smith, *The Acoustic World of Early Modern England: Attending to the O-Factor* (Chicago, 1999), p. 128.

14. K. Sharpe, *Reading Revolutions: The Politics of Reading in Early Modern England* (New Haven and London, 2000), p. 206. For early modern reading practices, see also C. Jagodzinski, *Privacy and Print: Reading and Writing in Seventeenth-Century England* (Charlottesville, Va., 1999), and the relevant essays in G. Cavallo and R. Chartier, eds., *A History of Reading in the West*, trans. L. G. Cochrane (Oxford, 1999).

15. Sharpe, *Reading Revolutions*, pp. 212–13.

16. M. Carruthers, *The Book of Memory: A Study of Memory in Medieval Culture* (Cambridge, 1990), pp. 165–6.

17. I quote from *The Riverside Milton*, ed. R. Flannagan (Boston, 1998), p. 1005. On the persistence of this topos, see Manguel, *A History of Reading*, pp. 170–1: 'Just as writers speak of cooking up a story, rehashing a text, having half-baked ideas for a plot, spicing up a scene or garnishing the bare bones of an argument, turning the ingredients of a potboiler into soggy prose, a slice of life peppered with allusions into which readers can sink their teeth, we, the reader, speak of savouring a book, of finding nourishment in it, of devouring a book at one sitting, of regurgitating or spewing up a text, of ruminating on a passage, of rolling a poet's words on the tongue, of feasting on poetry, of living on a diet of detective stories.'

18. *The Riverside Milton*, p. 1008; S. Achinstein, *Milton and the Revolutionary Reader* (Princeton, 1994).

19. Quoted in W. H. Sherman, *John Dee: The Politics of Reading and Writing in the English Renaissance*, (Amherst, Mass., 1995), p. 61.

20. Sherman, *John Dee*, p. 61.

21. Burton, *The Anatomy of Melancholy*, vol. 1, p. 25.

22. *The Riverside Milton*, p. 541.

23. Wright, *The Passions of the Minde*, pp. 69–70.

24. This section of the essay draws heavily on the pioneering and erudite work of two previous studies: L. Barkan, *Nature's Work of Art: The Human Body as Image of the World* (New Haven, 1975), particularly chapter 2; and D. G. Hale, *The Body Politic: A Political Metaphor in Renaissance English Literature* (The Hague, 1971).

25. See N. Siraisi, *Medieval and Early Renaissance Medicine* (Chicago, 1990), pp. 81–2; and F. D. Hoeniger, *Medicine and Shakespeare in the English Renaissance* (Newark, Del., 1992), pp. 131–7.

26. I discuss this in more detail in *Bodies and Selves in Early Modern England*. See also J. Le Goff, 'Head or Heart? The Political Use of Body Metaphors in the Middle Ages', *Fragments for a History of the Human Body*, part 3, eds. M. Feher, R. Naddaff and N. Tazi (New York, 1989), pp. 13–26.

27. J. G. Harris, *Foreign Bodies and the Body Politic: Discourses of Social Pathology in Early Modern England* (Cambridge, 1998).

28. F. Bacon, *The Essay, or Counsels, Civil and Moral*, ed. Brian Vickers (New York, 1999), 'Of Empire'.

29. Aristotle, *Politics*, 1235a, 20, trans. T. A. Sinclair (Baltimore, 1969), p. 29; cited in Barkan, *Nature's Work of Art*, p. 65.

30. W. H. Sherman, 'Anatomizing the Commonwealth: Language, Politics, and the Elizabethan Social Order', in E. Fowler and R. Greene, eds., *The Project of Prose in Early Modern Europe and the New World* (Cambridge, 1997), pp. 104–21.

31. *Policratus*, in *The Statesman's Book of John of Salisbury*, trans. J. Dickinson (New York, 1927), chapter 5, section 2, p. 65; cited in Barkan, *Nature's Work of Art*, p. 72.

32. I discuss the order of the temperate body in book 2 of *The Faerie Queene* in *Bodies and Selves in Early Modern England*.

33. Edward Forset, *A Comparative Discourse of the Bodies Natural and Politique* (London, 1606), in J. Winny, ed., *The Frame of Order: An Outline of Elizabethan Belief Taken from Treatises of the Late Sixteenth Century* (London, 1957), p. 101. For Forset, see also Le Goff, 'Head or Heart?', p. 17.

34. Forset, *A Comparative Discourse*, p. 13.

35. W. Harvey, *The Circulation of the Blood and Other Writings*, trans. K. J. Franklin (London, 1963), p. 3.

36. Ibid.

37. P. Fletcher, *The Purple Island, or The Isle of Man* (Cambridge, 1633), p. 20, marginalia, note to canto 2, stanza 14.

38. T. Healy, 'Sound Physic: Phineas Fletcher's *The Purple Island* and the Poetry of Purgation', *Renaissance Studies*, 5 (1991), pp. 350–1.

39. F. Bacon, *Historia Vitae et Mortis*, in *Works*, ed. J. Spedding *et al.* (14 vols., London, 1857–74), vol. 5, p. 294.

40. In *Fables of Power: Aesopian Writing and Political History* (Durham, N. C., and London, 1991), pp. 134–6, Annabel Patterson notes that '*The Belly and the Members* functioned as a metaphor for political theory by a rather remarkable act of abstraction – by translating the essentially carnal acts of eating and

digestion into a political consensus as to how and by whom the financial resources of a state (or church) should be controlled.'

41. John of Salisbury, *The Statesman's Book*, p. 257.
42. *Coriolanus*, 1.1.98–101 and 131–46, from *The Riverside Shakespeare*, ed. G. Blakemore Evans *et al*. (Boston, 1974), pp. 1397–8.
43. M. Healy, *Fictions of Disease in Early Modern England: Bodies, Plagues and Politics* (Basingstoke, 2001), pp. 214–15.
44. T. Mun, *England's Treasure by Forraign Trade* (London, 1664; written 1622–3), p. 70; cited in Healy, *Fictions of Disease*, p. 214.
45. T. Hobbes, *Leviathan*, ed. R. Tuck (Cambridge, 1991), p. 174.
46. Barkan, *Nature's Work of Art*, pp. 113–14.
47. Hobbes, *Leviathan*, p. 9.
48. Ibid., p. 221.
49. Ibid., p. 225.
50. Ibid., pp. 225–6.
51. Ibid., p. 226.
52. G. Winstanley, *The Law of Freedom in a Platform, or True Magistracy Restored*, ed. R. W. Kenny (New York, 1973), pp. 66–7.
53. F. Quarles, *The New Distemper*, in *Complete Works*, ed. A. B. Grosart (3 vols., 1880; repr., London, 1967), vol. 1, p. 153; cited in Hale, *The Body Politic*, p. 118.
54. R. Lovelace, 'A Mock-Song', *The Poems of Richard Lovelace*, ed. C. H. Wilkinson (Oxford, 1930), pp. 154–5; cited in Hale, *The Body Politic*, p. 119.
55. P. Sidney, *The Countesse of Pembrokes Arcadia* (1590), in *The Works of Sir Philip Sidney*, ed. A. Feuillerat (4 vols., Cambridge, 1912–26), vol. 1, p. 187; cited in Hale, *The Body Politic*, p. 73. Sidney's politics are explored by Blair Worden in *The Sound of Virtue: Philip Sidney's Arcadia and Elizabethan Policy* (New Haven, 1996).
56. Sidney, 'A Discourse . . . to the Queenes Majesty', in *Complete Works*, vol. 3, p. 52; cited in Hale, *Body Politic*, p. 73.
57. J. Ponet, *Short Treatise of Politick Power* (Strasbourg, 1556), sig. D7; cited in Hale, *The Body Politic*, p. 81. See also Healy, *Fictions of Disease*, pp. 214–19.
58. R. Parsons, *A Conference about the Next Succession to the Crowne of England* (London, 1594), p. 38; cited in Hale, *The Body Politic*, p. 81.
59. T. Craig, *Concerning the Right of Succession to the Kingdom of England*, ed. J. G. [London, 1703], p. 167; cited in Hale, *The Body Politic*, p. 81.
60. J. Nickolls Jr, ed., *Original Letters and Papers of State* (London, 1743), pp. 31–2; cited in D. Norbrook, *Writing the English Republic: Poetry, Rhetoric and Politics 1627–1660* (Cambridge, 1999), p. 271.
61. J. Rawlinson, *Vivat Rex* (Oxford, 1619), pp. 9–10; cited in M. Walzer, *The Revolution of the Saints: A Study of the Origins of Radical Politics* (New York, 1970), pp. 173–4.
62. See Walzer, *The Revolution of the Saints*, chapter 5.
63. H. Palmer, *Scripture and Reason Pleaded* (London, 1643), p. 14; cited in Walzer, *The Revolution of the Saints*, pp. 180–1.

64. S. Rutherford, *Lex Rex, or The Law and the Prince* (London, 1644), p. 71; cited in Walzer, *The Revolution of the Saints*, p. 181.

65. *London's Liberties, or A Learned Argument of Law and Reason*, December 1650; cited in A. S. P. Woodhouse, ed., *Puritanism and Liberty: Being the Army Debates (1647–49) from the Clarke Manuscripts with Supplementary Documents* (London, 1938), p. 375.

66. J. Streater, *Observations Historical, Political, and Philosophical upon Aristotles First Book of Political Government*, no. 1, sections 4–11, (London, April 1654), p. 4.

67. *The Kings Majestie's Speech to the Lords and Commons... on Wednesday the xxi of March, Anno Dom. 1609* (London, 1610), sig. B2; cited in Patterson, *Fables of Power*, p. 127.

68. *The Poems and Fables of John Dryden*, ed. J. Kinsley (London, 1958), p. 189.

69. See the politically attentive discussion of this preface in S. N. Zwicker, *Politics and Language in Dryden's Poetry: The Arts of Disguise* (Princeton, 1984), pp. 91–3.

70. J. Milton, *Of Reformation in England and the Cawses That Hitherto Have Hindered It* (1641), in *Complete Prose Works of John Milton*, ed. D. M. Wolfe et al. (8 vols., New Haven, 1953–82), vol. 1, pp. 583–84; Patterson, *Fables of Power*, p. 128.

71. Milton, *Of Reformation*, p. 599. Milton here paraphrases from his own commonplace book (*Complete Prose Works*, vol. 1, p. 442), where he had digested the political lessons of Sir Thomas Smith's *Commonwealth of England* (London, 1621).

72. Norbrook, *Writing the English Republic*, p. 113.

73. *The Riverside Milton*, p. 1020.

74. In Milton's letter 'To a Friend' of October 1659 (printed in 1698) he compared the troubles of the state to a disturbance of the bowels: 'these dangerous ruptures of the common wealth, scarce yet in her fancy, which cannot be without some in ward flaw in her bowels' (*Complete Prose Works*, vol. 7, p. 324).

75. Milton, *The Tenure of Kings and Magistrates*, in *Complete Prose Works*, vol. 5, p. 8.

76. On Hellish nationalism and its relation to the nationalist genre of epic, see the fine essay by Tobias Gregory, 'The Enabling Fictions of Hell: Devilish Agency and Renaissance Epic', forthcoming in *Huntington Library Quarterly*.

77. M. A. Radzinowicz, 'The Politics of *Paradise Lost*', in K. Sharpe and S. N. Zwicker, eds., *Politics of Discourse: The Literature and History of Seventeenth-Century England* (Berkeley, 1987), p. 224.

78. On the political component of Milton's attachment to the philosophical doctrine of monism, see J. Rogers, *The Matter of Revolution: Science, Poetry, and Politics in the Age of Milton* (Ithaca, 1996).

79. Milton, *Complete Prose Works*, vol. 8, p. 4; cited in A. Shifflett, *Stoicism, Politics and Literature in the Age of Milton: War and Peace Reconciled* (Cambridge, 1998), p. 153.

80. On Milton's complex attitude to autonomy amid an ethic of Christian obedience, see my essay, 'Obedience and Autonomy in *Paradise Lost*', in T. Corns, ed., *A Companion to Milton* (Oxford, 2001), pp. 363–79.
81. K. Sharpe and S. N. Zwicker, 'Introduction: Refiguring Revolutions', in Sharpe and Zwicker, eds., *Refiguring Revolutions: Aesthetics and Politics from the English Revolution to the Romantic Revolution* (Berkeley and London, 1998), p. 14.
82. I discuss the role of the emotions in *Paradise Lost* in more detail in ' "Commotion strange": Milton and Passion', in G. K. Paster, M. Floyd-Wilson and K. Rowe, eds., *Reading the Early Modern Passions* (forthcoming).
83. See C. B. Macpherson, *The Political Theory of Possessive Individualism: Hobbes to Locke* (Oxford, 1962).
84. Sharpe and Zwicker, eds., *Refiguring Revolutions*, p. 16.
85. M. Foucault, *The History of Sexuality*, vol. 1: *An Introduction*, trans. R. Hurley (New York, 1978), pp. 88–9.
86. S. Žižek, *Sublime Object of Ideology* (London, 1989), p. 126.
87. 'Modern sociobiology,' asserts Richard Sennett in his fascinating study of the body as a model for urban organization, 'is not too far from this medieval science [of the body politic] in its aim; it too seeks to base how society should operate on the supposed dictates of Nature. In either medieval or modern form, the body politic founds rule in society on a ruling image of the body' (*Flesh and Stone: The Body and the City in Western Civilization*, New York, 1994, p. 24). For nations as imagined communities, see B. Anderson, *Imagined Communities: Reflections on the Origin and Spread of Nationalism* (London, 1983).

CHAPTER EIGHT

Reading and experiment in the early Royal Society

Adrian Johns

The business of the Society as I sayd before [is] three fold to wit the
perusall of Bookes, the consulting of men & the Examination and
tryall of things... acquisitions shall be brought into and Read in the
Society at the usuall place & time & then recorded in their proper
place there to be perused at any convenient time by the members of
the Society & by none els whatsoever.

Robert Hooke[1]

READING IN THE HISTORY OF SCIENTIFIC PRACTICE

Back when everyone accepted that the Scientific Revolution was something that had actually happened, one of its defining features was always
said to be a turning away from the world of 'words' towards that of 'things'.
The existence and importance of the shift seemed incontrovertible. It was
everywhere visible and prominent. All the new philosophies of the seventeenth century, however erudite, obscure or occult they may have seemed
to modern eyes, loudly claimed to be abandoning slavish and idle adherence to ancient authority in favour of active and powerful engagement with
the powers of nature themselves. The general trend was exemplified by an
anecdote that Johann Joachim Becher, an enterprising mid-seventeenth-
century chymist, economic innovator and natural philosopher, was fond of
telling to anyone who would listen. The anecdote described an alchemical
adept who, on hearing a scholastic professor lecture on the impossibility of
transmutation, got up in front of the class and turned lead into gold there
and then. The adept demanded of the professor, 'solve me this syllogism!'
and, Pilate-like, left without waiting for an answer. Becher liked this story
so much precisely because no mere words could have stood against such a
demonstration. It evoked what Pamela Smith calls, excellently, 'the creative,
productive action of raw *ars*'.[2]

Yet if seventeenth-century natural philosophers turned ardently towards
things, they could never neglect words quite as conclusively as they liked to

claim in their looser polemical moments. After all, even the most neoteric of new philosophies remained dependent on articulating a view of the textual inheritance of antiquity, if only to distinguish itself from its predecessors. In practice, moreover, few adopted the radical position that ancient authority was actually worthless.[3] In fact, what the distinction between words and things did was to focus attention on questions about the proper use of both. And it is in this light that historians of science themselves have found fresh inspiration in the apparently hackneyed distinction.

So far historians of science have tended to pursue the study of scientific things rather than words. This is in large part simply because, thanks to the work of anthropologists, the social and cultural history of things in general came to be recognized as an interesting subject in the 1980s.[4] Historians of science since then have devoted a good deal of effort to reconstructing early modern naturalists' concern for things – finding them, making them, gazing at them, moving them about, collecting them, classifying them, and swapping them for other things.[5] Such a list itself suggests the real drive behind this renewed attention, which is to recover something of the past *practices* of natural philosophy and mathematics. We want to understand how knowledge was arrived at, and what it was used for; focusing on things has merely seemed a good way to achieve those ends. But seventeenth-century naturalists' uses of words have not yet been investigated in the same thoroughgoing fashion. Whilst the rhetoric of science has been subjected to intensive examination, we are only beginning to make progress in comprehending the actual dynamics of writing, circulation and reading that characterized early modern natural philosophy.[6] Such study is needed because the worlds of things and of words were never truly separate. As Anthony Grafton puts it, 'the laboratory could not exist without the library'. After all, things could no more speak for themselves in the Renaissance than they can now.[7]

What the historian of reading should now be offering the historian of science is therefore an approach to words parallel to those already devoted to things. That is, we need a taxonomy of literate practices, and an explanation of how they contributed to the development and distribution of knowledge. There are, it should be said, signs of progress in both respects. The history of scientific reading for this period is now starting to be written, taking advantage of the armoury of approaches developed in other historical realms. Andrea Carlino, for example, has examined physicians' views of textual authority in the context of practical anatomizing.[8] Nancy Siraisi's fine work on Girolamo Cardano shows how one Renaissance physician shaped his reading and his medical practice.[9] William Sherman has carefully analysed the

marginal annotations that John Dee made on the books he read, using them
to reconstruct his cultural world.[10] Grafton himself has described Kepler's
readings of ancient and recent authorities, from Tacitus to Galileo.[11] And,
in a bravura piece of reconstruction, William Newman has restored to view
a novice's reading of one of alchemy's notoriously opaque texts, such that
we can understand for the first time the detailed passage from iconography
to laboratory practice.[12] From such efforts it should soon prove possible
to propose a provisional taxonomy of natural-philosophical reading practices, classified in terms of the two axes of practice and cultural identity.
That taxonomy will surely find real distinctions between the readings of
mathematical practitioners, physicians, university philosophers, courtiers,
virtuosi and alchemists; and between such practices as commonplacing,
annotating and the intense, mystical experiences of the alchemists.[13]

In terms of practice, the major work that has been done in the history
of scientific reading has been on the technique of commonplacing.[14] This
was an extremely widespread practice in the Renaissance. Scholars would
maintain their own commonplace books, in which they would enter notes,
sentences and similar items from their reading. These then constituted discrete bits of information that could be called forth and deployed in various
rhetorical contexts. Historians have paid close attention to the compilation
strategies, classification schemes and uses of such commonplace books (and
I know of at least one modern professor who encourages students in his
writing class to adopt the technique themselves). A simple but intriguing
point about them is that the various entries were not subject to any principle
of coherence or compatibility. They were truly discrete entities. This helps
to explain the construction of books such as, most notably, Jean Bodin's
Theatrum Naturae, which display to modern eyes no clear argument. Such
books also seem replete with contradictory claims about nature. What we
see is that, given these past reading and composing practices, to look for
what we now would regard as a central argument and factual consistency is
anachronistic. Indeed, Ann Blair's study of Bodin is the single most persuasive account not only of how commonplacing was practised, but of how, in
being practised, it gave rise to further printed claims about nature – which
in turn were subjected to commonplacing by their readers. In other words,
Blair's work reconstructs the essential, but until now neglected, dynamic
of intellectual communication in the late Renaissance.

One of the more quietly compelling facts about the history of reading is
that the end of the commonplace book occurred at the same moment as the
advent of experiment. The last printed commonplace book was produced
by the great philosopher of empiricism, John Locke. On the face of it, this

is no more than appropriate. Experimental philosophy – a way of inquiring into nature that was pioneered in England in the mid-seventeenth century and first institutionalized during the Restoration in the Royal Society of London – represented the high point of early modern opposition to textual authority. The Society's motto, 'Nullius in verba', expressed its antagonism to such authority, and its own rhetoric was entirely of direct experience. Hence Abraham Cowley's lauding of Francis Bacon:

> From Words, which are but Pictures of the Thought,
> (Though we our Thoughts from them perversly drew)
> To Things, the Minds right Object, he it brought.[15]

Yet it is not difficult to see congruities between experimental practices and the world of the commonplace. Experimental 'matters of fact' were to be collected in great registers, the ancestry of which contemporaries such as Hooke traced to Bacon. Like commonplaces, these matters of fact were discrete items, the consistency of which only came to matter when they were subsequently deployed in argument. They were to be epistemic foundation-stones – tools for building a conversation rather than objects over which to dispute. And the most dedicated experimenter of them all, Robert Hooke, left recommendations for the construction of experimental registers on the page that clearly owed a debt to accepted commonplacing techniques. In the light of such prescriptions it is tempting to suggest a historical trajectory in which commonplacing did not disappear but shifted into a new area of practice. The commonplacing of words was supplanted by the commonplacing of facts.[16]

Yet the collecting practices devoted to experiments differed in one essential respect from earlier commonplacing techniques. They were not individual acts, but collective ones. All experimental philosophers stressed that, for experimental facts to count, they had to be witnessed collectively – and, ideally, on repeated occasions. Their kind of recording would therefore be an aspect of social civility in action. Much more than the commonplacing of a Bodin, it would record the existence and character of learned conversation. Its history is therefore part and parcel of the history of learned sociability itself – a history that has been the subject of much excellent work in recent years.[17] It is therefore this aspect of experimental philosophy that forms the subject of this chapter. It is concerned not with the private act of reading but with reading as a social gesture – and one taking place not in a pulpit or coffee house but amid a group of educated, privileged and (here, at least) sober gentlemen. Sometimes this means reading aloud to that group; on other occasions it means an act carried out alone, but with an eye to displaying its consequences to the group on a regular weekly basis. In either case, social reading of this kind was a formal, even ceremonial, act.[18] And, as will become clear, its formalities had consequences.

Those consequences were both social and epistemic. Then as now, any paper containing knowledge claims was of course much more of a collective product than formal ascriptions of authorship typically acknowledged. Reading by other gentlemen helped forge the finished work. Such reading was an everyday and vital part of intellectual life long before the experimental philosophy was invented. The point was not that other readers read better, in any consistently definable way, than the writer. They just read differently; necessarily so, since reading is, at some level, irreducibly individual. Paradoxically, that individual character was what now made it such a key component of a learned activity to which collectivity was of the essence. It was the vetting of candidate claims by diverse readers in places such as Arundel House and Gresham College (the venues for Society meetings) that qualified virtuosi to regard such claims as robust. So the practice under examination here was at once a cementer of social bonds (it helped to constitute a community) and a guarantor that what was published should be accounted knowledge. Indeed, in philosophical or history-of-ideas idioms it is possible to find many modern writers characterizing objectivity itself in such terms.[19] That is why the story told here matters – for not just any kind of reading could have served these purposes.

Reflection on the distinction between words and things – or between bookish and experimental civilities – thus raises some intriguing questions. Whence did the distinction between formal authorship and informal labour of this kind arise? How old is it, where does it come from, and how is it sustained? And what has been its role in shaping the character of knowledge in different cultural settings? It is in order to address such questions that this chapter examines the practice of reading in early experimental philosophy. It seeks to understand how the shared practices of reading and experiment both constituted a community of experimental philosophers and warranted what that community produced as knowledge. To that end, its focus is on the major location for experimental displays and conversation, namely the Royal Society. There are three major reasons for this focus. First, the virtuosi of the Society themselves accepted that reading was a central component of their activity – whether it be the reading of their own papers, of their fellows', or of outsiders' contributions sent into its arena. Second, the practices that the Society developed were, it seemed, significantly novel – not in absolute terms, but in their context of use. And third, it was an important part of these practices themselves to make and preserve careful archival records of reading. Those records still exist. That the modern historian can excavate the reading practices at the Society in such close detail is, then, a pleasing consequence of the unusual character of those practices themselves.[20]

DOING, SEEING, WRITING AND READING EXPERIMENTS

If there is one thing that everyone knows about the experimental philosophy, it is that that philosophy was indeed experimental. It depended on *doing* things, and on showing the things that were done to other people. That is, the Royal Society created practical demonstrations of natural 'facts', the demonstrations themselves being called experiments.[21] But experimental philosophy also rested on repeated acts of writing, printing and reading. The Society – or more specifically its fellows – circulated reports of its experiments both within its own fellowship and abroad. Those reports needed to carry with them a degree of verisimilitude, to warrant the trust of distant readers. They were supposed to exhibit 'moral certainty'.[22] Their recipients had then to respond by entrusting their own documents to the Society, creating a fruitful circulation. Experimental philosophy thus depended on a widening network of correspondence and printed communication in order to build up the international acceptance of both particular 'matters of fact' and experimental conduct in general which its proponents sought. And the outcome of this circulation was reckoned to be knowledge. In effect, making craft (of the kind needed to run an experiment in the Society itself) into science (that was universal in scope) depended not only on the existence of these circulating documents, but on their use. The very existence of experimental philosophy relied on their circulation and credibility being sustained.

All this required constant low-level work on the part of experimental philosophers and their agents (editors, operators, secretaries, amanuenses and the like).[23] Creating experimental knowledge involved solving difficult problems of both authorship and reception. In the first place, whilst experiments were necessarily collective (and they involved the labour of anonymous subordinates at least as much as that of recognized gentlemen), authorship itself was to be ascribed to individuals. It should not accrue to the Society or fellowship as a whole, since it was an important principle that the Society as an institution be seen to remain neutral in any controversy. It was to be the *arena for* debate, not a *participant in* debate. As William Petty put it of one of his own volumes, 'the *Society* have been pleased to order it to be published; (I dare not say, as approving it, but as committing it to Examination.)' This distinction between collectivity and singularity, and between examination and authorship, had to be publicly restated many times, and within the ranks of the Society itself it had repeatedly to be renegotiated. There is evidence that foreign readers were sometimes sceptical of it, or even affected to find it incomprehensible. Yet the Society's stance was nevertheless useful. Many fellows regarded it as a neat rhetorical excuse for projecting themselves as authors at all – something otherwise redolent of immodesty. As Edward Tyson said, once approved by the fellowship, authorship became 'allowable boldness'.[24]

If being an experimental author was problematic, so was being an experimental reader. It was certainly important that a virtuoso be well read. He would want to be acknowledged as a reliable witness to natural and experimental facts, and retaining the character of a good witness might depend on a reputation for literary competence. Thomas Molyneux, for example, gave a negative assessment of the microscope pioneer Leeuwenhoek's credibility on the grounds that he was not as well read as might have been expected. 'I found him a very civil complaisant man,' Molyneux reported, 'and doubtless of great natural abilities; but, contrary to my expectations, quite a stranger to letters, master neither of Latin, French, or English.' This was 'a great hinderance to him in his reasonings upon his observations; for being ignorant of all other mens thoughts, he is wholly trusting to his own, which, I observe, now and then lead him into extravagancies, and suggest very odd accounts of things, nay, sometimes such, as are wholly irreconcileable with truth'.[25] This was a rather extreme example of the denial of plausibility to the claims of someone who seemed less than fully acquainted with the world of books. But it reflected what was a consistent perception on the part of the virtuosi. In practice, an experimentalist could not truly shun words for things, if only because his reputation as a spokesman for things would depend on his acquaintance with books.

Reading in the Royal Society was conventional in character. That is, experimental philosophers could readily display some kinds of reading, but not all. Other reading practices were considered inappropriate in what seventeenth-century people called 'public' – which is to say, in the presence of select friends and peers purportedly representative of polite society. There are a number of places in which these conventions left traces. They appear, as noted already, in the records of the Society itself – although these are partial, and sometimes constructed after the fact. There are also diaries, especially of Robert Hooke – although Hooke's is laconic and tricky to interpret.[26] And there are the letters of the Society's secretary, Henry Oldenburg – but Oldenburg, as a good diplomat, knew when to put a polite gloss on

London views in order to keep his correspondents content.[27] There are also annotations made by virtuosi of their own readings, of the kind that historians in other spheres have found so fruitful. An unusually intriguing example is the 'Extract out of Col. Sidn. letter concerning ye change of Engl.' that Oldenburg himself wrote out just before making notes on Harrington's *Oceana*; it looks very much like an excerpt from a work by Algernon Sidney, and its content matches Sidney's known sentiments, but it does not seem to be from any of Sidney's known writings.[28] But with isolated exceptions such as Oldenburg's – and, of course, the vast anomaly of the Newton manuscripts – records of this kind are not as common or as illuminating as we might like. In sum, the best the modern historian can do is draw particles of evidence from all these sources, correlate them as well as possible, and infer a general picture accordingly. This section describes the general picture that thus emerges.

In the Royal Society, overt reading practices manifested four relatively discrete stages. They may be called presentation, perusal, registration and publication (or, more broadly, circulation).[29] Not every text entering the Society passed through all four stages, but many did, and they seem to have constituted a process that was tacitly accepted as normal. The process typically began with the presentation of a book or manuscript – and it could be either, for at this stage the distinction was not always paramount. Manuscripts might be finished works, after all, and printed books might be works in progress (especially if they were in foreign languages other than Latin, since the intention in such cases was often to generate a translation). Natural objects such as fossils were, of course, also presented, as were artifacts such as calculating engines. In this respect literary creations were treated much like technological devices or natural things. The sequence at a meeting would go something like this: books presented by fellows; books presented on behalf of outsiders; manuscripts; and things. But whatever the character of the object, a representative (often Oldenburg, or else an eminent fellow who knew the writer personally) would produce it before the group, and give it to them as a corporate recipient. Originating in the earliest days, such presentations rapidly became regular weekly occurrences. They furnished the Society's major 'occasions for discourse', and as such constituted a significant prop for its continued vitality.[30]

Presentation was here a 'public' act of clearly understood implications. It was quite distinct from *showing* a book, for example, which was a less formal and obliging gesture.[31] It therefore became the starting point for a series of further actions. At the outset, some response was required: the initiating of a correspondence, perhaps, or even the granting of a fellowship.

But many presentations also warranted more. The major response in such cases was an act of reading. It is very important to realize that for the most part this Society reading was *delegated*. It took the form of a 'perusal', which was an assessment of the work carried out on behalf of the Society by, generally, two of its fellows. In its public representations, however, a perusal was generally described as a reading by the Society itself. Indeed, some less than scrupulous beneficiaries used it as advertising for their latest patent medicine or subscription publication. This made a certain sense, because, whatever its outcome, the mere act of perusal signalled the Society's regard for the contributor and his claims. It was the major social gateway into philosophical conversation, experimental work and quite possibly dispute. Without perusal, it was unlikely that a presentation would lead to any conversation, and hence to anything that might be recognized as new experimental knowledge.

A perusal typically took a week to complete. One or two selected fellows would be assigned to perform the task. They would take the text away, 'peruse' it, abstract or translate it, and report back a week or two later – perhaps more, if the work were long, complex or controversial. A lengthy report might be read piecemeal over several meetings. Conversation and experiment would then ensue, inspired by the perusal – and they too might continue for several weeks, or even months (and, on rare occasions, years).[32] This was the mainstay of the Society's work, and its journal books are full of transcripts of such reported perusals and their conversational and experimental consequences.

Registration could occur before, after, or, sometimes, instead of perusal.[33] It meant the entry of the contribution into a manuscript volume, which was held under lock and key by the secretary. The principal purpose of the register was to record and protect authorial achievements. It existed, as Robert Boyle remarked, to 'secure [authors] against usurpations'. The register thus stood as an internal archive of discoveries and authorship. It was in theory immune from all tampering. But, partly for that very reason, it was of limited use. To preserve its reputation as privileged arbiter, it had to remain cloistered. So no register could insulate experimental philosophers from contests over authorship, since such contests were themselves not cloistered at all – they took place in the hugger-mugger of the coffee house and the tumult of Amsterdam bookshops. This was a major reason why, after five years, Oldenburg and the Society's grandees sought to extend the security of the register into what was slowly becoming recognized as a public realm. Certain papers were therefore singled out for publication. In being circulated, they became what one virtuoso called 'ambassadors' for the Society and for the conduct of experimental philosophy itself.[34]

Circulation need not involve printing. Oldenburg would often transmit short claims by written correspondence, to selected competent and honoured recipients. This was a way of linking the presentation–perusal–registration regime of the Society to equivalents that might persist elsewhere, without submitting fellows to the vicissitudes of the book trade. If long, however, the Society might recommend that the piece be printed. But it would not and could not act as publisher itself – the only time it tried, with Francis Willughby's *History of Fishes*, it failed so dismally that it almost bankrupted itself. Nor was it very happy to underwrite sales, although this did happen rather more frequently, especially with mathematical works, for which London booksellers showed notoriously little enthusiasm. After the beginning of 1665 contributions would most often be directed to a new publishing venture, designed to be, in Martin Lister's phrase, the Society's 'public register'. This was the printed periodical invented and administered by Oldenburg, and which he called the *Philosophical Transactions*. Starting out as a peculiar mixture of printed book, correspondence, and coffee house pamphlet, the *Transactions* soon became a great social success, even if its economic footing remained precarious. It was a periodical – itself rather an unusual concept at the time – aspiring to a printing schedule of an issue every month. That schedule both signalled a continuing commitment to the new philosophy and exemplified the back-and-forth, conversational character of that philosophy. But above all the *Transactions* was launched, succeeded and gained respect because it was an extension of the register into the printed realm. As the journal filtered through the channels of the international book trade, so it took with it an image of the Royal Society's conventions, and the responses of continental philosophers sustained those conventions even when local interest waned.

Many examples could be cited of how these conventions could act to stimulate conversation and provoke questioning about natural knowledge. One occurred in July 1679, when the Society received from the grand duke of Tuscany (via his resident in England) two copies of Stefano Lorenzini's *Osservazioni intorno alle torpedini*. They were given to Sir John Hoskyns and Robert Hooke for perusal. The following week, Hoskyns read a detailed account of the book, which was an anatomical study of the torpedo. He particularly noted three things. First, he remarked that parts of the fish would continue to move for hours after being cut from its body. Second, he mentioned Lorenzini's account of how the fish 'takes in water by several holes near the stomach, and throws it out at the other end, washing in its way the bronchia'. And third, Hoskyns referred to the question of the torpedo's 'benumming quality', by which it caused numbness and pain in anyone touching two muscles around its thorax. Immediate conversation then started from these points. Had Lorenzini said that the 'benumming liquor' was colder than the rest of the body, asked the physician William Croune? At the same time, Abraham Hill was moved by the account of the fish's internal washing to recall a different piece of natural experience: a Mr Torriano, who had drunk Epsom waters and died when they had not 'passed well'; on autopsy, 'his guts were found gangrenous'. The following week conversation returned to Hoskyns's report, this time centring on creatures that continued to move after being killed. Hoskyns himself recalled a passage written by Malpighi on insects that did just that. Thomas Henshaw suggested that the phenomenon might be ascribed to the viscosity of the 'juice' in which animal spirits moved in some creatures, which might be such as to hinder the 'evaporation' of those spirits after death. (This was a line of argument that Thomas Willis, among others, had used to explain spectres and similar events.) Hoskyns then added that the purpose of the numbing power might be to prevent attacks by predators that knew exactly where to strike in order to kill at one blow; that would explain its location in the body, to protect the heart. Hill, returning to Croune's question about cold, mentioned another death, this time of a person struck by a blast of cold air known as cold fire 'by the country-people'; on autopsy, he too was found to be gangrenous. Since the annual recess was fast approaching these exchanges went no further, but they had already allowed for conversation on natural history, the animal spirits (a key subject in medical anatomy) and other subjects.[35]

A second example is likewise partial, but it is interesting because it concerns an alchemical work (and thus an artifact of a very different kind of writing and reading practice) emerging from another courtly context. In mid-1684, the secretary received from Germany a work reportedly called *The Chemical Touchstone* by Johann Kunckel, who was one of Becher's counterparts and occasional competitors. It had been sent by a representative of the elector of Brandenburg, so was immediately recognized as warranting a civil gesture in response. Since the Society was in its summer recess, the book was first given to Boyle for perusal. Despite its grand title, the work proved to be a polemic in German on the spirit of wine. Boyle expressed himself reluctant because he understood little German, but on the society's resuming its meetings he presented an account of the text in Latin; physician Frederic Slare, the other peruser, gave his account in

English. Part of Slare's perusal was read aloud by the secretary, the rest being deferred to the following meeting. On that occasion the Society ordered the secretary to wait on Boyle with its thanks, and request Boyle's views as to a controversy involving Kunckel's views. Boyle replied that it was not the Society's business to resolve such disputes by framing systems. The following week, Slare showed three experiments from the book to prove the acidity of wine, and remarked on a series of unusual chymical operations mentioned by Kunckel. This, at last, met with Boyle's approval. He would not 'pass any judgment' on Kunckel's work, he declared, but would be 'glad to see controversies managed by experiments', as was now occurring. Until these experiments had run their course, 'he thought they should not prescribe to others'.[36] It was a restatement of the Society's goal of avoiding formal closure in such processes in favour of continued, fruitful discourse. And, indeed, Papin continued to report experiments for weeks afterwards, alongside Boyle's reported testimony as to their outcomes.[37] Here, then, the presentation of a book had produced perusal, translation, reciprocation, conversation, experiments both in the Society and elsewhere, and even reflection on the proprieties of the Society's own practices *vis-à-vis* learned dispute. Similar sequences of events played themselves out for a considerable proportion of the texts presented at the Society. In fact, it would not be unreasonable to see the Society's journal books as recording a long, nested and interlocking series of readings and the experimental variations played on them.

There were, of course, alternatives to these conventions. In some respects the compelling logic of mathematical works, like that of scholastic syllogisms and Cartesian system-building, contravened the Society's norms.[38] The chymical philosophers were also widely perceived to have different practices – practices characterized by personal transformation and literary obscurity.[39] Boyle himself apparently wrote a tract 'Of the difficulty of understanding the books [of] Hermeticke Philosophers'. The relation between such conventions and those of the experimentalists was, however, more complex than their overt antagonism might suggest. Principe has recently brought to light a dialogue written by Boyle which portrays the introduction of alchemical manners into a Royal-Society-like setting (the spagyrists win the ensuing debate).[40] Moreover, the Society's own conventions could be breached – or, which is to say much the same thing, such a breach could be proclaimed by those present. Hooke was especially prone to detecting heinous contraventions, not least by Oldenburg and Newton. Some of the more violent learned disputes of the later seventeenth century (for example, Hooke's controversy with Huygens over spring watches, or,

less notoriously, the Scottish philosopher George Sinclair's accusations that
Oldenburg had manipulated the Society's reading protocols to attribute his
discoveries to Boyle) hinged on accusations that the perusal, registration
and publication regime had been subverted.[41] Yet it is at least equally striking that such outbursts did not, in the end, destroy the system. Such was
the value placed on these protocols that they were preserved in the face of
apparently blatant contraventions, even by Hooke himself. For example,
Hooke must have come very close to breaching the bounds of propriety in
reporting his perusal of Obadiah Walker's *Propositions Concerning Optic-
Glasses*, which he did on the same day that Hoskyns gave his discourse
on Lorenzini. Hooke's report, unlike Hoskyns's, was brief and apparently
final: he 'had not found any thing in it, which was new', he declared, and 'it
contained some propositions about the place of the image, which were not
true'. In all, 'it came well short of the theory of optics now well known'.[42]
Yet even this damning assessment gave rise to discussions, experiments and
(Hooke claimed) inventions in optics over several succeeding weeks. That
it did so is a measure of how hard the virtuosi tried to sustain their conversations even in the face of a curator of experiments who saw in their source
little to detain him.[43]

Register and periodical thus became twin certificates of a new, ambitious
form of learned practice, serving to secure experimental civility within and
without the institution that gave rise to it. The important thing about
these highly visible practices is that together they manifested reason in action. They operated, moreover, in a cyclic fashion. Perusal gave rise to experiments, conversation and circulation, and subsequent publication then
restarted the cycle. The point about all this is that the intersection of reading
and experiment – two sorts of experience, as seventeenth-century educational writers often stressed – was the key to how the new philosophy was
supposed to succeed. Quite simply, this was how the Royal Society worked:
it tied words to things with knots of civility. This was how early modern
science came into being as a self-sustaining process – a kind of social perpetual motion machine that, in some respects, has not stopped turning
since.

ISAAC NEWTON AND THE REJECTION OF PERUSAL

The dominating figure of English natural philosophy in the later Restoration was, obviously, Isaac Newton. Whilst Newton has been the subject
of selectively exhaustive research by historians, it is nonetheless instructive to discover that his career took shape around repeated cycles of the

perusal–registration–circulation sequence. This is particularly clear in his first encounters with the Royal Society. Newton was introduced to the Society in early 1672; six years later he declared that he was withdrawing from fellowship and ceasing all philosophical correspondence. This trajectory of engagement and retreat – one that he repeated several times in later decades – may be understood as emerging from his reaction to the Society's conventions. In the very first instance these conventions were applied to a technical device. Thereafter, they were devoted to written texts that were subjected to the Society's mechanisms – mechanisms that, from Newton's study in Cambridge, looked less like courtesy than affront.

Newton introduced himself by sending to the Society a remarkable new telescope 'to be examined' by the virtuosi. Being based on reflection rather than refraction, his new instrument eliminated chromatic aberration and was a vast improvement on existing designs. The device had already been seen at Whitehall by the king and the president of the Society, together with Hooke, Wren and others. Newton also sent a paper in the form of a letter to Oldenburg, expanding upon his design, and requesting his 'review, before it should go abroad'. The Society acted immediately. Newton's description was read aloud, and ordered entered in the register together with its 'scheme' (that is, an image of the telescope – the drawing that is frequently reproduced today). On the motion of Seth Ward, Newton was proposed and elected a fellow of the Society. Forewarned that this would occur – Ward had actually suggested it before the formal presentation of the telescope – Newton affirmed in his letter that he would convey his gratitude by continuing to forward whatever his 'poor and solitary endeavours' effected in the future. Oldenburg now wrote a laudatory reply on the Society's behalf, informing Newton of his election, thanking him for communicating his new telescope, and assuring him that 'the society would take care, that all right should be done him with respect to this invention'. To ensure that this happened, he simultaneously wrote to Huygens in Paris 'to secure this contrivance to the author'. Meanwhile the Society ordered the instrument-maker Christopher Cock to make its own version of Newton's telescope.[44]

Responses from distant correspondents soon began to arrive. Over succeeding months they came in, from Gregory, Huygens, Pardies, Auzout and Denis. These letters would be edited by Oldenburg to ensure that they manifested the civility required to keep converse going, and then forwarded to Newton. All required further written responses from him. But despite the Society's solicitude, competition was to come from closer to home, in the shape of Robert Hooke. As usual, the reading of a submission and the examination of a device prompted fellows to advance their own claims; this was what such events were supposed to achieve. But when Newton's telescope was shown to and applauded by the fellows, Hooke announced his own decisive discovery in the making of burning-glasses – a discovery that would, Hooke said, allow for the perfection of telescopes. He refused to reveal it expressly, but lodged his claim in the form of a cipher, the President of the Society urging him to 'impart the thing itself' to him as soon as possible for examination. This use of a cipher was an accepted technique in the mathematical sciences to preserve priority while concealing a potentially lucrative discovery.[45] In future meetings, more hints were announced from both Newton and Hooke. Then, on 2 February, Newton's letter arrived announcing his new theory of light and colours, and 'importing, that light is not a similar, but a heterogeneous body, consisting of different rays, which had essentially different refractions'. Now the reading conventions came fully into play.

The letter was registered, and Oldenburg was ordered to convey thanks to Newton. The text was then given to Ward, Boyle and Hooke to 'peruse and consider it, and bring in a report of it'. Oldenburg further asked Newton to consent to publication, 'as well for the greater convenience of having it well considered by philosophers, as for securing the considerable notions of the authors against the pretensions of others'. He agreed, and the letter, edited by Oldenburg to become a paper, appeared in the *Philosophical Transactions* for February.[46] It seemed that the conventional mechanism was operating with unusual efficiency.

As was usual, however, the perusal produced a response. At the next meeting, Hooke stood up and delivered as the result of his perusal a set of 'considerations' on Newton's letter. There was nothing very unusual about his comments by the standards of most such perusals, since they were supposed to suggest interesting queries for future discussion and experiment. Hooke concurred with Newton's experimental reports, but declined to find them conclusive in confirming Newton's theory and refuting Descartes's. So more would need to be done. It was a typical perusal, but Newton was not a typical contributor, and Hooke's remarks launched what would become a fundamental bone of contention. In effect, Hooke claimed that Newton was demanding excessive credibility for unique and unwitnessed experimental facts. In other words, Hooke claimed that Newton violated the norms of the experimental philosophy itself. This would eventually lead to a catastrophic collapse of relations. In the meantime, however, Hooke himself was thanked for his 'ingenious reflections', which were registered in their own right and sent to Newton. The fellows clearly realized the risk of a battle: Newton's own discourse must be published unaccompanied, they decreed, 'if he did not contradict it'. Hooke's paper could only be issued later, 'it not being thought fit to print them together, lest Mr. Newton should look upon it as a disrespect, in printing so sudden a refutation of a discourse of his, which had met with so much applause at the Society but a few days before'.[47]

The engagement proceeded quietly at first. Newton tactfully expressed himself pleased that Hooke had confirmed so much of his argument and confident that its certainty would soon be accepted. Hooke, for his part, performed his duty as curator of experiments by creating experimental variations derived from his original reading. Over the course of several weeks he brought in his own prisms, advanced his own plans for telescopes, proclaimed a better way of grinding lenses, and displayed his own series of phenomena of colours. He also proposed a way of communicating 'intelligence' across great distances by using telescopes and a secret character, and the following week the fellows trooped out of Arundel House to see it tried between the garden and a boat on the far shore of the Thames. Interestingly, Hooke himself showed the first doubts about the Society's protocols – doubts that in fact had been growing in his mind for years. His discourse on the communications device was read, but he demurred when asked that it be registered. This, like his use of the cipher, was an indication of his growing scepticism about the fidelity of the Society's practices.[48] He also had to be reminded, in giving his defence of refracting telescopes, 'to deliver in to the Society some account of what was done on this subject, to be registered, to preserve his discoveries from being usurped'.[49] And his exchange with Newton on light was itself registered only when Newton's more formal response arrived as a letter to Oldenburg and was once more submitted for 'perusal' to Wren and Hooke.[50]

The exchange then died down temporarily. Hooke was required to undertake more perusals of the books and letters that arrived so regularly at the Society and demanded to be recognized. But he had raised important questions, and they surfaced again, perhaps inevitably, in 1675. Newton now found himself challenged by the Liège Jesuits Francis Line, Anthony Lucas and (Line's protégé) John Gascoines.[51] This 1675 series of exchanges was to prove even more damaging, because it breached unambiguously the protocols of civility that were supposed to govern experimental philosophers' reading of their counterparts' reports. Whereas Hooke had accepted Newton's reported observations but denied their conclusiveness, Line in particular denied some of Newton's actual experimental findings. The Society therefore undertook 'upon the reading of a letter of his to

Mr. Oldenburg' to perform the experiment in question. But its experimenter, Hooke, failed to repeat Newton's result. The experiment took
place, moreover, just as the Society was engaged in the open reading of
Newton's second and far more comprehensive paper on light. This finally
sparked open hostility between Newton and Hooke.

The exchange centred on claims of authorship. Newton remarked that,
on a rare visit to the Society, he had heard Hooke discourse of diffraction.
Newton himself had then observed that refraction might be a special case
of refraction. 'To this Mr. Hooke was then pleased to answer, that though
it should be but a new kind of refraction, yet it was a new one', Newton
recalled.

What to make of this unexpected reply, I knew not; having no other thoughts,
but that a new kind of refraction might be as noble an invention as any thing else
about light; but it made me afterwards, I know not upon what occasion, happen
to say, among some that were present to what passed before, that I thought I had
seen the experiment before in some Italian author. And the author is Honoratus
Faber, in his dialogue *De Lumine*, who had it from Grimaldo; whom I mention,
because I am to describe something further out of him.

The implication was unmistakable, and Hooke responded in kind. When
Newton's own discourse on light was read, he responded that 'the main of
it was contained in his *Micrographia*, which Mr. Newton had only carried
farther in some particulars'.[52] Newton in turn declared that Hooke himself
had 'borrowed' much from Descartes, and that in his newer discussions
he used as much from Newton's work as Newton had of Hooke's. He also
recalled that he had always openly acknowledged Hooke's authorship of
natural facts where he had used them.[53]

It is relatively well known that Newton withdrew from natural-
philosophical communication after this confrontation. He retreated back
to his alchemical and scriptural work in Cambridge, not to emerge again
for some six years. But in fact what happened was, in the short term at least,
a double withdrawal, for Hooke retreated too. The clash had occurred at
the same time as the final erosion of his faith in the mechanism of the register and Oldenburg's *Philosophical Transactions*. This was almost exactly
the time when Hooke persuaded John Martyn (printer to the Society) to
add a postscript to the published text of his Cutlerian lecture, *Lampas*, a
violent attack on Oldenburg. And he resolved never to trust his discoveries
to Oldenburg's 'snares' again. Essentially, Hooke believed that Oldenburg
was acting as a 'spy' for foreigners, chiefly Huygens, who were seemingly
intent on appropriating the designs and benefits of English inventors,

particularly Hooke himself. Hooke henceforth declined to use the register or to publish in the *Transactions*. When Oldenburg died, he rifled the erstwhile secretary's rooms looking for evidence of duplicity. And as late as 1683 he got himself nominated to reread the Society's journal books in search of 'vacancies... omissions of things and names, and mistakes', and to draw lines in any empty spaces 'that for the future there may be no new thing written therein'.[54] Hooke, even more than Newton, had come to distrust the perusal–registration–circulation system so much that he doubted even the written record that remains to us today.

On Newton's part the retreat proved more lasting and (perhaps partly for that reason) more fruitful. He had intended to publish a book on light and colours – it would have been his first. But the conventions of the Society, pushed to the hilt by Lucas and Hooke, drove him to abandon the project. Already by December 1674 he had told Oldenburg that he wanted to 'concern my self no further about the promotion of Philosophy'. In 1678 he declared his final exasperation at the relentless demand for responses that the Society's conventions seemed to him to generate. 'I see I have made my self a slave to Philosophy', he complained; 'I see a man must either resolve to put out nothing new or to become a slave to defend it.' Of Lucas he demanded:

Am I bound to satisfy you? It seems you thought it not enough to propound Objections unless you might insult over me for my inability to answer them all, or durst not trust your own judgement in choosing the best. But how know you that I did not think them too weak to require an answer and only to gratify your importunity complied to answer one or two of the best?

As late as 1724, Newton remembered the withdrawal as a conscious and correct decision. It was then, he remembered, that he had begun to 'decline correspondencies by Letters about Mathematical & Philosophical matters[,] finding them tend to disputes and controversies'.[55]

There was, as Peter Dear has pointed out, an epistemic bite to Newton's complaints. The conventions of Boylean experimental philosophy proclaimed by the Royal Society placed high value on experiments that were evident, carried out before witnesses, and integrated into an endless sequence of conversations, writings and readings. They should also be repeated many times. In the course of his encounter with the virtuosi, if not before, Newton had come to disagree fundamentally with central elements of this protocol. What mattered was 'not number of Experiments, but weight', he insisted. 'Where one will do, what need of many?' And Newton maintained that the matters of fact he reported from his rooms in Trinity

College should be regarded as possessed of near-mathematical certainty. In this light, he interpreted Lucas's repeated probing as a straightforward challenge to his own veracity, and demanded that the Jesuit 'take off all suspicion of my misrepresenting matter of fact'. In Newton's eyes, Lucas was questioning 'the credit of my being wary, accurate and faithfull in the reports I have made'.[56]

By 1678–9 Newton had therefore arrived at a position which departed markedly from the Royal Society's conventions of experimental philosophy and from the practices of collective reading ('perusal') that they included. Hooke, too, had abandoned faith in the civilities represented by Oldenburg's correspondence network, but Hooke, as a paid employee of the Society, did not have Newton's freedom to withdraw altogether. He remained as curator of experiments, repeatedly reminding fellows of his priority in the discoveries claimed by correspondents. Obviously, there is not space here to rehearse Newton's subsequent career in detail. But the conventions of experimental reading continued to play a part in most of the episodes and controversies that gave that career its distinctive shape: the production of the *Principia* in 1687; its criticisms by Leibniz and the subsequent dispute over the authorship of the calculus; the angry feud with the Astronomer Royal, John Flamsteed; and Newton's development of a cohort of apostles who were entrusted with the 'correct' reading of his work.[57] For example, the *Principia* emerged when Newton was finally coaxed into reconnecting with the experimental community after his withdrawal in 1678. With infinite patience, Edmond Halley negotiated him through the same sequence of presentation–perusal–registration–publication in order to generate the book. What began as an apparently casual spoken reference, when Newton told Halley in Cambridge in 1684 that he had demonstrated that an inverse-square law would produce elliptical orbits (something that, in London, Hooke was claiming to have proved while refusing to reveal his proof), developed through the steps of this process into the revolutionary three-book work that would be published in 1687. Halley first exhorted Newton to send a text to the Society 'to be entered upon their register'. The Society itself reminded him to tell Newton that it would act 'for the securing his invention to himself till such time as he could be at leisure to publish it'. And in 1686, when the first manuscript draft of the *Principia* was presented at the Society, it was Halley who was given it to peruse. It was eventually printed at Halley's personal expense and licensed by the Society.[58]

That experience may have helped Newton determine his strategy with respect to the Society's reading protocols in later years. He continued to sway between dramatic public statement and reclusive silence. That much is well known, and historians tend to explain it in terms of Newton's own character.[59] But such explanation is asymmetrical: we need also to appreciate his decisions in terms of the realm of the literary practice into which Newton was venturing. His apotheosis into scientific hero resulted from a series of encounters with the Society's protocols of reading and circulating texts. At first, however, he was subject to them; after the *Principia* he became their master and their manipulator. That process was not only a result of his success, but a major component of it. The Newton who in 1712–13 masterminded the demolition of Leibniz's claim to the calculus – a demolition based squarely in the textual archives of perusal and registration – was a far more artful exponent of Society reading protocols than the distant scholar who had been hounded back to Cambridge by Hooke and the Jesuits.

PRECEDENTS, PROTOCOLS AND PRIORITY

What made it necessary to adopt these conventions, rather than others – or for that matter none at all? There are two answers. Both of them relate to existing social practices, the first in the realm of natural philosophy, the second in that of print.

The first answer relates to the practice of natural philosophy and mathematics in courts and academies. It is not the case that the Royal Society was so radically new that fellows could see no precedents for their actions at all. The practice of presentation, for instance, plausibly derived from royal courts, where books had long been important elements in strategies of patronage. At court, whether a 'scientific' debate occurred and how it proceeded were as likely to depend on a book's patrons, dedicatees, presenters and channels of reception as on its intrinsic technical merit. Or rather, as Mario Biagioli has argued, technical merit was something that was sought and achieved as part of negotiating the processes of courtly science.[60] Since then, continental academies and circles of virtuosi had adopted the practice. Not only was it a necessary one if the virtuosi were to interact with court society; it was also seen as fertile in its own right, and symbolic of polite engagement in the developing republic of letters.

The Royal Society therefore appropriated what had already become an accepted reciprocal relation between presentation and legitimation. Like other, earlier academies it was keenly attuned to the idea that illustrated books in particular (and other printed objects, like planispheres and globes) would make 'very acceptable presents' to court officials.[61]

Both Willughby's *Historia Piscium* (published by the Society) and, later, Flamsteed's *Historia Coelestis* (produced against Flamsteed's opposition by Newton and Halley) had something of this character.[62] Moreover, earlier academies – in Richelieu's France, for example, in the form of Théophraste Renaudot's Bureau d'Adresse, some of whose conversations were reprinted in England in the early Restoration[63] – had had their secretaries, their methods of printing and their own processes for reading and responding to texts in polite situations. The Society certainly knew of these, through various channels including the personal experience of men such as John Evelyn and (ironically) Thomas Hobbes. But it was not altogether uncritical of them. Even before the Royal Society itself existed, Oldenburg was characterizing these older academies as dedicated only to 'puerile knowledge'. They were 'apt to chatter', he remarked, 'unripe', and 'useless for creative work'. They produced only dispute, and were sterile of consequential achievements. By contrast, experimental philosophy would judge as knowledge only that which 'does not disquiet the mind, but settles it; and which confers the ability not to dispute on any topic, but to deduce causes from effects and effects from causes in turn'.[64] So in adopting its own conventions the Society sought a balance between the perceived failings of existing scholarly groups – between, in effect, futility and dogmatism. Its compromise lay in conversation; that was why Newton found it so frustratingly interminable.

The second answer is a little less obvious. It relates as much to how we ourselves think of printed books and their reading as to how seventeenth-century people thought of them. Briefly, some of the characteristics which we most take for granted in printed materials – uniformity of content across an edition and authorial approval of publication, to name two important ones – were not necessarily so evident to our early modern counterparts. In particular, the reliability of print as a vehicle for learned converse was still unproven. There had not yet been a successful and sustained academic press anywhere in Europe. The virtuosi themselves therefore had to prove print a viable tool for 'science'. Users had to develop techniques for determining how best to employ these objects as tools for creating and sustaining knowledge across cultural boundaries. That need is what lies at the root of their devotion to these conventions of reading, appraisal and distribution. We need to remember, for example, that the *Philosophical Transactions* entered a world where a periodical was *ipso facto* untrustworthy and discreditable. Pamphlets were to be repudiated as a major cause of civil war, in Holland and France as much as in England. Hooke's fury when Molyneux casually described one of his works as a pamphlet may have smacked of the martinet, but it was nonetheless comprehensible.[65]

It is worth remembering that the reliability of a printed text, before and beyond academic institutions and readers, was *already* an achievement. It was an artifact of some involved cultural, ritual and ceremonial practices. Printers and booksellers sought to achieve respectability for their craft and its products themselves, by enforcing conventions of conduct on their own community. These centered on what they called 'propriety' – a notion which combined property and civility, and which would eventually transmute into copyright. This 'propriety' was embodied in a 'register' – a book that was held in a central location and in which all titles were supposed to be entered before publication. Conflicts over what later came to be called piracy were resolved by reference to this volume, at a regular 'public' court. ('Public' here meant that the court harmonized with the standards and conventions of a stable kingdom – in terms of access, it was resolutely and determinedly private, to the extent of out-and-out secrecy.) This underpinned the claim that the craft could make itself into a reliable, trustworthy culture of communication within the realm. Different polities in Europe had slightly different regimes – in Paris, for example, there was a register, but printers and booksellers relied more on direct royal privileges (a difference that reflected, and was taken to reflect, serious differences between the two political cultures) – but all regimes had had to develop some such system. The Royal Society's register was in part a genteel equivalent of the register regimes maintained by these craft communities. And the virtuosi worked to extend its influence into the domain of the printers and booksellers themselves. They developed alliances with particular Stationers, seeking to join forces with a community they could not truly master. And the Society became a licenser, endorsing the legitimacy of its printed works by means of an *imprimatur*. In short, it is reasonable to see the conventions of perusal, registration and circulation at the Society as betokening an effort not only to join polite culture to the realm of scholarship, but to ally craft propriety with learned gentility.[66]

Yet there was a price to pay. As with the Stationers' register, so the Scientists' register proved a double-edged asset. The point of regimes such as the Society's was not to suppress disputes but to limit and manage them in ways recognized and accepted by participants. Indeed, genteel civility itself implied not bland endorsement in one's readings but limited criticism; as Kevin Sharpe might have put it, criticism *was* compliment. A witness to a French literary academy expressed the point well. He 'observed in what manner works were there examined', he told his friends, seeing 'that it was not a businesse of compliments and flatteries, where each one commends that he might be commended, but that they did boldly and freely censure

even the least faults'. By this 'he was filled with joy and admiration'.[67]
Accordingly, the Society's conventions defined disagreement as much as
they facilitated consensus. And just as the transgression of 'piracy' in the
book trade was defined by one register, so here another register gave rise
to its own offence. The perusal–registration—circulation sequence itself
explains why scientific disputes now almost always took the particular form
of contests for priority. It was almost inevitable that when Hooke and
Newton clashed they would clash over rival claims to authorship. Whatever
the original debate, the criteria for victory in the Society were set according
to the terms of its cluster of conventions, and those conventions focused on
propriety of authorship. In short, the experimental philosophers elevated
the importance of protecting authorship so far that they made the priority
dispute into the archetypal scientific controversy.

NOTES

1. Royal Society, Cl.P. XX, fol. 92r.
2. P. Smith, *The Business of Alchemy: Science and Culture in the Holy Roman Empire* (Princeton, 1994), p. 45. For the controversial status of the 'scientific revolution' nowadays, see N. Jardine, 'Writing Off the Scientific Revolution', *Journal of the History of Astronomy*, 22 (1991), pp. 311–18, and the provocative introductory sentences in S. Shapin, *The Scientific Revolution* (Chicago, 1996), pp. 1–4.
3. See, for example, N. Jardine, *The Birth of History and Philosophy of Science: Kepler's 'A Defence of Tycho against Ursus' with Essays on Its Provenance and Significance* (Cambridge, 1984), and the discussion of 'apostolic succession' in mathematicians' histories in P. Dear, *Discipline and Experience: The Mathematical Way in the Scientific Revolution* (Chicago, 1995), pp. 93–123.
4. For example, A. Appadurai, ed., *The Social Life of Things: Commodities in Cultural Perspective* (Cambridge, 1986); A. Bermingham and J. Brewer, eds., *The Consumption of Culture, 1600–1800: Image, Object, Text* (London, Routledge, 1995); J. Brewer and R. Porter, eds., *Consumption and the World of Goods* (London, 1992).
5. For example, Smith, *The Business of Alchemy*; P. Findlen, 'The Economy of Exchange in Early Modern Italy', in B. T. Moran, ed., *Patronage and Institutions: Science, Technology and Medicine at the European Court 1500–1700* (Woodbridge, 1991), pp. 5–24; Findlen, *Possessing Nature: Museums, Collecting and Scientific Culture in Early Modern Italy* (Berkeley, 1994), pp. 293–392; M. Biagioli, 'Galileo's System of Patronage', *History of Science*, 28 (1990), pp. 1–62; L. Daston and K. Park, *Wonders and the Order of Nature, 1150–1750* (New York, 1998), pp. 67–108.
6. For example, R. W. F. Kroll, *The Material Word: Literate Culture in the Restoration and Early Eighteenth Century* (Baltimore, 1991), pp. 183–238; P. Dear, '*Totius in Verba*: Rhetoric and Authority in the Early Royal Society', *Isis*, 76

(1985), pp. 145–61; Dear, 'Narratives, Anecdotes, and Experiments: Turning Experience into Science in the Seventeenth Century', in Dear, ed., *The Literary Structure of Scientific Argument: Historical Studies* (Philadelphia, 1991), pp. 135–63; A. Gross, *The Rhetoric of Science*, 2nd edn (Cambridge, Mass., 1996), pp. 97–128; Gross, 'The Rhetorical Invention of Scientific Invention: The Emergence and Transformation of a Social Norm', in H. W. Simons, ed., *Rhetoric in the Human Sciences* (London, 1989), pp. 89–107; J. T. Harwood, 'Science Writing and Writing Science: Boyle and Rhetorical Theory', in M. Hunter, ed., *Robert Boyle Reconsidered* (Cambridge, 1994), pp. 37–56; J. D. Moss, *Novelties in the Heavens: Rhetoric and Science in the Copernican Controversy* (Chicago, 1993); C. Bazerman, *Shaping Written Knowledge: The Genre and Activity of the Experimental Article in Science* (Madison, Wisc., 1988), pp. 59–79; D. Atkinson, *Scientific Discourse in Sociohistorical Context: The 'Philosophical Transactions' of the Royal Society of London, 1675–1975* (Mahwah, N.J., 1999).

7. A. Grafton, *Commerce with the Classics: Ancient Books and Renaissance Readers* (Ann Arbor, Mich., 1997), p. 224.

8. A. Carlino, *Books of the Body: Anatomical Ritual and Renaissance Learning* (Chicago, 1999), especially pp. 194–225.

9. N. Siraisi, *The Clock and the Mirror: Girolamo Cardano and Renaissance Medicine* (Princeton, 1997), pp. 52–65.

10. W. H. Sherman, *John Dee: The Politics of Reading and Writing in the English Renaissance* (Amherst, Mass., 1995); bizarrely, however, Sherman chooses to avoid discussing Dee's alchemical books even though they were his most densely annotated volumes (p. 89). For this aspect of Dee's practice, see now D. Harkness, *John Dee's Conversations with Angels: Cabala, Alchemy, and the End of Nature* (Cambridge, 1999).

11. A. Grafton, 'Kepler as a Reader', *Journal of the History of Ideas*, 53 (1992), pp. 561–72, and Grafton, *Commerce with the Classics*, pp. 185–224.

12. W. R. Newman, *Gehennical Fire: The Lives of George Starkey, an American Alchemist in the Scientific Revolution* (Cambridge, Mass., 1994), pp. 114–69.

13. P. Findlen and T. Nummedal, 'Words of Nature: Scientific Books in the Seventeenth Century', in A. Hunter, ed., *Scientific Books, Libraries, and Collectors*, 4th edn (Aldershot, 2000), pp. 164–215.

14. A. Blair, 'Humanist Methods in Natural Philosophy: The Commonplace Book,' *Journal of the History of Ideas*, 53 (1992), pp. 541–51; Blair, *The Theater of Nature: Jean Bodin and Renaissance Science* (Princeton, 1997), pp. 49–81; Sherman, *John Dee*, pp. 60–5; A. Moss, *Printed Commonplace-Books and the Structuring of Renaissance Thought* (Oxford, 1996).

15. A. Cowley, 'To the Royal Society', in T. Sprat, *The History of the Royal Society of London* (London, 1667), sig. B2r.

16. R. Hooke, *The Posthumous Works of Robert Hooke*, ed. R. Waller (London, 1705), pp. 18–19, 24, 34–6, 63–5, 139–40; L. Mulligan, 'Robert Hooke's "Memoranda": Memory and Natural History', *Annals of Science*, 49 (1992), pp. 47–61, especially pp. 50–3.

17. There is now an extensive literature on this subject, but see especially S. Shapin, *A Social History of Truth: Civility and Science in Seventeenth-Century England* (Chicago, 1994); Shapin, 'The House of Experiment in Seventeenth-Century England', *Isis*, 79 (1988), pp. 373–404; M. Biagioli, 'Etiquette, Interdependence, and Sociability in Seventeenth-Century Science', *Critical Inquiry*, 22 (1996), pp. 193–238; Biagioli, 'Knowledge, Freedom and Brotherly Love: Homosociability and the Accademia dei Lincei', *Configurations*, 3 (1995), pp. 139–66; Biagioli, *Galileo, Courtier: The Practice of Science in the Culture of Absolutism* (Chicago, 1993).

18. Compare the remarks in D. F. McKenzie, 'Speech–Manuscript–Print', in D. Oliphant and R. Bradford, eds., *New Directions in Textual Studies* (Austin, Tex., 1990), pp. 87–109, and R. Chartier, 'Leisure and Sociability: Reading Aloud in Early Modern Europe', trans. C. Mossman, in S. Zimmerman and R. F .E. Wiessman, eds., *Urban Life in the Renaissance* (London and Toronto, 1989), pp. 103–20.

19. For example, H. Longino, *Science as Social Knowledge* (Princeton, 1990), pp. 62–132, and L. Daston, 'Baconian Facts, Academic Civility, and the Prehistory of Objectivity', *Annals of Scholarship*, 8 (1991), pp. 337–63; Daston, 'The Ideal and Reality of the Republic of Letters in the Enlightenment', *Science in Context*, 4 (1991), pp. 367–86.

20. M. Hunter, ed., *Archives of the Scientific Revolution: The Formation and Exchange of Ideas in Seventeenth-Century Europe* (Woodbridge, 1998), especially chapters 8, 9 and 11.

21. S. Shapin and S. J. Schaffer, *Leviathan and the Air-Pump: Hobbes, Boyle, and the Experimental Life* (Princeton, 1985), pp. 22–79.

22. B. J. Shapiro, *A Culture of Fact: England, 1550–1720* (Ithaca, 2000), pp. 105–67; Dear, *Discipline and Experience*, pp. 227–43.

23. This work is revealed most effectively in a continental context in A. Goldgar, *Impolite Learning: Conduct and Community in the Republic of Letters, 1680–1750* (New Haven, 1995).

24. E. Tyson, *Phocaena, or The Anatomy of a Porpess, Dissected at Gresham College* (London, 1680), sig. A2r–v; compare (among many other examples) A. M.[ullen], *An Anatomical Account of the Elephant Accidentally Burnt in Dublin* (London, 1682), p. 3, W. Petty, *The Discourse Made before the Royal Society... Concerning the Use of Duplicate Proportion* (London, 1674), sigs. A3r–A4r, A8r–v, and C. Havers, *Osteologia Nova* (London, 1691), sigs. A3r–A4v.

25. T. Birch, *The History of the Royal Society of London for Improving of Natural Knowledge, from Its First Rise* (4 vols., London, 1756–7), vol. 4, pp. 365–6.

26. R. Hooke, *The Diary of Robert Hooke MA, MD, FRS 1672–1680*, ed. H. W. Robinson and W. Adams (London, 1935); Hooke, 'The Diary of Robert Hooke, Nov. 1688–Mar. 1690 and Dec. 1692–Aug. 1693', ed. R. T. Gunther, in Gunther, ed., *Early Science in Oxford* (15 vols., Oxford, 1923–67), vol. 10, pp. 69–265.

27. H. Oldenburg, *The Correspondence of Henry Oldenburg*, ed. A. R. Hall and M. B. Hall (13 vols., Madison, Wisc., and London, 1965–86). For his diplomatic background, see especially vol. 1, covering the period before he became secretary at the Royal Society. At that time Oldenburg still called himself a 'secretary', but it was in much the same sense that Milton – one of his correspondents – was a secretary in Cromwell's government.

28. Royal Society, MS 1, fol. 89r. If it is indeed not a passage from a book by Sidney, then the most likely alternative is a letter to Oldenburg himself that is now lost. I am grateful to Jonathan Scott for conversations about this passage.

29. These stages are also discussed, in a different context, in A. Johns, *The Nature of the Book: Print and Knowledge in the Making* (Chicago, 1998), pp. 475–91.

30. For example, Birch, *The History of the Royal Society*, vol. 1, p. 487.

31. See, for example, Theodore Haak's conduct in presenting and showing different books at the same meeting: Birch, *The History of the Royal Society*, vol 4, p. 98.

32. The pursuit of conversation in weeks following a perusal report was expressly recommended by the Society in 1674, because such reports were becoming technical enough to preclude immediate responses: Birch, *The History of the Royal Society*, vol. 3, p. 153.

33. For remarks on registration and civility, see Shapin, *A Social History of Truth*, pp. 302–4.

34. Johns, *The Nature of the Book*, chapter 7, p. 489. For the origins of the public sphere in this period, see D. Zaret, *Origins of Democratic Culture: Printing, Petitions, and the Public Sphere in Early-Modern England* (Princeton, 2000).

35. Birch, *The History of the Royal Society*, vol. 3, pp. 494–5, 498, 500; S. Lorenzini, *Osservazioni intorno alle torpedini* (Florence, 1678).

36. Birch, *The History of the Royal Society*, vol. 4, pp. 325–6, 327–9; J. Kunckel, *De Acido et Urinoso Sale Calido et Frigido* (Berlin, 1684). For this incident, see also M. Boas, *Robert Boyle and Seventeenth-Century Chemistry* (Cambridge, 1958), pp. 153–4.

37. For example, Birch, *The History of the Royal Society*, vol. 4. pp. 332, 336.

38. S. Shapin, 'Robert Boyle and Mathematics: Reality, Representation, and Experimental Practice', *Science in Context*, 2 (1988), pp. 23–58.

39. For the civic implications of such alchemical practices, see O. Hannaway, *The Chemists and the Word: The Didactic Origins of Chemistry* (Baltimore, 1975), pp. 58–72 and passim.

40. L. Principe, *The Aspiring Adept: Robert Boyle and His Alchemical Quest* (Princeton, 1998), pp. 63–76.

41. For Hooke's controversy, see R. C. Iliffe, ' "In the Warehouse": Privacy, Property and Priority in the Early Royal Society', *History of Science*, 30 (1992), pp. 29–68; for Sinclair, see G. S.[inclair], *The Hydrostaticks* (Edinburgh, 1672), p. 146, and the separately paginated *Vindication of the Preface* appended to this volume, esp. pp. 4–8.

42. Birch, *The History of the Royal Society*, vol. 3, p. 499; O. Walker, *Propositions Concerning Optic-Glasses* (Oxford, 1679). It may be that Hooke was freer to

say what he thought because the book had only been 'produced' by Haak, and never formally 'presented'.

43. Birch, *The History of the Royal Society*, vol. 3, pp. 499, 500–3.
44. Ibid., vol. 2, p. 501; vol. 3, pp. 1–3.
45. Iliffe, 'In the Warehouse'.
46. Birch, *The History of the Royal Society*, vol. 3, pp. 4, 9, 20.
47. Ibid., vol. 3, pp. 10–15.
48. Ibid., vol. 3, pp. 16, 18–19. What Hooke was proposing was a variation on the standard way of testing telescope lenses, which was by using them to read distant printed letters. See M. L. R. Bonelli and A. Van Helden, 'Divini and Campani: A Forgotten Chapter in the History of the Accademia del Cimento', *Annali dell'Istituto e Museo di Storia della Scienza di Firenze*, 6 (1981), pp. 3–176.
49. Birch, *The History of the Royal Society*, vol. 3, p. 63.
50. Ibid., p. 52.
51. Ibid., p. 318; S. J. Schaffer, 'Glass Works: Newton's Prisms and the Uses of Experiment', in D. Gooding, T. Pinch and S. J. Schaffer, eds., *The Uses of Experiment: Studies in the Natural Sciences* (Cambridge, 1989), pp. 67–104, especially p. 85.
52. Birch, *The History of the Royal Society*, vol. 3, p. 269. In fact, Hooke bought Grimaldi's tract only in 1679: Hooke, *Diary*, p. 417.
53. Birch, *The History of the Royal Society*, vol. 3, pp. 278–9.
54. Johns, *The Nature of the Book*, pp. 521–31; Birch, *The History of the Royal Society*, vol. 4, p. 196; Gunther, ed., *Early Science in Oxford*, vol. 7, pp. 434–6.
55. *The Correspondence of Isaac Newton*, ed. H. W. Turnbull, J. F. Scott, A. R. Hall and L. Tilling (7 vols., Cambridge, 1959–77), vol. 1, pp. 317–19, 328–9, 358–65.
56. R. S. Westfall, *Never at Rest: A Biography of Isaac Newton* (Cambridge, 1980), pp. 274–80, 310; Schaffer, 'Glass Works', pp. 89–91.
57. For Leibniz's reading of the *Principia*, see D. B. Meli, *Equivalence and Priority: Newton versus Leibniz* (Oxford, 1993), pp. 95–125. For Newton's manipulation of the Royal Society's perusal, registration and publication mechanisms in the debate over the calculus, see A. R. Hall, *Philosophers at War: The Quarrel between Newton and Leibniz* (Cambridge, 1980). For the battle with Flamsteed, see Johns, *The Nature of the Book*, chapter 8. For Newton's use of favoured apostles, see R. C. Iliffe, ' "Is He Like Other Men?" The Meaning of the *Principia Mathematica*, and the Author as Idol', in G. MacLean, ed., *Culture and Society in the Stuart Restoration: Literature, Drama, History* (Cambridge, 1995), pp. 159–76.
58. Birch, *The History of the Royal Society*, vol. 4, pp. 347, 480; I. Newton, *The Principia*, trans. I. B. Cohen and A. Whitman (Berkeley, 1999), pp. 11–13.
59. Most famously in F. E. Manuel, *A Portrait of Isaac Newton* (Cambridge, Mass., 1968), for example, pp. 141–2, 156, 159; but in less thoroughgoing terms the tendency remains prevalent in many studies of Newton.

60. Biagioli, *Galileo, Courtier*, pp. 90–101; Findlen, *Possessing Nature*, pp. 352–65. More generally, see N. Z. Davis, 'Beyond the Market: Books as Gifts in Sixteenth-Century France', *Transactions of the Royal Historical Society*, 5th series, 33 (1983), pp. 69–88.

61. Birch, *The History of the Royal Society*, vol. 3, p. 434.

62. F. Willughby, *De Historia Piscium Libri Quatuor*, ed. J. Ray (Oxford, 1686). For Flamsteed on the use of the *Historia Coelestis* as a gift from Newton, see Johns, *The Nature of the Book*, pp. 609–10.

63. H. M. Solomon, *Public Welfare, Science and Propaganda: The Innovations of Théophraste Renaudot* (Princeton, 1972), especially pp. 60–122; G. Havers (trans.), *A General Collection of Discourses of the Virtuosi of France* (London, 1664); G. Havers and J. Davies (trans.), *Another Collection of Philosophical Conferences of the French Virtuosi* (London, 1665).

64. Oldenburg, *Correspondence*, vol. 1, pp. 112–14 (Oldenburg to Thomas Coxe, 24 January 1656/7).

65. Southampton Civic Record Office, MS D/M 1/1, fols. 95r–96r. For the general opprobrium about pamphlets in England, the Netherlands and France, see D. Freist, *Governed by Opinion: Politics, Religion and the Dynamics of Communication in Stuart London, 1637–1645* (London, 1997); C. E. Harline, *Pamphlets, Printing, and Political Culture in the Early Dutch Republic* (Dordrect, 1987), pp. 2–5, 44; J. K. Sawyer, *Printed Poison: Pamphlet Propaganda, Faction Politics, and the Public Sphere in Early Seventeenth-Century France* (Berkeley, 1990).

66. Johns, *The Nature of the Book*, pp. 187–265.

67. P. Pellison, *The History of the French Academy* (London, 1657), pp. 6–7.

PART V

Reading texts in time

CHAPTER NINE

Martial, Jonson and the assertion of plagiarism

Joseph Loewenstein

I have only a mildly surprising fact of cultural history to report here, that Martial seems to be the single most important influence on Ben Jonson's thinking about intellectual property in particular, and about the material culture of early modern books in general. I unearthed this datum during work on a central chapter of a study of the institutions of intellectual property in early modern England. My goal had been to specify the hard, material determinants of authors' imaginings of what they were making, but I couldn't escape the fact that Jonson's imagination of books was influenced not only by the manifold instances of English monopolistic competition, but also by a vivid and idiosyncratic first-century collection of poetry.

Such an observation is obviously encouraged by long-standing traditions of analysing influence, traditions central to the study of the history of writing, yet the editors of this volume have insisted that their contributors get over to the reader's side of things for this occasion. As a practising literary critic, I might find it slightly disingenuous, if not exactly perverse, to offer a short essay treating Jonson simply as a reader of Martial, or as a *simple* reader of Martial – that is, not as someone who reads in order, especially, to write but as someone who reads in order, say, to make private sense of Martial, or perhaps to staple *this* feature of the classical text to *that* feature of the Jacobean world – though this has been done effectively with a less gifted writer such as Gabriel Harvey. But it could be done. Such an essay might be prosecuted by means of attention to Jonson's annotations to his copy of Martial's works: I would be observing that Jonson's annotations to the Scriverius edition of Martial, annotations that are heaviest in the earliest books, suggest Jonson's special interest in Martial's rich vocabulary for the description of oral sex. Piquant as this might be, and probably useful as a means of extending our understanding of Jonson's unusually rich imaginative engagement with the mouth and throat, an essay of larger focus is in order here.

Looking only at these very specific annotations would be misleading, however, and quite possibly eccentric. There is every reason to believe that Jonson had once owned – and not simply borrowed – other copies of Martial's poems. He would certainly have owned Thomas Farnaby's 1613 edition of Martial, for example, for he had exerted himself to help Farnaby secure a pre-publication copy of Scriverius's emendations and so to free his friend from the scholarly embarrassment of having to base his text on sixteenth-century expurgated Jesuit texts – 'castrated' in Jonson's words.[1] Farnaby makes a fuss over Jonson's efforts in the front matter of the edition, and would surely have given Jonson a copy of the volume. And Farnaby's Martial would not have been the first that Jonson owned, for he had been reading Martial intently for at least a decade and a half prior to the appearance of that edition. And if, at the outset, we ask what a reader such as Jonson would find in a Renaissance edition of Martial, the first and not so simple answer would have to be *words*. Not just words for oral and other sites of sex, but words for cosmetics and wine making, for commercial negotiation and legal struggle, words for caustics and for unguents, for blandishment and insult, words to describe a savoured and coruscated life of things. A volume written in 85 CE, the *Xenia* or *Mottoes*, is a collection of texts to accompany gifts of delicacies – cheeses, young peaches, fowl; a companion volume, the *Apophoreta*, provides texts to accompany miscellaneous trinkets.

To read these texts at any historical remove is to encounter a difficult language that encoded the delightful and particular *quidditas* of a very civilized culture of consumption. It is no wonder that Martial came back to life in Italy, in the middle of the fifteenth century, during a great instauration in lexicography. Reviving, Martial forced the best Quattrocento editors to abandon the merely philological and paleographic norms of their practice. Scandalized by the textual deficiencies of the two *editiones principes*, Niccolò Perotti, for example, undertook a scholarly study of Martial, but if he ever intended an edition he forsook the project quickly. His *Cornu Copiae* was published posthumously in 1489, not an edition, but a rich commentary on Martial's *Liber Spectaculis* and book 1 of the *Epigrams*. Perotti had written the first modern Latin grammar and the *Cornu Copiae* is similarly pedagogical in motive, but the goal of synthetic and systematizing analysis was betrayed, for by the very nature of his representational disposition Martial obliged Perotti to reconstruct a dishevelled array of Roman material practices; and that diverse plenitude meant that Perotti could assert no principle of organization more abstract than line-for-line commentary. Perotti's research makes the *Cornu Copiae* one of the foundations of the

Stephanus Latin dictionaries compiled many decades later, and it informs the editions that Jonson would read several decades after that. These later editions – of which Scriverius was perhaps the best – would continue to collect a discontinuous and anecdotal Rome from the shining spatter of Martial's words. One way of charting the development of Jonson's Roman imagination would be to trace the marginalia – to check which words caught Jonson's eye in the Martial he was reading in the 1590s and which words provoke an underlining in Farnaby's edition, as he makes his reader's progress towards the middle-aged salaciousness marked in the Scriverius edition. But Jonson's reputedly well-stocked library went up in flames in 1623, and the earlier Martials do not survive. My own 'Execration upon Vulcan', then, is that the fire in Jonson's library impedes my doing as the editors have asked by cutting off one path over to the reader's side. I am obliged, therefore, to do things the old-fashioned way and to infer Jonson's reading habits from his writing habits and to infer a developing address to book culture that surges out of an intellectual apprenticeship to Martial that began in the 1590s.

Still, we would do well to keep the fact of the fire in mind, for it indicates a feature of early modern reading at once salient and usually neglected. Elaborating themes originally worked out in the study of literacy, Elizabeth Eisenstein encouraged us to think of the print revolution as decisively stabilizing the textual experiences of readers.[2] Her central themes of fixity, linearity and accumulation require steady critique, to which Jonson's fire can make a modest contribution. The library was fragile, vulnerable not only to fire – and apparently another nearly took off Jonson's lodgings a decade later – but also to poverty. Gloomily reworking the figure of reading as ingestion that meant so much to him, Jonson remarked to William Drummond that 'Sundry tymes he heth devoured his bookes... [that is,] sold them all for Necessity.'[3] 'Sundry tymes' and 'all' may exaggerate, but they remind us that, whatever Jonson's bibliophilia and commitments to scholarship, his books were a liquid asset.[4] The unsteady flow of new books and new editions and the ebbs and flows in his own library and in his access to others' libraries made reading distinctly contingent for Jonson and this would have been more than intellectually frustrating. Jonson was a brutal critic of others' obsessions with similarly configured contingencies, of fashion, news and esteem, and he seems to have found the dependencies of his own reading especially nettling. The 'Execration upon Vulcan' is not the work of a poet at ease.

Serious reflection on the material contingencies of reading has the odd effect of making it impossible to obey the editors' injunction to stay on the reader's side of literary history: for Jonson, as for others, writing is a very serious response to, resistance to, the contingency of reading. We are accustomed to tracing a range of imitative literary practices to the routines of the humanist schoolroom, with its translations and double translations, but this overshadows a more archaic and fundamental genealogy, writing as a work of conservation. Translation, imitation and even composition are variously preservative; apparently the deep reproductive drive in language was no more to be repressed in a printing culture than it had been within older cultures of writing. Certainly Jonson was a willing vector of reproduction, translating, imitating, recycling his own and others' writings, repeating and transcribing his own and others' spoken witticisms (some of them embarrassingly stale), making sure that his plays and masques were performed and revised and printed, copying and copying. Surely there were many motives for the energy of Jonson's submission to the reproductive drive in language; the 'Execration' suggests a special and heated resistance to the contingencies and scarcities of reading.

Although the general influence of Martial on Jonson has been casually remarked, it has not been assessed to date in a more concentrated way than it was by the Oxford editors, who devoted half a dozen pages to the subject.[5] They, and Richard Peterson, Thomas Greene and Ann Coiro after them, document Jonson's frequent and frequently close imitations of Martial – in the plays and, above all, in the *Epigrams*.[6] Their detailed focus on imitation has been unfortunately narrow, I think, failing to register some important general matters of influence – that Jonson learned a language of vituperation from Martial (more than from Catullus or Juvenal), that he learned from him how *many* vocabularies could be forced into the service of a sophisticated literary practice, that Martial taught Jonson – and such of Jonson's heirs as Herrick – to try to render the scent, tang and texture of good things (of good things *and* vile) and so set for them a standard of alerted sensuousness. It should be said – and here I am preceded by Ann Coiro – that it was also Martial (more than Ovid or Horace) who taught Jonson to think about the book, the verse collection, as a unit of composition. I propose to extend the account of how appreciatively Jonson read Martial by beginning with the much-discussed instance of *imitatio*, Jonson's small and securely central poem 'Inviting a Friend to Supper', which recalls and adapts several of Martial's invitation poems.

I've discussed this poem before.[7] When I first wrote about it, I concentrated on what its meditation on deliberate and moderate dining tells us about Jonson's sense of a nervous continuity between his physical and his literary corpus. I also sought to explain how the poem extends traditional ideas about imitation by taking classical figures of imitation as incorpora- tive ingestion and juxtaposing them with figures of modern iterability – the dangerous repetitions of those spying stoolies, Polly and Parrot, referred to in line 36, and the uncanny reproductions evoked ten lines earlier, where Jonson imagines the pastry to be served at his dinner party as repeating his verses. I've glossed the figure as staging the tension between a public market in printed books and a private culture of connoisseurship, for Jonson here fantasizes that the pastry he has purchased has been wrapped in unsold sheets of his own poems and that, by an unanticipated overextension of mechanical reproduction, the pastry therefore bears the inverted secondary image of the printed poem.[8] I want to continue this analysis by showing that this compounded reflection on reiteration is the product of Jonson's ongoing reflections on Martial.[9]

This imagined circuit of the poem, from privacy through the press to the pastry shop to the dessert plate, the return of the expressed, is a special case of a fantasy that recurs frequently in Jonson's non-dramatic verse. In an important study of early modern manuscript culture, H. R. Woudhuysen remarks that 'for Jonson, part of the pleasure of writing the poem' – he's referring to an epigram to Lady Digby from *Underwoods* – 'lay in thinking about its immediate circulation in manuscript'.[10] Jonson's fascination with the itinerant independence of poetry in its public state recalls Martial more than any other poet, ancient or modern.[11] And this node of recollection had long been habitual with Jonson. We can see it marked explicitly in 1601, in the text of *Cynthia's Revels*. There is no colophon to the edition of that year, so the last words of that quarto text are authorial and they show us a Jonson already thinking of publication – and of reading – in Martial's terms: '*Ecce rubet quidam*', he quotes: 'Look, somebody turns red, turns pale, is dazed, yawns, is disgusted. This I want. Now my poems please me.'[12] Private reading becomes a public spectacle, staged for the author's delight. This is a fantasy of especially personal reception, of course, and very different from that imagining of an impersonal and merely commer- cial circulation which we find in 'Inviting a Friend to Supper'. But the sunny, bold-faced egotism with which Martial contemplates the *social* cir- cumstance of Roman poetry is regularly complemented by an attention to the commercial and material life of poems unrivalled in the Silver Age or before. Imitating Horace, who had counselled *his* verses to preserve their pre-publication modesty, Martial gives a rougher evocation of what lies in store for the book that dares to forsake his *scrinium*, his writing cabinet, for the shops of Argiletum. He warns his poems of the 'rhinocerote's nose' of Rome's typical critic – I give Jonson's rendering here, from *Epigrams*, 28 – though Martial understands that the rhinoceran sneers of the Roman literati may seem preferable to the punishments inflicted by the author – his brutal scorings and rough erasures (1.3). Martial's Augustan predecessors might frequently write fables on the fate of their lines or books, but when Martial speaks of his books, they are represented as objects, susceptible to vermin (6.61, 11.1, *et al.*), to rain (3.100) and to fire (5.53). Another vocabulary is sedimented in Martial's texts: the Renaissance historian of the book was to be as gratified by Martial's lexicon as was the enthusiast of erotica, for Martial directs his reader's attention to the language and labour of binding, scouring and trimming pages for a codex (1.117 and 4.10); he designates the sizes of various codices, tablets and scrolls (1.2, 2.1, 2.6); he preserves the name for the purple covers that adorn especially valued scrolls and for the precious headpieces of their *umbilici* (3.2, 5.6, 8.72); and he focuses on the stains and fraying that the papyrus suffers when a scroll is frequently rolled and rerolled (10.93), or when it is gripped by the carelessly shaven chin of a coarsely skimming reader. We are alerted to the way poems fit the page of a codex (10.1, 10.59) and so encouraged to an attention to layout that may have powerfully influenced Jonson's largely idiosyncratic practice. Here again, to read Martial is to be less philologist than archaeologist. But what was even more influential than Martial's attention to the shape, heft, texture and material substance of books was his rendering of the social mechanics of Roman literary circulation – or, rather, of Rome's various literary circulations, for Martial is particularly sensitive to the several disarticulated systems of exchange in which the physical book participated.

Jonson would find the variable circumstance of Jacobean literature adumbrated in Martial's description of Roman book culture: 'Not alone does Rome's leisure rejoice in my Pipleis, nor do I give these pieces only to empty ears', he observes in *Epigrams*, 11.3; 'My book is thumbed by hard centurions beside Mars's standards in Getic frosts, and Britain is said to recite my verses.' The norms of Latin literary consumption were radically transformed by the simple fact of Rome's imperial expansion; a Renaissance English reader could reflect that English literary consumption had also changed, albeit as a result of the more complex interaction of expanded and altered schooling, print publication and subtly augmented physical and social mobility in the course of the preceding century. Martial's observations on the sheer geographical extent of his audience recurs to a topos recognizably Augustan, but he extends the observation in ways that would resonate in early modern England.[13] For Martial, the effect of expanded consumption is to unsettle an old image of the social relation of reader and writer; patronage relations based on direct contact were now felt to be incongruous with the reality of contemporary consumption.[14] He makes this the occasion of complaint: '*quid potest? nescit sacculus ista meus*... What's the use? My purse knows nothing of all that' (line 6). As Jonson's would be, Martial's response is conservative (although Martial's conservatism has a nice whiff of cynicism), for his purse gapes reverently for the advent of a new Maecenas (lines 7–10), a single patron to distill the poet's popularity into cash.[15] Here *exactly* is Jonson's straddling social posture, the dual presence in coterie and market, the poem as gift and as goods.

Almost whenever Jonson seems a particularly astute analyst of early modern book culture, we can find his analyses anticipated in Martial. One of the important features of the English book trade in the late 1590s and at least half a century earlier on the Continent was the marketing of authorial attention, the emphatic advertisement of books as newly revised by their authors. Jonson is, of course, one of Jacobean England's most notorious revisers, a poet who recovers creative control of plays and masques by rewriting them for print publication, and who perhaps revises already published plays in order to assist a friendly stationer in invading another stationer's copyright. He might have learned to measure the value of revision when he was asked to update Kyd's *Spanish Tragedy*, but he might have learned to reflect on the social economy of revision from Martial. In a particularly insinuating poem, Martial describes authorial revision in terms that perfectly evoke the author's nervous poise between social intimacies and the publicities of the market, the Martialian / Jonsonian straddle: to the library of an elegant country villa he commends seven slim volumes, hand-corrected: '*haec illis pretium facit litura*... the corrections give them value' (7.17.8).[16] Don't miss the crucial commercial flicker in 'pretium': the effect of autograph can be described only in terms of 'pretium', price, value added. The countervailing effect of 'litura' is harder to render: it means a correction by erasure or striking out. The paradox is that these poems are improved – or, rather, that their value is constituted – by a personal or characteristic blot, a copy made fair by being fouled. The paradox would be powerfully reinforced in the era of print, when the difference between autograph and publicly circulating printed text would be sharpened, and the personality of handwriting inflated.[17] Strenuously as he exerted himself to control the layout of the printed masques, Jonson nonetheless knows to write his presentation copies for Prince Henry by hand, and to inscribe them with variants. He knows, that is, how to privatize reading.

Despite such important studies as William V. Harris's *Ancient Literacy* it remains quite difficult to reconstruct the literary sociology and economics of imperial Rome, but a good deal of what we know of this subject has been gleaned, as Jonson and his contemporaries would have gleaned it, from Martial's poems.[18] From the epigram cited above we gather that, by the first century C E, modest networks had been established for distributing contemporary literature to the imperial provinces – though this can also be inferred from Pliny the Younger, and from Horace, Ovid and Propertius before them.[19] Although there is no reason to allege new norms of mass scriptorial book production (Atticus's efforts on behalf of Cicero and Varro were almost certainly unusual), we can also learn from Martial's *Epigrams* (4.72) that booksellers had begun stocking their shops with at least a certain number of exemplars so that a purchaser did not have to come up with a copy text himself. Martial's feeling that Rome was rather short of Maecenases is inflected, skewed, by an awareness that book acquisition no longer depended on a chain of more or less intimate social connections linking the purchaser to the author – a feeling that is refelt in the opening of Jonson's *Epigrams* and throughout that volume.[20] And although most Roman copying would still have been undertaken at the behest of an individual purchaser, some copying was now initiated by the bookseller himself, so that a book buyer could occasionally make a purchase on the spur of the moment (1.117). Booksellers must therefore have concerned themselves with anticipating the taste of their clientele, thus providing some slight commercial focus and reinforcement to the more diffuse patterns of literary connoisseurship.[21]

Martial's own imagination plainly warmed to this small adjustment towards a *market* in books. An author would normally benefit only indirectly from his literary achievements, much as an amateur with a fine singing voice might benefit from that skill today. Such gifts attracted notice, confirmed admiration, or otherwise consolidated social connections to those who could confer benefits, but Martial, whose own fame was built on ingenious insolence, contrived to flaunt the value that accrued to his poems in the booksellers' new, more impersonal system of exchange. He is amused by their cost: when an unpleasant acquaintance asks that Martial give him a copy of his poems – Martial employed a copyist to make such presentation copies – he refers him to the bookseller Tryphon.[22] He refers his readers to Tryphon more than once: '*Omnis in hoc gracili Xeniorum turba libello . . .* The entire assembly of mottoes in this slender little book will cost you four sesterces to buy. Is four too much? It could cost two, and bookseller Tryphon would still make a profit' (13.3.1–4). Scandalously, the volume declares itself to have been composed *for* sale. Both the *Xenia* and the *Apophoreta*, Martial's two collections of stylish gift enclosures, are guides to hospitable expenditure, but Martial undercuts the spirit of such largesse in a turn to which Jonson could only have aspired: '*hac licet hospitibus pro munere disticha mittas* . . . You can send these couplets to your guests *instead* of a gift, if sesterces are as scarce with you as with me' (lines 5–6). This disruption of the niceties of gift giving simply maintains the implicit force of the opening four lines from which the niceties of literary connoisseurship and community are banished, giving way to a culture of cheapening commerce.[23] Jonson might wish to rise above the smirking cleverness of such lines, but he could not but find them arresting. Here is a book that – like 'Inviting a Friend to Supper' – exposes the fragility of hospitality, that exposes hospitality to the market; as in 'Inviting a Friend to Supper', we are to savour verse fragments that rival food.[24]

Both the *Xenia* and the *Apophoreta* were compiled for disintegration and distribution, but Jonson's predecessor and model in bibliographic fantasy imagines the disintegrating book in other ways. Like his early modern imitator, Martial enjoys referring to the fate of unpopular books, the papyrus re-used to wrap fish, olives, pepper, or incense.[25] But the contrivance of the *Xenia* and the *Apophoreta*, released quite early in Martial's writing career, in 85 CE, suggested other market disintegrations, in this case the detachment of Martial's poems from Martial's name:

Erras . . . You are mistaken, greedy purloiner of my books, in thinking that it costs no more to become a poet than the price of copying and a cheap length of papyrus . . . You must look for private, unpublished work, poems known only to the parent of the virgin sheet, which he keeps sealed up in his book-box, work not rubbed rough by hard chins. A well-known book cannot change author . . . *mutare dominum non potest liber notus*. (1.66.1–9)

Here, of course, is the Martialian topic that most concerns me since it was the Martialian topic that most concerned Jonson, the proprietary back-formation that a burgeoning and relatively indiscriminate market in books produces. Here is where Jonson's reading of Martial emerges as a central seventeenth-century event, where the influence of Martial's bibliographic imagination becomes more historically pointed than the diffuse influence of, say, Horace's model of social poise or even Cicero's (fantastic) model of determining eloquence.

It should be insisted that Martial refers here to a figurative crime, since the poems are not authorial property, but it is not so clear that the poet is not proposing a real transaction.[26] As in the introduction to the *Xenia* the spirit of Tryphon's market insinuates itself into an older, non-commercial culture of writing and connoisseurship. Martial pre-empts Tryphon, having learned the lesson of his market: '*tales habeo; nec sciet quisquam*... I have such poems, and nobody will be the wiser' (line 12). He is not simply offering his poems for sale. Martial proposes, rather, that the attributes of cultured personhood, his literary 'gifts', can be put up for sale by the mere detachment of his name from his poems.[27] Of course, the quietly impudent subtext is that the purchaser will not be able to carry off the imposture, but, as always, Martial's impudence has an analytic, clarifying force: '*aliena quisquis recitat*... Whoever recites other men's productions and seeks fame thereby, ought to buy – not a book, but silence' (lines 13–14). With cheeky aplomb, Martial polices the market, insisting that skill is inaccessible to commerce, that poetic 'gifts' cannot be made the object of sale. He casually denigrates the marketable book in order to emphasize and protect the value of those personal arrangements for which the book is only a vector: what Jonson could find clarified in such poems is the overlapping incommensurability of two very different economies, the one of book selling, the other of clientage, the one of personal property or goods, the other of personal attributes or skills. So from Martial Jonson would learn to make poems about the buying and selling of poems; he would learn that one way in which the satirist can quickly penetrate the manners of a culture is to observe its commerce in books; he would learn to consider the effect of a burgeoning market in books on a fragile culture of clientage; he would learn to wonder – as Heywood, Marston and the printers of their day were independently learning to wonder – what the market value of an authorial name and style might be. No editor has traced lines from Jonson's epigram 'To Fine Grand' to any particular classical models, but his mere '*In primis*, Grand, you owe me for a jest' demonstrates that Jonson had learned to read and to locate himself in the economy of Jacobean culture by reading Martial. Martial may not have taught Jonson the craft of impersonation, but in such gestures as that which concludes the bill in verse to Grand –

> *Item*, an epitaph on my lord's cock,
> In most vile verses, and cost me more pain
> Than had I made them good, to fit your vein.

– it becomes clear that Martial had made Jonson early modern England's most self-conscious *analyst* of market impersonation.

However casually Martial had distinguished between the forms of reification that variously shape literary culture, Jonson found that act of distinction useful, and he infuses Martial's archly satiric address to the literary economy with a hint of historically momentous urgency. In the print version of *Hymenaei*, the first masque that Jonson prepared for print, he takes great pains over the cultural grammar of attribution. Hence the conclusion to his description of the scenic effects:

The *Designe*, and *Act* of all which, together with the *Device* of their *Habits*, belongs properly to the Merit, and Reputation of Maister YNYGO JONES; whom I take modest occasion, in this fit place, to remember, lest his owne worth might accuse mee of an ignorant neglect from my silence.[28]

He goes on in quite a different vein to name, praise and pledge his friendship for Alfonso Ferrabosco, who wrote the music, and to acknowledge his own inability properly to assess or praise the dances of Thomas Giles: Jones is thus singled out as the proprietary stickler. But Jonson concludes these acknowledgements with a quotation from Martial that shows him to be as much the stickler: 'What was my part, the Faults here, as well as the Vertues must speake. *Mutare dominum nec potest Liber notus*' – a well-known book cannot change its author or – to render 'dominum' more precisely – cannot change its lord, its master.

That Jonson was fascinated by the question, the possibility, of intellectual dominion is news to no one. The same concerns shape Jonson's commentary at the end of his next published masque, *The Haddington Masque*:[29]

The two latter [dances] were made by M. THO. GILES, the two first by M. HIE HERNE ... The tunes were M ALPHONSO FERRABOSCO'S. the device and act of the scene, M. YNIGO JONES his, with addition of the Trophæes.

And then, in a grave act of imitation that anticipates the more capacious one of 'Inviting a Friend to Supper', Jonson returns to the same bibliographic *auctor*:

For the invention of the whole and the verses, Assertor qui dicat esse meos, Imponet plagiario pudorem.[30]

'The prosecutor who calls them mine will shame the plagiarist.'[31]

Both the fastidiousness of these acknowledgements and the quotation from Martial mark this as a nearly seismic moment in modern literary culture. I cannot give a full account of the Roman thought that strikes Jonson here, but I can start. He is adapting Martial's epigram 1:52, a text that turns out to be the locus classicus in the cultural history of plagiarism.[32] Martial was not the first to criminalize intellectual appropriation by referring to falsely attributed texts as stolen property, but in the epigram to which Jonson turns here Martial does seem to have invented a new term. The thief of book-slaves is a kidnapper, 'plagiarius'. This figurative use of the legal term apparently did not become part of the vocabulary of commonplace Latin metaphors – conditions were not right for the establishment of a permanent analytic vocabulary, much less a regular legal or institutional reification, of the social, personal, or commercial aspects of the intellectual artifact.[33] Thanks to Renaissance scholars, however, this use of the Latin term was revived, and appears, for only the second time in English, in *Poetaster* (1602). Jonson's use of *plagiary* in that context seems unresponsive to the most obvious force of Martial's figure, the way the imputed crime ascribes personality to the misappropriated literary work. Actually *Poetaster* misses a good deal more, for Martial's figurative work is extraordinarily complex: Martial had described the kidnapped poems as manumitted slaves, freed by the poet into informal manuscript circulation – as opposed to more formal *edition* – and illegally seized, hauled back into slavery, by the plagiarist. '*Commendo tibi, Quintiane*' – the epigram is addressed to the patron-reader, whose function is also given figurative extension:

If they complain of harsh enslavement, come forward to claim their freedom and give bail as required. And when he calls himself their owner, say they are mine, discharged from my hand. (1.52.1–7)[34]

The dense specificities of the legal situation figured here would appeal to the formalist – the metrist, the grammarian, the bricklayer – in Jonson: Martial submits the uncertain sociology of literary production and appropriation to the extraordinarily elaborate schematics of the Roman law of slavery.[35] Although Jonson drops all reference to manumission – to the figurative personhood of the poem, to the drama of freedom and enslavement – he preserves Martial's sharply analytic address to the contingencies of aesthetic production: 'The tunes were M. ALPHONSO FERRABOSCO'S. the device and act of the scene, M. YNIGO JONES his, with addition of the Trophæes.' Jonson has turned to Martial not for his breezy poise but for his distinctive sensitivity to the competitive underpinnings of patronage. He knew to whom he could turn to gloss a mood provoked by collaboration.

Up to this point I have been emphasizing the historical commonalities that bind Jonson to Martial, but I do not wish to imply that they are distinguishable only by temperament. At this key juncture, Jonson is at once enlarging on Martial and measuring those specific contingencies of the early modern cultural market. We can speak of an enlargement by virtue of the mere fact that reference to antique plagiaristical appropriation takes its place as part of a larger attributive parsing in *The Haddington Masque*; we can also speak of an enlargement specified to the place of the bookseller in early modern London as distinguished from his place in late antique

Rome. A deeper gloss on Martial's poem will enable us to see the Jonsonian distinction.

The figured narrative of the manumitted then kidnapped poem reflects on the relation between two distinct states in the social ontology of Roman poems, both of which survive, transmuted, in modern systems of text propagation, though the first sometimes evades critical notice. The *second* state of a poem, the poem 'as published', has remained a central object of critical scrutiny, whereas the first, the poem 'circulated in draft', is usually treated uneasily as part of a poem's *pre*-history, a datum for the literary biographer (though recent studies in early modern manuscript circulation may be changing the disposition of scholarly readers). Classicists, however, recognize the period in which a poem circulates among an ostensibly exclusive coterie of ostensibly friendly connoisseurs as an important phase in the social being of a poem, however difficult its reconstruction may be.[36] It is useful to remember here the habit enjoined on the aspiring poet by Horace in the *Ars Poetica*, that the poet withhold a manuscript from public circulation for nine years, in the meantime seeking the advice of skilled critics: '*nescit vox missa reverti*', he warns: 'that which has been uttered, cannot be recalled' (line 390). The Latin cognates of 'edition' refer with some specificity to this moment of missive, a release that marks the end of a writer's control over a work and the beginning of the second, autonomous phase of its social being.[37] Before this release, the poem serves as a vector of intellectual and social intimacy, constituting or sustaining a circle of cognoscenti; afterwards – if all goes well – wider approval will redound to the poet's credit and will confirm the literary authority and exclusivity of the group within which it circulated before.[38] The Horatian idea, of the absolute (and, sometimes, licentious) freedom of the edited poem, became a classical commonplace, but, in a hopeful resistance to which Jonson would subscribe, Martial's figure imagines limits on that freedom: like the manumitted slave, the edited poem owes its author loyalty. At the same time, Martial dwells on the precariousness of that freedom – the edited poem, circulating widely, is vulnerable to vulgar misappropriation in the form of plagiarism (and not, say, in the form of misprision or criticism). For Martial – and for the Jonson of 'Inviting a Friend to Supper' – the bookseller represents a threat, albeit a small one, to the intimacies of 'pre-editorial' circulation in general, and of patronage in particular. For Jonson, however, print was emerging as the sphere of a self-assertion, a court of more public opinion when patrons at Whitehall, or in the theatre, proved fickle. Given the uncertainties of his competition with the designer Jones or with the more proximate rival poet Daniel, Jonson turns to the press for vantage. Even after the moment of edition, we find Martial calling on the patron-reader to redeem the kidnapped poems – '*Commendo tibi, Quintiane*' – whereas Jonson's 'assertor' is indefinite. The printed text of the masque acknowledges the uncertainty of the sphere of edition, even as it attempts to enfold that sphere into a very personal embrace: 'I adventure to give that abroad, which in my first conception I intended honorably fit'; his detractors 'have found a place, to powre out their follies, and I a seate, to sleepe out the passage' (lines 11–12 and 20–2).

Jonson's 'assertor' is not entirely indefinite, for one of his avatars is the stationer Thomas Thorpe. Jonson could have observed the alliance between his rival, Daniel, and Samuel Waterson, an alliance that had begun in 1585 and had yielded the irksomely impressive *Works of Samuel Daniel* in 1601 – and would, in the coming years, confer on Daniel more power over the production and marketing of certain of his printed works than had ever accrued to an English author not himself a stationer.[39] Jonson seems to have sought such an alliance with Thorpe, who had facilitated Jonson's finicky intervention in the printing of *Sejanus* in 1605, and had then published *Hymenaei*, *Volpone* and, finally, *The Masques of Blacknesse and Beautie* ('Invented by BEN: IONSON') and *The Haddington Masque* ('Devised by BEN: IONSON'). It is difficult to describe the intensifications of authorship towards which Daniel and Jonson, each in his way, labour, but something new is being 'invented' and 'devised' by the mere fact of being 'adventured abroad' in the sphere of print. These terms grope their way over the plastic surface of the Written, even as Martial's odd metaphor of the poem as manumitted slave, at once independent and attached, person and thing, gropes its way over the uncertain ontology of edition. Jonson suppresses the drama of freedom in Martial's poem so that early modern invention might be unembarrassed by the personality (however curtailed) of the slave; Jonson's suppression does not so much assert absolute property in the printed work as prepare for such assertion. And despecification serves Jonson's ends in another way as well. Where Martial wittily imagines a specific patron as 'assertor', Jonson more earnestly entrusts his inventions to a more unspecific readerliness 'abroad', as if the moment of courtly performance could only constrain new and *newly contingent* forms of originality and property.

Martial taught Jonson to watch the reader. In 1601, Jonson had ended the printed *Cynthia's Revels* with his pleasure in the reader's blush: '*Ecce rubet quidam... nunc nobis carmina nostra placent.*' A few months later, on the title page of *Poetaster*, he disclaimed any unprincipled desire for the reader's blush: '*Et mihi de nullo fama rubore placet.*' '*Hoc lege*... Read this, of which Life can say, "this is mine"', wrote Martial, and Jonson picked up the passage on the title page of *Sejanus* in 1605: '*Non hic Centauros, non Gorgonas, Harpyasq[ue] / Invenies: Hominem pagina nostra sapit*... You'll find no centaurs, gorgons or harpies here; our pages taste human.' Our *pages*, not our words: Jonson transcribes Martial for print and not for performance, for epigraphs, concluding mottoes, glosses. We might say, then, that the other avatar of the '*assertor qui dicat esse meos*' is Martial himself: it was from reading Martial that Jonson learned to observe the modern reader reading invention itself from the printed page.

NOTES

1. D. McPherson, 'Ben Jonson Meets Daniel Heinsius', *English Language Notes*, 44 (1976), pp. 105–9. The same figure may be found in Donne's little epigram 'On Raderus'.

Farnaby gratefully records Jonson's assistance in preparing the edition, not least his help in securing some of the emendations of the Dutch scholar Scriverius, whom Jonson had visited in 1613. The two men had worked together closely – in addition to assisting with the Martial edition, Jonson had written Latin commendatory poems to Farnaby's editions of Juvenal (1612) Persius (1612) and Seneca (1613) – and Farnaby knew Jonson well enough to know how pleased he would be to be praised as '*dignus... meliori theatro quam quo malevolorum invidiam pascat*... deserving...a better theatre than that by which he feeds the envy of detractors' (*Ben Jonson*, ed. C. H. Herford, P. Simpson and E. Simpson (11 vols., Oxford, 1925–52), vol. 11, p. 134). Both non-dramatic poetry and print provided Jonson with just such a 'melior theatrum', and one might suppose him to have been referring directly to Farnaby's phrase when he concludes his dedication to the *Epigrams* by referring to the collection as 'my *Theater*, where *Cato*, if he liv'd, might enter without scandall'. But Jonson is no doubt referring not to Farnaby's Martial but to Martial, whose own letter prefatory to the first book of *his Epigrams* concludes by banning Cato from 'meum theatrum'. Instead of feeding his detractors in a public theatre, Jonson, who has fed on Martial, will repossess his plays by revising them for presentation, like epigrams, in a theatre more properly his.

It cannot be seriously proposed that Jonson owes the conception of the non-dramatic as a refuge from dramaturgy, or the notion of print as an alternative to performance, to Martial. But it should not be supposed that Martial's influence on such thinking was trival. The self-consciousness that dogs Jonson shaped his engagement with Martial; the strength of that engagement is evidenced by the depth of the self-consciousness it yielded – and by 'self-consciousness' I mean both a consciousness of the self compounded of, at least, bodily hungers and the aspirations of the craftsman *and* an awareness of those contemporary conditions least assimilable to the historical circumstances that Martial and his poems represent. In the course of reading Martial's *Epigrams*, Jonson sharpened his sense of contemporary literary conditions and would have conspicuously sharpened his sense of the various claims a poet might assert on his readers, his publishers, his imitators and his poems; to specify this further, rereading and rewriting Martial as he does in 'Inviting a Friend to Supper', Jonson discovered the book market as such.

2. I have tried to keep the fire in mind in a different way on another occasion: 'Personal Material: Jonson and Book-Burning', in M. Butler, ed., *Re-Presenting Ben Jonson: Text, History, Performance* (Houndmills, 1999), pp. 93–113.

3. The latter portion of this page of Drummond's 'Informations be Ben John-ston' could not be more revealing as a map of one sector of Jonson's psyche, for it records how Raleigh's son made a spectacle of Jonson by getting him dead drunk in Paris and of how Jonson 'drank out all the full cup of wyne' at his first communion following his return to the Anglican church; how Jon-son measured his declining place in Salisbury's esteem by his lost access to the food on Salisbury's own plate; and how 'he heth consumed a whole night in lying looking to his great toe, about which he hath seen tartars & turks Romans and Carthaginians feight in his imagination' (*Ben Jonson*, vol. 1, pp. 140–1): these agglomerate as a suite on consumption, visionary imagination and alienation.

4. Of course, the instability of his own library does not exhaust the instabilities of his access to books. Jonson read in others' collections, like modern scholars, and like modern scholars he borrowed books, hoping not to have to return them too quickly. A reader of Eisenstein might lapse into thinking that all books in print were always available to a Renaissance scholar, whereas they were no more so then than they are now.

   Drummond records a related detail on the same page of his notes on Jonson's remarks: 'every first day of the new year he hath 20lb sent him from the Earl of Pembroke to buy bookes' (p. 141).

5. *Ben Jonson*, vol. 2, pp. 342–57, but see also W. D. Briggs, 'Source-Material for Jonson's *Epigrams* and *Forest*', *Classical Philology*, 11 (1916), pp. 169–90.

6. R. S. Peterson, *Imitation and Praise in the Poetry of Ben Jonson* (New Haven, 1981), passim; T. M. Greene, *The Light in Troy: Imitation and Discovery in Renaissance Poetry* (New Haven, 1982), pp. 278–88; A. B. Coiro, *Robert Herrick's 'Hesperides' and the Epigram Book Tradition* (Baltimore, 1988), p. 83. As Coiro shows, by the 1590s the influence of Martial was pervasive, in large part because of the use of his poems as models for writing exercises in schools such as Winchester. She goes on to discuss Sir John Davies' *Epigrams* of the mid-nineties, in which Martial's persona is reproduced, save for the greed and libidinousness.

7. 'The Jonsonian Corpulence; or, The Poet as Mouthpiece', *English Literary History*, 53 (1986), pp. 491–519; reprinted in R. N. Watson, ed., *Critical Essays on Ben Jonson* (New York, 1997), pp. 192–216.

8. Note that the fantasy of Jonson's printed poems as wrapping paper for groceries provides the punch line for 'To My Bookseller', the third poem in Jonson's collection of *Epigrams*.

9. I'm going to neglect Jonson's address to Martial's delicacy, his interest in the Pretty that he keeps firmly tethered to his committed insolence. Such neglect is merely strategic: it's not my subject here. But if Jonson isn't as committed to an attempt to render the Martialian Pretty as, say, Herrick, he's probably more successful insofar as he cleaves to the insolence. In Martial's spirit, he places his most tinklingly charming gestures in satiric contexts – they are set pieces in plays or are kept within such suites as the 'Celebration of Charis'.

10. H. R. Woudhuysen, *Sir Philip Sidney and the Circulation of Manuscripts, 1558–1640* (Oxford, 1996), p. 153. The 'Epigram to My Muse, the Lady Digby, on Her Husband, Sir Kenelm Digby' bears citation at this juncture:

> Goe, *Muse*, in, and salute him. Say he be
> Busie, or frowne at first; when he sees thee,
> He will clear up his forehead, thinke thou bring'st
> Good *Omen* to him   (*Underwoods*, 78.19–22)

And from this focus on the physiology of reading, Jonson proceeds to the economics and sociology of reception:

> O! what a fame't will be?
> What reputation to my lines, and me,
> When he shall read them at the Treasurers bord?
> . . . .
> . . . Then, what copies shall be had,
> What transcripts begg'd? how cry'd up, and how glad,
> Wilt thou be, *Muse*   (lines 25–7, 29–31)

11. After Jonson, there would be others who would relish this Martialian topos. In *MacFlecknoe*, Dryden looks askance at the complicity of print in the 'coronation progress' of Thomas Shadwell:

> No Persian carpets spread th'imperial way,
> But scattered limbs of mangled poets lay;
> From dusty shops neglected authors come
> Martyrs of pies and relics of the bum.
> Much Heywood, Shirley, Ogleby there lay
> But loads of Sh— almost choked the way.
>   (lines 98–105)

12. '*Ecce rubet quidam, pallet, stupet, oscitat, odit. / Hoc volo: nunc nobis carmina nostra placent*', *Epigrams*, 6.60.3–4. To some extent, the motto on the title page of *Poetaster*, the next of Jonson's plays to see print, will seem to retract this particular exultation, for there Martial is quoted in a moment of caution: '*Et mihi de nullo fama rubore placet* . . . Nor do I desire fame from any man's blush' (7.12.4).

13. For other poems on provincial literary consumption, see 9.84 and 10.78.

14. This is to *explain* what Gordon Braden remarks in passing, Martial's 'interminable concern with grubby matters of literary politics' (*The Classics and English Renaissance Poetry*, New Haven, 1978, p. 185). For the transformation

of literary fame in the imperial period, see E. Auerbach, 'The Western Public and Its Language', in Auerbach, *Literary Language and Its Public in Late Latin Antiquity and in the Latin Middle Ages*, trans. R. Mannheim (New York, 1965), pp. 237–47.

15. But cf. 4.27. Martial describes the new instability of the poet's position as essentially aleatory in the obscure first poem of book 13. It is tempting, but it would be misleading to suppose that its conclusion – '*haec mihi charta nuces, haec est mihi charta fritillus / alea nec damnum nec facit ista lucrum* . . . This paper is my nuts, this paper my dice-box; such gambling brings neither loss nor gains' (lines 7–8) – suggests the modern uncertainties specific to a retail market.

16. And cf. 7.11.

17. For a sustained discussion of the augmentation of autograph in early modern England, see J. Goldberg, *Writing Matter: From the Hands of the English Renaissance* (Stanford, 1990). Goldberg glances at the relation between printing and handwriting, but does not pursue this particular line of analysis.

18. W. V. Harris, *Ancient Literacy* (Cambridge, Mass., 1989). See also R. Starr, 'The Circulation of Literary Texts in the Roman World', *Classical Quarterly*, 37 (1987), pp. 213–23; and E. J. Kenney, 'Books and Readers in the Roman World', in Kenney, ed., *The Cambridge History of Classical Literature*, vol. 2: *Latin Literature* (Cambridge, 1982).

Despite the fire that destroyed many of Jonson's books in 1623, three copies of Martial's poems known to have been owned by Jonson survive: the 1615 London edition of Farnaby, the 1617 Paris edition and Scriverius's 1619 Leyden edition, the latter quite heavily annotated. Jonson is particularly fond of glossing allusions to oral sex – finds such allusions where many readers would not – and more than once defends Martial against the strictures of fastidious commentators. See D. McPherson, 'Ben Jonson's Library and Marginalia: An Annotated Catalogue', *Studies in Philology*, 71/5 (December 1974), pp. 67–70.

19. Hence the story from Pliny in which Tacitus tells a stranger of equestrian status, 'you know me by my writings' (*Epistles*, 9.23.2); see Auerbach's gloss in 'The Western Public', pp. 237–9. See also Starr, 'The Circulation of Literary Texts', p. 220 n. 58.

20. Classical scholars now speak with much more caution about antique book production than they did forty or fifty years ago. For a useful summary of the current literature on the subject, see Harris, *Ancient Literacy*, pp. 223–5.

21. Booksellers could, of course, err in their anticipations. E. J. Kenney adduces Catullus, 95.8, and Horace, *Epistles*, 2.1.269–70, on the use of unsold, 'prewritten' copies as wastepaper, though he shrewdly stipulates that 'it is hazardous to press the significance of what was clearly a literary *topos*' ('Books and Readers in the Roman World', p. 22).

22. ' "*Aes dabo pro nugijs et emam tua carmina sanus? / non,*" *inquis, "faciam tam faciae." nec ego . . .* "Am I to give cash for rubbish?" you say, "and buy your verses in my right mind? I'll be no such fool." No more will I' (4.72.3–4). See also the more expansive 1.117, in which the bookseller is Atrectus, not Tryphon.

23. See also the brilliantly sharp couplet: '*Exigis ut nostros donem tibi, Tucca, libellos / non faciam: nam vis vendere, non legere* . . . You demand that I give you my little books, Tucca. I won't, for you want to sell them, not to read them' (7.77).

24. McPherson, 'Ben Jonson's Library', pp. 69–70. Although the surviving copy of Jonson's Scriverius Martial dates from 1619, Farnaby tells us in the preface to his 1615 edition (sig. A4r) that several of his emendations came from Scriverius via Jonson, who had met the Dutch scholar in Leyden in 1613 (*Ben Jonson*, vol. 11, pp. 134–5). The first edition of Scriverius's Martial appeared in 1618, so Jonson seems to have been permitted to see Scriverius's work in manuscript and to make transcriptions from it. For Jonson's encounters in Leyden, see McPherson, 'Ben Jonson Meets Daniel Heinsius', pp. 105–9.

25. 3.2, 4.86, 6.61, 13.1; cf. Jonson's *Epigrams*, 3.

26. See also I.29, one of the several poems addressed to the plagiarist, Fidentinus, which concludes, '*si mea vis dici, gratis tibi carmina mitam: / si dici tua vis, hoc eme, ne mea sint* . . . If you want the poems called mine, I'll send you them for nothing. If you want them called yours, buy out my ownership' (lines 3–4). Also 1.38, 1.53 and 1.72.

27. This may put us in a position to gloss the gnomic poem (4.10) in which Martial instructs his servant to deliver a freshly completed book of his poems to a friend:

> comitetur Punica librum
> spongea: muneribus convenit illa meis.
> non possunt nostros multae, Faustine, liturae
> emendare iocos: una litura potest

> Let a Punic sponge accompany the book; it suits my gift. Many erasures cannot mend my jests, Faustinus, but one erasure can. (lines 5–8)

Will the crucial emendation be the removal of Martial's name?

28. And see the remark in the dedicatory epistle of Volpone: 'My workes are read, allow'd, (I speake of those that are intirely mine).'

29. It's one of three in the same volume; the other two are *The Masque of Blacknesse* and *The Masque of Beautie.*

30. *The Haddington Masque*, lines 348–55.

31. Martial becomes one of the proprietary markers for Jonson, a kind of *ex libris*. Quotations from Martial appear on the title pages of three masques that appeared after the printing of the folio, masques whose publication seems to have been instigated and supervised by Jonson himself.

32. For a more sustained discussion of the conceptual structure of Martial's epi-gram, see chapter 3 of my *Jonson and Possessive Authorship* (Cambridge, 2002).

33. The kidnapping of slaves is actually one of the principal areas in which conflict arises about their status: as persons they were covered under the 'lex fabia de plagiariis', but as things their misappropriation could be treated as theft. It is perhaps worth noting that the analogy of book and slave gapes in the words of the poem. '*Plagiario pudorem*': the kidnapper will be *ashamed*, not guilty,

the book now not only a person but also merely a book, the misappropriation merely improper. Again, the disproportion of affect suits both slave and book – the slave usually standing lower *at law* than in the human environment in which he or she operated; the book a trivial thing, yet the source and object of uncanny affect for reader and writer and plagiarist.

34. I cite from the Loeb edition of D. R. Shackleton Bailey (Cambridge, Mass., 1993).

35. Since it was customary, if not quite compulsory, for manumitted slaves to take the *nomen* or both the *praenomen* and *nomen* of the man who had freed them, Martial figures in manumission a convention of enduring affiliation of poem to poet.

36. For a helpful summary of the available information concerning the phases of literary circulation, see Starr, 'The Circulation of Literary Texts'.

37. The most useful study of edition remains B. A. van Groningen's 'Εκδωσις', *Mnemosyne*, 4th series, 16 (1963), pp. 1–17.

38. See, for an eminent example, the last poem in the first book of Horace's *Epistles*.

39. For more on Daniel's work with Waterson, see chapter 4 of my *The Author's Due: Printing and the Prehistory of Copyright* (Chicago, 2002) and chapter 5 of my *Jonson and Possessive Authorship*.

CHAPTER TEN

The constitution of opinion and the pacification of reading

Steven N. Zwicker

My subject is the conduct of reading at the close of the seventeenth century, but I want to draw an arc over habits of reading from Renaissance humanism to the mid-eighteenth century in order to set the late seventeenth century within a broad chronology and continuum of social practices and intellectual protocols. Such a context will help us to understand the formation and the long history of reading practices as well as the habits of particular moments. It will also suggest why the creation and prizing of opinion – the recognition and the critique of opinion as a sphere of social exchange – should emerge simultaneously, late in the seventeenth century, with the fashioning of increasingly passive consumers of texts. Charting the confluence of reading and opinion allows us to explore relations between the consumption and production of texts and ideas, perhaps even to explain how and why different spheres of mental activity get articulated together. Indeed, the creation and valorization of opinion might be seen as intimately tied to and dependent on a pacification and mechanization of humanist habits of reading.

In *The Battle of the Books* Swift dramatized the contest between the ancients and the moderns, between learning and opinion, as armed conflict on the shelves of the royal library at St James's Palace.[1] But some of the most revealing sites of reading and opinion are not to be found within the confines of the library; they are to be discovered instead in the twinned localities of coffee house and theatre, those prized and feared localities of social and intellectual exchange so characteristic of late seventeenth-century London. Not, of course, that the theatre is peculiar to this moment, and even the origins of the coffee house should be dated earlier, to the interregnum rather than the Restoration,[2] but the confluence of theatre and coffee house in the late seventeenth century represented new possibilities for social and intellectual mixture and for the production, consumption and exchange of ideas. The late seventeenth-century coffee house was a site, at once commercial and sociable, for drink and talk and news and print. For us the fascination of this scene is the fluidity of its ingredients, the novelty, danger and attractions of exchange; but even the Londoners who were doing the talking and drinking, the performing and reading, understood the implications of their own moment; they were, after all, pretty relentlessly educated in its meaning by contemporary satire.

Indeed, by the 1690s satire and social commentary more than hint at the interdependence, even complicity, of contemporary intellectual and social habits. In the coffee house, fops and beaux revel in wit, joust for social distinction, and delight in the creation, display and application of opinion. Over a dish of politic or poetic coffee,

Painters, Fiddlers, Poets, Minor Authors, Beaux, and the rest of the illiterate Block-heads, promiscuously dissect the poor Play, to be sure of the Author's disadvantage. This, indeed, is the Scene of the Wits, where a pert young Fop (fresh come from the University, with his Head fuller of Notions and Authors Names than Sense, from seven Years poring over his Books, and the height of his reading, the indexes of those authors he names) shall pass for a profound Scholar. Another, that under-stands not so much English as to write a Billet-doux, shall, with the help of reading Mr. Rimer's Criticisms on the Plays of the last Age, the Translation of Theocritus, Mr. Dryden's Essays of Drammatic Poesis, or some of his Prefaces, give you Critical Observations on the Greek Poets; when all the Knowledge is of the Labours of those I have mention'd, or else from some old Translations which have served a Patriarch's age till discarded for the value of one single Penny.[3]

The scene is fopland, and the sketch a sharp send-up of theatrical culture, that much embattled territory of the 1690s; the satire takes aim within and beyond theatre and coffee house targeting a generation that debases learning, cribs from the ancients, cobbles together sentences, and hunts for opinion in digests, extracts and abridgements. The whole is a brilliant assemblage, but we might pause specifically over the fop's habits of reading, for these take us to the heart of intellectual culture c.1690. Vital to this moment are printed index and epitome; we are in the first age of the reader's digest; we have entered a world that prizes the monthly abstract of books.

Swift ridiculed *The Hind and the Panther* as that 'masterpiece of a famous writer now living [viz in the year 1698] intended for a complete abstract of sixteen thousand schoolmen from Scotus to Bellarmin',[4] but what Swift found so laughable in Dryden's digest of the church fathers, others made a point of pride. The history of learning could now be got out of books de-voted to abstracts of recent publications;[5] philosophy, mathematics, physic, history, philology and other arts and sciences – all were now available on a monthly, even a weekly, basis.[6] On a single-sheet broadside Hobbes's philosophy has been abstracted into an anthology of sentences;[7] with a single book in hand, readers might consult the wisdom of a generation, and booksellers boasted of volumes that would at once compress and inform, that would democratize learning, liberate the reader from the burden of long books, and please by variety and brevity.[8] The whole of learning could now be imagined as a kind of 'common theatre' for all and sundry readers,

> where every person may act or take such part as pleases him best, and what he does not like, he may pass over, assuring himself that every ones Judgment not being like his, another may choose what he mislikes, and so every one may be pleased in their Turns.[9]

In such a readerly world, where the aim was to please every taste – indeed, where the aim was pleasure itself – we should not be surprised to find that even night walkers were catalogued in print and published monthly ''till a discovery be made of all the chief prostitutes in England, from the Pensionary Miss, down to the Common Strumpet'.[10]

The 1690s are a decade of catalogues and compendia, of keys and codes, of paraphrases and translations. Fop and university wit take paratext for text, shell for substance, the name of learning and its accents for the thing itself. But the fop's methods are not merely adventitious: he combs the indices of books as a short cut to commonplaces and depends on translation and critical essay for the generation of what can only be called opinion. The irony in the satiric sketch of the coffee house is sparked not by potted wisdom – the commonplace is, after all, as old, as venerable, as humanism itself – but by the fraudulent getting of sentences. The image of the fop hunting mechanically for places and lifting opinions from others neatly juxtaposes older methods of learning with the new; the fop is a figure that might just remind us of Swift's brilliant caricature of Dr Bentley, that worthy modern whose learning is 'patched up of a thousand incoherent pieces' lifted from index and lexicon.[11] Indeed we might take the figure skimming indices as an emblem of the technologies of reading *c*.1700.

Of course, patching together 'a thousand incoherent pieces' was no new readerly practice. For generations, schoolboys had been taught to annotate while they read, to draw wisdom from the printed page, to mark and transfer choice sentences from text to manuscript commonplace book where quotation and paraphrase would be mixed and newly framed under various topical schemes.[12] Commonplacing was practised across the social spectrum of early modern literacy and over the whole of the early modern period. It urged a close and particular attentiveness to the text, enforcing a readerly dialectic between consumption and production. Commonplacing prized the syntax of moral example and aphorism, of epithet and precept, and everywhere it called for the active participation of the reader as transcriber, collector, indeed collaborator in the work of recording, circulating, even fashioning the texts of antiquity and modernity. What we have come to appreciate from recent work on the various modes of manuscript and print publication in the Renaissance is how active were the processes of early modern reading, how intimate the relations between writing and reading,[13] how implicated in the dynamic of production was consumption, and not only because consumption always creates a field of expectations in which writing is imagined and into which texts are issued but because the practices of humanist learning made the work of commonplacing and annotation almost second nature to reading itself.

And such habits are shared broadly across two centuries and more. Commonplacing and annotation were fostered by the educational practices of sixteenth-century humanism and they flourished throughout the seventeenth century; even as late as the mid-eighteenth century we can find Samuel Johnson scolding readers out of their old commonplacing habits.[14] But the move away from extractive reading began well before Johnson's urging. By the end of the seventeenth century we can already detect the waning of humanist habits: printed index and epitome have begun to short-circuit manuscript annotation, and the printed commonplace book itself has appeared as a strong alternative to the manuscript compilation.[15] In 1673 Marvell's *Rehearsal Transpros'd* was advertised in the form of 'A Common Place-Book digested under [the] heads of his Logic, Chronology, Wit, Geography, Anatomy, History, and Loyalty',[16] and in 1697 Locke published a commonplace book to the Bible.[17]

It had not been so long since the university wit would have gathered sentences from his own reading. In 1660 we can still hear a father sagely, though perhaps in a nostalgic mood, counsel his son to

Read seriously whatever is before you, and reduce and digest it to practice and observation...Trust not to your Memory, but put all remarkable, notable things you shall meet with in your Books under the sound care of Pen and Ink, but so alter the property by your own Scholia and Annotations on it, that your memory may speedily recur to the place it was committed to.[18]

By the 1690s, the world of humanist annotation is in eclipse, crowded out by other kinds of marking and other methods of reading and recalling. What had been a practice once devoted to the creation of a mind stocked with a fund of commonplaces, a communal system of wisdom, had been transformed into a method that liberated opinion from the labour of its production and valued mere difference and distinction. From Swift's point of view the failure of modern commonplacing was not the commonplace itself, not Bentley armed with a thousand incoherent pieces, but the absence of learning that underpins and might render coherent a scattering of commonplaces. The coffee house wit is taken to task not for the possessing of commonplaces, but for his ways of getting them, and for habits of reading that make the index central to modern learning, that liberate opinion from knowledge, and that translate wit from the very synonym of learning and wisdom into mere virtuosity and archness:

Wit, without knowledge, being a sort of cream, which gathers in a night to the top, and by a skilful hand may be soon whipped into froth; but once scummed away, what appears underneath will be fit for nothing but to be thrown to the hogs.[19]

Not, of course, that such liberation derived simply from printed index and digest, or that index and epitome were inventions of the late seventeenth century. Abstract and epitome had long been features of the trade in law books and histories; what is notable is the growth, late in the seventeenth century, in the volume and variety of abstracted learning. And the valorization of opinion was driven by other intellectual currents, by a growth of the sceptical habits and particularist techniques of science, by the rise of news and the widening bases of literacy, and perhaps most by the proliferation of dissenting practices of reading and interpretation that prized individual conscience and personal applications of Scripture. Heterodox beliefs and intellectual habits flourished from the time of the Reformation and they created repeated outbursts of religious and social controversy. The cultural contests staged in the Marprelate tracts of the late sixteenth century derived from Reformation impulses, as did the crises over Laudian practice in the 1630s and perhaps even the fury over popery in the 1680s; and these crises stimulated a variety of political, literary and religious dissent.

But in the world of Renaissance humanism dissident reading was a minority practice, balanced against other impulses and examples. The more important and by far the more dominant models of Renaissance literary consumption, and the more prominent intellectual features within a broad field of readerly habits and protocols, were imitation, exemplarity and admiration.[20] The detailed portraits we possess of Renaissance humanists argue not simply the active and applied agency of the intellect, but an overarching model of exemplarity that guided the reading of courtiers, aristocrats and connoisseurs, and of their professional servants and protégés.[21] Exemplary reading – the careful study of texts for patterns of virtue, the imbibing of classical wisdom, and the exportation of models of conduct and expression – was reinforced by a culture of imitation which spread far beyond the study or the diplomatic and courtly conference. Imitation and admiration inhabited the schoolroom and the rhetorical handbook, they informed literary experimentation, and they animated the creation of a rhetorical culture of extravagance and amplification that we see everywhere in late sixteenth-century literary performance, in Spenser's *Hymns* and *The Faerie Queene*, in the Elizabethan sonnet sequences, and in the burgeoning miscellanies, songbooks and madrigals.[22] These texts evidence a particular node of cultural style and literary habit, a kind of complicity between consuming and producing, of reading for wonder, for admiration and imitation, and of writing into that very market. But modes of reading and writing not only inform one another in and through the economy of demand and supply – though that is surely an important economy – but also create a nexus of social and psychological circumstances shared by all those who read and wrote, circumstances transformed by the challenges and upheavals of civil contest that took place in the mid-seventeenth century.

By the time of the civil wars, the habits of religious contest and cultural dissent fostered by Reformation controversy had spread far beyond the materials of religion itself. Acts of dissent and distinction, of all kinds, were marked, with increasing vehemence, on the pages of printed texts, and in succeeding decades such marking grew boldly to dominate annotation as the conflagration of opinion and arms swept across decades of civil war and political experimentation. The civil wars loosed a tide of verbal and physical contest that found its way into every corner of social, political and intellectual life and translated habits of admiring, annotating and absorbing texts into acts of contest and combat. Reading, indeed, had been transformed from the work of exemplarity and admiration into the assertion of distinction and difference, and marginal annotation became a skill not in identifying, acquiring and replicating the wisdom of the text, but in asserting, contesting and denying mere opinion. The great cataclysm of the mid-seventeenth century tipped the intellectual balance so that exemplarity no longer remained in tension with animadversion but was overwhelmed and transformed by anger and partisanship.

Hobbes argued that the civil wars were born out of the unsupervised reading of classical texts,[23] and whatever the analytical force of the argument, the perception of the polemical, indeed revolutionary, power of reading is undeniably important. What distinguished the heirs of humanism in the growing turbulence of the 1630s and 1640s, and in the nervous and disillusioned decades that followed, was the willingness not only to abandon sweet similitude and sage sentence, but to press controverting habits well beyond the tracks of religious controversy where they had been so deeply laid by the Reformation, to cover with increasingly hostile response a broad field of texts, to arm and intensify annotation – indeed, at points, almost to flood with suspicion and hostility an entire marketplace of texts from broadside and pamphlet (where we might well expect the mark of controversy) to song and strophic ode.[24]

The years of civil war and republican triumph afford a multitude of examples of reading as anatomy and destruction, but no text demonstrates the assumptions and techniques of reading as combat more effectively than Milton's response to Charles I's *Eikon Basilike*.[25] Milton engaged the king's book chapter by chapter; he contested the king's text phrase by phrase, at times word by word. *Eikonoklastes* decried the habits and materials of Royalist reading, challenging a king who favoured the reading of play texts over the scripts of statecraft. Nor was Milton satisfied with an attack solely on the intellectual habits of Charles I; he aimed to spread the argument beyond the king's closet, to address not only the vacuity of royal reading but to ridicule all those who read by adoring the false images, conceited portraiture and 'quaint emblems and devices begg'd from...some Twelf-nights entertainment at Whitehall' that, for Milton, characterized the king's text.[26] His close and strenuous address to the *Eikon Basilike* may suggest the force of humanist training, but nothing could be further from the affect of *Eikonoklastes* than admiration and exemplarity.

It may not be surprising that books of such notoriety as the *Eikon Basilike* drew the attention of readers armed for combat. But if the practice of contestative reading were exclusive to such programmatic texts we would extend our understanding of only one aspect of civic culture. In fact, what we witness through the decades of civil war, republicanism and Restoration is a wholesale transformation of intellectual practices, of reading as suspicion and combat applied to a wide range of texts and textual practices. Once the field of reading had been transformed into a territory of combat, it was impossible to imagine it, and to experience it, otherwise. What Milton had done to *Eikon Basilike* might be the very model for the reading of a broad range of texts and forms, though perhaps in cooler and more oblique ways. And evidence of contestative reading exists not only in published acts of hostility and suspicion; combat and contest also mark the work of less articulate expressions of reading – acts that took place in the margins of books and between lines of print, at times even over the printed line itself, and at times over other marginalia in the form of deeply incised cross-hatching which aimed to efface and obliterate.[27] And when such reading intended more than obliteration, it contested and engaged through correction, denial and repudiation. Throughout the years of the Civil War and for decades thereafter marginal annotation – itself, as we have seen, a venerable humanist practice – turned partisan and harshly polemical. Insults were scrawled across title pages, scandals were cast on 'schismatics' and 'delinquents', aspersions were written on flyleaves and up and down the sides of pages.[28] Politics drove the consumption of texts and writing was absorbed to 'partie Projects'.[29] Books from these years were covered with signs of active reading, but they no longer gave evidence of a commonwealth of meanings; they exemplified rather a world of politics, partisanship and passions.

Although the pressures of partisanship would change, they would not get any simpler when the strenuous republicanism of the 1650s gave way to that force field of ironies and brutalities that constituted Restoration culture.[30] It is possible to see the rise of party politics over the course of the Restoration as a civilizing innovation, a gradual reduction of the stakes of political combat from armed conflict to paper skirmish, but we should not exaggerate the rapidity with which civic violence was translated into mere partisanship, or a consequent sense of diminished dangers or diminished stakes for the invention, publication, distribution and reading of texts. On 17 August 1681 Stephen College was brought to trial on charges of high treason; the next day a jury proclaimed him guilty, and by the end of August College had been drawn on a hurdle to the gates before the castle at Oxford and there 'hung by the neck, cut down alive, his privy members cut off, his bowels taken out and burnt before his face, his head cut off from his body, and his body divided into four quarters'.[31] All as a consequence of the writing, singing and publicly distributing of a ballad called 'A Raree Show'.[32] The trial of Stephen College aimed to demonstrate not only the authority of the Crown and the force of its justice, but also the high stakes of writing and reading in the aftermath of the Exclusion Crisis. Nor was College the only victim of such a campaign. Algernon Sidney was also trapped and destroyed by writings that gave supposed evidence of 'compassing and imagining' the death of the king; in Sidney's case the writing was private, a manuscript seized from Sidney's closet, but any words on paper, Lord Justice Jeffreys demonstrated, might be read into dangerous places.[33]

If anything, both manuscript and print in the Restoration are ever more closely and overtly implicated in politics and the field of reading more volatile. The dense topicality of civic texts is one sign of that implication; more broadly, the entire culture of hints and allusions, of masking, allegory and innuendo, suggests the intimate, at times claustrophobic, relations among readers and texts in a world where narratives, histories and poems became significant party players, and where not only the writing, producing and circulating of texts might be driven by party allegiance but where reading itself took place under bold new party signs:

> 'Tis not my intention to make an apology for my poem; some will think it needs no excuse, and others will receive none. The design, I am sure is honest; but he who draws his pen for one party must expect to make enemies of the other. For wit and fool are consequents of Whig and Tory; and every man is a knave or an ass to the contrary side. There is a treasury of merits in the Fanatic Church, as well as in the Papist; and a pennyworth to be had of honesty, and poetry, for the lewd, the factious, and the blockheads; but the longest chapter in Deuteronomy has not curses enough for an anti-Bromingham. My comfort is, their manifest prejudice to my cause will render their judgement of less authority against me.[34]

So Dryden began, with a kind of mock wariness, and hidden behind a veil of anonymity (a veil that functioned more to excite and exasperate than to conceal), the author's 'apology' to *Absalom and Achitophel*. We have come in recent years to appreciate what Dryden's contemporaries knew instinctively – that the dialectical arrangements and arguments of the preface define and seize on moderation as a sanctioned political ground, and that they do so both to anticipate and to disarm, insofar as they can, suspicions against moderation as mere rhetoric. And we also understand the ways in which Dryden's mixture of generic signals in preface and poem allowed him to cast a kind of plasticity of form and ambiguity of literary kind over the whole of his proceedings so that no single genre might seem to dominate or delimit the poet's strategies and, in turn, the readers' responses.

But what modern students of Dryden's text have not fully appreciated is the work that this preface also performs in anatomizing, in attempting to override, and finally in accepting the force of partisanship as the very principle of reading in the midst of political crisis. From its opening gestures – its denial of the aims of apology, its acknowledgement that partisanship has divided the reading public, its urging of aesthetic primacy and innocence – the preface would both comprehend and override the fact that partisanship creates readers and that ideology inhabits the aesthetic. The poet in Dryden argues that the sweetness of good verse disarms its victims, but there is little evidence among contemporary readers of this poem that aesthetics as such had much to do with the reception of *Absalom and Achitophel* or that any of the victims of Dryden's brilliant cartooning forgave the sweetness of his savagery.[35] And the polemicist in Dryden not only understood but both mocked and articulated the ways in which Whig and Tory allegiance had come to organize the very idea of the aesthetic. Though Dryden claims to discount the tow of partisanship in the creation of his poem – he aimed only to please the 'honest' middle – everything about the texts of *Absalom and Achitophel* seems pitched into the political divide. What the record of response indicates is the intricate and enduring ways in which the aesthetic was imbedded within the partisan, and the ways in which partisanship created, from Dryden's point of view, neither political wisdom nor statecraft but mere opinion. 'Stiff with opinions, always in the wrong', so Dryden wrote of the duke of Buckingham, chief strategist of Exclusion, and the sting of his language was meant as a rebuke at once to the intellectual vacuity, the aesthetic incoherence and the political folly of a man reduced by restless vanity and variety to a mere laughing-stock.

That brew of partisanship and opinion are the very circumstance not only of this masterpiece of Tory argument but of the conditions of reading *c*.1681 and of the crisis years that followed. In the preface to his poem, Dryden turned, over and over, the meaning of the absorption of reading to mere opinion. Although he had begun to learn this lesson in the texts of literature and politics from the mid-1660s onwards, nothing demonstrated its force better than the Popish Plot and Exclusion. The events of the Plot were spun out narratives, depositions, transcripts, pamphlets and prophecies. The capacity of Whig publicists to turn a paper crisis into a pitched political battle over the succession to the throne demonstrates the degree to which the partisan production, circulation and consumption of texts might determine the fate of the political nation. This Dryden understood exactly in his calculating definition of the 'honesty party' for whom he claims to have crafted his poem; but the ways in which Dryden's poem was marked by readers raises a question as to whether there were any honest – in the sense of non-partisan – readers.[36] Nor did the effort to achieve honest readers have much success in the years that followed, when such crises as the Rye House Plot, the Trial of the Seven Bishops and finally and most critically the Glorious Revolution divided, rescripted and redefined the reading nation. In such a climate we should not be surprised by the work that readers performed with and on books of Dryden's poetry and prose. The annotation of his work went on not only in the crisis years of the 1680s but also after the Glorious Revolution, when Dryden's literary identity came to be constituted out of his religious and literary politics: his conversion to Rome, his sustained, if weary, allegiance to the Stuart cause and his status as defanged literary lion of the 1690s.

Listen, as one reader who dated his annotation 16 August 1696 takes Dryden's sly, concessive and ironic description of King David as a mere

'Officer in Trust' and rebukes the text: 'in Eng: the Law makes them so and no more'.[37] Another reader of the 1690s marked his copy of Dryden's *Discourse Concerning Satire* with a series of sarcastic rejoinders.[38] Where Dryden wrote of fame, 'in it self a real good, if we may believe Cicero who was perhaps too fond of it', the marginal note reads, 'Not fonder of it than Mr. Dryden – nor halfe so fulsom'. When Dryden points to the work he must do to 'give the Definition and Character of true Satires', the reader snipes, 'He means his own!' When Dryden apologizes to Dorset for his digressive manner, 'By this time, My Lord, I doubt not but that you wonder, why I have run off from by Biass so long together', the word 'wonder' is underscored, and the reader comments, 'And well He might, had not his Lordship known your Vanity!' When Dryden writes of Juvenal's tenth Satire, 'But this, tho' the Wittiest of all his Satires, has yet the least of Truth or Instruction in it', the manuscript hand intrudes, 'Forgive me (Mr Dryden) if I am of opinion that you think otherwise.'

Nor of course do Dryden's texts provide the only such opportunities. In his copy of Bacon's *Advancement of Learning*, Defoe recorded his smart rejoinders to the Lord Chancellor.[39] Bacon wrote of James I, 'there hath not beene since Christ's time any king or temporall Monarch which hath been so learned and humane', and Defoe comments, 'Who but a blind sot cou'd brook such and so much gross flattery !! or who could think, that of all men, a Bacon shou'd prove such a sycophant.' And when Bacon cites learned authority in his text, Defoe remarks, 'Can there be a greater pedantry than this frequent quoting of Latin. But his Patron was a Royal pedant and he therefore aped him.' And if we look at the texts of explicitly political writing, we note similar rejoinders, expostulations and exceptions. James Tyrrell's Exclusion Crisis tract, *Patriarcha Non Monarcha*, is sharply applied, by manuscript annotation, to the 1690s: 'Mark those which doat on Arbitrary power,' one reader observes, 'and you'll find them either hot brain'd fools; or needy bankrupts.'[40] Henry Wharton's *Specimen of Some Errors and Defects in the History of the Reformation of the Church* (1693) is, in one copy, marked throughout with cross-hatching and arch corrections, and on the fly leaf of a copy of the *Dialogue at Oxford* (1681) one reader asserts:

Whosoever reads over this Booke, may easily perceive, that the Author of it is an insolent, audacious, Republican fellow, who takes upon him to affront his Soveraigne; & hath written this piece, as an intended Answer to his Majesties Declaration publish't after his having dissolved Parliament at Oxford; & is, in it, very desirous to argue the English Monarchy into a Venetian Republike, or less, if he could.[41]

Books are issued into a hostile world, full of rejoinder, of censure, contempt and ridicule.

And of course not only texts but also authors came to be constituted and refashioned for readers by political forces and partisan perceptions. We might think that Andrew Marvell was first constituted a poet not in the gardens and meadows of Nun Appleton but by the publication in 1681 of a folio of his verse, supposedly got into print and authorized by his 'widow', but without question a product of those who would promote the cultural elevation and respectability of Whiggery and antipopery in the midst of Exclusion.[42] The contemporary force of the volume is surely attested to by the printer's cancellation of the three Cromwell poems from the folio. Whether the poems were cancelled at the urging of friends to Marvell's memory who may not have wished the image of Cromwell too closely associated with the designs of late seventeenth-century toleration, or at the insistence of a government that may have seen the celebration of the Lord Protector as a threat to Stuart monarchy, the potency of Cromwell's name and the dangers of reading its celebration, even two decades after Cromwell's death, could not be doubted.

Nor was Milton, in the 1660s and again in 1688 and in the 1690s and beyond, any less than Andrew Marvell, constituted and reconstituted by publishers, booksellers and readers. In 1667 the poet and his epic were deeply entangled by the reputation of republicanism and regicide;[43] booksellers of impeccably dissenting credentials put *Paradise Lost* to sale;[44] and only gradually was 'Milton' removed from the turmoil and tensions of partisanship. In 1688 the commissioning by Jacob Tonson of a set of plates for a new edition of *Paradise Lost* and his offering of the sumptuous folio for sale by subscription were efforts to aestheticize and surely to elevate the reputation of the old radical; the willingness of readers to enroll their names in a subscription list that cut across political parties and cultural divides works a similar socialization of poet and text.[45] John Toland's biography of 1699 spiritualized Milton and rendered him a hero of liberty, and further separated the poet from the radical publicist.[46] The final pacification of *Paradise Lost* and the utter removal of the poet from the turmoil of seventeenth-century politics were effected by Joseph Addison in a series of essays for the *Spectator*, which rendered safe and respectable, indeed polite, the once radical poet and his text.[47]

In 1667 the episcopal licenser Thomas Tomkins smelled treason lurking in the corners of Milton's poem; Tomkins's responsiveness to the text is a compelling illustration of the ways in which partisanship typed reading and reputation in the 1660s.[48] No less, Addison's classicizing and moralizing of

the poem in the early eighteenth century, his concentration on taste, sentiment and politeness – on its 'most exquisite Words and finest Strokes'[49] –
demonstrate the transformation of *Paradise Lost* from a dangerous script of
literary radicalism to a repository of timeless aesthetic values which required
not the engagement of the political capacities of the reader as subject and
citizen but the discovery and assent to beauty and sensibility.[50] And how
perfectly one John Gay, an early eighteenth-century reader (but not likely
the poet of that name), performs in this capacity when he annotates his
copy of *Paradise Lost*, marking not politics and treason but aesthetics, and
not his own responses but opinions gleaned from others, from Milton's
late seventeenth- and early eighteenth-century editors: Benson, Bentley,
Helyn, Hume and Newton.[51] Gay's system was to insert, together with an
abbreviation of the editor's name, a system of letters indicating the good,
the bad and the beautiful: 'b' for 'bene', 'm' for 'male' and 'p' for 'pulchre'.
It is nearly impossible to imagine a reader in 1667 conceiving of the work
of reading *Paradise Lost* in such terms, and it is equally unlikely for this
eighteenth-century reader – intent on the cultivation and collation of taste
and the identification of opinion – to have detected the treason so lightly
veiled for Thomas Tompkins in Milton's language of disastrous eclipses and
fallen monarchies.

Nor is it difficult to see that the point of transit between politics and
aesthetics, between argument and opinion, might be located in the very
coffee house where fop and university wit fashioned their own aesthetics out
of received opinion, out of Rymer on the theatre, out of Dryden on dramatic
poetry, and out of scanned lists and indices, prefaces and translations. The
formation of a Whig aesthetic, of a canon and market for Whig culture, is
the creation of a certain kind of editing, book making and reading, but it
was also, and we might well expect this of the late seventeenth century, the
product of contest with the texts and totems of Royalism and loyalism. And
yet at the very heart of this enterprise, and at a moment that seems to exult
in opinion, the marginal comment, the act that challenges the text, that
liberates – indeed, we might think, generates – opinion, is itself challenged
by the growing complexity of the printed page in which notes and textual
apparatus (once reserved for the humanist edition of classical texts), now
set in type, subsume and mechanize manuscript contestation, and in so
doing seem to predict, and participate in, a pacification of reading.

Renaissance books are crowded with underscoring, nota benes and pointing fingers that signal an active participation in the text, the inclusion of
the reader, by way of manuscript note and commonplace book, in the production of wisdom. By the early eighteenth century, the printed page has

absorbed a number of these acts, and it features print mechanisms to ease the way, typography designed to encourage skipping and skimming. In the preface to a book on gardening, the author announces that he has devised, just as his book went to press, a method to allow those that

> do not care for what relates to Geometry . . . to read only what the Table or Margin will shew him to be most for his use. And lest the nicest Reader should have any occasion to complain, and think it too great a trouble for him to chuse what he may read, and what he may pass over, I have all along set, in the Margin, some Commas, over against such places, as any one, not skilled in Mathematicks, may freely avoid.[52]

Of course the pointing fist is a venerable typographical tradition, but here the marking seems designed not to call attention to what should be noted but to allow the bored or indifferent reader to skip the detail. And John Arbuthnot's comic dialogue, *The Invitation to Peace*, gives a wonderfully self-conscious instance of the growth of just such print apparatus:

> Lastly we do insist, that the Englishman, alias Ironsides, do at his own Expence cause forthwith to be printed, a new Edition of Cato, with a large Margin, and a Hand in the said Margin, pointing to such Lines in the said Play, which in any way belong to the D. of M. and also there shall be another Hand of a different make, which shall declare what Lines in the said Play do belong to Us, or to our Kinsman and early ally Abel Roper.[53]

Nor should it surprise us that Swift, another ally of Arbuthnot, would, even at the beginning of his career, understand how much of the work of supervisor and simulator of reading he, as author, would have to perform in and through his text. In *The Battle of the Books* he adopted the disinterested, slightly dim voice of the bookseller to arrange a fastidiously neutral setting for his pamphlet; then he supplied ironic footnotes with which to needle the reader; and finally he arranged gaps in the text itself got up with smart scholarly apparatus and brief Latin tags to indicate missing patches of text, lacunae that supposedly rendered inconclusive the final disposition of that great battle between the ancients and the moderns.[54] But who could have been in doubt about the losing rearguard action that the ancients fought in the world of opinion, vanity and folly that for Swift comprised modernity in the 1690s? And how symptomatic that Swift should have set at the centre of his superb allegory the figures of Criticism and Opinion, daughters to Ignorance and Pride – the father 'blind with age', the mother dressed up 'in the scraps of paper herself had torn'. In this family constellation, it was to the portrait of Opinion, that constant muse of modernity, that Swift gave his most brilliant turn:

There was Opinion her sister, light of foot, hoodwinked, headstrong, yet giddy and perpetually turning. About her played her children, Noise and Impudence, Dulness and Vanity, Positiveness, Pedantry, and Ill-Manners. The goddess herself had claws like a cat, her head, and ears, and voice resembled those of an ass, her teeth fallen out before, her eyes turned inward as if she looked only upon herself.[55]

Though Swift would deny the debts he owed to Dryden in the analysis of opinion (and elsewhere), they are obvious enough; equally clear is the example that Swift gave here, and in *A Tale of a Tub*, with its layered prefaces and mock footnotes, its anonymous editorializing and its printed marginalia, to Pope, who became absolute master of print apparatus, the writer who would learn most exquisitely to play every angle of the printed page. There is no text more brilliant in its deployment of print annotation than *The Dunciad*; on its pages Pope ventriloquized all the roles of production and consumption: author, editor, reader, annotator, misconstruer, impartial critic. In 1681 Dryden had produced a political allegory that caught the attention of a generation of readers. As we have seen, a number of the surviving copies of *Absalom and Achitophel* are covered with manuscript notes indicating the English identities of the poet's scriptural politicians, hacks and tools. But by the late 1720s Pope could not rely on the device of initial letters and hints in order to engage the reader in his gallery of dunces. The 1728 edition of *The Dunciad* deploys exactly such devices, and Swift remarked of that edition,

The Notes I could wish to be very large, in what relates to the persons concerned; for I have long observed that twenty miles from London no body understands hints, initial letters, or town-facts and passages; and in a few years not even those who live in London.[56]

Dryden had perfectly calculated the effect of his poem; he knew that every veiled identity would induce the interventions of curiosity, gossip and scandal. Pope might have wished for such a readerly culture, but he understood the changes that had occurred; his *Dunciad Variorum* leaves nothing to readerly chance. Pope claimed that the 1728 edition was unauthorized and that to correct errors and avoid misunderstandings Lawton Gilliver had printed a corrected text with identities revealed.[57] Perhaps there were legal reasons to print the concealed names, but I suspect Pope feared that the initial letters and hints, rather than produce legal action, might well induce boredom, passivity and indifference.

Of course the transformations of social and intellectual culture are never quite so steady and seamless as we might hope; even as late as the 1760s

Samuel Johnson was scolding those readers who note important passages and strong arguments in their books and

load their minds with superfluous attention, repress the vehemence of curiosity by useless deliberation, and by frequent interruption break the current of narration . . . and at last close the volume, and forget the passages and the marks together.[58]

The key to Johnson's passage is surely the phrase 'current of narration', for the novel, that now dominant literary form, demanded a new kind of readerly attention, one which imagined the work of reading not as the humanist production of commonplaces, or the partisan expostulation of opinion, but as the internalization of narrative and the expression of feeling. For that work, it is hardly surprising that different sites and techniques of reading would need to emerge. The novel demanded fluency and rapidity of consumption; its narrative arc had transformed plot from a space marked and dwelled within, a site that invited accretion and repetition,[59] to a dimension of time, experienced not as territory but as movement, and noted not by the marking pen but, if at all, by the moving finger.

Although we must be careful to understand and evaluate as emblematic and expressive the rhetoric of representation, we can gauge this transformation of both the geographies and techniques of reading if we follow the visual record. The most familiar site of Renaissance reading is the scholar's closet or study.[60] Surrounded by the equipment of reading – by oil lamps, pens, penknives, inkpot and scissors, by sand, eraser-knife and paper, and most of all by books, books with their fore-edges turned outward to display the identity of the text, books casually strewn on the work table, books actively marked, books tagged with pieces of paper, held open to points of reference, displayed to reveal a text or a collation of texts – the reader sits amidst his work. And in our apprehension of the Renaissance reader the emphasis should properly fall both on the masculine gender of the reader and on all the signs of his engagement, the work in which aristocrat, saint or scholarly male is repeatedly and typically engaged in these portraits.[61] Not only is the book an emblem of masculine and aristocratic authority; the reader's engagement with the text demonstrates the signs of those actions which we can discover from other traces of reading: from the annotations, commonplace books and manuscript compilations that are the practices and products of humanist reading and scholarship.

And how differently the reader emerges from the eighteenth-century visual record. The book has now fallen away from the hands and portrait postures of English aristocrats, figures most often displayed not reading the texts out of which they might have once composed their intellectual authority but surveying the real properties out of which they constitute their social identity. Of course readers have not wholly disappeared from the visual record, but he and she are now rather to be discovered in more casual sites and circumstances, within different domestic spaces, and, most emblematically, out of doors, alone and with a single book in hand, the reader intent not on the collation of texts but on the scripts of the book and nature as alternative and intermingled ways of narrating the self.

The eighteenth-century reader has not, however, wholly disappeared from the congress of society; we should not forget the circulation of texts through the coffee house in eighteenth-century London, nor should we neglect the importance of the theatre for the ways in which it mingled texts and spectators and helped to fashion and replicate new technologies of reading. Indeed, where better to observe the new fashions of reading than in the scripts of the eighteenth-century theatre, in Sheridan's plays, for example, which are so attentive to the circulation of language through gossip, newsletter and book, and so observant of new techniques of reading which privileged not the commonplacing pen but the 'observing thumb'. In this world one character might remark of another that the books she borrows from the circulating library reveal the presence of the previous reader who 'cherishes her nails for the convenience of making marginal notes'.[62] From pen, and ink, and sand, from all the studied equipment of humanist reading, we have come to reading as the articulation of a fingernail. This is a scene that Swift, for his own dyspeptic reasons, would have cherished; but it is as well a superb and expressive emblem of the ways in which form and technology, novel and novel reading, are so exactly, so beautifully, expressive of one another. The site, the work, even the gender of reading have been transformed from the strenuous, masculine world of the humanist schoolroom to the leisured boudoir of the novel reader intent less on the production of learning than on the generation of feeling and opinion.[63]

NOTES

1. J. Swift, *A Full and True Account of the Battel Fought Last Friday, between the Antient and the Modern Books in St James's Library*, ed. A. Ross and D. Woolley (Oxford, 1984); Swift wrote the pamphlet in the late 1690s and published it in 1704.
2. See S. Pincus, ' "Coffee Politicians Does Create": Coffeehouses and Restoration Political Culture', *Journal of Modern History*, 67 (1995), pp. 807–34.
3. *The Humours and Conversations of the Town, Expos'd in Two Dialogues. The First, of the Men. The Second, of the Women* (London, 1693), pp. 105–6.

4. J. Swift, *A Tale of a Tub*, ed. A. C. Guthkelch and D. Nichol Smith (Oxford, 1920), p. 69.
5. See *The History of Learning, or An Abstract of Several Books Lately Published, as Well Abroad, as at Home* (London, 1691); or *The History of the Works of the Learned, or An Impartial Account of Books Lately Printed in All Parts of Europe. With a Particular Relation of the State of Learning in Each Country. For the Month of January, 1699. Done by Several Hands* (London, 1699).
6. See the *Gentleman's Journal, or The Monthly Miscellany* (London, 1692–4), which mixes news, history, philosophy, poetry, music and translation; or *The Politics of Europe, or A Rational Journal Concerning the Present Affairs of the Time... Now Published Every Saturday in a Single Sheet* (London, 1690–1).
7. *Memorable Sayings of Mr Hobbes in His Books and at the Table* (London, 1680).
8. See, too, the argument against the reading of long books in *Aesop at Tunbridge* (London, 1698), sig. A2r: 'Whosoever would be sure of Pleasing must not be tedious; it happens but to a few great Books to be read through; and many good Authors have defeated their own purpose of instructing the world, by frightening the Reader with three or four hundred Pages'; or the epitome made of Boyle's works, *The Works of the Honourable Robert Boyle... Epitomiz'd* (London, 1699), which is prefaced by a defence of the epitome, sig. B2r: 'Although it is the general consent of all learned men, that the Author's Works deserve the highest esteem... yet it is as common a complaint that long apologies and too frequent excursions interspers'd through his writings make 'em less serviceable to vulgar readers, who are unable to carry his sense along with them.'
9. *The History of Learning*, p. 2.
10. *The Night Walker, or Evening Rambles in Search after Lewd Women* (London, 1696).
11. Swift, *The Battle of the Books*, p. 17; see also the attack on modern learning in *A Tale of a Tub*, p. 131: 'we of this age have discovered a shorter and more prudent method to become schollars and wits, without the fatigue of reading or of thinking. The most accomplished way of using books at present is twofold; either first, to serve them as some men do lords, learn their titles exactly and then brag of their acquaintance. Or secondly, which is indeed the choicer, the profounder, and politer method, to get a thorough insight into the index, by which the whole book is governed and turned, like fishes by the tail.'
12. For commonplacing and the Renaissance reader, see T. Cave, 'Problems of Reading in the *Essais*', in I. D. McFarlane and I. Maclean, eds., *Montaigne: Essays in Memory of Richard Sayce* (Oxford, 1982), pp. 136–7.
13. See P. Beal, *In Praise of Scribes: Manuscripts and Their Makers in Seventeenth-Century England* (Oxford, 1998); A. F. Marotti, *Manuscript, Print, and the English Renaissance Lyric* (Ithaca and London, 1995); and H. Love, *Scribal Publication in Seventeenth-Century England* (Oxford, 1993). Of course, at the lower ends of literacy, writing and reading were not invariably on intimate terms and sometimes not linked at all; see K. Thomas, 'The Meaning of Literacy in Early Modern England', in G. Baumann, ed., *The Written Word:*

Literacy in Transition (Oxford, 1986), p. 100, who points out that reading and writing were different skills in the Tudor period and that it was 'perfectly possible in the Tudor and early Stuart period for someone to be able to read print fluently, but to be quite incapable of deciphering a written document'.

14. S. Johnson, *Essays from the Rambler, Idler and Adventurer*, ed. W. J. Bate (New Haven, 1968), p. 231.

15. See A. Moss, *Printed Commonplace-Books and the Structuring of Renaissance Thought* (Oxford, 1996).

16. *A Commonplace-Book out of The Rehearsal Transpros'd* (London, 1673).

17. *A Commonplace-Book to the Bible* (London, 1697).

18. A. Douglas, *Instructions to a Son* (Edinburgh and London, 1661), pp. 101–4.

19. Swift, *The Battle of the Books*, p. 2.

20. For Renaissance imitation and admiration and on the twin themes of teaching and delight, see B. Weinberg, *A History of Literary Criticism in the Italian Renaissance* (Chicago, 1961); and R. R. Bolgar, *The Classical Heritage and Its Beneficiaries* (Cambridge, 1958), p. 329ff. But see also, for a more sceptical estimate of the Renaissance preoccupation with exemplarity, the essays collected in the *Journal of the History of Ideas*, 59/4 (October 1998), *The Renaissance Crisis of Exemplarity*.

21. See the work on Gabriel Harvey by Lisa Jardine and Anthony Grafton, ' "Studied for Action": How Gabriel Harvey Read His Livy', *Past and Present*, 129 (1990), pp. 30–78; William Sherman on John Dee, *John Dee: The Politics of Reading and Writing in the English Renaissance* (Amherst, Mass., 1995); and Kevin Sharpe on Sir William Drake, *Reading Revolutions: The Politics of Reading in Early Modern England* (New Haven and London, 2000).

22. Terence Cave provides the best introduction to the rhetoric and arts of Renaissance copia, *The Cornucopian Text: Problems of Writing in the French Renaissance* (Oxford, 1979).

23. *Behemoth* (London, 1679), p. 38: 'For 'tis a hard matter for Men who do all think highly of their own Wits (when they have also acquired the Learning of the University) to be perswaded, that they want any ability requisite for the Government of a Commonwealth, especially having read the glorious Histories, and the sententious Politiques of the ancient popular Governments of the Greeks and Romans, amongst whom Kings were hated, and branded with the name of Tyrants, and Popular Government (though no Tyrant was ever so cruel as a Popular Assembly) passed by the name of a Liberty.'

24. See R. A. Beddard, 'A Traitor's Gift: Hugh Peter's Donation to the Bodleian Library', *Bodleian Library Record*, 16 (April 1999), pp. 374–91, which documents the disillusionment with humanist education in the 1650s: 'As a senior member of Merton College, Anthony Wood had closely followed the menacing dispute. He bound in one volume many of the pamphlets in the controversy, and labelled it, "For and against, humane learning".'

25. See S. N. Zwicker, 'Milton, Marvell, and the Politics of Reading c. 1649', in A. Boesky and M. T. Crane, *Form and Reform in Renaissance England* (Newark, Del., 2000), pp. 288–305.

26. *Eikonoklastes* is cited from *Complete Prose Works of John Milton*, vol. 3, ed. M. Y. Hughes (New Haven, 1962), p. 343.

27. See, for example, the Folger Library copy, P4109, of W. Prynne, *The Treachery and Disloyalty of Papists to Their Soveraignes* (London, 1643), which is marked by a score of marginal comments, each one defaced and rendered illegible.

28. See the Folger Library copies of Prynne's *New Discovery of the Prelate's Tyranny* (London, 1641), Folger Library copy, P4018; *Cabala, Mysteries of State* (London, 1654), Folger Library copy, C7175; and J. Vicars, *Former Ages Never Heard of, and After Ages Will admire, or A Brief Review of the Most Materiall Parliamentary Transactions* (London, 1656), a collection of eight pamphlets, Folger Library copy, V306.2

29. See W. Ashhurst, *Reasons against Agreement with a Late Printed Paper, Intituled, Foundations of Freedome* (London, 1648), p. 14: 'But let us lay aside this Paper, and all dividing and partie Projects'.

30. See S. N. Zwicker, 'Irony, Miscellany, and Modernity in the Stuart Restoration', in H. Nenner, ed., *Politics and the Political Imagination in Later Stuart Britain* (Rochester, N.Y., 1997), pp. 181–95.

31. *A Compleat Collection of State Tryals and Proceedings upon Impeachments for High Treason* (4 vols., London, 1719), vol. 2, p. 323.

32. See G. deF. Lord *et al.*, eds., *Poems upon Affairs of State* (7 vols., New Haven, 1963–75), vol. 2, pp. 425–31.

33. See William Cobbett, *State Trials* (34 vols., London, 1816), vol. 9 (1682–4), pp. 821–9.

34. *The Poems of John Dryden*, ed. J. Kinsley (4 vols., Oxford, 1958), vol. 1, p. 215.

35. A number of the annotated copies of *Absalom and Achitophel* reveal pronounced party bias; see S. N. Zwicker, 'Reading the Margins: Politics and the Habits of Appropriation', in K. Sharpe and S. N. Zwicker, eds., *Refiguring Revolutions: Aesthetics and Politics from the English Revolution to the Romantic Revolution* (Berkeley and London, 1998), pp. 108–10.

36. See Zwicker, 'Reading the Margins'; for a dissenting view, see A. Roper, 'Who's Who in *Absalom and Achitophel*', *Huntington Library Quarterly*, 63/1–2 (2000), pp. 98–138.

37. *The Fourth Volume of the Works of Mr John Dryden* (London, 1693), Folger Library copy, D2208, p. 41.

38. See *The Satires of Decimus Junius Juvenalis. Translated into English Verse. By Mr Dryden* (London, 1693), pp. ii–li.

39. Defoe's copy of Bacon's *Advancement of Learning* is in the Robert H. Taylor Collection, Rare Books Division, Firestone Library, Princeton University.

40. Folger Library, Accession no. 146555.

41. Huntington Library copy, D1290.

42. See W. Empson, *Using Biography* (Cambridge, 1984), 14ff.; and A. Patterson, 'Miscellaneous Marvell?', in C. Condren and A. D. Cousins, eds., *The Political Identity of Andrew Marvell* (Aldershot, 1990), p. 191.

43. See N. von Maltzahn, 'The First Reception of "Paradise Lost" (1667)', *Review of English Studies*, 47 (November 1996), pp. 482–7.

44. Their publications records may be consulted through P. G. Morrison's *Index of Printers, Publishers and Booksellers in Donald Wing's Short Title Catalogue* (Charlottesville, Va., 1955).

45. For the politics of the subscription list to the Tonson *Paradise Lost*, see G. Foster, 'Re-Reading the Heroic in Restoration and Augustan England' (Ph.D. dissertation, Washington University, St Louis, 2000).

46. J. Toland, *Amyntor* (London, 1699).

47. See Addison's *Spectator*, nos. 267, 273, 292 and 297, *Selections from 'The Tatler' and 'The Spectator'*, ed. A. Ross (Harmondsworth, 1988), pp. 412–29.

48. See von Maltzahn, 'The First Reception of "Paradise Lost" (1667)', pp. 482–4.

49. Addison, *Spectator*, no. 291, in *Selections*, p. 423.

50. See eighteenth-century anthologies such as *The Shepherdess's Golden Manual to Which Is Annex'd, Elegancies Taken out of Milton's 'Paradise Lost' by a Person of Quality* (London, 1725), which stress the aesthetic and pictorial dimensions of the poem.

51. See the Houghton Library copy of *Paradise Lost* (London, 1669), *EC 65. M6427 P. 1669ag.

52. [N. Fatio de Duillier,] *Fruit Walls Improved* (London, 1699), pp. 2–3.

53. *An Invitation to Peace, or Toby's Preliminaries to Nestor Ironsides Set Forth in a Dialogue between Toby and His Kinsman* (London, 1713), p. 34.

54. In *A Tale of a Tub*, p. 90, Swift plays the sceptical and ironical editor, and says of such lacunae, 'Here is pretended a defect in the manuscript; and this is very frequent with our author either when he thinks he cannot say anything worth reading, or when he has no mind to enter on the subject, or when it is a matter of little moment; or perhaps to amuse the reader (whereof he is frequently very fond) or lastly, with some satirical intention.'

55. Swift, *The Battle of the Books*, p. 12.

56. J. Swift, *Miscellaneous and Autobiographical Pieces, Fragments, and Marginalia*, ed. H. Davis (Oxford, 1962), p. 295.

57. See James Sutherland's introduction to *The Dunciad* (London, 1953), pp. xviiff.

58. Johnson, *The Rambler, Idler and Adventurer*, p. 231.

59. For Renaissance plot and its spatial dimensions, see L. Hutson, 'Fortunate Travelers: Reading for Plot in Sixteenth-Century England', *Representations*, 41 (1993), pp. 83–103.

60. See D. Thornton, *The Scholar in His Study: Ownership and Experience in Renaissance Italy* (New Haven, 1997).

61. There are of course notable exceptions among aristocratic girls and women throughout this period. The best known is Anne Clifford, who records her reading in her diary, *The Diary of Anne Clifford, 1616–1619: A Critical Edition*, ed. K. O. Acheson (New York, 1995). Clifford is also painted, at her direction, among her books; see G. Parry, 'The Great Picture of Lady Anne Clifford', in D. Howarth, ed., *Art and Patronage in the Caroline Courts* (Cambridge, 1993),

pp. 202–19. And other women are similarly learned and well read. See, for example, Lady Jane Lumley's manuscript translation of *Iphigenia at Aulus*, British Library, Royal MS, 15A.ii, printed in *The Malone Society Reprints* (London, 1909), and Anne Cornwallis Campbell, countess of Argyll, who kept a commonplace book which shows wide contemporary reading, Folger Library, MS V.a.89.

62. R. B. Sheridan, *The Rivals*, ed. C. Price (Oxford, 1968), 1.2.13–21.

63. See Lady Bradshaigh on reading *Clarissa*, *The Letters of Jonathan Richardson*, ed. A. Barbauld (4 vols., London, 1804), vol. 4, pp. 240–1:

I verily believe I have shed a pint of tears, and my heart is still bursting, tho' they cease not to flow at this moment, nor will, I fear, for some time.

Talk not of tragedies, I can now bear any; the deepest pain they give is momentary and trifling, compared with your long-dwelt upon, and well-told story.

It was purely out of gratitude, and to oblige you, I read the last three volumes. I expected to suffer, but not to that degree I have suffered ... Had you seen me, I surely would have moved your pity. When alone, in agonies would I lay down the book, take it up again, walk about the room, let fall a flood of tears, wipe my eyes, read again, perhaps not three lines, throw away the book, crying out, excuse me, good Mr Richardson, I cannot go on; it is your fault – you have done more than I can bear; threw myself upon my couch to compose, recollecting my promise (which a thousand times I wished had not been made); again I read, again I acted the same part: sometimes agreeably interrupted by my dear man, who was at that time labouring through the sixth volume with a heart capable of impressions equal to my own, tho' the effects shewn in a more justifiable manner, which I believe may be compared to what Mr Belford felt when he found the beauteous sufferer in her prison room: 'Something rose in my throat, I know not what, which made me gurgle as it were for speech.'

CHAPTER ELEVEN

Cato's retreat: fabula, historia and the question of constitutionalism in Mr Locke's anonymous Essay on Government

Kirstie M. McClure

> There are books that are of the same chemical composition as dynamite. The only difference is that a piece of dynamite explodes only once, while a book explodes a thousand times.
>
> Yevgeny Zamiatin[1]

In the autumn of 1689 London publishers Awnsham and John Churchill offered up a timely, if badly printed, anonymous tract that would long outlive the concatenation of hands and purposes that first gave it life. Two further anonymous editions followed, in 1694 and 1698. With the fourth edition of 1713, nine years after the death of its author, the official fame of the *Two Treatises of Government* accelerated apace as the work of the celebrated philosopher John Locke. Over the next two centuries, the second of the treatises accumulated its modern reputation as a freestanding whole. Severed from the first initially in the French translation of 1691, under the title *Du gouvernement civil* it saw seven further French language editions between 1724 and 1790. With successive waves of translation from the French it developed a life of its own in a variety of European vernaculars – German in 1718, Italian in 1773, Spanish in 1821, Russian in 1902.[2] Thus associated with an unfolding history of European revolutions and popular agitations, the *Second Treatise* has few rivals as a paradigm case of exploding print.

Like *The Prince*, *The Social Contract* and *The Communist Manifesto*, it was endlessly reprinted, embraced and repudiated by generations of readers, marshalled to illuminate the dilemmas of disparate political presents. Like these, too, it has been elevated to canonical status in the history of political thought, made at once a staple of the undergraduate curriculum and an ongoing site of scholarly dispute. And, perhaps surpassed by the *Manifesto* alone, amidst the ideological struggles of the twentieth century it has been seen by many as a singularly resonant site of historical and intellectual authority for the elaboration of modern political understandings.

In 1932, for example, on the occasion of the tercentennial of Locke's birth, Ernest Barker epitomized the historical meaning and significance of the *Treatise* by recounting its place in the broad sweep of modern history, a history narrativized as a triumphalist account of representative government. In addition to summarizing its premises, arguments and doctrines, Barker cast 'Locke's political theory' itself as a narrative subject and recounted its adventures across time and place: it 'penetrated into France, and passed through Rousseau into the French Revolution; it penetrated into the North American Colonies, and passed through Samuel Adams and Thomas Jefferson into the American Declaration of Independence'. Despite its abstract accounts of natural law, natural right and government as a trust, 'abstract doctrines can form a creed, and a political creed can fire and inspire a political party'. Its doctrines, Barker continued, 'became the creed of a great party, and of a succession of great statesmen . . . who between 1688 and 1832 worked out a system of Parliamentary government that may justly be called the great contribution of England to Europe, and beyond Europe, to other continents'.[3]

This placement of the *Treatise* within a history of constitutionalism inaccessible to both its author and its original publics has, in more recent scholarship, taken on a different cast. Pressured by the new gods of discourse the old gods of authorial genius have grown feet of clay, and Locke is no exception. As sometime secretary to the proprietors of Carolina, co-writer of that colony's first constitution and investor in companies engaged in the slave trade, the author Locke these days appears nothing if not all too human. Scholarship concerned with the *Treatise*'s participation in the formation of colonial discourse, however, has not infrequently rewritten rather than abandoned Barker's historical account. Indeed, the closing decades of the twentieth century found Barker's credal interpretation and narrative augmentation of the *Treatise* treated as an element internal to the text itself and opened to the scrutiny to which such triumphalist accounts are now generally and duly subject by post-colonial criticism.[4]

Salutary though this shift may be from any number of contemporary political and ethical perspectives, the narrative dimensions of both earlier triumphalist and more recent critical accounts nonetheless pose problems. While the former relied upon an uninterrogated metanarrative of constitutionalist progress to recommend the *Treatise*'s doctrinal virtues, the latter typically embrace that narrative as a matter of historical fact and reference only to up-end its triumphalist evaluation by attending to the imperial practices it was used to justify. Though their critical and political commitments differ, in other words, both approach the *Treatise* as the site of a creed made fact, and in their shared emphasis on the analysis of discursive argument *cum* credal elaboration both are unprepared to interrogate its relationship to the overarching narrative of modern constitutionalism that it is commonly taken to subtend.

Perhaps the most challenging and thoroughgoing post-colonial critique of the *Treatise* is that of James Tully. Tully presents the book as an exemplary instance of the complicities between modern constitutionalism and imperial expansion, particularly with regard to the suppression of cultural diversity and the extension of an 'empire of uniformity' in the history of colonial encounter.[5] Tully's broader theoretical compass, especially his emphatic differentiation of 'ancient' and 'modern' constitutionalism, is a significant intervention in contemporary theorizations of both constitutional politics and cultural pluralism. And yet, for all its virtues, Tully's critique also reiterates the conventional identification of the *Treatise* as an icon and a founding text of modern constitutionalism – albeit now as a bad example of historical developments that might have been otherwise in light of the political languages available in the period, and more particularly in view of the resources for cultural negotiation proffered by ancient constitutionalist alternatives.

In *Strange Multiplicity*, for instance, Tully reads the *Treatise* as epitomizing the features characteristic of modern constitutionalism that link it to imperial expansion.[6] In the essay that follows I am not concerned to address each of these features in their particularity, much less in the complexity of their mutual imbrication in Tully's critique. Rather, I am interested in the relationship of the anonymous editions of the *Treatise*, in the context of late seventeenth-century print culture, to two aspects of modern constitutionalism upon which Tully's specifications of these features repeatedly converge: on the one hand, to doctrinal considerations that privilege modern institutions of representative government, the rule of law and the separation of powers as matters of principle; on the other hand, and more broadly, to the stadial view of human history that codes those doctrines and institutions as the end or culmination of the progress of civilization. At issue here, in other words, is not Tully's theorization of modern constitutionalism *per se*, but the ostensibly narrower question of the extent to which, in the context of its original publication, the anonymous *Treatise* merits the status of an exemplum within that frame. This, I would suggest, is more than simply a matter of historical quibbling, for it opens the possibility of distinguishing between the political meanings, sensibilities and purposes tapped by the original text and those that, under other political developments and pressures, it could be made to serve by later readers encouraged or beset by the weight of its association with the authorial Locke.

To raise this question is not to suggest that the *Treatise* offers no evidence of participating in what we now understand as the historical vicissitudes of constitutionalism. Its commitment to the rule of law, of course, is undeniable, but this alone is insufficient to distinguish its 'modernity' from myriad ancient texts, Stoic and otherwise, that conveyed similar sentiments. More promising, it would seem, might be its differentiation of legislative, executive and federative powers, its account of the subordination of powers, and its treatment of prerogative power, all of which have provided resources for such readings in modern scholarship. To speak of powers, however, is not necessarily to speak of principles, nor is it to privilege the manifestation of such powers in particular institutional forms in doctrinal terms. As a matter of textual fact, these various discussions arrive late in the order of the book, congregating in roughly its third quarter – and the various powers there named are strangely unattached as a matter of doctrine or principle to specific institutional forms.[7] More oddly still, these attentions follow directly on the heels of the text's middle and briefest chapter, the scant two paragraphs of which are devoted to clarifying definitionally that what is at issue in the essay is not forms of government at all, much less representative government, the separation of powers and other now standard doctrinal features of modern constitutionalism. Instead, as we find them there, democracies, oligarchies and monarchies both hereditary and elective mingle promiscuously under the general term 'Commonwealth' – by which the erstwhile anonymous author claims to mean 'not a Democracy, or any Form of Government, but any *Independent Community* which the *Latines* signified by the word *Civitas*, to which the word which best answers in our Language, is *Commonwealth*, and most properly expresses such a Society of Men, which Community or Cittie in English does not'.[8]

There is a riddle in all this, to be sure. But in light of the *Treatise*'s now institutionalized history of ideological saturation, its answer is unlikely to be found in the protocols of reading and interpretation that have generated its status as an icon of modern constitutionalism. Recent perspectives on the history and historicity of print culture, however, suggest the possibility of a new point of departure – not, perhaps, a path beyond ideology so much as a passage beneath it, an excavation, if you will, of patterns of meaning sedimented in the materiality of the book in its initial, anonymous seventeenth-century variants. My interest in this possibility, I should note at the outset, is political and theoretical as well as historical – an effort in what might be called historically inflected political theory. The question to be raised here is whether the place conventionally accorded to the *Treatise* in the history of political thought is the only history within which we can imagine the book to function – and what, if we can imagine an alternative historicity of that printed work, this might imply for our sense of the duration and dilemmas of political modernity. The essay that follows is intended as a spur to that imagination.

READING THEORY: BENEATH THE EIGHTEENTH-CENTURY FORM

In speaking of the history of political thought, contemporary political theorists typically identify that 'thought' not with readers and the history of print culture, but with the political ideas and arguments articulated by historical writers. For some these ideas, read as principles or concepts, are intrinsically worthy of study and philosophical reflection. For others, they signify as elements of more general, overarching conceptual structures that arise and change in time – traditions, ideologies, *mentalités*, or, in more recent terms of art, discourses or languages. Almost never do we pause to consider the material form of the books in which such ideas appear or the activities of generations of readers who encountered them, much less the question of the historicity of the relationship between the materiality of print and the agency of readers. The issue of material form we trust to specialists in bibliography and textual criticism, upon whose largely unsung labour the whole enterprise rests. Readers, on the other hand, we tend to neglect entirely – with the exception, of course, of such notable readers as those who, having made their mark as writers, are themselves recognized as significant contributors to what we now call Western political thought. As for the interaction between such things, well, this we imagine as the territory of cultural historians, too immersed in the particularities of the archive for proper theory. None of the three, we tend to think, has much pertinence for the business we are about as theorists.

For the purposes of both history and theory, however, these tendencies give pride of place to conventions of modern philosophical writing and reading. Scholarly attention to the 'arguments' of historical writers, for example, privileges an analytical understanding of the term that focuses on premises, assumptions, propositions, statements, inferences, chains of reasoning and the like – as if the activity of theorizing were essentially circumscribed by purely cognitive or didactic purposes. That 'argument', in the rhetorical traditions that dominated pedagogy until the nineteenth century, could also refer to narration – itself aimed at soliciting the affects of its audience – is quite neglected. Also abandoned is the broader and more complex notion of the ends of writing characteristic of rhetorical culture more generally: that is, the hope not simply of teaching or instructing its audience of address, but of delighting them and moving them to action as well. Excluded, too, is consideration of the power of images painted in words, akin to but not identical with rhetoric, that Renaissance and early modern readers might have recognized as the provenance of poetics.

Similarly neglected are dimensions of print culture recently raised to scholarly attention by bibliographical and text scholarship – most notably, the ways in which various physical aspects of the printed book may collaborate in the process of signification.[9] That typography and layout, chapter divisions, headings, marginal apparatuses and the like may pivot meanings in specific directions is not something that contemporary theorists take as pertinent to theoretical understanding. Neither do we typically worry about practices of editing and annotation or wonder about such paratextual elements as titles, authorial names, dedications and inscriptions, epigraphs, prefaces, intertitles, illustrations and notes. So it is hardly a surprise that we're little concerned with the question of the ways in which such paratextual elements might have engaged a book's original readers, much less with how changes in these elements over time might spawn changes in the meanings elicited by particular books amongst diverse historical publics, up to and including our own.

In effect, in the absence of historical consideration of such conventions of reading, writing and printing, theorists' scholarly habits of reading for argument yield a philosophical variant of what one literary scholar has called 'the incarnational text'.[10] For such readings the 'theory' immanent within the dross matter of the book can be distilled, its political meaning separated from the contingent mire of the printed page and returned to its essence as a collocation of political concepts, ideas or principles. And at this level the result is the same whether the texts to which such readings are directed are understood as self-sufficient objects of philosophical inquiry or as collections of utterances to be puzzled out in the context of the ideological or discursive conventions of their time and place. By both procedures the political meaning of the arguments gleaned from any particular text are typically dissociated both from the historicity of the printed form of the book and from the activities of successive generations of readers over time. In short, where arguments are essences materiality doesn't matter.

Or so it seems. On the other hand, perhaps, like the ground beneath our feet, the stability of such matter is simply taken for granted. Whatever might be the case for other canonical works in the history of political thought, the print history of the *Second Treatise* makes it a book ripe for reconsideration along these lines.

By the time of the American Revolution the *Two Treatises* had become widely regarded, by admirers and foes alike, as a work of considerable authority on the 'Revolution Principles' of 1688.[11] In the eighteenth century, however, the books that circulated under that title were not materially the same books that percolated through Anglophone print culture in the turbulent decade of the 1690s. Though its authorship had been suspected, and occasionally suggested in print, until Locke's death in 1704 the book remained, as it were, officially anonymous.[12] Only with the fourth edition, of 1713, did its title page announce it to its publics as the work of an eminent philosopher. Here, too, and more often than not in subsequent editions, a serene portrait of the by then increasingly illustrious Locke appeared opposite the title page.[13] These, however, were not the only changes in the material form of the book between its three appearances as an anonymous tract in the late 1680s and 1690s and its later anointment as a summary statement of various, and not always approving, interpretations of the principles of 1688. Beginning with the edition of 1713, the book also began to be invested with the bibliographical codes of a learned or otherwise authoritative work. In addition to its appearance under the posthumous auspices of a great name, for instance, it was at this time first formatted with footnotes.[14] Admittedly, there wasn't much to work with, there being only two short Filmer passages in the first *Treatise* and nine passages from Richard Hooker's *Laws of Ecclesiastical Polity* in the second. But given Hooker's continuing stature as an Anglican theologian what was there carried considerable weight. In the new format, however, unlike the old, these passages were pegged to specific sentences in the main text, a convention that prompted readers to regard Hooker as the source or authority for the statements thus referenced, and through them for the *Treatise*'s associated arguments more generally.[15]

Though these features remained basically constant, over the course of the eighteenth century the material form of English language editions of the book divided further along two general lines of development.[16] On the one hand, supported by subscription, it appeared as a series of expensive folio editions of Locke's collected works. In this form, appropriated to the conventions governing editions of the life and works of famous authors, it became part of the 'good literature' towards which 'good society' was increasingly inclined.[17] On the other hand, it was repeatedly issued in cheaper duodecimo or octavo volumes of the *Two Treatises* as a single work, and twice as still cheaper pamphlets of excerpts from the *Second Treatise* alone.[18] In these assorted variants, until the nineteenth century appearances of the *Treatises* tended to follow the tempo of political life rather than the roughly once-a-decade-or-so pattern that typified editions of the *Works*. Within this initially more popular or plebeian line of development, and consistently absent from the folio editions, a particularly visceral Latin passage from Livy (invoking divine vengeance on tyrants) found a brief life on the title pages of the 1713 and 1728 printings, only to disappear from the print history of the book until Peter Laslett's scholarly edition of 1960.[19] Finally, among a flurry of printings towards the end of the eighteenth century, the separate publication of an annotated critical edition of the *Second Treatise* not only contributed to its status as an authoritative text but also directed critical attention to it as an autonomous and freestanding whole.[20]

In short, over the course of the eighteenth century the book then widely known as *Mr Locke's Essay on Government* underwent a substantial histor- ical transformation both in reputation and in physical form – a change, we might say, from anonymity to authority. The vicissitudes of the in- terpretive history of the book suggest that these changes were less than successful in stabilizing its meanings among diverse publics; nonetheless, they increasingly marked it as a book that aimed to instruct – indeed, as a book both admired and criticized for the substance of its arguments.[21] But if some aspects of the *Treatise's* meaning had to do with moving and delighting as well as teaching, and if attention to philosophical argument tends to sidestep the rhetorical and poetic gestures through which these tasks were attempted, the question of what meanings might lie beneath the bibliographical and interpretive traditions through which we now con- ventionally read it would seem well worth asking. Is it possible today to recover the delights and provocations it offered before it became freighted with authority? How might such a reading proceed?

In the absence of evidence from late seventeenth-century readers scrib- bling away in the margins of the *Treatise's* anonymous editions, the at- tempt to pursue such questions in the service of political theory might seem quixotic. That observation itself, however, in a sense helps us along. Fanciful labour, illusory jousts with imaginary windmills – many of us have a sense of what 'quixotic' connotes whether or not we've ever actually worked through Cervantes's novel. And this, perhaps, may be precisely the place to begin – that is, with the associative connections of books with books, of meanings in one with meanings in another. By considering the relation- ship between various details of intertextual reference within the anonymous

Treatise and the literary categories and cultural resonances available to its early modern readers we might glimpse elements of its political meaning sidelined by the familiar protocols of philosophical argumentation.

As it turns out, the *Second Treatise* hosts a number of such elements. Interestingly, particularly in light of Paul Ricoeur's insistence that narratives are typically 'apprehended from the angle of praxis', with few exceptions these intertextual moments are intensely involved with the narrative dimensions of the text.[22] Some of these narrations are elaborately extended, others are highly condensed – others still are simply noted as examples, as if readers were presumed sufficiently familiar with the stories as to make further prompting unnecessary. All point to books widely available to the late seventeeth-century reading public, ranging from biblical stories, to travellers accounts of distant places, to ancient writings that functioned as valued texts in humanist education.[23] To unfold the question of constitutionalism in the *Treatise*, let me focus initially on one particularly pointed intertextual moment, from which I will work outwards – first to the literary convention it might have marked for early modern readers, and then to the sorts of political meanings elicited by that convention in the anonymous form of the book.

CATO'S RETREAT

The once common view that the *Second Treatise* was intended as a counter-argument to Hobbes's absolutism has been amply laid to rest by sustained historical scholarship.[24] As a matter of textual fact, the larger work offers but one reference to *Leviathan*, and that merely in passing in the *Second Treatise*. There may be more here, however, than meets the eye. Appearing early in the chapter entitled 'Of the Beginning of Political Societies', *Leviathan* is mentioned iconically as part of the condensed summary of the invention of government that prefaces the chapter's numerous narrative examples of the founding of particular polities. There, favouring a majority of a previously constituted 'Body Politick' or 'Political Society' as the origin of government, the alternative of unanimous consent is rejected as 'next impossible ever to be had':

[T]he Infirmities of Health, and the Avocations of Business . . . in a number though much less than that of a Common-wealth, will necessarily keep many away from the public Assembly. To which if we add the variety of opinions, and contrariety of Interests, which unavoidably happen in all Collections of Men, the coming into Society upon such terms, would be only like Cato's coming into the Theatre, *tantum ut exiret* [only to go out again]. Such a Constitution as this would make the mighty *Leviathan* of a shorter duration than the feeblest Creatures; and not let it outlast the day it was born in; which cannot be suppose'd till we can think that Rational Creatures should desire and constitute Societies only to be dissolved. For where the *majority* cannot conclude the rest, there they cannot act as one Body, and consequently will be immediately dissolved again.[25]

As a doctrinal justification of majority rule or majoritarian democracy, these passages are more notable for their generation of dilemmas than for their capacity to secure the principle or doctrine they are generally taken to defend.[26] As an instance, however, of the power of narrative to combine and layer meanings by orchestrating a variety of resources from a culture's available stock of stories, the passage merits further consideration.[27]

To begin with, it is not only the case, as Laslett suggests, that Hobbes's covenant story is here subjected to irony or sarcasm.[28] It is also the case that this is accomplished by recourse both to the *Treatise*'s previous narrative accounts of the state of nature and paternal power and, more curiously, to an anecdote about Cato the Younger widely circulated in the period by Martial's *Epigrams*. Wryly cautioning those offended by the liberties of the epigram form to rest content with the introduction alone, Martial observed that epigrams 'are written for those who are accustomed to look on the Games of Flora', then closed the preface with a verse:

> You knew the rites to jocund Flora dear,
>   The festive quips and license of the rout;
> Why on our scene, stern Cato enter here?
>   Did you then enter only to go out?[29]

The story to which this alluded – and, we might say, to which the *Treatise*'s allusion alluded as well – was recounted also by Valerius Maximus, in a work owned by Locke in multiple editions, widely available to late seventeenth-century English readers, and standardly used in grammar schools as a sourcebook for the memorable deeds and sayings of ancient Romans.[30] The Floralia, one of a series of plebeian agrarian festivals devoted to as-suring the fertility of crops and beasts, had, by Cato's time, taken on a bacchanalian rather than rustic aspect, including nude theatrical per-formances and mock gladiatorial combat between naked prostitutes.[31] As Valerius tells the story, Cato's exit from one of these performances was memorable as a token of his virtue, but not, as it turns out, because he was offended by its licence. In Cato's austere presence, it seems, the people were ashamed to ask that the actors 'should appear naked'. Cato, understanding from a friend that his presence was inhibiting 'the custom of the show', departed. On Valerius's telling, that departure epitomized Cato's political virtue not because it valorized his severity, but because it exemplified his understanding of its limits: accompanied by popular applause, Cato's retreat affirmed popular liberties and 'renewed the ancient custom of Jesting in the Scenes'.[32]

The meanings set in motion here are not easily slotted into doctrinal accounts of modern constitutionalism as an empire of uniformity. As a literary allusion to a story distant from accounts of political foundings, the anecdote of Cato's retreat relies on analogical association rather than logic, and its sarcastic edge turns the story's Roman sources to new purposes. Picturing the invention of government amidst a 'society' whose incorporated members are engaged with other concerns, Cato's brief appearance suggests that the austerity of unanimous consent threatens 'the custom of the show' there as well. As an anecdote it is historical; as a brief yet pointed narrative it is more broadly meaningful, for it evokes by allusion and suggestion a world of robust sociability, a 'political society' of social bodies likely to be struck silent, in danger of being stilled or arrested, by a too rigid or austere criterion of public will. A matter less of argument than of imagery, the 'majority' alternative it supports thus functions as a default position for a 'constitution' minimally cast as that which renders such a society capable of acting 'as one Body'. Beyond this vindication of consensual originals, however, the particularities of such constitutions remain open-ended.

Were this the beginning of the *Treatise*'s account rather than its eighth chapter, we might, with Laslett, pronounce it unsatisfactory.[33] But to the extent that narrative generates meaning through evocation and association, these passages are quite effective. The Cato story, in this regard, is no more than suggestive. But it is no less than suggestive either, for it invites recollection of the variegated range of narratives that preceded it. And these, it should be noted, are not limited to the opening story of the metamorphosis of the 'original' of political power into 'governments' in the first five chapters.[34] Increasingly dense thickets of narrative follow on the heels of that account in chapters 6 and 7 – the first cluster of which distinguishes paternal from political power, then recounts the 'tacit' and 'insensible' changes by which 'the fathers of families' might have become 'politick Monarchs', while the second distinguishes 'political society' from various other forms of voluntary association, then relates how even such monarchies might have been prudentially altered or augmented by further institutional innovation.[35] In effect, rather than a twinned doctrinal elaboration of majority rule and modern constitutionalism, we might here read 'majority' not literally, as a nose-counting exercise at some historically actual original contract, but rather as a name applied retrospectively to all those narrations – a name that, by affirming 'consent' and refusing unanimity, gathers them in all their variety into an ensemble of similar instances.[36]

But this is not all that is accomplished here, for the assemblage thus collected points forward as well. Indeed, it is precisely here, immediately following Cato's retreat, that the *Treatise* takes up the objection that 'there are no Instances to be found in Story' of such beginnings and opens prospectively onto the enumeration of particular historical polities.[37] And among these are not only the oft-cited foundings of Rome and Venice, but references to Spartan and Hebrew history, as well as to Peru, Brazil and other Amerindian examples, as instances of the contingent generation of a variety of political forms by societies divergent in both time and space.[38] In the print culture of the last decade of the seventeenth century, all these are not simply 'historical examples' but intertextual references, pointing to widely available Latin and vernacular sources – none of which has any apparent relation to what later moderns have come to understand as either the contractarian tradition or modern constitutionalism more generally.

That Cato's retreat explicitly forges the *Treatise*'s link to historical exempla of the consensual beginnings of government is generally passed over by modern scholarship. Worry we do about the *epistemological* status of the *Treatise*'s state of nature – as 'historical fact' or 'moral fiction', as 'an axiom of theology', or as an illicit naturalization of the commercial relations of early capitalism.[39] What we don't discern, and what a good many seventeenth-century readers might have found familiar, is what late Renaissance poetics understood as a distinction between *fabula* and *historia*, a distinction irreducible to that between the irreality of fiction and the certainty of known facts. As courtier-poet Philip Sidney framed the issue, the latter pertained to the deeds and events attested to by the historical record, to the particularities of 'true stories what have bin', while the former entailed universal considerations, 'pictures, what should be'.[40] The definitional clarity of this distinction between history and poetics notwithstanding, any number of early modern narrative texts creatively intertwined the feigned and fictioned with the particularities of historical fact.[41] In the English context More's *Utopia* famously worked the boundary between the two, as did Bacon's *New Atlantis* and Harrington's *Oceana*, among others too numerous to mention. To the detriment, I would suggest, of its easy assimilation to the political principles and stadial history underpinning modern constitutionalism, the *Second Treatise* can be productively read as similarly oscillating across that boundary.

OF FABULA AND HISTORIA

The issue to be raised here is not Sidney's 'influence' on Locke,[42] but rather whether the poetic distinction between *fabula* and *historia* – understood both as a compositional strategy in the order of the book and as a protocol of reading – changes the horizons of meaning within which we typically understand the *Treatise* to operate. Considered experimentally, what do we *notice*, what reads *differently*, if we allow that distinction to inform our own reading?

As my concern here is with the *Treatise's* relation to the conceptual architecture of modern constitutionalism, I would prefer to limit my remarks to such things as bear directly on that question. But the suggestion that the *Treatise* might be read in light of early modern poetics may seem so preposterous to late modern readers that a preliminary digression seems in order. Starkly put, the question is this: could a writer widely considered one of the rationalist founders of modern liberalism – or, alternatively, one of the philosophical fonts of modern empiricism – be thought remotely sympathetic to the powers of narrative and poetics? Strange though it may seem, I think so, and on two counts: first, in light of Locke's own assessments of the power and usefulness of stories, and particularly fables, for the purposes of ethical instruction and reflection; second, in light of later readers' remarks on the fabulous character of the *Treatise's* representation of the state of nature for the purposes of political argument. Let me speak briefly to each of these, then return to the materiality of the book and the question of its relation to modern constitutionalism.

On the first count, we might consider Locke's various letters to Edward Clark, written from exile, recommending the usefulness of stories in the education of children.[43] As he observed in one of these, Aesop's fables might provide Clark's son with the sorts of 'delight' and 'entertainment' that 'might draw him on and reward his pains in reading'.[44] The suggestion, however, was not merely a matter of child's play. The fables, Locke noted in a later letter, 'being stories apt to delight and entertain a child, may yet afford useful reflection to a grown man; and if his memory retain them all his life after, he will not repent to find them there among his most manly thoughts and serious business'.[45] 'Stories' are similarly recommended to focus biblical reading. Youths' 'promiscuous reading' of the Scriptures 'by chapters as they lie in order', he observed, neither advances their reading skills nor principles their religion, for it offers no 'pleasure or encouragement' and 'is very disproportionate to their understanding'. Other parts of Scripture, however, are recommended for 'reading and instruction together' – most notably 'the story of Joseph and his brethren, of David and Goliath, of David and Jonathan, etc.', and others as might offer such plain moral instruction as 'What you would have another do unto you, do you the same unto them.'[46] Three years later – curiously enough, roughly about the time Locke must have decided to publish the *Two Treatises* – another letter notes that while children 'should be treated as rational creatures and therefore argued with as grown men', 'longe discourses and philosophical reasonings' are likely to 'amaze and confound both'.[47] It is not, Locke observed, chains of argument that are wanted in such cases, but examples of things to be done or avoided in the practice of others. Such exempla, he continued, are 'of more force to draw or deter their imitation than any philosophical discourse'; they 'will make deeper impressions' than 'any rules or instructions' – and this for adults no less than for children.[48] Given such acknowledgement of the power of fabulation, it is perhaps no wonder, though the fact is little noted, that among Locke's last works was an edited Latin–English edition of *Aesop's Fables*, the avowed purpose of which was to further the learning of either language for those 'not having a master'.[49] But there should be little wonder, too, that the *Treatise* might have been written with an eye to the affective powers of its *fabula*.

And so, on the second count, was it read by various members of its successive publics – most explicitly, though not exclusively, by its critics. Charles Leslie, for instance, in the first sustained attack on the *Treatise*, called its account of political origins a 'Romance' of impossibility and contradiction.[50] In similar terms, the third earl of Shaftesbury pronounced its state of nature 'chimerical'.[51] More approvingly, if apparently oblivious to the question of affect, by the 1760s the American James Otis saw the representation of that state as simply a philosophical convenience: rather 'an abstract way of considering men than agreeable to the real and general course of nature', it was nonetheless useful as a way to 'form an idea' of natural rights.[52] In the same decade, however, George Horne fulminated against this 'way of ideas' and linked all such notions of an original compact to the 'visionary systems' of ancient historians, philosophers and poets. The product of imagination rather than information, such imagery might display the ingenuity of former ages, but it was 'an imperfect and disjointed tradition, disguised in the dress of fable'.[53] Likewise, Jonathan Boucher regarded its 'imaginary compact' as an ancient and dispensable residue, its political edge tapping 'the decline, perhaps, of some fabulous age of gold'. Such a 'visionary idea of government', Boucher noted, though once regarded as 'merely another Utopian fiction', nonetheless appealed to the corrupt imaginations of creatures restive under restraints. '*Ignes fatui* of our own fancies or "feelings" ', such things represented wishes rather than truths.[54]

To return to the *Treatise* with these things in mind, we might begin by noting a seemingly simple paratextual detail, the heading of the chapter in which Cato's retreating figure appears: 'Of the Beginnings of Political Societies'. The *Treatise*, it seems, offers not one but two *sorts* of account of political beginnings. If Cato's retreat leads on to historical actualities, to something like Sidney's 'true stories what have bin', what precedes his entrance become fabulations of what might or could have been the case, historical records being absent, in the first ages of the world. Read in these terms, what is at issue in the earlier chapters is perhaps less the logic of propositions than the artistry of persuasion, the marshalling less of a creed directed to cognition than of images aimed to engage the affects. The *Treatise*'s representation of the state of nature is, of course, one of these, as the above-mentioned eighteenth-century critics insisted. It is not, however, the only one, for the seven chapters preceding Cato make repeated narrative recourse to familial relations in 'the beginning and first peopling of the world', to the innocence of 'the first ages', and to other such formulations of a time preceding historical records.[55] Aligned with the sense of Sidney's 'universal consideration' such things are feigned probabilities – strictly speaking neither fact nor fiction, they are nonetheless meaningful as 'pictures, what should be'.[56]

A second paratextual detail emerges in this context as well, and this has to do with the passages from Hooker's *Laws of Ecclesiastical Polity* that eighteenth-century and later editions formatted as footnotes. In the original anonymous editions, however, these materials were neither pegged to specific passages in the body of the text nor printed flush with the bottom of the page. Rather, they floated freely in italic in the shoulders of the main text, always printed in full on a single page and nestled into the paragraph/s with which they were associated. In this respect their placement aligns them perhaps more closely with the print conventions of commentary than those of citation, an impression strengthened by the fact that when Hooker *is* invoked as an authority the passage is included in the main text.[57] Most interesting, though, are the series of Hooker passages that float in the margins of the two chapters immediately preceding Cato's arrival. Clustered at the end of each chapter, these excerpts tend to converge with the paragraphs they accompany as extended narrative moments. Viewed more specifically in relation to the paragraphs they border, they read less as philosophical evidence than as parallel fabulations of the first ages, while the paragraphs thus edged read as extensions or amplifications of the extracts that hover around them. In effect, as they are composited on the printed page of the anonymous editions, the paragraphs of the main text read rather like commonplace entries – that is, as commentaries, elaborations or inventions, confected from striking passages copied out from an admired author, for they characteristically retell or expand upon brief narratives extracted from Hooker. And the political sense of all these fabulations repeatedly condenses on two basic themes: the consensual origins of government and the thoroughgoing contingency of political forms.[58] The prudential wisdom of living under laws rather than the will of rulers is also mentioned, but nothing resembling either the form or formulae of modern constitutionalism is feigned as a 'universal consideration'.

But let us consider the other side of Cato's retreat – the answer to the objection that 'there are no Instances to be found in Story of a Company of Men independent and equal one amongst another, that met together and in this way began and set up a Government'.[59] The intertexts there adduced as historical exempla of consensual beginnings range in time from the ancient world to the *Treatise*'s present and in space from the valleys of Palestine and the shores of Magna Graecia to Italy and the Americas. Rome and Venice are mentioned in passing, familiar instances of republican forms for seventeenth-century readers, but they receive no elaboration or discussion. Other and more unusual examples, however, find more space. The first draws on Joseph Acosta's *The Naturall and Morall Historie of the Indies* to suggest that 'in parts of America there was no government at all', while Acosta's speculations about Peru analogize it to known examples which '*for a long time had neither Kings nor Common-wealths, but lived in Troops, as they do this day in Florida, the Cheriquanas, those of Bresil, and many other Nations, which have no certain Kings, but as occasion is offered in Peace or War, they choose their Captains as they please*'.[60] The second example is from Justin's *History*, the instance of Palantus and his cohort 'who went away from Sparta', here adduced as '*Freemen independent* of one another' who 'set up a Government over themselves, by their own consent'.[61]

Further exemplifications touch on the question of political form as well, acknowledging that such consensual beginnings commonly settled on monarchical rule but insisting that these were contingent upon local conditions. Even for known monarchical foundings, it is suggested, if one king died another might be chosen by consent, a point instanced by another reference to those parts of America whose people lived 'out of the reach of the Conquering Swords, and spreading domination of the two great Empires of Peru and Mexico'. These 'enjoy'd their own natural freedom, though, *caeteris paribus*, they commonly prefer the Heir of their deceased

King; yet if they find him in any way weak, or uncapable, they pass him by and set up the stoutest and bravest Man for their Ruler'.[62] Such rulers, we're told – in an unsubtle diminution of regality – were 'little more than Generals of their Armies', a 'pattern' or type of 'the first Ages in *Asia* and *Europe*', and one evidenced by the Old Testament books of Judges and I Samuel as well. Thus Jephtha was elected to defend Israel against the Ammonites, Gideon is mentioned only for 'what he did as a General', and Abimelech, Saul and David are likewise figured as captains over Israel.[63] So "in *Israel* it self, *the chief Business of their Judges and first Kings* seems to have been to be *Captains in War*, and Leaders of their Armies'.[64] Like the fabulations that came before, such exempla of consensual rule are re-mote from modern constitutionalist doctrine. The issue they engage is not what forms of government *should* be, but the groundlessness of divine right and patriarchalist perspectives that naturalize both the monarchical form and political obligation. And it is precisely at this point, after the last of these 'instances found in story', that the chapter turns once again to fabulation. Here, the rhetorical pitch is heightened, Ovid links hands with Hooker in parallel narrations to lament the viciousness and corrup-tion of later ages, and the doctrine of *jure divino* is decried as a modern innovation.

The two brief chapters that follow in the order of the printed book (chapters 9 and 10), titled 'Of the Ends of Political Society and Govern-ment' and 'Of the Forms of Government', recur in retrospect to a more consistently analytic voice. The first of these recapitulates in summary form what might loosely be called the philosophical sense of the eight chapters that precede it, enumerating in turn the need for known law, indifferent judges and a power of execution. The second briefly asserts the variety and contingency of political forms that may answer these needs by con-stituting a 'Commonwealth', then announces, paradoxically by the more stringent lights of modern constitutionalism, that 'by *Commonwealth*' is meant 'not a Democracy, or any form of Government, but *any Independent Community*'.[65] And it is only after this, the tenth and central chapter of the book, that elements of constitutionalist language begin to populate the *Treatise*. Indeed, elaborated through sequenced discussions of legislative, executive, federative and prerogative powers, that language is central to the next four chapters. But if, as I have suggested, something like the distinc-tion between *fabula* and *historia* can be understood as both a strategy of composition and a protocol of reading available in the period, we might be wary of the temptation to read them as statements of doctrinal commit-ment to a specific political form, much less as a principled commitment, *avant la lettre*, to the sort of teleologically coded 'universal history' favoured by the stadial models of the Scottish Enlightenment.

Approached with this distinction in mind, the analytic language that dominates these later discussions begins to oscillate as well, this time between the poles of conceptual generality and English particularity. No longer pictures painted in words but conceptual abstractions, the powers there elaborated in general terms repeatedly recur to the contingency and open-endedness of actual institutionalizations: 'Legislative power may be placed in one or more'; 'Whatever Form the Commonwealth is under, the Ruling Power ought to govern by *declared* and *received* Laws'; 'Government into whatsoever hands it is put' has no power over anyone's property without their consent.[66] Powers that are conceptually differentiated by their function, however, are institutionally differentiated in practice not by principle but by prudential considerations. Thus the legislative and executive powers can be put in different hands to avoid the 'temptation . . . to grasp at Power' that could make governors exempt themselves from the law to pursue their own advantage – but if the legislative 'be a single Person, it cannot but be always in being, and so will as Supreme, naturally have the Supreme Executive Power, together with the Legislative'.[67] At the same time, as the account proceeds dilemmas specific to English politics accumulate as examples. Taxation, the franchise, the calling and proroguing of parliaments, and, finally, the ambiguous virtues of prerogative power – over the course of these four chapters the discussion is repeatedly turned to the operation of political powers in specifically English institutions. As an early reader of the first anonymous edition observed, the 'Scheme of Government' forwarded by the then unknown author of the *Treatise* in the latter portions of the book 'is not erected as the most perfect, but seems designedly adapted to what he takes our Government to be, tho not expressly named'.[68]

Again, as was the case in the turn from *fabula* to *historia*, the compositional strategy appears to be that of exemplification. Given the contingency of political forms, England's 'constitution' – its 'legislative' of king, lords and Commons – thus arrives not as a model of a 'universal consideration' but rather as a manifestation of historical particularity, an instance of what one consensual beginning did with its freedom. It offers, in other words, not an ideal or paradigm case of 'modern constitutionalism' but a municipal institution of powers that might be and had been constituted otherwise elsewhere. Taken as a late instance in the book's series of historical exemplifications, these institutions may signify a history of political prudence but they carry no ontological or moral privilege. Theoretically speaking – like the Israel of Judges and 1 Samuel, like Rome, Venice, Tarentum and the Amerindian examples that preceded it in the order of the book – the English 'constitution' represents a contextually specific case of a political society or social body that generated governing forms, institutions and practices appropriate to its then perceived needs, however these might have been obscured by the mists of time. In effect, by making all such constituting moments coeval in relation to the 'universal considerations' of natural freedom and consent, the English constitution becomes a local invention, a home-grown response to a general dilemma rather than the culmination of a universal historical process that favours the modern constitutional state as a matter of principle.

Drawn from an internalist practice of close reading, an account that runs so athwart our conventional beliefs will probably be regarded as the product of a fevered imagination. There is, however, external evidence to be weighed in its support, for the construals and complaints of a number of eighteenth-century readers tend to corroborate the interpretation just advanced. As Goldie notes, from the Kentish Petition onwards the *Treatise* was appropriated to the cause of populist agitations, yet for roughly the first half of the century these perspectives were advanced from within, rather than in opposition to, the convention of regarding the English 'constitution' as a matter of king, Lords and Commons assembled in Parliament.[69] Even for these, however, the irreducible contingency of political forms remained an oft-stated commonplace. It was not until the later decades of the eighteenth century, and then largely through the ministrations of rational dissent, that the populist edge of the *Treatise* became aligned with universalizing normative arguments for an expanded franchise, representative institutions, the rights of man and other such now familiar elements of modern constitutionalism. In this latter trajectory of reception, it is perhaps hardly surprising that the historical exempla I've emphasized here fall by the wayside. Indeed, the new, democratic, modern constitutionalist 'Locke' of the late eighteenth century might as well not have wasted his time writing much of the *Treatise*, as these later readers attended principally to such passages as could easily be read as universalizing statements of philosophical grounding for constitutionalist principles. On such readings Old Testament exempla, ancient foundings and travellers' tales disappeared from view in favour of rational arguments, clearly deduced from first principles of natural freedom and equality, and critically applied to current facts in support not simply of representative government but of democratic sovereignty as well.[70]

Among critics of this tendency, however, there were disgruntled rumblings over the book's new repute as a source of political edification for self-described enlightened and civilized Europeans. Far, it would seem, from nestling comfortably into either the imperial complacencies or stadial histories of the time, the text seems to have struck various readers of the period as incommensurable with 'progressive' understandings of European civilization. Its heathen and ancient exempla, in particular, seem to have raised hackles for such as continued to read the text closely for the relationship it suggested between its examples and the principles they were taken to exemplify. Unenlightened nations, as Josiah Tucker wrote in 1781, could prove no guide to their betters, and the *Treatise*'s use of Amerindian exempla in this respect was wrong-headed in the extreme. Distinguishing these into 'savages', 'half-savages', and 'almost-civilized', Tucker went on at great length about the impropriety of such exempla. 'Let the Lockians,' he intoned, 'not din our Ears with the Examples of the Savages of *America*... as Proofs and Illustrations of their Hypothesis', for these, 'when thoroughly discussed and accurately examined, prove and illlustrate quite the contrary'.[71] George Horne, somewhat earlier, was similarly irritated by the *Treatise*'s examples. Characterizing Amerindians as bereft of revelation and running wild 'like brutes in the woods', he mocked the 'polite philosopher, in these enlightened days' who would 'send us to study politics under Cherokee tutors!' The *Treatise*'s use of the founders of Rome, Venice and Tarentum drew his fire as well. The first were 'a gang of robbers'; the second, conquered by the Goths, were simply 'obliged to shift as they could, and chase governors in their distress'. Palantus and his Spartan cohort, for their part, 'were an extraordinary breed of bastards', generated by a 'promiscuous concubinage', who invaded the city of Tarentum, exiled its inhabitants, 'settled, grew seditious, and at last banished forever that same Palantus, the cause of their birth, and the guide of their peregrinations'.[72]

In effect, even as the book's friends came to ignore its instances 'found in story', its foes came to sense a yawning gap between its examples and the universal norms they were supposed to exemplify. No longer resonant with late Renaissance notions of *fabula* as 'pictures, what should be', over time the *Treatise*'s then apparent invocation of such norms seems to have been held critically accountable to a standard of empirical generalization that rendered suspect its recourse to ancient and non-European instances. Jonathan Boucher, for instance, put the issue in probabilistic terms when he expressed doubt that 'any large concourse of people, in a rude and imperfect state of society', could rationally and collectively consent 'to subject themselves to various restrictions, many of them irksome and unpleasant, and all of them contrary to their former habits'. To imagine otherwise, he noted, was 'to suppose them possessed of more wisdom and virtue than multitudes in any instance of real life have ever shown'.[73] By the 1830s, as the notion of social laws and empirical regularities had become more and more the common coin of Anglophone critical exchange, the *Treatise*'s exempla could be simultaneously recognized as facts and rejected out of hand as a way 'to prove a universal law'. The 'wonder', one writer observed – explicitly citing the *Treatise*'s use of Brazil, 'other Indian nations' and Tarentum – is 'that the examples are not greatly more in number, nay, that they are not exhibited by every government under the sun'.[74]

REMAINDERS

Considered in light of the historicity of the *Second Treatise*'s material form, such variations in readers' responses suggest that its transformation from anonymity to authority was accompanied by its sometimes subtle, sometimes blatant, assimilation to philosophical languages and political purposes alien to its initial contexts of composition, dissemination and consumption. That the book *became* an icon of modern constitutionalism is beyond question. That it was written and anonymously published in the service of that historical phenomenon should, I think, be regarded as doubtful. On the basis of the account I've given here, we might see its reputation as such an icon as forged by simultaneous processes of amnesia and augmentation. Forgotten were the rhetorical and poetic sensibilities that permitted narrative the status of argument and read exempla as ethical models of actions to be done or avoided. Added were more rigorous distinctions – on the one hand, between fact and fiction, on the other, between fact and norm, both of which tended to flatten or literalize the book's rhetorical and poetic gestures in the eyes of later generations of readers. And as some literalized its *historia* into the primitive and unsavoury facts of a world they regarded as well lost, so others literalized its *fabulae* into universal moral imperatives.

By attending to the *Treatise*'s anonymous editions, by burrowing beneath the protocols of reading we've inherited from those literalizations, I've tried to unsettle a few of the ideological complacencies and antagonisms that dominate contemporary readings of the *Treatise*. Though maintaining the prudential privilege the text accords to representative institutions, I've called into question the *Treatise*'s reputation as a philosophical defence of modern constitutionalism. Relatedly, and on the same grounds, I've also suggested that the book's relationship to later Enlightenment accounts of human progress from savagery to civilization bears critical reassessment – not least of all because the coeval status it grants to all actual political beginnings defies the very possibility of a teleologically coded universal history. Perhaps, though I will not pursue the point here, this might link the *Treatise* rather with the cyclic imagery of particularized histories – histories of founding and decay, corruption and renewal – widely circulated in late Renaissance modernity. But in any case, a similarly doubtful eye might be cast on post-colonial theory's evaluatively inverted assimilation of conventional triumphalist frameworks as a protocol for reading the *Treatise*. However its phrases might have been appropriated by later readers to the self-images of progressive universal history, and however such selective readings may have been used to justify imperial conquest, on its own terms the book's images of both history and indigenous peoples serve other, more particularized political purposes. In its fabulated emphases on consent and the contingency of all beginnings it remains a document of political radicalism. But in refusing ontological privilege to any particular political form it leaves its readers to their own devices, their own resources, their own prudence, even their own habits, should they find themselves confronted with the difficult prospect of beginning anew.

NOTES

1. 'Fragment for an Anthology on Books', in *A Soviet Heretic: Essays by Yevgeny Zamiatin*, ed. and trans. M. Ginsburg (Chicago, 1970), p. 131.

2. This information is drawn from Peter Laslett's checklist of printings (1689–1960), published as Appendix A to the introductory essay of his critical edition of the *Two Treatises of Government* (1960; repr. with amendments, Cambridge, 1963), pp. 136–45.

3. *The London Times*, 29 August 1932. These remarks were inserted by Barker in the introduction (p. xvi) to his collection titled *The Social Contract*, first published in The World's Classics series of Oxford University Press (London, 1947) and issued in paperback by the Press in 1960. In light of post-colonial criticism, it is difficult to encounter such triumphalist accounts without embarrassment or irritation, but it may not be impertinent to recall that the political dynamics of the years 1932–47 revolved around other sorts of imperatives. Even in that context, Barker's narrative might be situated within a historical movement within which the Englishness he attributed to the *Treatises* was becoming discursively assimilated to the construction of a broader 'European' culture – itself framed by a notion of 'civilization' that pivoted most significantly on a contrast less to the 'rude ages' imagined by Renaissance thinkers or the 'primitive peoples' of eighteenth-century stadial history and nineteenth-century historicism than to the new barbarism of National Socialism. For an account of these and other elements of Barker's work, see J. Stapleton, *Englishness and the Study of Politics: The Social and Political Thought of Ernest Barker* (Cambridge, 1994).

4. See, for instance, H. Lebovics, 'The Uses of America in Locke's *Second Treatise of Government*', *Journal of the History of Ideas*, 47 (1986); J. Tully, 'Rediscovering America: The *Two Treatises* and Aboriginal Rights', in Tully, *An Approach to Political Philosophy: Locke in Contexts* (Cambridge, 1993), pp. 137–76; Tully, *Strange Multiplicity: Constitutionalism in an Age of Diversity* (1995; repr., Cambridge, 1997), chapter 3, especially pp. 71–82; B. Parekh, 'Liberalism and Colonialism: A Critique of Locke and Mill', in J. N. Pieterse and B. Parekh, eds., *The Decolonization of Imagination: Culture, Knowledge, and Power* (London and New Jersey, 1995), pp. 81–98; and B. Arneil, *John Locke and America: The Defence of English Colonialism* (Oxford, 1996).

5. Tully, *Strange Multiplicity*, especially chapter 3. See also Tully's 'Rediscovering America', and his 'Placing the *Two Treatises*', in N. Phillipson and Q. Skinner, eds., *Political Discourse in Early Modern Britain* (Cambridge, 1993), pp. 253–82.

6. Tully elaborates seven of these: (1) the notion of a culturally homogeneous sovereign people who come to agree on a form of constitutional association, (2) a contrast with an 'ancient' or earlier form of association, in the sense of either pre-modern European forms or those of non-European societies at more primitive levels of historical development, (3) uniformity, by way of contrast with the 'irregularity' of 'ancient' constitutions, (4) the recognition of custom as part of a stadial theory of progress towards uniformity in manners and institutions, (5) the linkage of a 'modern' constitution with a converging uniformity of European institutions – 'representative government, separation of powers, the rule of law, individual liberties, a standing army, and a public sphere' – necessary to that stage of development, (6) the possession of an identity as a 'nation' with a corporate identity or personality, and (7) the notion of a founding moment that grounds and regulates democratic politics. These seven features are elaborated at length in *Strange Multiplicity*, pp. 62–70; the account of the *Treatise* as an exemplary expression of these follows at pp. 70–8.

7. Chapters 11–14 of the *Second Treatise* address the topics, respectively, 'Of the Extent of Legislative Power', 'Of the Legislative, Federative, and Executive Power of the Commonwealth' 'Of the Subordination of the Powers of the Commonwealth' and 'Of Prerogative'.

8. *Two Treatises*, part 2, p. 133.

9. In thinking about the implications of these issues for political theory, I've found the following particularly interesting or incisive either in relation to the period I'm interested in or more generally. As an overview of the fields of textual study, D. C. Greetham, *Textual Scholarship: An Introduction* (New York, 1994). On the signifying aspects of typography and layout, D. F. McKenzie, 'Typography and Meaning: The Case of William Congreve', in G. Barber and B. Fabian, eds., *Buch und Buchhandel in Europa im achtzehnten Jahrhundert: The Book and the Book Trade in Eighteenth-Century Europe* (Hamburg, 1981); J. McLaverty, 'The Mode of Existence of Literary Works of Art: The Case of the *Dunciad Variorum*', *Studies in Bibliography*, 37 (1984), pp. 82–105; and

R. Cloud [Randall McLeod], 'Tranceformations in the Text of *Orlando Furioso*', in D. Oliphant and R. Bradford, eds., *New Directions in Textual Studies*, (Austin, Tex., 1990), pp. 60–86. On annotation, marginalia and editing, A. Middleton, 'Life in the Margins, or What's an Editor to Do?', also in Oliphant and Bradford, eds., *New Directions in Textual Studies*, pp. 167–83; R. Hannah III, 'Annotation as a Social Practice', in S. Barney, ed., *Annotation and Its Texts* (Oxford, 1991), pp. 178–84; W. E. Slights, 'The Edifying Margins of Renaissance English Books', *Renaissance Quarterly*, 42 (1989), pp. 682–716; E. B. Tribble, *Margins and Marginality: The Printed Page in Early Modern England* (Charlottesville, Va., and London, 1993); M. Spevak, 'The Editor as Philologist', *Text*, 3 (1987), pp. 91–106; D. C. Greetham, 'Textuality and Literary Theory: Redrawing the Matrix', *Studies in Bibliography*, 42 (1989), pp. 1–24; and J. J. McGann, 'Shall These Bones Live?', *Text*, 1 (1984), pp. 21–40, and 'What Is Critical Editing', *Text*, 5 (1991), pp. 15–30. More generally, see J. J. McGann, *A Critique of Modern Textual Criticism* (Chicago, 1983); D. F. McKenzie, *Bibliography and the Sociology of Texts* (London, 1986); and G. Genette, *Paratexts: Thresholds of Interpretation* (Cambridge, 1997).

10. M. de Grazia, 'The Essential Shakespeare and the Material Book', *Textual Practice*, 2/1 (Spring 1988), pp. 69–86.

11. Laslett's introductory discussion of the print history of the book, as well as the checklist of printings in Appendix A noted earlier, are invaluable resources for thinking about the materiality of the text. Beginning with the French translation of 1691, which printed only the second of the two essays under the title *Du gouvernement civil*, this was the norm for the dissemination of the book in languages other than English. Subsequent translations into German, Italian and Spanish were from this or later French editions. Laslett refers to this as the French form, which changed the numbering conventions for paragraphs, dropped the initial preface to the work as a whole as well as the original first chapter of the *Second Treatise* – all of which alterations pivoted the work in the direction of the Enlightenment by carving off aspects that tied it to its initial political context of production and consumption. The only American printing of the book before the twentieth century, the Boston edition of 1773, also adopted the French format but dropped paragraph and chapter numbers entirely. In the Anglophone context, interest in the *Treatises*, and particularly in the *Second Treatise*, apparently accelerated about the middle of the eighteenth century. For accounts of this, see J. Dunn, 'The Politics of Locke in England and America', in J. W. Yolton, ed., *John Locke: Problems and Perspectives* (Cambridge, 1969); M. P. Thompson, 'The Reception of Locke's *Two Treatises of Government*, 1690–1705', *Political Studies*, 24/2 (June 1976), reprinted in R. Ashcraft, ed., *John Locke: Critical Assessments* (6 vols., London and New York, 1991), vol. 1, pp. 100–9; I. Kramnick, *Republicanism and Bourgeois Radicalism: Political Ideology in Late Eighteenth-Century England and America* (Ithaca, 1990), pp. 4, 170–5; and M. M. Goldsmith, ' "Our Great Oracle, Mr Lock": Locke's Political Theory in the Early Eighteenth Century', *Eighteenth-Century Life*, 16 (1992), pp. 60–75. The most

comprehensive discussion of the reception history of the *Treatises*, as well as of Locke's other published writings, is Mark Goldie's superb introductory essay to his landmark six-volume edition of responses to Locke's work between 1690 and 1838, *The Reception of Locke's Politics* (London, 1999), hereafter cited as *Reception*.

12. By 'official' I mean acknowledged publicly by its author, which Locke did for the *Treatises*, as well as for other hitherto anonymous publications, in the 15 September 1704 codicil to his will. This is available in J. S. Yolton, ed., *A Locke Miscellany* (Bristol, 1990), pp. 359–62. To note the official anonymity of the text in these terms is not to suggest that Locke's authorship was wholly unknown. Richard Ashcraft noted five book-auction catalogues, circulating between 1696 and 1700, that identified Locke as the author ('John Locke's Library: Portrait of an Intellectual', in Ashcraft, ed., *John Locke: Critical Assessments*, vol. 1, p. 28 n. 27). There was also an unpleasant exchange of letters between Locke and his friend James Tyrrell over the matter, but the first suggestion in print culture of Locke as a possible author was that of William Molyneaux, in *The Case of Ireland's Being Bound by Acts of Parliament in England Stated* (Dublin, 1698), reprinted in Goldie, *Reception*, vol. 1, pp. 211–82, especially pp. 225, 274. As Goldie notes in the introduction to Molyneaux's work, the critical 'arrival' and dissemination of the *Treatises* on the tides of public contestation was more explicitly occasioned by the Kentish Petition controversy of 1701, when the text was both appropriated and lambasted as a populist appeal to the people against a sitting parliament (see especially pp. xxx–xxxii).

13. The convention was one that Locke both knew and hoped to follow in the one book of the early nineties that he acknowledged as his own: the first edition of *An Essay Concerning Humane Understanding. In Four Books* (London, 1690). Indeed, the correspondence shows that he was quite clear about the image he wanted, though at this time he was unsuccessful in obtaining it. See *The Correspondence of John Locke*, ed. E. S. de Beer (8 vols., Oxford, 1976–89), vol. 1, letter 748, vol. 2, letter 1020, vol. 3, letter 1165. Hereafter cited as *Correspondence*.

14. Indeed, the first American edition, a small quarto of the *Second Treatise* alone published by Edes and Gill in Boston in 1773, announces itself as 'by the late learned John Locke'. Parenthetically, this appears to be the only American printing of the *Treatise* as a whole until 1937. For the proliferation and peregrinations of the footnote in the eighteenth century, see A. Grafton, *The Footnote: A curious History* (London, 1997), especially chapter 4.

15. In the editions of 1689, 1694 and 1698 these passages are neither pegged to specific passages in the body of the text nor printed flush with the bottom of the page. We will return to these below. Regarding Hooker as an authority in more general terms, William Atwood's observation in *The Fundamental Constitution of the English Government* (London, 1690) might be apt: 'Many have cited the Authority of the *Judicious Hooker* till it is threadbare, to prove, that it is impossible there should be a lawful Kingly Power which is not mediately, or

immediately, from the Consent of the People where it is exercised' (cited from the selection reprinted in Goldie, *Reception*, vol. 1, p. 39). Atwood was an attentive and generally favourable reader of the *Treatise*, though he questioned whether the situation of 1688 qualified as a dissolution of government given the specificity of English institutions.

16. The following observations are based on Peter Laslett's checklist of printings, included as Appendix A to his 1960 edition of the *Treatises*.

17. Jürgen Habermas, among others, has seen in such inclinations the formation of subjectivities appropriate to the 'bourgeois public sphere' of the eighteenth century. See *The Structural Transformation of the Public Sphere* (Cambridge, 1989), especially chapters 1–4. Habermas's focus on the print culture of 'good society' leaves unaddressed the less genteel arenas of print culture through which early modern political contestation so often proceeded. For a challenging account of the latter in late eighteenth- and early nineteenth-century Britain, see D. Herzog, *Poisoning the Minds of the Lower Orders* (Princeton, 1998).

18. The latter pamphlets are particularly notewothy, for each quite explicitly condensed and reformatted the *Treatise* into a handbook or system of principles. The first, having no references to author, printer or publisher, and titled simply *Of Civil Polity* (1753), combined various of its passages with excepts from other sources to settle it into the mainstream of mid-century Hanoverian concerns (reprinted in Goldie, *Reception*, vol. 2, pp. 359–77). The second, also a rationalizing epitome, reduced the *Treatise* to a seventy-eight-page duodecimo, titled *The Spirit of John Locke on Constitutional Government, Revived by the Constitutional Society of Sheffield* (Sheffield, n.d.), and pitched it headlong into British domestic controversies over the French Revolution. The date tentatively assigned to the latter work by the Library of Congress is 1794.

19. The passage, in Laslett's 1960 edition on the verso of the title page, is from Livy's *History of Rome*, 9.1: 'Quod si nihil cum potentiore juris humani relinquitur inopi, at ego ad Deos vidices humanae superbiae confugiam: et precabor ut iras suas vertant in eos, quibus non suae res, non alienae satis sint quorum saevitiam non mors noxiorum exatiet: placasti nequeant, nisi hauriendum sanguinem laniandaque viscera nostra prae buerimus' – in Laslett's Englishing, 'But if, in dealing with the mighty, the weak are left no human rights, yet I will seek protection in the Gods, who visit retribution on human pride. And I will beseech them that they turn their anger against those who are not content with their own, or with that of others, who will not be sated with the death of the guilty. They are not to be placated unless we yield to them our blood to drink and our entrails to tear out.' Laslett goes on to explain that this passage appears in Locke's hand on the flyleaf facing the title page of his copy of the third edition of 1698, the copy used as copy-text for the edition of 1713. Its arrival as part of the printed form of the book in the 1713 and 1728 editions but not in the folios of the works provides an interesting historical puzzle, and one that can't be explained by the various editions being brought out by different publishers. John Churchill, who published the 1713 edition in

duodecimo, also published the 1714 and 1722 folio editions of the works, while A. Bettesworth published both the 1727 folio edition of the works and the 1728 octavo of the *Two Treatises*.

20. T. Elrington, ed., *An Essay Concerning the True Original, Extent, and End of Civil Government* (Dublin, 1798). Elrington's annotations are printed in Goldie, *Reception*, vol. 4, pp. 365–87.

21. One might also consider the fact that the period witnessed considerable debate over the stylistics of philosophical writing and the proprieties of philosophical argument in the public sphere – some of which may have had to do with an evolving appreciation of Locke himself, at least in the conversational manner of the *Essay Concerning Human Understanding*, as a style-setter for philosophical reflection. For an account of this, see J. V. Price, 'The Reading of Philosophical Literature', in I. Rivers, ed., *Books and Their Readers in Eighteenth-Century England* (Leicester, 1982), pp. 165–96. The discursive notion of conversation, however, particularly insofar as it supported the persistence of rhetorical elements, was also taken to task as diminishing the power of philosophical reasoning. In 1751, for example, John Brown's *Essays on the Characteristics of the Earl of Shaftesbury* chastised their appeal 'to Eloquence, rather than Argument', and their tendency at key points to proffer their readers 'a Metaphor instead of a Reason' (p. 179). By the nineteenth century, no less a figure than Adam Smith fell prey to a similar criticism. Irritated with the profusion of narratives, examples, digressions and illustrations that populate the pages of Smith's *Theory of Moral Sentiments*, James MacIntosh regarded such writing with undisguised disdain. In his *Dissertation on the Progress of Ethical Philosophy* of 1836, he complains that such things 'embellish the book more than they illuminate the theory'. 'For purely philosophical purposes,' he continued, 'few books more need abridgement: for the most careful reader frequently loses sight of principles buried under illustrations' (repr., Bristol, 1991, p. 223). I am grateful to Douglas Dow for drawing MacIntosh's observations to my attention.

22. P. Ricoeur, *Time and Narrative*, vol. 1 (Chicago, 1983), p. 81. In light of Ricoeur's insistence that narrative provides an orientation to praxis, I would suggest that it is the narrative dimensions of the text that best answer the rhetorical goal of not simply teaching but delighting its readers and moving them to action as well. As I've argued more generally in 'Speaking in Tenses: Narrative, Politics, and Historical Writing', *Constellations*, June 1998, pp. 234–49, this doesn't mean that narrative is necessarily 'applied' in any determinate way, but rather that it invites readers into a particularized perspective onto the world.

23. Aside from the Hooker passages noted above, these intertextual references include Robert Knox's *Historical Relation of Ceylon* (London, 1679), Joseph Acosta's *Naturall and Morall Historie of the Indies* and Garcilaso de la Vega's *Royal Commentaries*, as well as such humanist educational staples as Martial's *Epigrams*, Ovid's *Metamorphoses*, Juvenal's *Satires*, and Justin's *Epitome of the Philippic History of Pompeius Trogus*. By the time the *Treatises* were published,

I should add, all of the Latin works noted here were commonly available in the vernacular in numerous editions.

24. See especially *Two Treatises*, introduction, section 4, 'Locke and Hobbes'. Laslett suggests that Sir Frederick Pollock, in 'Locke's Theory of the State', *Proceedings of the British Academy*, 1 (1903–4), pp. 237–49, was largely responsible for the view now discredited. Interestingly, and now more particularly in light of Tully's placement of the *Treatise* in the 'modern' rather than 'ancient' constitutionalist camp, what Laslett doesn't mention is that Pollock reads it not simply as a constitutionalist tract opposed to Hobbesian absolutism, but as an 'ancient constitutionalist' view resistant to Hobbesian notions of sovereignty, notions that Tully regards as standing at the font of the 'modern' constitutionalist tradition. This may or may not be little more than a curious footnote to the history of the historiography of the *Treatises*, but Pollock's reading was no less caught up in the political questions of its day than Barker's triumphalism, more recent post-colonial critiques and, doubtless, my own reading as well. At the turn of the century, in any case, what was on the table for Pollock (like Maitland, Figges and a more youthful Barker, among others variously involved with turn-of-the-century English pluralism) was the possibility of writing a history that countered the monism of both Austinian and neo-Hegelian notions of sovereignty. Though unconcerned with the likes of either Pollock or Locke, I've touched on this moment in the context of the emergence of pluralist theories of the state in 'On the Subject of Rights: Pluralism, Plurality, and Political Identity', in C. Mouffe, ed., *Dimensions of Radical Democracy: Pluralism, Citizenship, Community* (London, 1992).

25. *Two Treatises*, part 2, p. 98. The Latin tag, from Martial as we'll see below, was Englished for the fourth edition of 1713.

26. Among modern scholars see, for example, W. Kendall, *John Locke and the Doctrine of Majority Rule* (Urbana, Ill., 1941); and H. Pitkin, 'Obligation and Consent', parts 1 and 2, *American Political Science Review*, 59/4 (1965), pp. 990–9, and 60/1 (1966), pp. 39–52.

27. See H. White, 'The Value of Narrativity in the Representation of Reality', in White, *The Content of the Form* (Baltimore, 1987).

28. *Two Treatises*, introduction, p. 85 n. 14, part 2, p. 98 n. to lines 13–16.

29. Martial, *Epigrams*, trans. W. C. A. Ker (2 vols., New York, 1919), vol. 1, preface, lines 29–31. Though in his educational writings Locke deplored the practice of requiring youths to memorize ancient writers by heart before they were capable of understanding their complexity, he made frequent recourse to such texts to convey or condense meanings to a point. In his correspondence with both friends and other denizens of the republic of letters, Roman writers are prominent. Among Locke's books, too, there stood an array of humanist favourites. Some of these books clearly dated from his student years, yet many – most notably, perhaps, various editions of Horace, Ovid and Seneca, but also Martial – continued to draw Locke's attention. John Harrison and Peter Laslett's catalogue of Locke's books lists five editions of Martial, one of which,

a 1661 edition in use at Westminster School, Locke gave as a gift to Francis Cudworth Masham, the son of his friend Damaris Masham. See *The Library of John Locke* (Oxford, 1965), entries 1917–21 and notes.

30. For example, *Factorum et Dictorum Memorabilium*, Englished as *Valerius Maximus His Collection of the Memorable Acts and Sayings of Orators, Philosophers, Statesmen, and Other Illustrious Persons of the Ancient Romans, and Other Foreign Nations, upon Various Subjects: Together with a Life of That Famous Historian* (London, 1684). The English Valerius was also picked up by the Churchills, the publishers of the first four editions of the *Treatises* – and it is listed in the printers' 'Advertisement' for their books in the second, still anonymous edition of the *Two Treatises* that was issued in 1694. Locke owned three Latin editions, entries 1946–8 in Harrison and Laslett's catalogue. Here I've relied on the 1684 edition, but a new translation, by D. R. Shackleton Bailey, has recently been issued by the Loeb Classical Library (London and Cambridge, Mass., 2000). Another rendering of the story is in Seneca's *Epistles*, 97.8.

31. See F. Altheim, *A History of Roman Religion*, trans. H. Mattingly (New York, 1938), especially pp. 122–3; and H. H. Scullard, *Festivals and Ceremonies of the Roman Republic* (London, 1981), pp. 110–11. For more general discussions of the plebeian games, see also B. S. Spaeth, *The Roman Goddess Ceres* (Austin, Tex., 1996), pp. 36, 89–90.

32. *Valerius Maximus*, 2.10.8, p. 99.

33. *Two Treatises*, II.98 n. See also Laslett's brief discussion in the introduction, pp. 84–5.

34. Though the point can't be developed here, I mean the term metamorphosis to resonate as yet another intertextual possibility unnoticed by modern readers. To date, no one has remarked on the parallels between the *Treatise*'s famous account of property in the state of nature – as a series of transformations of the human relationship to the land and its products – and the Ovidian topos of the four ages so popular in early modern European literature. From gathering, to planting, to the unearthing of precious metals, the story of humanity according to that view was one not of progress but of corruption, and there is reason to believe that Locke's account was a creative adaptation, a humanist reinvention, of Ovid's familiar narrative. In textual terms, in a variant of the story of corruption, the *Treatise* invokes the *Metamorphoses* by a Latin tag at part 2, p. 111. The correspondence, too, evidences frequent use of the trope in various forms throughout Locke's life, and among other Ovidiana in Locke's library were four editions of the collected works (in Harrison and Laslett, *The Library of John Locke*, entries 2154–6 and 2159) and two editions of the *Metamorphoses* (entries 2159 and 2159b), one of which Locke also gave to Damaris Masham's son.

35. See, for example, chapter 6, where the task of distinguishing paternal from political power offers a series of narratives on the emergence of political from familial orders, and chapter 7, where narratives help distinguish political societies from other forms of association.

36. As Goldie's collection of responses to Locke's work makes clear, the *Treatise*'s earliest foe, like many of its subsequent critics in the later years of the eighteenth century, held it to the nose-counting criterion with great relish. See, for example, C. Leslie, *The New Association* (London, 1703), and *Rehearsal*, no. 38 (14–21 April 1705), in Goldie, *Reception*, vol. 2, pp. 62–9 and 13–17, respectively; G. Horne, *The Origin of Civil Government and Some Considerations on Mr Locke's Scheme of Deriving Government from an Original Compact* (London, 1769 and after), in Goldie, *Reception*, vol. 3, pp. 229–46; J. Boucher, *A View of the Causes and Consequences of the American Revolution*, discourse 12, 'On Civil Liberty, Passive Obedience, and Non-Resistance' (London, 1775), in Goldie, *Reception*, vol. 3, pp. 281–316, especially pp. 292–4; J. Bowles, *Thoughts on the Origin and Formation of Political Constitutions…Reflections on Mr Locke's System* (London, 1798), in Goldie, *Reception*, vol. 4, pp. 347–64, especially pp. 349–51; and the more equivocal criticism of Thomas Elrington, editor of a 1798 edition of the *Treatise*, in his note to the offending paragraph on majorities (*Two Treatises*, II.98), in Goldie, *Reception*, vol. 4, p. 380.

37. *Two Treatises*, II.100.

38. For Peru, Brazil and other Amerindian 'Politick Societies' instanced at II.102, the source is J. Acosta, *The Naturall and Morall Historie of the Indies* (London, 1604); for Palantus and his Spartan cohort's founding of Tarentum, noted at II.103, the source is Justin's epitome of the lost Roman history of Pompeius Trogus, a commonly cited source in the period and also available in English. Examples of Hebrew history at II.109 are drawn from the Old Testament books of Judges and 1 Samuel, texts that since the late sixteenth century had provided standard sites for English defences and criticisms of kingly power.

39. See R. Ashcraft, 'Locke's State of Nature: Historical Fact or Moral Fiction', *American Political Science Review*, 68/3 (1968), pp. 898–914; J. Dunn, *The Political Thought of John Locke* (Cambridge, 1969); and C. B. Macpherson, *The Political Theory of Possessive Individualism: Hobbes to Locke* (Oxford, 1962).

40. P. Sidney, *Defence of Poetry*, in *The Works of Sir Philip Sidney*, ed. A. Feuillerat (4 vols., Cambridge, 1912–26), vol. 3, p. 29.

41. For an extended discussion of the problems attending this, see W. Nelson, *Fact or Fiction: The Dilemma of the Renaissance Storyteller* (Cambridge, Mass., 1973).

42. Considered in line with the historiographical convention of the 'influence' of the philosophical tenets of earlier writers upon their successors, the suggestion would border on the absurd. That said – though at present political theory has no term of art to consider the pertinence of such things – the possibility of Locke's imaginary relation to the likes of Sidney is opened by the pseudonym taken by his friend and interlocutor, Damaris Masham, in their long correspondence. As her 'Philoclea' evokes a character in Sidney's *Arcadia*, so does his 'Damon' evoke, among other things, the politically complex pastoral imagery

of a Virgilian shepherd. At the same time, and again as a challenge to conventional notions of 'influence', Locke's 'Damon' signified in other registers of meaning as well, not least of all as the famed Pythagorean friend of Pythias, whose loyalty so softened the heart of an ancient tyrant. As Annabel Patterson has argued, pastoral poetry could carry a distinctive political edge (*Pastoral and Ideology*, Berkeley, 1987). And while Locke's library catalogue includes neither the *Arcadia* nor Sidney's *Defence of Poetry*, he refers to 'Sir Ph. Sidney's two verses' from the *Arcadia* in a letter to Benjamin Furly. Perhaps collapsed into the coded/canting languages that the exiled radicals used amongst themselves, the letter as a whole would break the teeth of anyone chewing it for direct reference (see *Correspondence*, vol. 3, letter 1004).

43. Later revised and published, initially anonymously, as *Some Thoughts Concerning Education* (London, 1693).

44. *Correspondence*, vol. 2, letter 829, p. 734. Harrison and Laslett note six editions of Aesop in Locke's library (*The Library of John Locke*, entries 31–35a), three of which bear imprints from the 1690s. Two, judging only from publication dates (1605, 1660), might have belonged to him prior to the composition of the *Treatise*, while the last, John Ogilby's verse paraphrase with annotations of 1683–4, was published during Locke's exile in the Netherlands. For recent accounts of the political character and uses of Aesopian and other fables in the period, see A. Patterson, *Fables of Power: Aesopian Writing and Political History* (Durham, N. C., and London, 1991); J. Lewis, *The English Fable: Aesop and Literary Culture, 1651–1740* (Cambridge, 1996); and, more generally, M. Loveridge, *A History of the Augustan Fable* (Cambridge, 1998).

45. *Correspondence*, vol. 2, letter 844, p. 773.

46. Ibid., pp. 773–4. It might be noted that in this form the 'golden rule' doesn't necessarily reference the good Samaritan. The stories here recommended – of Joseph and his brothers, David and Goliath, and David and Jonathan – are, after all, also stories of treachery, monstrous force and conspiracy. As it appears in the *Treatise* at II.109, among the various lessons discoverable in the last of these, drawn from 1 Samuel, is the notion that royal authority might be limited to generalship and available by consent.

47. Correspondence, vol. 3, letter 1098, p. 535. As Locke noted further, '[t]he foundations on which several duties are built and the fountains of right and wrong from which they spring are not perhaps easily to be let into the minds of grown men not used to abstract their thoughts from common received opinions' (p. 535). However such matters might pertain to the compositional history of the *Two Treatises*, we might nonetheless find them pertinent to the decision to publish it, as this letter was penned shortly before Locke's departure, in the entourage of the princess of Orange – soon to be Queen Mary – for England, where Parliament had but recently invited William to succeed the newly absconded James II. Parenthetically, this invitation, in addition to various of William III's initial proclamations, was printed and disseminated by Locke's publishers Awnsham and John Churchill.

48. Ibid., p. 536.

49. *Aesop's Fables, in English and Latin, Interlineary, for the Benefit of Those Who Not Having a Master, Would Learn Either of These Tongues. With Sculptures* (London, 1703).

50. *Rehearsal*, no. 59 (1705), in Goldie, *Reception*, vol. 2, p. 44.

51. Third earl of Shaftesbury, letter to James Stanhope, 7 November 1709, in B. Rand, ed., *The Life, Unpublished Letters, and Philosophical Regimen of Anthony, Earl of Shaftesbury* (London, 1900), in Goldie, *Reception*, vol. 2, p. 131 n. 13.

52. J. Otis, *The Rights of the British Colonists Asserted and Proved* (Boston, 1764), in Goldie, *Reception*, vol. 3, p. 24.

53. Horne, *The Origin of Civil Government*, in Goldie, *Reception*, vol. 3, pp. 235–6.

54. Boucher, *A View of the Causes and Consequences of the American Revolution*, discourse 12, in Goldie, *Reception*, vol. 3, pp. 294–6.

55. *Two Treatises*, II.35, 36, 37, 45, 49, 74, 94. The image recurs again as analepsis (II.111), replete with Ovidian tag, with the mention of a 'golden age' of virtue eclipsed by the corruption of future ages given over to luxury and ambition.

56. Or so, I'm suggesting, might we consider the terms in which the *Treatise* was written. By the mid-eighteenth century, commitment to a harder distinction between fact and fiction apparently led the author/compiler of *Of Civil Polity* (1753) to recast such feigned probabilities as an exercise of imagination. Noting that the formation of governments in various parts of the world is 'a Question of Fact, that can only be determined by Historical Evidence', the writer observes further that 'if we indulge our Imagination upon the Subject' reasonable suppositions about 'the Infant-Ages of the World' might be generated. The tract then goes on to renarrativize in condensed form various elements of the *Treatise*'s chapters 6–8 in combination with other similar sources. Printed in Goldie, *Reception*, vol. 2, pp. 357–77; the passage referenced here is at 367–9.

57. *Two Treatises*, II.5 and 15, 60 and 61, in chapter 2, 'Of the State of Nature', and chapter 6, 'Of Paternal Power', respectively. In these cases Hooker's authority is appealed to explicitly.

58. All of these are drawn from *The Laws of Ecclesiastical Polity*, 1.1.10, the point at which Hooker himself had recourse to the resources of *fabula*. The *Treatise*'s chapter 6, 'Of Paternal Power', closes with Hooker's observation that 'It is no improbable Opinion, therefore, which the *Arch-Philosopher* was of, That the chief Person in every Household was always, as it were, a King: So when Numbers of Households joyn'd themselves in Civil Societies together, Kings were the first kind of Governours amongst them, which is also, as it seemeth, the reason why the name of Fathers continued still in them, who, of Fathers, were made Rulers; as also the ancient Custom of Governours to do as *Melchizedec*, and being Kings, to exercise the Office of Priests, which Fathers did, at the first, grew perhaps by the same Occasion. Howbeit, this is not the only kind of Regiment that has been received in the World. The Inconveniences of one kind have caused sundry other to be devised; so that, in a word, all

publick Regiment of what kind soever, seemeth evidently to have risen from the deliberate Advice, Consultation and Composition between Men, judging it convenient, and behoveful; there being no impossibility in Nature, considered by itself, but that Man might have lived without any publick Regiment' (II.74).

Chapter 7, 'Of Political Society', draws on two further passages. First, on Hooker's observation that for the removal of injuries and grievances – and the text adds 'i.e. such as attend Men in the State of Nature' – 'There was no way but only by growing into Composition and Agreement amongst themselves, by ordaining some kind of Government Publick, and by yielding themselves subject thereunto, that unto whom they granted Authority to Rule and Govern, by them the Peace, Tranquility, and happy Estate of the rest might be procured. Men always knew that where Force and Injury was offered, they might be Defenders of themselves; they knew that however Men may seek their own Commodity; yet if this were done with Injury unto others, it was not to be suffered, but by all Men, and all good Means to be withstood. Finally, they knew that no Man might in reason take upon him to determine his own Right, and according to his own Determination proceed in maintenance thereof, in as much as every Man is towards himself, and them who he greatly affects, partial; and therefore that Strifes and Troubles would be endless, except they gave their common Consent, all to be ordered by some, whom they should agree upon, without such Consent there would be no reason that one Man should take upon him to be Lord or Judge over another' (II.91). Second, and closing the chapter, it adds Hooker's supposition that 'At the first, when some certain kind of Regiment was once appointed, it may be that nothing was then farther thought upon for the manner of governing, but all permitted unto their Wisdom and Discretion, which were to Rule, till by experience they found this for all parts very inconvenient, so as the thing which they had devised for a Remedy, did indeed but increase the Sore, which it should have cured. They saw, that <u>to live by one Man's Will, became the cause of all Mens misery</u>. This constrained them to come unto Laws wherein all Men might see their Duty beforehand, and know the Penalties of transgressing them' (II.94). (The underlined emphasis appears in the *Treatise*.)

Parenthetically, the last of these passages appears a second time, at the end of the list of historical examples in chapter 8's account 'Of the Beginning of Political Societies'. There, it borders the culminating discussion, cited in note oo above, that invokes a 'golden age' with a tag from Ovid's *Metamorphoses*.

59. *Two Treatises*, II.100.
60. *Two Treatises*, II.102. Acosta was translated by Edward Grimstone and published in London in 1604.
61. *Two Treatises*, II.103. Justin's epitome of the history of Pompeius Trogus was widely avaliable in both Latin and English, and commonly used in grammar schools. Like Valerius's account of Cato's leaving the theatre, the story of Palantus carries a salacious effect for such as might remember it. It seems

the Spartans, laying seige to the Messenians, vowed that none would leave until victory was won. A decade later they were still there and their wives were complaining about their long absence. Worried about Sparta's declining population, they sent a cohort of youthful reinforcements who had not shared the vow to mate promiscuously with the Spartan women. Palantus was one of the children of such couplings. With others of that brood, illegitimate and thus without patrimony, he left to conquer Tarentum, where he and the others established themselves as a new polity. See Justin, *Epitome of the Philippic History of Pompeius Trogus*, trans. J. C. Yardley, introduction and notes by R. Develin (Atlanta, 1994), 3.4.1–11.

62. *Two Treatises*, II.105.
63. Ibid., II.108, 109.
64. Ibid., II.109.
65. Ibid., II.133.
66. Ibid., II.135, 137, 139.
67. Ibid., II.143–4, 153.
68. W. Atwood, *The Fundamental Constitution of the English Government. Proving King William and Queen Mary Our Lawful and Rightful King and Queen* (London, 1690), in Goldie, *Reception*, vol. 1, p. 48.
69. Goldie, *Reception*, vol. 1, introduction, pp. xxi–xxxvi.
70. See, for instance, J. Priestly, *An Essay on the First Principles of Government* (London, 1768), and R. Price, *Observations on the Nature of Civil Liberty* (London, 1776), in Goldie, *Reception*, vol. 3, pp. 97–165 and 317–75, respectively, as well as the condensed tract *The Spirit of John Locke on Constitutional Government, Revived by the Constitutional Society of Sheffield* (Sheffield, n.d.) (see note 18 above).
71. J. Tucker, *A Treatise Concerning Civil Government* (London, 1781), chapter 2, answer to objection 3, in Goldie, *Reception*, vol. 4, pp. 93–113, especially, p. 112.
72. Horne, *The Origin of Civil Government*, in Goldie, *Reception*, vol. 3, pp. 243–4.
73. Boucher, *A View of the Causes and Consequences of the American Revolution*, discourse 12, in Goldie, *Reception*, vol. 3, p. 295.
74. R. Ward, 'The Opinions of Locke', in *An Historical Essay on the Real Character and Amount of the Precedent of the Revolution of 1688*, in Goldie, *Reception*, vol. 4, p. 414. For the more general historicity of the *Treatise's* relation to later notions of empirical generalization, see the epilogue to my *Judging Rights: Lockean Politics and the Limits of Consent* (Ithaca, 1996).

Parts of this chapter appeared in my essay 'Between the Castigation of Texts and the Excess of Words: Political Theory in the Margins of Tradition', in A. Botwinick and W. E. Connolly, eds., *Democracy and Vision: Sheldon Wolin and the Vicissitudes of the Political* (Princeton, NJ, 2002), pp. 193–231.

Index